After the Nazi Racial State

Recent Titles

For a complete list of titles, please see www.press.umich.edu

After the Nazi Racial State

Difference and Democracy in
Germany and Europe

*Rita Chin, Heide Fehrenbach, Geoff Eley,
and Atina Grossmann*

The University of Michigan Press

Ann Arbor

Published in the United States of America by
The University of Michigan Press
Manufactured in the United States of America
⊚ Printed on acid-free paper

2012   2011   2010   2009   4   3   2   1

A CIP catalog record for this book is available from the British Library.

Library of Congress Cataloging-in-Publication Data

After the Nazi racial state : difference and democracy in Germany and
    Europe / by Rita Chin ... [et al.].
        p. cm. — (Social history, popular culture, and politics in
    Germany)
      Includes bibliographical references and index.
      ISBN-13: 978-0-472-11686-7 (cloth : alk. paper)
      ISBN-10: 0-472-11686-X (cloth : alk. paper)
      ISBN-13: 978-0-472-03344-7 (pbk. : alk. paper)
      ISBN-10: 0-472-03344-1 (pbk. : alk. paper)
      1. Racism—Germany—History—20th century.   2. Germany—Race
    relations—History—20th century.   3. Europe—Race relations—
    History—20th century.   4. Alien labor—Germany—History—20th
    century.   I. Chin, Rita C-K, 1970–
    DD74.A38   2009
    305.800943—dc22   2008047855

        ISBN-13 978-0-472-02578-7 (electronic)

Preface

The first spark of recognition that we were engaged in similar quests to puzzle out the ongoing relevance of "race" in the wake of Nazi defeat and postwar democratization came in an elevator on the campus of the University of Illinois in the fall of 2003. Two of us, Rita and Heide, had just become acquainted at the Midwest German History Workshop and, in discussing our current research interests, realized we shared compatible assessments—and frustrations—regarding the historiography of the postwar period and the absence of attention to issues of "race." Over the next few years, while completing our individual projects, we began collaborating and recruited our coauthors, Atina Grossmann and Geoff Eley, for a panel on the subject at the German Studies Association in 2004. Their expertise has substantially broadened and deepened the comparative analysis we agree is so sorely needed for exploring connections between notions of "difference" and practices of democracy in the postwar German and European context and has greatly enriched our collective understanding.

What has emerged from our ongoing collaboration is a rather odd species of book. It is neither a synthetic narrative of the evolution of "race" after 1945 nor an edited collection that presents the full range of topics, and historians, this theme could encompass. Rather, it offers a brief critical analysis of certain key debates and developments in German and European history since 1945. Each of us has authored a separate chapter, connected to our expertise and research interests; the introduction and chapter 4 are coauthored. Taken together, the essays aspire to make a spirited historiographical intervention on behalf of establishing the continued salience of notions and practices of "race" both for the post-1945 period and for contemporary German and European society more generally. The introduction lays out the theoretical and historiographical ambitions of our collaboration in more detail.

This volume has been several years in the making and has benefited from the generous support of various institutions and individuals. We acknowledge the University of Michigan's Department of History, Department of German Studies, Institute for the Humanities, and in particular, Center for European Studies, which provided the funds and support for a daylong workshop in February 2006. This event served as a forum for the four of us to present our chapters publicly and was instrumental in helping us tighten our arguments, both in individual chapters and in the volume as a whole. We wish to thank Charlie Bright, Kathleen Canning, Matthew Countryman, Shirli Gilbert, Kali Israel, Kader Konuk, Damani Partridge, Roberta Pergher, and Geneviève Zubrzycki for their contributions to the workshop, as well as other Michigan colleagues and graduate students whose energetic participation from the audience went a long way to making the event such a rich intellectual experience. The authors would also like to thank Claudia Koonz for her helpful comments early in the project, and more recently Frank Biess and an anonymous reader for the Press for the useful criticisms and thought-provoking questions they offered on the manuscript as a whole.

In addition, Rita Chin and Heide Fehrenbach are grateful to the Woodrow Wilson International Center for Scholars and the John Simon Guggenheim Memorial Foundation, respectively, for the fellowships during the 2007–2008 academic year that allowed them to complete this book project and begin work on others. They also acknowledge Robert Moeller and Uta Poiger for helpful criticisms and comments on the Introduction. Rita Chin thanks Kathleen Canning, Jay Cook, Alex Stern, and the members of the German Women's History Group in New York for reading and providing incisive critiques of Chapter 3. Geoff Eley is especially grateful to Mica Nava and David Feldman, who at the final stage of writing Chapter 5, challenged him to clarify his arguments. For similar intellectual help, he is also indebted to innumerable friends and colleagues, but especially Charlie Bright, Kathleen Canning, Joshua Cole, Jessica Dubow, Paul Kramer, Gina Morantz-Sanchez, Sonya Rose, Bill Schwarz, Todd Shepard, Miriam Ticktin, and Geneviève Zubrzycki.

Contents

Introduction

What's Race Got to Do With It?
Postwar German History in Context

Rita Chin and Heide Fehrenbach

In June 2006, just prior to the start of the World Cup in Germany, the *New York Times* ran a front-page story on a "surge in racist mood" among Germans attending soccer events and anxious officials' efforts to discourage public displays of racism before a global audience. The article led with the recent experience of Nigerian forward Adebowale Ogungbure, who, after playing a match in the eastern German city of Halle, was "spat upon, jeered with racial remarks, and mocked with monkey noises" as he tried to exit the field. "In rebuke, he placed two fingers under his nose to simulate a Hitler mustache and thrust his arm in a Nazi salute."[1]

Although the press report suggested the contrary, the racist behavior directed at Ogungbure was hardly resurgent or unique. Spitting, slurs, and offensive stereotypes have a long tradition in the German—and broader Euro-American—racist repertoire. Ogungbure's wordless gesture, moreover, gave the lie to racism as a worrisome product of the New Europe or even the new Germany. Rather, his mimicry efficiently suggested continuity with a longer legacy of racist brutality reaching back to the Third Reich. In effect, his response to the antiblack bigotry of German soccer fans was accusatory and genealogically precise: it screamed "Nazi!" and labeled their actions recidivist holdovers from a fanatical *fascist* past. Ironically, since his Hitler mustache was accompanied by the raised arm of a Nazi salute—a gesture banned in Germany—Ogungbure was briefly investigated by German authorities. His tormenters, it appears, melted into the crowd and evaded legal action.

The incident on this German playing field, of course, was far from unique. Distasteful taunting and outright racist insults are part and parcel of soccer culture in Europe. The problem has been acknowledged in the sport since at least 1993, when Great Britain established "Kick It Out," an organization to fight racism in football throughout the country. In 1999, Football Against Racism in Europe was founded as a European forum to combat racism in all aspects of the sport. But the impending World Cup generated more attention than usual to "friendly" matches leading up to the tournament and exposed the routine and continuing abuse heaped on black players in pro stadiums across the Continent. These events prompted Thierry Henry, at the time a professional player for the London club Arsenal and key member of the French national team, to initiate a highly publicized campaign urging fans to reject racism in football with the help of his corporate sponsor Nike. FIFA (Fédération Internationale de Football) recognized the issue as urgent enough to make "No to racism" an official slogan of the 2006 World Cup. Given the public hand-wringing by German politicians and FIFA officials, Germany's ability to avoid major incidents of outright racism during the monthlong event was a cause for celebration. The achievement served to confirm that the nation had indeed overcome its previous racist tendencies. Ironically, this self-congratulatory posture came at a moment when Islamic xenophobia and, to a lesser degree, antisemitism have gained increasing currency in Europe.

Acknowledging the prevalence of racism in European soccer and the more recent emergence of a racialized discourse around Muslim immigrants on the Continent as a whole, we would also like to suggest that the Ogungbure incident and its aftermath are particularly emblematic for Germany in the ways they invoke and transgress postwar taboos surrounding "race" and the term's association with the Third Reich. If the "surge" of racist behavior in public was portrayed as Germany's shameful secret, it was also linked to the post–Cold War challenges confronting the unified German state. Contemporary German racism, in other words, is routinely described as perpetrated by hooligans inhabiting a specific geography— namely, the provinces of the former East Germany.[2] It is characterized as a recidivist impulse from the German margins: the persistent psychological and behavioral residue of economic stagnation, unemployment, and a population insufficiently socialized in democratic forms. Despite its often neofascist fashioning, contemporary German racism has been interpreted as the ugly legacy of the repressive state politics of socialism and the uncomfortable adjustment to capitalist democracy: somehow not-yet modern, not-yet Western, not-yet democratic or socially progressive. Centered in disaffected, unemployed white male youth, it is perceived by and large as a product of the social malaise and political immaturity of the still economically stunted East.[3]

Ogungbure's angry gestures too denounced racism as recidivist. In contrast to journalists and social scientists, the soccer player suggested contemporary racism's origins in, and affinities with, Nazism. His charge was one of historical continuity rather than rupture. But due to the Federal Republic's successful postwar conversion to a stable democracy, now over a half century old, this struck some observers as immoderate, offensive, and indeed technically illegal. Ogungbure, unlike his attackers, felt compelled to apologize: "I regret what I did . . . I should have walked away. I'm a professional, but I'm a human too. They don't spit on dogs. Why should they spit on me? I felt like a nobody."[4] Some sixty years after the demise of the Third Reich, even in the face of dehumanizing racism, it was somehow inappropriate and historically inaccurate to trace racist infractions back to the days of Hitler and thereby suggest continuities of racial ideology and practice between the Nazi era and the democratic Federal Republic.[5] After all, Germans—whether civilians or scholars—no longer even speak the language of "race." The term *Rasse* has virtually disappeared from the German lexicon and public discourse since 1945 despite the persistence of social ideologies and behaviors that look an awful lot like racism.

Racism, theorists agree, has "no single characteristic form"; although a product of modernity, its specific manifestations and targets vary across space and time.[6] After World War II, historians of Europe and the United States began to bifurcate the study of racism and antisemitism, in effect treating these as two distinct social, psychological, and historical phenomena. This scholarly response echoed a broader post-Holocaust trend to disaggregate the historical treatment and experience of Jews from that of other racialized populations, particularly those of color, as decolonization and the American civil rights movement were gaining force. This approach, moreover, has altered contemporary understandings of "racism," a term that was coined and gained currency in the 1920s and 1930s and explicitly *included* anti-Jewish discrimination in its original definition. The postwar distinction between racism and antisemitism was accompanied by a new social conception of Jews, at least in scholarly and public venues: instead of constituting a "race" they came to be understood (and came to understand themselves) as an "ethnicity." As this example makes evident, notions of race and ethnicity are fluid, contingent, and unstable. Here, we want to insist on the analytic value of exploring processes of racialization both comparatively (across groups) and historically (across the 1945 divide).[7]

First, though, it seems important to offer some rudimentary observations regarding our use of the terms *race* and *ethnicity*. *Ethnicity* connotes a sense of peoplehood based upon shared customs, language, and (sometimes) religion. It derives from a "belief in common descent" and therefore tends to be self-ascribed and embraced as a positive collective identity.[8] *Race,* on the other hand, implies a "harder" or "deeper" sense of difference from some specified or unspecified norm. Unlike ethnicity, which evokes (although doesn't necessarily enact) an unhierarchical social landscape of coexisting diversity, racial ascription is at least implicitly hierarchical and therefore initially imposed from without. Race, like ethnicity, is an ideology that achieves political, social, and psychological expression via institutions, structures of thinking, social policy, and social practice. It thereby profoundly affects the racialized subject's life. Race doesn't exist in nature; rather, groups *become racialized* when their difference is registered and invested with heightened negative social meaning. Race differs from ethnicity, then, in the perceived intensity, character, and implications of its difference. As historian George Frederickson put it, race "is what happens when ethnicity is deemed essential or indelible," innate, hereditary, transgenerational, unchangeable, ineradicable, and most of all unassimilable. While frequently justified by a fetishistic focus on skin color or other phenotypical traits perceived as markers of political, social, physical, intellectual, or moral inferiority, "race"—in the eyes of the contemporary beholder—need not be embodied or biologized in ways characteristic of the "old racisms" prior to 1945. Rather, racialized thinking can be found in institutional patterns, policies, social practices, and behaviors that target, stigmatize, treat as unequal, exclude, or adversely affect individuals on the basis of their perceived ethnoracial membership, "even if *conscious* belief that they are inferior or unworthy is absent."[9]

The Ogungbure case, of course, is only one of countless examples of "race" and racialized thinking that have surfaced in contemporary Germany—from the so-called Muslim test developed by the Baden-Württemberg naturalization office and that same state's ban of the headscarf, to the recent judgments handed down for an attack on eight Indian men in the eastern town of Mügeln, and even to the now prevalent public anxiety over the clash between Judeo-Christian and Muslim civilizations. Indeed, it is no exaggeration to say that "race" is a veritable moving target in current German public discourse. For precisely this reason, we do not aspire to provide an on-the-spot, comprehensive analysis of "race" in the present conjuncture. Rather, we seek to counter the long-dominant and unspoken assumption that the problem of "race" disappeared at the level of public discourse and policy-making with the defeat of the Third Reich.[10] This assumption has made it more difficult to perceive the racialized response that underlies much of the contemporary debate in Germany around immigrants and asylum seekers, Turks, Jews, and other native minorities. Our goal, then, is to trace the thread of continuity across the 1945 divide and sort through key analytical categories in order to help better understand the current discourse and the ways it is implicated with "race." In the pages that follow, we ask a number of basic, yet crucial questions: How and when did "race" become taboo in Germany? Why has it disappeared as a significant category for understanding German society since 1945? And perhaps most important, what are the social and epistemic consequences of this determined retreat from "race"?

Race and Rupture: Interrogating the *Stunde Null*

Over the last two decades, historians of Germany have systematically deconstructed the myth of "zero hour," arguing for the numerous ways in which 1945 did not and could not represent an absolute rupture from all that came before. We now take for granted that West Germany did not emerge sui generis from the ruins of war and occupation, that its society, politics, and culture can only be fully understood as part of the longer continuum of German history. This perspective, for example, has made it possible to grasp the multiple meanings of 1945. The armistice of 8 May, on the one hand, terminated the war in Europe and spelled the collapse of the Third Reich. The subsequent occupation period (1945–49) resulted in the establishment of two German states and helped usher the new Federal Republic into the Western alliance. Ordinary Germans, on the other hand, did not perceive an end to the war so much with the signing of the armistice, but rather with the introduction of the new currency and impending division of their nation. And many experienced 1945 as the moment when one repressive regime (Hitler's dictatorship) was replaced by another (Allied occupation).[11]

Yet in terms of the all-important question of race, assumptions of a *Stunde null* remain largely unchallenged. The Third Reich, scholars agree, was a hyperracialized society. Virtually every aspect of life was determined by Nazi race thinking; at its most extreme, the state made decisions about the fate of its citizens—and during the war, its European subjects—based on racial categories and distinctions. At the same time, most historians have operated on the unspoken assumption that the problem of race disappeared after the Nazi defeat, reflexively accepting that the postwar taboo against the term *Rasse* also meant the question of how to define and deal with difference was no longer central. This book, by contrast, wants to insist that the same challenges to the zero hour thesis leveled in other areas of historical analysis also apply to the issues of race and difference.

As a first step, our intervention seeks to demonstrate that the question of race remained at the very center of social policy and collective imagination during the occupation years, as the western Allies worked to democratize Germany, and during the Bonn Republic. Our goal is to begin to trace the development of race and ethnicity debates after the collapse of the Third Reich's racial state, exploring how and in what forms these issues resurfaced and were reconstituted in the post-1945 period, even as explicit public discussion of "race" gradually subsided and Germans became habituated to democratic forms and practices. Our primary focus is the Federal Republic of Germany—"West Germany" prior to unification in 1990—for both practical and analytical purposes. Because of its status as the German successor state, its historiography at the moment is somewhat deeper and richer than that of the now defunct German Democratic Republic. This same status, moreover, convinces us that it is urgent to explore the historical dynamics and mythologies that have produced and sustained its democratic polity and culture. Nonetheless, our introduction is intended as a clarion call for comparative and contextualized approaches to the study of the postwar period, and we indicate in what follows our desiderata for the reconceptualization of contemporary German and European history, both West and East.

While this introduction sketches out a rather ambitious program of historiographical reorientation, the following three chapters present synthetic summaries of some of the innovative arguments of our recent research on Black Germans, Jews, and immigrant Turks after 1945.[12] The aim of our collaboration is to highlight, in abbreviated form, and bring into dialogue with each other some of the historical work that has already been done to explore processes of racialization and democratization in postwar Germany. In doing so, we hope to demonstrate the new perspectives opened up by such a focus.

Chapter 1, by Heide Fehrenbach, traces the postwar "devolution" of the Nazi racial state. It follows the shifting language and taxonomy of race across the 1945 divide within Germany, investigating the impact of international impulses—especially segregationist U.S. military policies and liberalizing American social science—on postwar reformulations of racial policy and practice in West German society. Discussions regarding postwar occupation children of color, Fehrenbach argues, were crucial in reconstituting notions of race in West Germany, shifting the terms of postwar debate about race away from Jewishness and toward a black-white binary.

Chapter 2, by Atina Grossmann, examines how Jews became *Ausländer* in postwar West Germany. Focusing on East European Jewish Holocaust survivors who resided in the displaced persons (DP) camps of occupied Germany, it considers the ways in which victims of the Third Reich were quickly cast as parasitic "foreigners," who threatened to siphon off precious resources. Germans insistently remembered their own victimization and refused to recognize their new/old prejudices and resentments as antisemitism, in part because notions of difference were recast in the language of resources and "rights."

Chapter 3, by Rita Chin, shifts temporal frames to consider Turkish guest workers during the early 1980s, a moment when public debates began to acknowledge that two million foreigners and their families now constituted immigrants in the Federal Republic. It examines conservative and progressive ideas about *Ausländer* and integration. While German conservatives tended to see migrant culture as timeless, essential, and fixed, their liberal counterparts generally insisted on the mutability of migrant culture. Yet both patterns of thought and discourse came to emphasize incommensurable differences between Turkish and German cultures and ultimately treated integration as a one-way process. Through these case studies, it is possible to glimpse the outlines of postwar West Germany's efforts to both redefine and deal with difference across three distinct minority groups. But this is just a start. Our hope is that the picture will become more detailed and nuanced through the work of other scholars.

The final two chapters in this volume are, like this introduction, more interpretive in character and offer reappraisals of significant developments in postwar German and European history. Chapter 4, by Rita Chin and Heide Fehrenbach, revisits some milestone moments in the history of the Federal Republic from 1945 through the early 1990s in order to trace the interconnections (sometimes explicit, but mostly implicit) between the shifting ways Germans understood democracy—as secured by economic recovery, achieved through a condemnation of fascism and capitalism, earned through historical commemoration—and their conceptions of difference. The essay also explores unification and its aftermath—including the specific analytical terms that German social scientists and the media deployed to test the democratic stability of the expanded Federal Republic *and* that minority intellectuals used to illuminate unified Germany's unacknowledged ethnonational self-conception.

Finally, chapter 5, by Geoff Eley, broadens the geographical lens, arguing that other Western European countries also absorbed the lessons of the German Holocaust and shied away from the language of race in the decades after 1945. Some, like France, appealed to a longer tradition of republican universalism that emerged from the Enlightenment and French Revolution, even as they repeatedly reinscribed racial difference in their social and political conceptions of colonials and postcolonials across the past two centuries. Eley then turns to Britain to explore in more detail how "race" as a central category of analysis emerged only fitfully from the neo-Marxist thinking of mostly minority intellectuals like Stuart Hall and Paul Gilroy, whose theorizing gained international influence by the 1980s and beyond. In tracing the analytical turn toward "race" over the past couple of decades, Eley trains a critical eye on discussions of European culture and commonality as well as the recent embrace of anti-Islamicism in efforts to consolidate European identity.

It is important to be clear that this book by no means represents the first attempt to address the continuities of racism and xenophobia in German history. Minority writers, intellectuals, and scholars have been commenting on the processes and effects of racialization in contemporary German society since the mid-1970s. As early as 1973, Aras Ören published poems that highlighted the ways in which assumptions of essential ethnic difference prevented German and Turkish workers from recognizing their shared oppression within the capitalist system of production.[13] May Ayim and Katharina Oguntoye wrote *Farbe bekennen* in 1988 with the explicit purpose of exposing "the social underpinnings of racism" and demonstrating that the invisibility of Afro-Germans was a "consequence of the suppression of German history."[14] In the months after the fall of the Berlin Wall, Zafer Şenocak pointed to the racializing effects of the Federal Republic's citizenship law, which continued to treat German descent as the crucial criterion for citizenship. This residue of genealogical thinking, he observed, meant that ethnic Germans from Eastern Europe with only distant family ties to Germany and little ability to speak the language were considered German, while second- or third-generation Turks who knew German better than Turkish remained perpetual foreigners.[15]

Despite their trenchant critiques, these authors have generally gone unrecognized by most German historians. Part of the problem is that their writing has been categorized as "foreigner literature." This designation marked their texts as primarily of interest to literary scholars. It also relegated their work to "migration" or "minority" studies, fields often perceived as marginal to the main currents of modern German history. These important early efforts to engage the question of race and to insist on the continued relevance of racial assumptions in the Federal Republic have thus failed to register as integral to our understanding of German society, politics, and culture in the postwar period.

For the future, a thorough unpacking of the zero hour thesis in terms of race and difference would involve further interventions in the broader field of modern German history that can only be gestured at here. First and foremost, this task would require considering continuities across the 1945 divide. It is worth pointing out that a significant, authoritative historical literature has emerged that investigates continuities in racialized thinking and social policy from the Imperial period, including colonialism, through the Weimar Republic *into* the Third Reich.[16] The question of continuity has been taken up by looking backward from the 1930s to earlier decades and across prior political regimes. In recent years, historians have exhibited a great deal of interest in tracing the evolution of German racism and its mobilization by the German state through the last days of the Nazi regime. A primary concern is to test the radicalism of National Socialist policies toward German and European minorities, which emerged from a longer historical commitment to racial hierarchies and eugenic practices, and culminated in state-mandated sterilization, medical experimentation, and mass murder. But the question of continuity also needs to be posed for the period after 1945. While the most egregious racialized violence of the Nazi regime ceased with defeat, Claudia Koonz has suggested that other, more localized and everyday practices were not rooted out so easily. What, in other words, happened to the everyday racism that was also very much a part of German social life, social policy, and the social imaginary during the Third Reich?[17]

Pioneering work has begun on this question, but its central insights and critical approach have yet to be integrated into synthetic accounts of modern German history. Thus far, studies that have raised the issue of race after 1945 have primarily focused on postwar German interactions with, and responses to, American culture and American military occupation. In her study of the reconstruction of national identity and gender norms in the two postwar German states, Uta Poiger explores the social and cultural threats that the import and youthful consumption of "black" American music like jazz and rock 'n' roll represented to both East and West German authorities. In detailing the convergences and divergences of this Cold War dialogue about the meaning of American cultural forms for "Germanness," Poiger exposes continuities in eugenic language and racist stereotype across 1945 in both German states and thereby highlights the racialized content of social and cultural reconstruction. Maria Höhn, on the other hand, considers ground-level social interactions between German civilians and American soldiers in western Germany. She pays special attention to interracial (black-white) sexual fraternization, including the hostile reception it provoked among Germans and Americans alike, and ultimately shows how American practices of race were transferred to German garrison towns in the form of racially segregated bars and entertainment venues. Heide Fehrenbach examines transnational debates regarding the "mixed-race" children of postwar fraternization between black troops and white German women from the end of the war through about 1960, suggesting that responses to the children were central to the ideological transition from National Socialist to democratic approaches to race and, moreover, that these early years helped shape contemporary German racial understanding. Her essay in this volume compares the racial typologies of the Nazi period with those that emerged under U.S. occupation, while Atina Grossmann's piece, like her recent book, highlights the everyday ways in which antisemitic prejudices (re)surfaced during the interregnum.[18] More recently, the emergent body of work around guest workers in West Germany has also begun to consider the issue of race. Analyzing national public debates about foreign labor recruits, Rita Chin argues that the figure of the guest worker effectively marked imported workers as temporary sojourners who were completely separate from German society. Her essay shows how West Germans applied racialized notions of cultural difference to guest workers (and especially Turks) once the presence of labor migrants was officially acknowledged as permanent. As a whole, this scholarship on the postwar period represents an important start, but the line of investigation needs to be extended.[19]

Taking seriously the issue of continuity would also open up new avenues of inquiry across the entire span of modern German history. If the racial ideologies of the National Socialist regime are no longer perceived as an absolute break with what came before and after, then it becomes possible and even necessary to think about racial or ethnic "difference" as an ongoing, constitutive question in the nation's development.[20] One of the primary tasks of consolidating the nation-state, after all, was defining the legal and ideological parameters of membership in order to differentiate insiders from outsiders. In this respect, nineteenth-century antisemitism, anti-Slavism, and antiblack racism served a function similar to that of late-twentieth-century xenophobia. Each form of prejudice became a kind of weapon in the effort to assert a uniquely German identity; each singled out a specific group of people as antithetical and antagonistic to the German social body in an attempt to create ethnic homogeneity. Germany's protracted struggle to achieve national unification—with the debates over a greater or lesser Germany—made the need to clearly demarcate "others" especially urgent. And defeat in both world wars, along with more recent reunification, produced moments of crisis that required (re)constructing national identity and hence clarifying belonging. Our point is not to claim that these engagements with "difference" were exactly the same or that they produced equivalent historical effects. We simply want to suggest that they ought to be explored in relation to one another rather than treated as isolated, discrete episodes.

A Jewish-Turkish comparison, for example, yields several potentially illuminating insights. In terms of the status of religion, Christian anti-Judaism offers a counterpoint to the Islamization of Turkish immigrants after 1945. In medieval and early modern Europe, religion served as the primary marker of absolute difference: Jews were viewed as religiously misguided and even the source of deicide. The perception of religious alterity dictated the way Jews were treated in German Christian lands. Even when they were tolerated, the population understood them as separate from and inferior to the rest of society. This status was most visible in terms of the restrictions placed on Jews' free movement, trades, and clothing. Their social and economic standing as well as their physical security were highly precarious and ultimately dependent on the goodwill of the rulers in whose territory they resided. With the recognition of Turkish permanent residence in postwar Germany, religion has resurfaced as a crucial explanation for incompatibility. In this case, the problem is not so much a clash of doctrinal interpretations or theological understandings that set one community off from another, but rather a sense that Islamic religious practices cannot be accommodated within a Western liberal democracy. For many Germans, the Turkish custom of female head-covering is the ultimate sign of Islam's deeply patriarchal nature and tendency to oppress women. These aspects of the religion are deemed antithetical to the liberal principle of equality. Islam, in this view, represents a major challenge and threat to postwar Germany's hard-won democracy.

Another point of comparison is the question of integration or assimilation. For Jews in German lands, the issue emerged as a matter of serious public debate once emancipation became a real possibility. To the extent that the Enlightenment principle of individual equality paved the way for Jewish equality of rights over the course of the nineteenth century, it also led to the expectation that Jews would "merge with the rest of the citizens" and forgo "a nation of their own, completely isolated by religious customs, ways of thinking and acting."[21] One unanticipated consequence of Jewish emancipation, then, was an expectation of assimilation that was ultimately hard to distinguish from the eradication of Judaism pure and simple. Similarly, a main tension around Turkish immigrants in contemporary Germany has been the putative failure of integration. For many Germans on both the right and the left, the integration of Turks requires relinquishing cultural particularities and pathologies that they associate with Islam, such as the wearing of headscarves or the perpetuation of gender inequality (through arranged marriages, domestic violence, and "honor killings"). Islam, these Germans fear, encourages Turks to live in a *Parallelgesellschaft* with its own rules, values, and institutions that isolate them from mainstream society. The existence of enclaves in major German cities where Turkish is the primary language, worship takes place in mosques, businesses are predominantly Turkish-owned, and seemingly backward customs and behaviors predominate often serves as proof of the Turkish community's unwillingness or inability to integrate.

By juxtaposing the push for assimilation or integration at two very different historical moments, we begin to see Christianity as a constitutive but sometimes unnamed element of German cultural identity.[22] Jewish emancipation often came with the expectation of conversion, while the Islam of Turkish migrants has been understood as clashing with a secular state even as that state still maintains special privileges for Judeo-Christian institutions. At the same time, German anxiety over the failure to eradicate difference grows out of a distinct set of concerns in each case. Antisemitism, which first emerged as a term in German public debate during the late nineteenth century, specifically condemned Jews for causing and benefiting from the massive upheavals of global capitalism, industrialization, urbanization, and modernization.[23] On this score, the discourse around Turks presents an interesting contrast: Islam has often been blamed for encouraging backwardness and illiberal behavior among its Turkish-German adherents, a scenario that is perceived as especially dangerous because it reintroduces retrograde values into German society.

This comparison between Jews and Turks, moreover, productively foregrounds the complicated calculus that exists between cultural and biological conceptions of difference. After the murderous genocide of European Jewry committed in the name of racial purity, it became commonplace among Western democracies to reject the language of race. The 1950 United Nations statement on race, in fact, unequivocally denounced the validity of the concept as a scientific category and made biological notions of race unacceptable in a post-Holocaust world. The 1949 constitutions of both postwar German states declared civic equality under the law and prohibited racial discrimination.[24] One effect of this trend was the repudiation of biology and the growing preponderance of culture as an explanation for fundamental differences between peoples. Such explanations insisted that it was unnatural for different national groups to live together not so much because one was superior to the other but rather because each belonged to a different culture. In the early 1980s, for example, Christian Democrats condemned the far Right's claim that Turks and other guest workers threatened the genetic purity of the Federal Republic as obviously racist. But they went on to advocate restrictions on continued family reunion, arguing that the strength of Turkish culture prevented successful integration and thus imperiled the German way of life. Rejecting immigration and ethnic diversity, in this view, was not racist, but an honest acknowledgment of unbridgeable difference.[25]

In the last twenty years, scholars of Europe have criticized the postwar shift from biology to culture, noting the ways that cultural explanations of incommensurable difference escaped the tainted label of racism. Some of the most insightful work characterized this shift as the emergence of a "new racism," in which using the language of culture made racist assumptions of essential difference seem reasonable and respectable.[26] But these scholarly efforts to expose the racialist thinking lurking beneath cultural arguments against immigration and ethnic diversity (a project we enthusiastically endorse) have also produced unintended consequences. Culture often appears as an entirely novel mode for rationalizing the claim of absolute boundaries between peoples and nations.

What a broader temporal frame and comparative approach make visible are the ways in which culture and biology are routinely interwoven. Indeed, both the Jewish question and the guest worker question demonstrate that culturally based notions of difference have always existed alongside their biological counterparts. Within the framework of Christian anti-Judaism and antisemitism, Jews' religious beliefs and customs proved their fundamental distinction from Germans, even as those cultural traits were often understood as inherited. The Nazis conversely employed bloodlines to mark Jews as Other, while simultaneously pointing to Jewish cultural peculiarities to justify this exclusion.[27] In a similar vein, West German conservatives expressed anxieties about Turkish cultural difference by emphasizing Islamic faith and condemning what they perceived as Islamic-inspired forms of behavior. But they also retained a harder notion of immutability, insisting that Turkish culture was too strong to allow for successful integration no matter how long Turks and Germans lived together. In each case, neither the biological nor the cultural is fully absent from racialized conceptions of difference.

This broader approach also helps us to see that race, ethnicity, and nation are not so much discrete entities or things in themselves but rather modes of perception or ways of making sense of the world.[28] In this formulation, the salient question is not whether antisemitism and anti-Turkish xenophobia really count as racism? Or what differentiates regular old prejudice from dangerous racism? But rather how does race thinking get operationalized? When and why do people interpret social experience in racial or ethnic terms? What about a particular historical moment leads people to invoke race or ethnicity as an explanation for social relations, social resentments, or even social violence? Our intention here is not to offer definitive analyses of antisemitism or anti-Turkish xenophobia, or to explicate the relationship between them once and for all, but to draw attention to the kinds of questions opened up by making race *as a way of understanding the social world* an ongoing and central narrative within modern German history.[29]

At this point, it also seems necessary to ask what is to be gained and what is to be lost with an approach that insists on seeing "race" as a salient category, and racialization as a continuing practice, within German history. There is unease, especially among Europeans, with what seems to be the imposition of an American model—race—on a radically different European history, society, and set of values. To be sure, the concept of *Rasse* has been closely associated with the disciplines of anthropology and eugenics, traditionally involved a fixation on Jews and Slavs, and was generally treated as an ontological category. Thus, for many Germans born after

World War II, the idea of using the word is tantamount to validating the assumptions, beliefs, and false science on which it had been based. Yet what is consistent between "race" and "Rasse" is the insistence on looking for differences between people. In this respect, we are trying to open up a whole field of "race" and race thinking, a broader framework that would allow these two concepts to be seen as comparable but also never fully stable. Maxim Silverman has observed for a French society that has similarly rejected the word *race* that "the banishment of the term is no guarantee of the banishment of the practice."[30]

Our intention is certainly not to lend credence to the social category of "race" as a biological or ontological reality or to suggest that we accept such a view but rather to use the term as a critical concept that enables us to perceive processes of racialization, the ways German society has been and remains structured according to ideas about fundamental (and often hierarchical) differences among groups of peoples. It is important to be clear about the precise moments when racialized thinking became operational: when, how, and why specific sectors of the population are identified and targeted as constituting "groups" imbued with significant and meaningful differences from the majority population. When, how, why, and by whom is "groupness" mobilized, to borrow Rogers Brubaker's terminology, and to what political, social, and cultural effect?[31]

Fehrenbach demonstrates quite clearly that in the first postwar decades the American model of race did, in fact, have a major influence on West German parameters for thinking about and formulating social policy on Afro-German occupation children. At the same time, Chin suggests that racialized notions of difference only became necessary for understanding guest workers once the Federal Republic began to acknowledge these migrants as permanent members of society. Such examples vividly illustrate the necessity of opening our eyes to the historically contingent processes of racialization and ethnicization. Indeed, we cannot grasp the full range of social experience in postwar West Germany without this critical perspective.

Racial Ideologies in Transnational Perspective

Racial ideologies, although typically investigated and conceptualized in national terms, are fundamentally international and transnational in reference. This extends from specifically national regimes of belonging such as citizenship and immigration policy, which are grounded in conceptions of "us" and "other" and articulate the legal basis for inclusion in and exclusion from the nation, through social policy, to popular notions and cultural expressions of difference. In this, Germany was like other modern European nations of the eighteenth and nineteenth centuries, founded upon the language of ethnic self-determination and rights. What differed in the German case were the historical, geographical, and therefore the ideological particulars. German unification and nation building in the late nineteenth century resulted from a half decade of wars (against the Danes, the Hapsburg Austrians, and the French), which were orchestrated to forge a polity, citizenry, and, ultimately, a loyalty to the new German nation and its Protestant Prussian Kaiser among a diverse collection of central Europeans divided not only by region and religion but also by language and ethnic identification. The German nation that resulted was hardly a homogeneous ideal, but a more heterogeneous mix that included minority religions (Catholicism and Judaism) and ascribed ethnicities (Poles, Czechs, Danes, French, Sorbs, Sinti, and Roma). The quest to foster national loyalty and German identity involved explicit attempts by the state and its academic establishment to delineate the social and cultural differences between Germans and their Others, both domestic and foreign. This encompassed strategies as diverse as Bismarck's Kulturkampf (1873–79), which targeted Poles and Catholics; imperial expansion in overseas colonies prior to 1918 and in Europe proper through 1945; a nationality law (1913) based upon patriarchal descent and an ethnicized notion of *Deutschtum*; and the cultivation of social knowledges of race—such as colonial anthropology, *Ostforschung*, eugenics, and other racial sciences—that legitimated state initiatives ranging from conquest, colonization, nationalization, and deportation to adoption, abortion, Aryanization, sterilization, euthanasia, enslavement, mass expulsions, and eventually genocide. German national identity emerged and evolved according to a protracted *politics of difference* that established German subjectivity and superiority by delineating these from their historically, geographically, and politically relevant Others. By the early twentieth century, Germanness was defined in opposition to a number of racially defined categories of perceived aliens residing in Germany, its colonies, and its borderlands, namely, Jews, Slavs, Blacks, and "Gypsies."[32] Because this process was "enmeshed" with the quest for "national identity and cohesion," we call it a *nationalizing politics of difference*.[33]

This nationalizing politics of difference was responsive to more than merely the accidents of geography and localized international pressures, whether actual or perceived. It also developed in ongoing dialogue with a larger international marketplace of ideas and interactions. In this sense, German racial ideologies—though articulated through national laws, policies, and practices—have been shaped by a transnational dynamic.[34] Beginning in the nineteenth century, this involved, among other things, the professional interactions of biologists, anthropologists, and ethnographers within a growing international academic circuit of conferences, research institutes, and journals that resulted in the circulation of social knowledges of race, now unhinged from the national context within which they had been articulated, for selective borrowing or transplantation elsewhere.[35] Racial ideologies were also shaped by a range of interactions between normative Germans and perceived racial aliens in the workplace, neighborhood, street, shop, school, military, and even the home (in the case of domestic servants) in Germany proper, in Germany's colonial territories in Africa, Asia, and Europe, and during Germans' travels abroad.

A third crucial transnational network for the cultivation of social knowledge and cultural representations of race was the expanding global market. This unleashed a historically unprecedented increase in transnational migrant labor and the mass circulation of commercial media and products—such as movies, music, magazines, fashion, and cosmetics—that disseminated potent images and narratives of race.[36] Racial aesthetics and ideology are an integral expression of modernity, implicated in its political, social, cultural, and economic forms. Mobilized through processes of nationalization, racial aesthetics and ideologies have been perpetuated by an increasingly mobile and global capitalist economy.[37] The German politics of race must be situated in this larger international nexus.

The argument for investigating the politics of race as an ongoing, constitutive feature of modern Germany—and modern nations more generally—does not discount the dynamics of change. The years after 1945 in Germany are a case in point. With military defeat in May 1945, the wartime geography of race imposed upon Europe by the Nazi regime was thrust back into Germany, in particular into the western zones occupied by the British and the Americans. Defeated Germans witnessed the influx of their former racialized enemies in the form of Jewish, Slavic, and Soviet DPs, who were liberated from slave labor and the death camps or, a bit later, had fled westward in the face of pogroms in early postwar Poland.[38] Simultaneously, Germans were subordinated to the multiethnic militaries of the British, French, Soviet, and U.S. victors. In terms of political authority and social demographics, May 1945 represented an abrupt rupture for Germans. The resident population within their occupied borders increased and became ethnically diverse. Due to military occupation, moreover, Germans had lost their formalized political and social superiority. They no longer exercised authority at home or abroad. Their hierarchical social and racial order had become disordered. But exactly how interactions with foreign Allied superiors, protected DP survivors, and refugees—and contact with victors' own racial attitudes and ideologies—affected postwar Germans' notions of racial and national identity and their expectations concerning the content and social consequences of democratization is still insufficiently understood.

Nonetheless, it is clear that the altered international context and transnational interactions within occupied Germany produced a dramatic impact. Military occupation, combined with postwar Germans' observation of antiblack racism in the U.S. army and often violent reaction to the civil rights movement, a growing market for African American rock 'n' roll, jazz, and rhythm and blues, and the political destabilization caused by decolonization created a new lens through which Germans began to interpret "race."[39] As Germany abruptly receded as a global political and military power, the significant sites of race appeared to move elsewhere. In the decades after World War II, Germans on both sides of the Cold War border increasingly internationalized—and *Westernized*—the race problem.

By the turn of the 1950s, German commentators identified racist policy and behavior—and therefore preoccupations with "race" as a social category—primarily with the United States and, secondarily, with their Western European neighbors engaged in the painful process of decolonization. This was likely a function of several developments, all of which were connected to the drastically changed geopolitical situation after World War II and the emerging bipolar world. First was the adoption, in Germany, of an American model of race, based upon skin color and a black-white binary, and a corresponding disarticulation of antisemitism from racism. Second, the Federal Republic experienced a demographic decline, as a result of the Holocaust and avid emigration, of Jews and other minorities who were German citizens rather than German residents. Third, the emergence of the Cold War and proliferation of socialist states under Soviet patronage produced a new type of politicking that eagerly advertised the discrepancies between the lofty promises and the prejudiced practices of American capitalist democracy at home and abroad. At the same time, European socialist states actively supported the liberation movements of colonials against their Western European masters and concurrently shielded their *own* domestic social ills from scrutiny.[40] The rise of American international influence, combined with the social earthquake of the U.S. civil rights movement and a decline in Western European countries' ability to maintain their imperial power abroad, refocused the international battleground of "race" away from Germany. This development was likely further propelled by the New Left radicalism of the student movement, which was grounded in a critique of the oppressive social effects of global capitalism in general and American power in particular.[41]

To sum up, it might be useful to make a couple of observations. Definitions of race/*Rasse* are not historically stable and were in a period of tremendous flux in the post-1945 period in *both* Europe and the United States. The ideologies of "race" and *"Rasse,"* though associated with distinctive national-cultural traditions, did not evolve in splendid isolation but through intense mutual interaction, particularly after World War II. By the 1960s, Germans and their historians came to recognize "race" only in moments of overt racial violence and increasingly around problems of color—such as the eras of Nazi domination, decolonization, or the U.S. civil rights movement. As a result, the study of questions of race has been cordoned off to periods of high social drama or destruction. This has led to a neglect of the more subtle yet nonetheless significant ways that notions of difference have structured a more stable, democratic German society, economy, and culture since 1945.

The tendency of post-1945 Germans to internationalize the problem of race and uncouple it from the contemporary German context has extended to the historical scholarship of the postwar period, as we have noted. We want to insist that a nationalizing politics of race persisted after 1945, if in an altered form. Processes of racialization did not end with the demise of Germany's global political and military power. In fact, one could argue just the opposite: that in times of military defeat, foreign occupation, and perceived social and moral disorder, the impetus for a politics of national redefinition and reconstitution intensified. As the following essays make clear, racialized notions of both German cohesiveness and unassimilable difference persisted and informed this process in significant and insufficiently acknowledged ways. After all, Germany was divided into two Cold War states, each of which faced the task of national reconstruction via political, social, and ideological redefinition. How they defined themselves and their Others was key to this process. What lessons were learned? What models were employed? And although racial discrimination was outlawed in both states, did they envision societies built upon racial tolerance or integration? Did they, in practice, pursue both—or either?

Race and Democracy Reconsidered

What emerges from this transnational perspective, especially for the post-1945 period, is a more complex understanding of the relationship between race and democracy. As the U.S. case demonstrates most vividly, commitments to racial hierarchies and democracy were not incompatible. While American leaders in Germany preached democratization and sought to lay its foundation through denazification and reeducation, this mission was carried out initially by a segregated U.S. Army. Despite the American military's best efforts to downplay the racist practices of its own organization, the lesson that white supremacy and racial inequality could coexist with democracy came through loud and clear to occupied Germans.[42] During the initial efforts to mete out justice, moreover, American officials insisted on identifying Nazi victims on the basis of nationality and refused to recognize Jews as a special group that cut across national lines. This classification system had the effect of obscuring the deeply racialized distinctions that animated Nazi decisions about who should live or die.[43]

Yet by 1949, as Grossmann points out, key American diplomats such as U.S. high commissioner John McCloy insisted that the West German stance toward its remaining Jewish population would serve as a measure of the country's democratization. American leaders further suggested that commitment to the Western alliance compelled West Germans to acknowledge German responsibility for the Holocaust.[44] Acceptance into the family of Western democracies thus implicitly required a clear rejection of the Nazi racial project. In practice, this meant that the categories of race tainted by the Nazi legacy became taboo, and the language of race was largely purged from West German public discourse. At the same time, there was no uniform or consistent policy against racism; West German attitudes toward race shifted multiple times in this period of flux and upheaval. Different strands of racism were treated differently: whereas it was possible to accommodate the racialist binary of black/white in thinking about Afro-German *"Mischlinge,"* it simultaneously became impossible to invoke *Rasse* in relation to the Jewish remnant in the Federal Republic and, more generally, as a social category in public discussion.

This complicated relationship between race and democracy is worth emphasizing.[45] After all, one of the arguments in favor of German exceptionalism was its purportedly overly rigorous racism. There seems to be some residual acceptance of this thesis, since scholars have often operated on the assumption that West Germany was "cured" of this problem with the advent of democracy.[46] Or, in the case of East Germany, was blocked from expressing racist values and behaviors publicly by the repressive state structures of socialism—at least while these were in place. The lack of historical attention to postwar processes of racialization evinces an unquestioning acceptance of the mythology of Western democracy, which suggests that democracy actually enacts—and doesn't just represent itself as aspiring to—political and social equality. In the case of West Germany, taking the discourse of democratization at face value has made it difficult to grasp the ways in which assumptions of difference continue to shape social policy, social practices, and cultural representation.

While scholars have noted how German law has drawn exclusive boundaries around citizenship and national belonging to exclude migrant laborers, they have addressed this pattern in terms of economic and labor needs or immigration law. There has generally been very little scholarly discussion casting the issue in terms of racialized conceptions of nation, of a longer history of racial exclusion.[47] Yet democracy and race were intertwined in West Germany in at least two respects. One of the key foundations for establishing democracy in the Federal Republic was building a strong and stable economy. This goal was a priority for Western forces and German leaders alike because of the ways that economic volatility had undermined the Weimar Republic. As relations among the Allied powers shifted with the emergence of the Cold War, moreover, economic prosperity became a key component of the American and British efforts to preclude communist takeover and encourage democracy in their occupation zones. With its unexpectedly quick economic recovery, however, the Federal Republic required more manpower than the native population could provide, if it was also to fulfill the conservative social agenda of returning German women to the home. To address the shortage of acceptable workers, the government embarked in 1955 on an eighteen-year period of foreign labor recruitment from many southern Mediterranean countries, including Italy, Spain, Portugal, Greece, Yugoslavia, and Muslim Turkey. Ultimately, the decision to fuel the economic miracle with guest workers meant that the process of forging West German democracy necessarily involved a renewed engagement with difference.

But the successful building of German democracy also required another, very specific relationship to race: repudiation of Nazi racism and remembrance of German complicity in that racial project. By the time West Germany became an official state, federal leaders such as Konrad Adenauer understood that acceptance as a full partner in the Western democratic alliance demanded public admission of Germany's responsibility for the Holocaust.[48] For the 1968 generation a decade and a half later, it was their parents' stubborn silence about the details of the Nazi period that proved the thorough corruption of West German democracy. True democracy, according to many of these young people, was grounded in and could only be achieved by serious *Vergangenheitsbewältigung.*

This leftist generational critique helped solidify the deep connection between—indeed, the inseparability of—the West German democratic achievement and rejection of the racist past (along with an embrace of its more positive variant, Holocaust remembrance). Indeed, one of the reasons Chancellor Helmut Kohl provoked such an outcry during the 1985 Bitburg affair was the implicit suggestion that four decades of democratic commitment had bought West Germany the right to abandon its self-consciously circumspect posture of remorse for the past. His invitation to U.S. president Ronald Reagan to lay a wreath at the Bitburg military cemetery in spite of the presence of SS graves was roundly condemned—in large part because it seemed to assert that *Vergangenheitsbewältigung* no longer need be at the center of German democracy. The fact that a proper attitude toward the Nazi past has remained a cornerstone of German democracy was starkly illustrated in the recent response to the Hitler salute mimed by Nigerian soccer player Adebowale Ogungbure. Local authorities condemned his illegal gesture as improper and antithetical to a democratic German society, more concerned with the legality of his act than the fact that Ogungbure was responding to undisguised acts of racism.

This incident makes clear that the democratic impulse to eliminate all trace of Nazi racism has not rooted out racist action or racialized understandings of difference from German democratic society. The same is true for the habitual commemorations of the Holocaust since the 1980s. The postwar German inclination to define a new, democratic national identity in terms of "collective guilt" and a "community of fate" reinscribed an ethnically exclusive notion of belonging. Only those who could claim a genealogical connection to the perpetrators fit within this conception of German identity. Somewhat ironically, then, the very effort to embrace democracy by atoning for the Nazi past inadvertently became a tool for reconstituting a homogeneous German nation. The preoccupation with Holocaust remembrance prevented Germans from seeing other, more immediate forms of race thinking and racism that persist in their democracy.

From Postfascist to Post–Cold War and Beyond

What work does focus on "race" as a category do? We want to suggest that it would both provide a better understanding of German history and contemporary social problems and allow comparisons between the German experience and that of other European (and non-European) countries. An international perspective allows us to place the German case in dialogue with other national debates about race and difference—not only Britain, France, and other European countries that have struggled with diversity after World War II[49] but also the United States, Canada, and Australia.

Attention to the category of race and the processes of racialization also offers an opportunity to reframe the postwar period and substantially rethink its defining narratives. Since the 1950s, West Germans constructed for themselves and posterity the perception of having produced a "raceless" polity and society through the ready adoption of democratic forms and values. Although racist behaviors and racialized social and economic policies persisted after 1945, they were rarely recognized as such. To be sure, historians have noted "episodes" of antisemitism and xenophobia since 1945, but these have been understood as periodic phenomena marginal to the broader trajectories of the Federal Republic's history, which tends to be narrated through a more positive focus on democratization, reconstruction, prosperity, Atlanticism, and European integration.[50]

Given this perspective, it is perhaps not surprising that with the end of the Cold War, the demise of the East German socialist state, and the advent of German unification in 1990, incidents of racist and xenophobic slurs and violence—like those directed at soccer player Adebowale Ogungbure—were attributed to the racist proclivities of former East Germans. In this scenario, a progressive West German society now had to contend with its prejudiced East German counterpart. Since 1990, then, racism and xenophobia have been interpreted more often than not as an irascible inheritance of a now defunct East German socialist organization and political ideology. As such, they mark a persistent "difference" from the West German democratic ethos. It is noteworthy that this analysis continues to marginalize the place of racism in German society, if in a somewhat different way than before 1990. Rather than locate racism in the actions of a handful of hateful extremists, as had been done since the 1950s in West Germany, it is now located in the German East where western (German) democratic culture has not yet "taken." (After all, if there *is* an argument for "continuity" in postwar German history it is evident in scholarship connecting the Nazi dictatorship with the "second dictatorship" of the Socialist Unity Party, or SED.)

Such conceptual framing of the post–Cold War order seemingly derives from, and perpetuates, a celebratory narrative of the stability, strength, and success of West German capitalist democracy. It once again discourages a critical self-examination among (West) Germans when it comes to issues of native racial ideology and practice. In fact, one might say that unification allowed citizens and scholars of the Federal Republic to persist in ignoring issues of continuity across 1945 by off-loading concerns about racism to collective hand-wringing over the residual effects of socialism's corrosive impact on social behaviors and values. The lack of a more generalized attention to "race" in the contemporary Federal Republic may well be a function, in part, of Western triumphalism following the Cold War.

This is not to argue that the German Democratic Republic and East German society should be exempt from critical scrutiny. It is worth considering why questions of "race" are not frequently posed in relation to East German history—or even postwar Eastern European history more generally. In the case of East Germany, this too may be a legacy of Cold War politics. After all, the Socialist Unity Party (SED) by the late 1940s increasingly refused to speak the language of "race" in public in relation to its own society. Instead, they engaged in an ideological strategy of projecting "race" and its social ills onto the contemporary capitalist West and its contemptible Nazi predecessor.[51] However, despite official SED denunciations of Western and especially American racism and racist practices, the politics of difference persisted after 1945 in East Germany as well: whether in early postwar reactions to perceived racialized rape by Soviet soldiers and debates about who should cover the costs and care of unwanted "*Russenkinder*" of Soviet paternity or in later instances of antisemitism in purges of the East German socialist leadership.[52] By the 1970s, the SED participated in the official recruitment of "contract workers" from Poland, Vietnam, Cuba, Angola, and Mozambique, who were segregated into workers' housing and deliberately isolated from the daily lives of their German counterparts, but who nonetheless fueled East Germany's minor economic miracle.[53] We need to know more precisely how and to what political and social effect the GDR mobilized a socialist discourse and practice of difference.

Yet even this cursory glance yields intriguing analytical possibilities. It is worth noting, for example, that like capitalist West Germany, socialist East Germany too sought to cultivate postwar prosperity through the use of migrant foreign labor and policies favoring their social isolation rather than integration. Boldly put, one could argue that both Cold War Germanys ultimately structured *ethnicized economies* to meet labor needs and supply their national populations with acceptable levels of consumer goods. Yet the fact, and historical effect, of these ethnically articulated economic policies—and the ethnically segmented economies they produced—has not registered in burgeoning social and cultural histories of consumption and consumerism in the German and European context.[54] Rather than inform the broader historiography and historiographical debates of the postwar period, discussions of foreign labor are mostly consigned to the narrower purview of minority, labor, and to a lesser extent, economic history.[55]

The German experience, and its Cold War framing, may be instructive when considering Europe as a whole. After all, the impulse for racial reconstruction was hardly a uniquely German enterprise after 1945. An important legacy of Nazi military aggression, beyond the ideological division of Europe into two Cold War camps, was its demographic and ethnic reordering. One way of thinking about this is to pose a provocative question: How would we write the postwar history of the Nazi racial empire in Europe? How would we investigate the aftermath of racial and eugenic ideologies, policies, and practices that achieved such radical and murderous expression under the Nazi regime and its aggressive war of conquest? The consequences of the Nazi imperializing project in Europe are only beginning to be explored by historians, and more attention needs to be devoted to the war's aftermath as a constitutive period of contemporary Germany and Europe. Some historical attention has been devoted to the postwar experiences of individual groups of persecuted minorities across Europe, including Jews, Sinti, and Roma.[56] Here again, employing "race" as an analytical framework (focusing on what Brubaker has called "*processes* of racialization, ethnicization, and nationalization") seems especially productive.[57]

After all, during World War II, European countries experienced historically unprecedented forced population transfers and losses, and wartime displacements created a demographic revolution across much of

Europe, but particularly in the East.[58] By war's end, Europeans as a whole engaged in the project of reordering national societies. With the explicit agreement of Western democratic nations like the United States and Britain, mass expulsions of ethnic Germans occurred from Czechoslovakia, Hungary, Romania, Yugoslavia, Poland, and the Baltic states. In addition, Hungarians were deported from Czechoslovakia; Slovaks were deported from Hungary; Ukrainians and Belorussians were deported from Poland to the Soviet Union; Poles were deported from the Soviet Union to Poland. Violent postwar pogroms drove Jews out of Poland and the Soviet Ukraine and into occupied Germany. Within the Soviet Union, the Red Army and Secret Police undertook rigorous ethnic cleansing against national groups in the west and southwest,[59] and consigned thousands of other ethnicities to prison camps and slave labor.[60]

This was *not* primarily the result of postwar chaos. Rather, the victorious Allied governments of World War II agreed in principle that ethnic mixing had historically caused conflict in Europe. The "orderly migration" of minorities to their national homes was expected to secure peace and European stability. As Winston Churchill put it, "there will be no mixture of populations to cause endless trouble . . . A clean sweep will be made."[61] Following on the heels of Nazi Germany's demographic revolution in Central and Eastern Europe, early postwar efforts succeeded in producing ethnically homogeneous nations. The success of this process of ethnic homogenization was assured by Soviet might and may have aided the establishment of Communist rule throughout Eastern and Central Europe. The aim, according to historian Mark Kramer, was to "reshape the ethnic contours of the region psychologically as well as physically."[62]

So far, these forced population transfers in Central and Eastern Europe after World War II have been analyzed by specialists as examples of "ethnic cleansing" and an international strategy with two distinct agendas: first, to ensure political stability in a historically volatile region, and second, to facilitate Soviet control and the installation of communist governments throughout the region.[63] However, this heavy-handed attempt to defuse the national-ethnic demands of minorities within nations through forcible expulsion paradoxically reinforced a commitment to ethnic nationalism demographically, and perhaps politically and psychologically. By suggesting that "mixture" was politically dangerous and destabilizing, the postwar political strategy of ethnic cleansing contributed to the cultivation of a culture of purity.[64]

Certainly the rigorous attempts by numerous nations to homogenize their populations beg the question of not whether, *but in what specific ways,* the broader European project of postwar reconstruction was racialized. How did prewar racial ideologies and wartime Nazi racial policies affect postwar national reconstructions?[65] On the intimate social scale of the family, for example, it would be instructive to follow the postwar legal disposition and geographical dispersion of war children, numbering in the hundreds of thousands, whose final placement sometimes took a good half decade and the negotiation of multiple national legal codes to determine. This amorphous category of children encompassed the illegitimate children fathered by German troops in the conquered and occupied territories of wartime Europe; the predominantly Czech and Polish children kidnapped, "Aryanized," and adopted by German families in Nazi-dominated Europe; children of various nationalities and ethnicities, including Jewish, who miraculously survived being targeted for deportation, slave labor, or death; and the postwar occupation children of Allied paternity born to European women of various nationalities. The international debates and national politics concerning the "proper placement" of such children are only beginning to be explored by historians. Yet these negotiations constitute a rich trove of evidence and assumptions regarding emerging postwar notions of national and ethnic belonging in European societies. As such, they may suggest the legacy of Nazi violence and racial hierarchies for *postfascist* social ideologies throughout continental Europe.[66]

What would happen to our understanding of postwar European history, and our conceptualization of "Europe" more generally, if we attended to the moments when "race"—in the form of racialized language, policy, social behaviors, and valuative distinctions—gets engaged? How would we periodize the social politics of race in Europe? Would attention to such an alternative chronology alter the historical narratives of postwar European reconstruction? The historical narratives of Cold War politics? Of capitalist and socialist economies? And most particularly, of democracy and the processes of democratization, whether postwar or post–Cold War? We think so. Focusing on processes of ethnicization and racialization may be a useful way to begin to synthesize what have been relatively discrete historical narratives regarding population displacements, ethnic cleansing, decolonization and postcolonial adjustments, immigration, and labor migration.

Until now, histories of social integration and social disarticulation have continued to be structured in accordance with the political geography of the Cold War. There has been one narrative model for Western Europe, typically keyed to the challenges of postgenocidal Jewish-Gentile relations, postcolonial immigration, labor migration, and a growing multicultural population.[67] And another, possibly more contentious narrative for Eastern Europe, which has debated the socially stabilizing effects of socialist regimes, the socially *de*stabilizing effects of their demise, and whether or why Eastern Europe since 1990 has been more prone than its Western neighbors to pursue contemporary politics of ethnic, rather than civic, nationalism. The terms of such debates suggest that a rigorous rethinking of ideological biases may be in order. After all, the conceptual dichotomy of "civic" versus "ethnic" nationalism, in which the former describes the rational postwar West while the latter damns the fractious post–Cold War East, better serves purposes of moralizing than historical analysis.[68] Attending to the historical processes of racialization and ethnicization across postwar Europe would level the ideological playing field between East and West. Indeed, it may prove productive in breaking the stranglehold of Cold War conceptualizations and yield unpredictable answers to recent questions regarding the historical, political, social, and cultural coherence of "Europe" itself. At the very least it would allow us to begin to sketch a more expansive European history that not only includes Western (and select areas of Central) Europe but can accommodate the Baltic states to Bulgaria and beyond (to Turkey). A focus on the postwar politics of difference would provide one useful comparative framework for investigating social formations, social classifications, social practices, social understandings, and social representations across the European continent *as a whole.*[69]

To cite a contemporary example: Germany is not unique in struggling with a more visible Muslim presence, whether in the assessments of mainstream politicians, experts, and media coverage or in the perceived and actual social, political, and religious practices and prescriptions of European Muslims.[70] Isn't the challenge at the moment how to describe, interpret, represent, and evaluate *difference*? What, for example, does this difference mean for definitions of Europe in a legal, social, political, and cultural sense? To what extent are these conceptions historically unique? To what extent are they implicated in a longer history of racialization and ethnicization intended to protect, preserve, or produce specific notions of national or regional identity in opposition to groups judged to be different from, inassimilable in, or destructive of those visions? Would we learn something by considering the current situation in a broader conceptual frame that would allow us to compare contemporary assessments of "the Muslim problem" with diverse European articulations of "the Jewish problem" over the course of the nineteenth and twentieth centuries? Whether such comparisons would ultimately emphasize points of overlap or divergence is something we won't conjecture here. Our simple point is that such an approach would at least provide a *historical context* in which to make sense of the contemporary situation. Such a historical perspective would permit us to read current concerns in relation to longer ideological and cultural formations and strategies—whether national, European, or transatlantic in scope—regarding difference.

After 1945, the politics of difference remained a constituent part of the modern nation, both in Germany and indeed throughout Europe. Rather than be consigned to the marginalized subdisciplines of minority or (im)migration studies, questions of race and difference should be mainstreamed in historical inquiry and recognized as central to the larger political, social, and cultural articulation of national and European identities, institutions, economies, and societies. Only then can we assess the historical limits, fluidity, and possibilities of defining and diversifying both Germany and Europe.

CHAPTER I

Black Occupation Children and the Devolution of the Nazi Racial State

Heide Fehrenbach

Prior to 1945, children were a primary target in the Nazi regime's murderous quest to build a new order based upon fantastical notions of racial purity. In a determined drive to craft an Aryan superstate and realize a racialized empire in Europe, the Nazi regime enacted social policies ranging from sterilization to "euthanasia" and, ultimately, mechanized mass murder targeted at those deemed eugenically or racially undesirable. Children were not incidental victims of this fight for posterity. In demographic terms, they numbered among the Third Reich's earliest and most consistent casualties. Beginning in the 1930s, hundreds of Afro-German adolescents were sterilized, and thousands of disabled institutionalized children, regardless of ethnicity, were quietly starved to death or killed by lethal injection. Abortion and adoption law in Germany was recast along racial lines, resulting in the forcible termination of fetuses and families judged inimical to "the public interest" due to the presence of "alien blood." By the war years, Polish and Soviet youth were pressed into slave labor, while phenotypically pleasing Polish, Czech, and Yugoslavian children were kidnapped and Aryanized into German families. Once transports to the Nazi death camps began, children were seized from kindergartens without their parents' knowledge and shipped away on their own. Painfully few of the mostly Jewish children survived the initial hours following arrival at the camps. Due to their dependent and unproductive status, on the one hand, and fears about their future reproductive potential, on the other, children—some unescorted, others accompanied by mothers, siblings, or grandmothers—were inevitably "selected" for immediate death.[1]

After 1945 and the demise of the Third Reich, children remained a focus of racialized social policy in Germany, particularly in the decade and a half following the war. Although no longer subject to physical violence or death by state dictate, certain children continued to serve as objects of scientific study by anthropologists, psychologists, social workers, and school and state officials intent on documenting signs of racial difference. Children, that is, remained a central social category for the postwar production of national-racial ideology. The historical literature on state-sponsored racism and mass murder under the Third Reich is vast, and although scholars have recently published excellent work on the Nazi regulation of sex and reproduction, there has been little focus on children as a category of social analysis.[2] This essay aims to address this gap and argues that the study of social policy toward children has a lot to tell us not only about Nazi conceptions of race and nation but, more significant for the purposes of this volume, about the evolution of racial ideology during the transition from National Socialism to liberal democracy in postwar West Germany.

Here I explore some key features of how attention to children—in particular, black occupation children fathered by Allied troops of color and born to white German mothers—figured in what I have called the *devolution* of the Nazi racial state.[3] Informing this analysis is an insistence that we begin to consider two key postwar developments—namely, democratization and racial reconstruction—in tandem as mutually informing processes. The transition away from Nazi racial practice and understanding was hardly abrupt. Rather, this was a protracted social process lasting at least into the 1960s. It was through the articulation of social policy regarding abortion, adoption, schooling, and integration of these youth into the workforce that questions of German racial redefinition after 1945 were worked out.

Postwar responses to black occupation children represent a formative moment in the racial reconstruction of postfascist Germany. Military occupation between 1945 and 1949 produced some 94,000 occupation children. However, official and public attention fixed on a small subset, the so-called "*farbige Mischlinge*" or "colored mixed-bloods," distinguished from the others by their black paternity. Although they constituted a small minority of postwar German births—numbering only about 3,000 in 1950 and nearly double that by 1955—West German federal and state officials, youth welfare workers, and the press invested the children with considerable symbolic significance.

The years after 1945 were constituent for contemporary German racial understanding, and postwar debates regarding "miscegenation" and "*Mischlingskinder*" were central to the ideological transition from National Socialist to democratic approaches to race. The term *"Mischling,"* in fact, survived the Third Reich and persisted well into the 1960s in official, scholarly, media, and public usage in West Germany. But its content had changed. Rather than refer to the progeny of so-called mixed unions between Jewish and non-Jewish Germans as it had during the Third Reich, immediately after the war it came to connote the offspring of white German women and foreign men of color.[4] Thus *"Mischling"* remained a racialized category of social analysis and social policy after 1945, as before. But the definition of *which races* had mixed, as well as the social significance of such mixing, had fundamentally altered.

Contact Zones: The Social Meaning of Military Occupation

I begin with a few brief observations about the radically altered conditions that confronted Germans in 1945 since these helped shape the terms of social and ideological revaluation following National Socialism's demise. First, it is important to note that the postwar reformulation of notions of race in Germany was not a purely national enterprise but an international and transnational one as well. Defeat in the spring of 1945 brought military occupation and the victorious Allies' mandate for Germans to denazify and democratize themselves, their society, and their polity. The first decades after the war were dominated by debates regarding self-definition as contemporaries were forced to grapple with the question of what it would it mean to be German after Hitler and the Holocaust.

Second, debates about national self-definition necessarily involved confronting issues of race since Germany was occupied by the multiethnic armies of enemy nations. Former racial subordinates—whether Jews, Slavs, North Africans, or African Americans—now occupied a position of political superiority due to their membership in the Allied forces. The occupation challenged Germans to function within a context that was radically *postfascist* in terms of social composition and political authority, if not yet in terms of ideological disposition or social policy.

Third, the most explicit discussions of "race" after the war occurred in response to interracial sex and reproduction between German women and Allied soldiers of color. This was accompanied by an emerging unwillingness among German officials to speak openly about Jews in racialized terms—although antisemitic utterances and actions certainly persisted in informal private interactions, through the circulation of jokes and stereotypes, and even in anonymous exchanges on public transportation or desecrations of Jewish cemeteries.[5]

American practices of racial segregation and antiblack racism in the American occupation forces also helped shape racial ideology after 1945. This does not mean that postwar Germans learned antiblack racism from American occupiers. After all, Germans had a long tradition of such bigotry that predated and was intensified by Germany's short stint as colonial power prior to 1918 and shorter stint as National Socialist power between 1933 and 1945. Rather, informal contacts between occupier and occupied—along with the discriminatory policies of the U.S. military toward its minorities and the tense relations among occupation soldiers of differing ethnicities—affected the ways Germans perceived and received American political and social values after 1945. Although the American Military Government in Germany put a good deal of emphasis on official efforts to denazify and reeducate the German public, "race" barely figured in formal reeducation programs (beyond the legal language against discrimination that ultimately entered West Germany's *Grundgesetz* in 1949). As a result, racial reconstruction in early postwar Germany resulted primarily not from official Allied pronouncements or programs, but more spontaneously through Germans' interaction with, and observation of, the social and racial dynamics of occupation on the ground in Germany.

The United States defeated and occupied Germany with a Jim Crow army in 1945, and the hierarchical values of racial segregation affected social dynamics and perceptions of the American occupation, both among American soldiers and between American occupiers and Germans. In particular, interracial fraternization between African American GIs and white German women elicited a zealous rage—and frequent incidents of verbal and physical abuse—by white GIs. In a series of intelligence debriefings of U.S. troops returning from overseas in 1945, for example, numerous white officers and soldiers denounced interracial dating by black GIs abroad as the primary cause of racial violence in the military. On the ground in Germany, it was treated as an unbearable provocation. White GIs harassed German women in the company of black GIs and physically assaulted the men. American military police forcibly excluded black GIs from bars, in effect imposing racial segregation on German establishments, as Maria Höhn has shown. Where segregation broke down, violent brawls, serious injury, and even murder could result. White American hostility toward interracial sexual relations between African American troops and German women in Germany persisted for decades, but was especially vehement and violent during the late 1940s and 1950s—the years during which desegregation of the U.S. military, if not American society at large, was accomplished. What is more, it was assiduously reported in the German press and no doubt served to condone acts of violence directed at black GIs by German men, which were less frequent but not unheard of.[6] During the occupation, white men of American and German nationality employed a common epithet, *Negerliebchen* or "nigger lover," newly popularized in the German language, to slander women who associated with black troops. Although white Americans and Germans drew on distinct national-historical idioms of race, both agreed upon the necessity to "defend" white manhood and police white women.[7]

In the public behavior of U.S. troops on the German street, troubled American race relations were on display for all to see. Germans absorbed the *postwar* lesson, inadvertently taught by their new American masters, that democratic forms and values were consistent with racialist, even racist, ideology and social organization. German understandings of the content of "democratization" were conditioned by the racialized context within which this was delivered. As a result, military occupation initially reinforced white supremacy as a shared value of mainstream American and German cultures.[8]

Abortion and the Persistence of Antinatalism

The Nazi regime had been pronatalist regarding Aryan reproduction and antinatalist regarding non-Aryan. During the Third Reich, new laws were promulgated that restricted the social and sexual choices of "Aryan" women—those deemed racially and eugenically valuable as reproducers of the *Volk*—to "Aryan" male partners. Relations between such women and "racially foreign" men, whether Jewish, Polish, Soviet, or Black, were strictly prohibited and severely sanctioned.[9] The same did not hold true for Aryan men, who retained the license to engage in interracial sex and wartime rape provided it was nonreproductive. Indeed, archival evidence suggests that at least one Black German girl, who was sterilized in 1937 as a "Rhineland bastard," narrowly escaped being shipped to Eastern Europe to be pressed into prostitution for the Wehrmacht.[10] During its twelve-year rule, National Socialism forged a culture based upon a "racialization of sex" in which the bodies of Aryan women were stringently policed, while the bodies of non-Aryan women were violently or murderously exploited.[11] In both cases, female sexuality was instrumentalized for national purposes by a regime intent on forging a powerful racial state and European empire.[12]

German defeat and the influx of occupation forces ended a decade of prescribed Aryan exclusivity in white German women's heterosexual relations. What came home to the Germans after 1945 was not just their former state enemies, but their declared *racial* enemies as well: Blacks, Jews, Slavs, and other so-called "Asiatics" who served in Allied armies or were liberated as slave laborers, POWs, or concentration and death camp inmates. The result for German women was that the restrictive, state-mandated Aryanized sex of the Third Reich gave way to a broader range of choice in social relations and sexual partners.[13]

In 1945, German state officials attempted to nullify the reproductive consequences of conquest by temporarily relaxing Paragraph 218, which outlawed abortion. Under National Socialism, a state-sponsored policy of "coercive pronatalism" emerged in which access to abortion was severely restricted for Aryan women, who were prohibited from terminating pregnancies under penalty of death, unless there were severe medical problems or unless pregnancy resulted from sexual relations with "racial aliens."[14] In liberalizing abortion policy, German officials specifically targeted "miscegenist" rape by enemy soldiers. In early March 1945, just months before defeat, the Reich Interior Ministry issued a decree to doctors, health offices, and hospitals to expedite abortions of "Slav and Mongol fetuses."[15] Sometime during the spring the Bavarian state government followed suit, issuing a secret memo authorizing abortions in rape cases involving "colored" troops. In the months following defeat, state and municipal officials continued to refer to those orders.[16] So while compulsory abortions and sterilizations ceased in May 1945 due to the nullification of Nazi laws, the elective abortion of fetuses continued apace from the first months of 1945 and over the course of the year "became a mass phenomenon."[17]

The majority of abortions between early 1945 and early 1946 occurred in response to rape by perceived racial aliens—Allied troops of color and Soviet soldiers—indicating that a commitment to racial eugenics and anti-natalism persisted in abortion policy and practice after the Nazi state's demise.[18] This was possible because German authorities at the local and state level were left to deal with women's health and medical issues without firm instructions from the Allied occupation powers.[19] A German medical board of three doctors (preferably gynecologists) ruled on applications for abortion. Applications by women alleging rape by white Allied soldiers were often denied, since medical boards "doubted that physical or emotional problems would ensue" for women carrying such pregnancies to term.[20]

While notions of *Rassenschande* (racial pollution) continued to inform the language and social policy of abortion in the early years of the occupation, the rationale for such decisions changed. The diagnostic focus was transferred from the racialized body of the offspring to the emotional state of its mother. For example, one thirty-six-year-old woman who alleged she had been raped by a Moroccan soldier and was applying for permission to abort wrote that it "affects me mentally to think that I shall bring a Moroccan child into this world." In assessing the case, the district magistrate noted that "one has to be careful because the incident occurred in a forest without witnesses" and expressed concern that she hadn't told her husband about the attack, though she might have contracted a sexually transmitted disease. Still, this magistrate concluded that "if she really *was* raped by a Moroccan, which can't be disproved, then emotional injuries must also exist," and he approved the abortion.[21] This reasoning signaled a shift in racialist thinking after 1945 and anticipated a crucial development in the rhetoric and rationale of postwar social policy: namely, the transition from an emphasis on the *biology of race* to the *psychology of racial difference*.[22]

By early 1946, as the incidence of rape and legal abortions declined, the first "occupation children" were born. German officials and social policy came to focus on the implications of consensual sex between occupying soldiers and native women in the Western zones. Evidence from southern Germany suggests that in addition to American GIs, German women also chose French occupation soldiers—including those from Algeria, Morocco, Tunisia, and French Indochina—as lovers, bore their children, and in some cases married them and emigrated.[23] Despite this broader range of social interaction, American soldiers attracted the lion's share of Germans' attention and aggression.

In a survey conducted in the early 1950s, for example, German social workers asked German women why they had become involved with black troops. Similar questions were not posed to women involved with white foreign troops.[24] While almost half of the women surveyed expressed an intention to marry their black beaus, German and American officials could not accept that interracial relationships were based upon genuinely mutual love and desire. As a result, the women consorting with Black GIs were accused of wanton materialism and moral deficiency, and were characterized as mentally impaired, asocial, or as prostitutes.[25] In many cases, women found in the company of African American GIs were remanded to VD treatment clinics, jails, or workhouses where they could be held against their will for anywhere from a few days to many months.[26]

After 1949, moral assumptions about the women who engaged in interracial fraternization continued to affect the ways that the perceived problem of biracial occupation children was formulated in the Federal Republic. Through the 1950s, German commentators of various political viewpoints insisted that the child should not be made to suffer for the "sins" of the mother. The high number of births in Bavaria alarmed state officials there, and they sought in vain to negotiate with the American military government regarding the citizenship status of the children. Ultimately, all occupation children, including those of color, were grudgingly extended German citizenship—but only after Allied Military Government officials made it clear that they would not entertain paternity suits or grant citizenship to their troops' out-of-wedlock offspring born abroad.[27] Since marriage between GIs and German women, while legally permissible by late 1946, was virtually impossible for black soldiers due to the racial biases inherent in the screening process, such interracial marriages remained rare, rendering most black occupation children "illegitimate." By closing off the possibility of emigration, this policy ensured that the children and their mothers would remain German citizens on German soil.[28]

Counting "Coloreds," Documenting Difference: Toward a Postwar Taxonomy of Race

As a resident minority population of citizen-minors, black occupation children attracted increased official and academic attention with the end of military occupation and the founding of the West German Federal Republic in 1949. From the turn of the 1950s, social and scientific debates about the meaning of race—and its implications for postwar West German society—focused insistently upon these children. Such debates not only invoked but also reconstituted German understandings of race by revising racial classifications, often with reference to contemporary American race relations and social science.

Here I can only summarize the ways that attention to the children revamped and redeployed racial categories in the postwar period.[29] Over the course of the early 1950s, Afro-German children were subjected to special race-based censuses and anthropological studies beholden to methodologies of interwar *Rassenkunde.* Prior to 1945 and reaching back to the nineteenth century, Jews and Slavs, as well as Blacks, had been treated as alien to *Deutschtum* and, more tellingly, to the *Volkskörper,* or very "body of the nation."[30] After 1945, a number of factors, including Nazi-sponsored genocide and the subsequent emigration of surviving Jews, the westward expulsions of ethnic Germans from the eastern reaches of the former Reich, and an increasingly impermeable Iron Curtain dividing West Germans from Slavs (as much as capitalists from communists), imposed a type of ethnic unmixing on Cold War Central Europe. As a result, although "the East" continued as a political and ideological foe, by the 1950s, its perceived threat to West Germans' racial integrity was drastically diminished. Following geopolitical developments, the point of reference for West Germans shifted west to the United States.

By 1950, in fact, West German federal and state Interior Ministry officials explicitly constructed the postwar problem of race around skin color and, even more narrowly, blackness. That year, they surveyed state and municipal youth offices to determine the number and living arrangements of so-called "*Negermischlingskinder.*" By limiting the survey to West German states formerly occupied by the French and Americans (Baden, Bavaria, Hesse, Rheinland-Pfalz, Württemberg-Baden, and Württemberg-Hohenzollern) and drawing on a simplified appraisal of the racial and ethnic composition of those occupying armies, this survey established a postwar preoccupation with color/blackness in bureaucratic record-keeping and in official and public discourse regarding the reproductive consequences of defeat and occupation. What is more, this schematic racial binary—with its categories for national paternities on the one hand and colored paternity, or "*farbige Abstammung,*" on the other—set a precedent for a subsequent federal census of all occupation children in the Federal Republic undertaken in 1954.[31] In creating one explicitly racialized yet denationalized category keyed to "color," the official census in effect de-raced the offspring of Soviet paternity and rendered Jewishness invisible, implicitly coding the occupation children of these formerly racialized groups "white." As a result, the attribution of racialized identities previously, obsessively, and lethally targeted by the German state before 1945—whether Jewish, Slavic, or "Mongoloid/Asiatic"—disappeared from official record-keeping on postwar reproduction. What remained were distinctions of nationality, on one hand, and blackness, on the other.

Postwar Germans' telescoped focus on blackness was also evident in a number of anthropological studies of *"Mischlingskinder"* in the 1950s. During the first half of the decade, two young German anthropologists, Walter Kirchner and Rudolf Sieg, independently undertook studies on Black German children ranging in age from one to six. Assisted, respectively, by Berlin's youth and health offices and by Christian social welfare organizations in West Germany proper, Kirchner and Sieg minutely recorded the children's skin color, lip thickness, and hair texture; the breadth of their noses, shoulders, chests, and pelvises; the length of their limbs and torsos; the shape of their dental bites; and the circumference of their heads and chests. In keeping with the earlier practice of German ethnographers and racial scientists, Kirchner appended a set of photographs of the children to his work. Both anthropologists analyzed the children's medical and psychological records, as well as their social, family, and moral milieu, and subjected the children to a series of intellectual and psychological exams. The point of these exercises was to establish the extent to which *"Mischlingskinder"* deviated from the white norm (Kirchner) and to account for the children's "anomalies" (Sieg).[32]

In exploring the somatic, psychological, and behavioral effects of "racial mixing," both anthropologists drew on the earlier work and methodologies of German racial scientists and eugenicists Eugen Fischer, Wolfgang Abel, and Otmar Freiherr von Verschuer (along with Americans Charles Davenport and Melville Herskovits). Beginning in the 1910s, Fischer pioneered an early study on racial mixing based upon the so-called Rehobother bastards—the children of German fathers and Nama (or "Hottentot") mothers—and concluded that "racial crossing" led to "degeneration" or, at best, the inheritance of "disharmonious traits." Fischer continued his work into the Nazi years. Joined by Abel and others, he conducted racial examinations of the so-called "Rhineland bastards" (the biracial German children of French African occupation troops and German women born after World War I) and later of Jews, providing scientific expertise for the Third Reich's increasingly radical program of eugenic engineering that culminated in forced sterilization and murder.[33]

Though beholden to the earlier work of Fischer and others, the anthropological studies of the 1950s departed from that literature in small and self-conscious ways. As products of young anthropologists who had not established their credentials during the Third Reich but had been trained by those who had, their studies serve as transitional texts. While relying on the methodology of their precursors, they reworked aspects of the Nazi-era paradigm in search of a morally acceptable postwar alternative.

In its attention to the effects of race mixing, Kirchner's postwar work clearly continued his predecessors' tendency to think within a racist eugenicist paradigm. But what is peculiarly postwar is his choice of subject: the black Mischlingskind. This was not a logical choice in demographic terms. The vast majority of black occupation children resided in the southern states of mainland West Germany. Kirchner's study was based in Berlin, where less than 2 percent of the children (about eighty in total) were located.[34] A focus on Jewish children or so-called *Russenkinder,* the colloquial term for German children of Soviet paternity in the first years after the war, would have yielded a larger sample.[35] But there is no indication that Kirchner ever considered such a study, and that is precisely my point. It was politically impossible to contemplate studying Jewish or *Russenkinder* after the death camps, Nazi defeat, and the onset of the Cold War.[36] The postwar political situation influenced the postfascist study of race and the delineation of racial categories in Germany.

Kirchner's and Sieg's studies were also symptomatic in their exclusive emphasis on a subset of black occupation children: namely, those of African American paternity. Kirchner, for example, examined the medical records, social welfare and school reports of fifty "colored mixed-blood children" in Berlin ranging in age from one to twenty but focused his analysis on a subgroup of twenty-three children, aged one through five, of "American Negro" paternity. Similarly, Sieg had access to children of Algerian, Moroccan, and American paternity but deliberately excluded all but the latter from his study. This deliberate focus on black American paternity and the post-1945 circumstances of conception allowed these anthropologists to render a relatively rosy picture of the postwar *Mischlingskind's* physical, mental, and emotional health as compared to the supposedly more negative impact of Moroccan paternity on "Rhineland bastards" after the First World War. In accounting for the absence of serious disease among postwar *Mischlingskinder,* both Kirchner and Sieg credited the relative health and wealth of black American GIs. Unlike North African soldiers after 1918, who "presumably represented a thoroughly unfavorable selection" in eugenic and material terms, African Americans were assumed to have few serious maladies, in part because "Negros" were defined as mixed-race rather than pure-blooded Blacks and had ample resources with which to provide for their offspring.[37]

This assessment made all of the difference for the children. Neither anthropologist found significant deviations in the health, intelligence, or emotional disposition of postwar *Mischlingskinder* when compared to their white counterparts. However, they did note certain developmental, physical, and behavioral characteristics, which they attributed to the children's "Negroid biological inheritance," and that clearly echoed the stereotypes handed down by previous generations of racial scientists. For example, Kirchner and Sieg cited a disposition for respiratory disease (due to maladjustment to the European climate); abnormalities of dental bite; long legs; lively temperaments; a marked joy in movement, including dance; and well-developed speaking abilities, with particular talents for rhythmic speech, rhyme, and imitation. Although the children were described as open to social contact, they were also declared willful, impatient, uncooperative, and at times given to strong, although not necessarily ungovernable, impulses.[38]

As regards the children's mothers, Kirchner judged their influence as generally beneficial, which, he argued, was not the case when one considered the example of the earlier "Rhineland bastards" who were alleged to have suffered disproportionately from psychopathologies. Following earlier racial scientists, Kirchner blamed that interwar generation's poor mental health on the miserable genetic stock of their "asocial" mothers, who were deemed a "particularly negative" type of woman. "In the case of Berliner Mischlinge" born after 1945, he judged that "no such factor presented itself." As Sieg put it at the end of his study, "No detrimental consequences of bastardization were perceptible among *our* Mischlingskinder."[39]

Ultimately, then, postwar anthropologists arrived at a less negative assessment of "race-mixing" and "*Mischlingskinder*" by reading the contemporary episode in relation to earlier historical experience. Their upbeat prognostications rested on evaluating the distinct national and gender dimensions of each case: "Our *Mischlingskinder*" present fewer problems than those of the past because they were fathered by healthy, wealthy "American Negroes," rather than diseased and uncultivated Africans; because they were born to caring lower-class mothers, rather than asocial lunatics.

Finally, the postwar anthropological studies differed significantly from their precursors in their focus on social environment, and in particular its potentially mitigating effect on racial inheritance. While Kirchner and Sieg detected a tendency for hotheadedness, impulsiveness, and disobedience among Black German children, they also declared that these supposedly inherited racial qualities could be tempered by the proper positive influences of attentive mothers, childhood friendships, and a well-disposed public. The markers of "race," that is to say, were not destiny.[40] If

Kirchner and Sieg agreed with earlier anthropologists that racial difference persisted in the biology and psychology of their subjects, Kirchner's innovation was to permit the possibility of social solutions to the purported "problems of race."

In sum, official surveys and anthropological studies of "*Mischlingskinder*" of the 1950s articulated a revised taxonomy of race that would spur new social policy initiatives. In the process, West German official, academic, and media reports constructed a unitary origin for black occupation children. By consistently representing them as offspring of black American soldiers, such reports erased the actual national affiliation of the more diverse paternity by Allied soldiers. By the 1950s, "race" in West Germany was embodied in "*Mischlingskind*" and linked to America. German censuses and scientists had conceived a putatively "new" and peculiarly postwar problem of race.

Viewed in concert, the official censuses and anthropological studies of postwar Afro-German children recalibrated definitions of race by the early 1950s in West Germany. "Negro or Colored" rather than Jewish heredity was labeled, understood, and investigated in racial terms. This is not to argue that antisemitism disappeared from West German life or that Jews and other European minorities were not races in the eyes of many West Germans. There is ample evidence that they were.[41] Rather, it is to argue that West German social policy and academic scholarship of the 1950s did not authorize defining those differences as racial. In this sense, postwar West German definitions of race paralleled those of the postwar United States. For over the course of the 1930s and 1940s, American social scientists softened the differences among whites of European origin (including, in particular, Jews) to a cultural one and conceived of these groups in terms of "ethnicity." Race, as a concept, continued to be employed but was reduced to the radically simplified terms of the black-white binary (or at its most articulated, the black-white-yellow triad), redrawing the lines of meaningful difference according to stereotypical phenotype.[42] The result was a confluence of the broad forms of racial taxonomy in both West Germany and the United States.

Learning from America: Prejudice Studies and the Psychology of "Race"

The reformulation of notions of race after 1945 did not occur in a vacuum but was shaped by transnational influences and interactions between

Americans and Germans. One significant example for the postwar period was the creation of the *Gesellschaft für Christlich-Jüdische Zusammenarbeit* (Society for Christian-Jewish Cooperation), which was modeled on the National Council of Christians and Jews. Founded in the interwar United States to fight antisemitism and the racist violence of the Ku Klux Klan, the *Gesellschaft* was exported to Europe after World War II in response to the murderous racism of the Third Reich. By mid-1948, the U.S. Military Government supported the *Gesellschaft*'s efforts to recruit Germans to establish branches in major German cities to fight against racial and anti-Jewish discrimination in postwar Germany and to foster tolerance and interconfessional understanding.[43]

There were a couple of noteworthy consequences of the *Gesellschaft*'s founding. First, it transferred to the Federal Republic the American model of "intergroup relations" that had emerged in the United States in the 1930s and that sought to fight racism by building educational and activist communities across confessional, ethnic, and racial lines. Second, it introduced to Germans the reigning American social-scientific tool for investigating racism, namely, "prejudice studies," which emphasized the psychological costs of racism for victim and society alike. In doing so, it denationalized the postwar German problem of race by construing racism as a function and pathology of *human,* rather than a uniquely German, psychology. Finally, it helped pioneer the principles on which a liberal discourse of race would be constructed in West Germany.

Although the stated goal of the *Gesellschaft*'s 1952 conference was to facilitate the social acceptance and integration of Black German children into West German society and schools, the psychological approach to race could as easily authorize a policy of social segregation and emigration. Germans advocating these "solutions" professed to be motivated by concern for the well being of the children, who were considered too vulnerable, sensitive, or maladjusted to deal in healthy ways and on a daily basis with their difference from white classmates. As Blacks in a fundamentally white society, the children were considered at risk for developing severe emotional problems.

"Naturally, [they] mostly suffer from the fate of manifestly belonging to an alien race," observed a youth welfare official in Nuremberg. After all, she added, anthropologists had already established a tendency for premature physical and sexual development in *"Mischlingskinder"* that could lead to serious disturbances in school classrooms, orphanages, and foster homes. One ward of the Nuremberg youth welfare office, an Afro-German boy named Klaus who, by all reports had acclimated well to foster care, was removed from this successful placement at the request of his white foster mother. Although she acknowledged their good relationship thus far, she thought it necessary to take preemptive action as he approached puberty in order to avoid "difficulties" that she felt could ensue between Klaus and his younger foster sister. At the time, Klaus was a mere nine years old. That she could imagine the well-behaved boy as a sexual threat is a sad indication of the cultural currency—and potency—of stereotypes regarding black male sexuality and comportment.[44] The concerns expressed by the Nuremberg youth official and foster mother were not isolated. Rather, they were indicative of a more generalized fear—at the local, state, and even federal levels—that the children's troubled emotional development would culminate in social alienation or socially pathological behavior, such as licentiousness or criminality, once they approached puberty. Highlighting the psychological roots and emotional toll of racism did not necessarily advance integrationist thinking or undermine antiblack stereotypes. Rather, it could as readily translate into heightened wariness regarding the socially *de*stabilizing effects of perceived racial difference.

In the early 1950s, the West German federal Interior Ministry integrated German schools, in effect rejecting the segregationist culture of its powerful American mentor. Given the small, dispersed population of black German children, this was as much a pragmatic as ethical decision, since segregation was hardly a practical alternative. Nonetheless, German officials reveled in the celebratory reception they received from the National Association for the Advancement of Colored People (NAACP) and the African American press, which pointed out the great strides made by the formerly Nazi nation when compared to the United States. What *Ebony* magazine and others missed, however, was that the West German Interior Ministry also ordered German states to collect data on the intellectual, physical, and moral development of Black German children and to detail any academic deficits or problems of socialization that would hamper their "integration into our social and civil order."

The racial anxieties underlying this initiative are evident once considered from a broader demographic perspective. In the first decade after the war, ethnic German refugee children from eastern Europe entered West German schools in far greater numbers than Afro-German children. In the state of Bavaria alone they constituted between 15 and 30 percent annually of school children during this period; at the national level, ethnic German refugees represented more than 90 percent of population growth and a full one-quarter of West Germany's total population by the end of the decade.[45] Nonetheless, the federal Interior Ministry ordered school and youth officials to investigate the character, abilities, and integration prospects of only Afro-German children, despite their comparatively minute numbers. Clearly, then, the overriding concern was not to facilitate social integration. Rather, such selective study shows that official attention to racial difference and its presumptive national and social consequences persisted well into the postwar period. Simultaneously, West German officials explored the option of adopting Afro-German children abroad.[46]

International Adoption and Racialized Notions of Kinship

As early as 1947, the African American press covered the story of Germany's "brown babies."[47] Interested parties, on both side of the Atlantic, were intent on pursuing Afro-German children's most "proper" placement. Discussions revolved around issues of national belonging and racial fit. In West Germany, the children were typically imagined as *Heimkinder,* or unwanted institutionalized children, despite the fact that just over 10 percent resided outside of families.[48] Ignoring actual demographics, most West German authorities viewed the children as a social problem and advocated international adoption as the preferred solution.

Adoption by African Americans—described as "families of their own kind"—struck German social welfare authorities as a fitting solution since most Germans were unwilling to adopt children from perceived inferior biological or moral backgrounds. Under the Nazi regime, such adoptions by "Aryan" Germans had been legally prohibited in 1939 for "offending the public interest," and existing adoptions deemed "undesirable" could be terminated by the state.[49]

Concerns about heredity and racial-biological factors persisted after 1945 and discouraged adoptions of biracial children by white German couples. It bears noting that the American Military Government in Germany did nothing to counter this response. In fact, when German officials asked for clarification on adoption law in 1948 the American Legal Affairs Branch responded that it had not abrogated the Nazi-era law but found it "politically and ideologically neutral" (the British and Soviets ruled otherwise). The reason for American inaction on this issue was likely attributable to the rigorously racialized adoption practices in the United States at the time. Racial restrictions in forming German families attracted little

American attention after 1945 because the assumptions underlying such policy were similar to the principles and practices informing adoption in America, where whites cleaved to whites, blacks to blacks, and Jews to Jews. Consideration of race in creating elective families through adoption was therefore not viewed by American officials as necessarily Nazi or even undemocratic.[50]

Shortly after the end of military occupation, West Germans liberalized their adoption law. This was not done to encourage ethnic diversity within the German family. Rather, it was to facilitate the adoption of white (mostly ethnic German) children who had been separated from their parents or orphaned in the war.[51] Concurrently with adoption law reform, West German federal, state, and youth officials continued to seek ways to offload the costs and care of Black German children. In 1951, in fact, West German federal Interior Ministry officials pursued negotiations with representatives of the U.S. Displaced Persons Commission to press for the adoption of black occupation children to the United States using non-quota visas available for war orphans. Strikingly, German officials expressed interest in including in their plan children who had *not* been surrendered by their mothers for adoption, even if they were currently living in German families and would end up in orphanages in the United States.[52] While hundreds of adoptions of Afro-German children to the United States did ensue, most, in the end, appear to have been voluntarily arranged by the mothers.

Adoptions of Afro-German children to the United States were encouraged and pursued by African American civilians at home and in the U.S. military in Germany as well. From the late 1940s into the 1950s, the African American press in particular spread the word about the plight of unwanted "half-Negro" children abroad. The *Pittsburgh Courier* and Baltimore *Afro-American* published appeals to their predominantly black readership, urging them to send special CARE packages to "brown babies" and their unwed German mothers.[53] The NAACP and the Urban League also lobbied on behalf of Afro-German children, invoking them to chastise the American government and military leadership about its reluctance to engage in civil rights reform. The NAACP, for example, pointed out that the "problem of the children" was due to prejudicial official policies that didn't permit black GIs to marry their white German girlfriends.

However, the NAACP and Urban League also expressed doubts about whether the children's adoption to the United States, into an American culture of virulent antiblack racism, would be in the best interests of the child. As Lester Granger of the Urban League put it, "colored children in . . . [the U.S. state of] Georgia, for example, . . . are much worse off than colored children in Germany."[54] In 1952, Walter White of the NAACP issued press releases praising West Germany's decision to integrate schools without regard to race, noting with irony that the former fascist foe surpassed the democratic United States in racial tolerance and equality. In addition, by the mid-1950s, increasing numbers of Americans began adopting Amerasian children. Published exposés of these children's appalling living conditions in Japan and Korea made Germany's treatment of Afro-German children appear beneficent and broad-minded by comparison. As a result, American youth welfare workers—black and white—increasingly questioned whether intervention on behalf of the Germany's "brown babies" was necessary or advisable.[55]

Black Americans on the ground in West Germany saw things differently. Mrs. Mabel Grammer, occasional correspondent for the Baltimore *Afro-American* and wife of a U.S. warrant officer based near Mannheim, observed the miserable economic conditions of some of the children and their mothers in West Germany and actively sought black adoptive parents. Publicizing the children's plight and working closely with local German public and religious youth offices and orphanages, she facilitated up to 700 adoptions between 1951 and 1953 and remained active into the 1960s. Grammer received assistance from West German authorities, who preferred adopting the children to Americans—and especially African Americans—both for reasons of racial "fit" and to release German taxpayers from the costs of the children's care.[56]

Although West German state and local officials eagerly cooperated with Mrs. Grammer through most of 1950s, even permitting proxy adoptions, by late in the decade they began to have second thoughts. Economic recovery fueled more domestic German adoption requests, albeit for white children. Since white German children were also eagerly sought for adoption by white Americans, German federal officials began to demand more stringent regulation of international adoptions in order to keep such "desirable" progeny at home in the Federal Republic.[57]

As a result, the late 1950s marked a retreat from transatlantic adoptions. When it came to Afro-German children, however, West German authorities offered a different rationale for discouraging adoptions to the United States. To explain their policy shift, the federal ministries generalized from the case of "Otto." Charging that the boy suffered severe emotional trauma after being placed with an African American family, German ministry memos warned against similar future placements because of both the child's shock at and inability to adjust to an all-black adoptive family and neighborhood, and the child's subjection to racial segregation and Jim Crow laws in the democratic United States. Since white German families were still not adopting biracial children in any significant numbers,[58] the preferred destination for such children became Denmark where, German commentators curiously insisted, racial prejudice was nonexistent.[59]

By the early 1960s, international adoptions of Black German children to Denmark outpaced those to the United States.[60] In contrast to the troubling reports on adoptive Black German children in the United States, West German officials and social workers painted a picture of easy integration due to the elevated class background of the parents and their assured cultural competence in easing the children from a German context to a Danish one. Denmark was portrayed in terms of cultural similarity: it was like Germany, only better, since prospective Danish parents seemed "more broad-minded about the children's origins." Moreover, German psychologists concerned with the children's emotional development in the segregated United States now described Danish mothers as more culturally compatible and less overbearing than the "black mammies" who, a decade before, had been seen as "natural" nurturers to the children.[61] By claiming to act in the best interests of the child, the West German state cultivated its role as protector and used its experience in international adoptions to provide a critical comparative perspective on the social progress of American and German democracy. Within a decade and a half of Nazi defeat, West German officials could claim a moral victory when it came to race relations and declared the provisional period of postwar racial reeducation closed.

Integration . . . and Its Limits

By the turn of the 1960s, as the oldest of the postwar cohort of Black German youth concluded their education, the public and official focus shifted from the question of "where the children most properly belonged" to the issue of integration into the West German economy. Historically low unemployment aided this process. These were, after all, the early years of the "guest worker" program, when some major West German industries began to import southern European and, later, Turkish workers to address a growing labor shortage. As Black German teens joined the workforce, municipal and state employment offices tracked their movements and reported the ready cooperation of West German employers in providing training and jobs, as well as the teenagers' unbiased absorption into working life. Press reports, official memos, and academic assessments projected the image of a stable and prosperous democracy whose bureaucrats and employers operated according to principles of social equality and economic rationality. In brief order, integration was declared a success—but only because integration was defined and pursued in *exclusively economic* rather than more broadly social terms.[62]

While social policy interest in black German children subsided by the early 1960s in West Germany, sporadic media attention continued and centered on two general themes. The first concerned the alleged social progress and economic privilege accorded Blacks in Germany by the 1970s; the second concerned the allure of black female sexuality. Press coverage took the form of follow-up stories purporting to answer the question of how "the Germans with dark skin" were faring since they reached adulthood. While noting examples of racial prejudice and racist epithets Black Germans had weathered during their young lives, the articles were upbeat, optimistic, and self-congratulatory. In large measure, this was the result of media proclivity to profile the biographies of performers, personalities, and sports figures—in short, celebrities whose careers contrasted sharply with the mundane blue- and pink-collar work performed by most young Black Germans but who were nonetheless treated as representative of the entire postwar cohort of German "*Mischlingskinder.*" For example, weekly magazines highlighted the achievements of "Jimmy" Georg Hartwig, who grew up in miserable circumstances in Offenbach and braved childhood taunts of "nigger pig" and "whore's son" to become a soccer star in Munich. Or Georg Steinherr who had to learn to protect himself from bullies as a small child and put his resulting "aggressiveness" to good use as a professional boxer.

By the 1970s, the West German magazine *Quick* borrowed the American phrase "Black is beautiful" to report on the various ways that biracial German women benefited from the current mode and marketability of their black skin. *Quick* showcased Nicky, "a poor orphan child, abandoned by her parents," now transformed into a stunning long-legged temptress (and featured in a full-page magazine photo), who worked in a Munich boutique and turned the heads of men as she walked down the street. Rosi, who as a child tried to scrub her "dark skin clean" after being cruelly ridiculed as a "*Niggerkind*" by classmates, was now a fashion model earning a lucrative daily rate of six to eight hundred German marks thanks to her "dark, exotic" looks. Such magazine articles betrayed a voyeuristic fascination with black female physicality and sexuality, and incessantly invoked these as a powerful stimulant of white male desire.[63] Even respectable newspapers like the *Frankfurter Allgemeine Zeitung* could not help noting the young women's "attraktive Andersartigkeit," or attractive (racial) difference, in sociological discussions of the teens' integration into the workforce.[64] Illustrated weeklies ran racy photo-essays that promised an intimate peek into the personal lives and sexual relationships of Black German women and white German men. Interracial sex was titillating and therefore profitable for the print media.[65] However, there were limits. Relationships between Black German men and white German women did not become the subject of magazine features. That particular gendering of interracial unions apparently offended the boundaries of social acceptability and marketability in the 1970s—even for the West German tabloid press.[66]

In this connection, it is worth noting that one aspect of postwar German reconstruction to receive scant attention is the issue of continuity and rupture in social norms regarding sexual relations between white Germans and ethnic minorities. Indeed 1945 did not disturb the prerogatives of white German men to engage in nonmatrimonial, nonreproductive sexual relations with women perceived as racial others. These liaisons, while not openly condoned by the German majority, were nonetheless tolerated. By the 1970s, in the wake of the American civil rights and Black Power movements, interracial relationships appear to have become increasingly attractive to socially progressive, politically radical German men seeking to advertise their cosmopolitan taste, antiracist credentials, and therefore their irrepressibly un-German hip-ness.[67]

Afro-German women, on the other hand, suffered from their cultural image as sex objects. Carole, a child-care worker in her twenties featured in a 1975 article in the *Neue Illustrierte Revue,* noted that before she could reconcile herself to a relationship with her white German lover, she first needed to overcome the "I-just-want-to-seduce-you-complex" that she had internalized at a younger age in relation to white men. (This was likely not made any easier by the way her lover described his first impression of Carole: "As I saw her in the partial darkness of the cinema I thought, 'What a pretty exotic bird!' I was not averse to the usual little adventure.") Another magazine reported, in an article inexplicably titled "Skin color is no problem," that a young Afro-German woman attempted suicide after a one-night stand with a white partner.[68] In addition, a Black German woman who was born in 1946 and came of age in the 1960s has described being repeatedly subjected to explicit unwanted sexual advances by male acquaintances and strangers on the street. As a child, she was lectured by the nuns raising her that she—as a black girl—would need to choose between a future as a Christian missionary and life as a prostitute. To them, her race rendered her inherently more sexualized and morally abject than her white counterparts at the orphanage. However, media reports on Afro-Germans through the late 1970s did not focus on such feelings of debased objectification, profound alienation, and worthlessness produced by social interactions and cultural representations so relentlessly cued to notions of "racial difference."[69]

It took until the 1980s for Black Germans to forge a positive identity from the racial designation that had governed their lives. Tellingly, among the first to do so were young women who had been influenced by black feminists from abroad.

"I've never thought of Afro-German as a positive concept before," she said, speaking out of the pain of having to live a difference that has no name . . .

"Let us be ourselves now as we define us. We are not a figment of your imagination or an exotic answer to your desires. We are not some button on the pocket of your longings."[70]

So wrote African American poet Audre Lorde, describing the political awakening of her Black German students at the Free University in Berlin in the spring of 1984 in the original preface to *Farbe Bekennen* [*Showing our Colors*].[71] Considered a foundational text for the establishment of Afro-German identity and community, *Farbe Bekennen* was one of the first publications to establish the historical presence of Blacks in Germany, to explore their social experience, and to express the emotional and personal repercussions of being treated as alien in a country that is their own.[72] The articulation of "Afro-German" (later "Black German") as a positive personal and social identity emerged through intellectual contact with, and mentoring by, Black American women who, like Lorde, were poets, scholars, and not coincidentally, feminists. Asserting self and voice engaged the dual interlocking identities of race and gender: not only what it meant to be black in a predominantly white Germany but what it meant to be a black woman in that context as well.[73]

This is not to suggest that Afro-German identity was derivative of Afro-American, as it was then called. Rather, it is to recognize both that feminism developed a language with international application and resonance, and that the articulation of Black German identity occurred within the larger conceptual framework of an international Black Diaspora, based upon shared experiences of "oppression," as Lorde suggested, even as these experiences differed according to distinctive national contexts and histories. In the 1980s—as in the late 1940s and 1950s—reformulations of notions of race, identity, and nation in Germany were part of a larger transnational dialogue with African Americans and the American experience of race and gender. The critical concepts and terminology that Lorde and others introduced to their German students in the early 1980s assisted them in their social analysis and allowed them to reject their received identities as "*Mischlinge*," "*Besatzungskinder*," and "*Negerin*" and conceive of themselves in a self-affirmative way as Afro-Germans. Afro-German identity was galvanized through dialogue with African American intellectuals; nonetheless comparisons with the African American experience were only one point of reference for the development of Afro-German identity. Black Germans have also looked to postcolonial experiences and social theorizing of Africans and other Black Europeans. And since they hail from diverse family backgrounds, Black Germans have traveled to African nations, in addition to the United States, in search of self-knowledge, political subjectivity, and a sense of belonging—precisely the things that had eluded them in the Federal Republic.[74]

Social and Epistemic Consequences of West Germany's Retreat from "Race"

Following the defeat and international condemnation of National Socialism, West Germans made Afro-German children integral to their postwar process of national rehabilitation and social redefinition, albeit as *objects* of social policy. Unlike other minority groups in postwar Germany, Black German children were minors with German citizenship and therefore under German control, rather than that of the Allies or UN, as was the case for surviving Jews and other DPs. This allowed German officials to conflate issues of race with juvenile stewardship: whatever the policy proposed, Germans claimed to be working in the "best interests" of the child rather than the state.

West German anthropologists, psychologists, social workers, and officials, from the federal down to the local levels, learned from America to generate new scientific knowledge and social policies to confront the challenges of racial difference they believed the children embodied. It was by means of this process—and in explicit comparative reference to the practices of the still-segregationist United States—that German notions of race were renegotiated and revised. Along the way, the children were rendered a stimulus for, and a test of, West Germany's new democratic ethos.

In the early 1960s, having exhausted the children's use as advertisement of West Germany's successful democratic transformation, official and public attention to the children sharply subsided in the Federal Republic, and the "*Mischlingskind*" receded as an object of social policy. One significant step in this direction was the resistance encountered by the federal Ministry of the Interior when its officials in 1960 ordered West German *Länder* (states) to conduct another survey of the numbers of "*Mischlingskinder*" in their jurisdictions. The state cultural minister of Schleswig-Holstein refused outright, citing both pragmatic concerns (such as understaffing) and legal principle (such as the constitutional prohibition on singling out individuals on the basis of race). While these objections came from a state with a minuscule black population, the rebuke effectively nullified the German Ministry of the Interior's practice since the Nazi years of keeping separate statistics on black children.[75]

As a result, official and public discussions regarding the role of race *within* the Federal Republic subsided. As "*Mischlingskinder*" disappeared as a racialized object of social policy, the use of the word *Rasse* and reference to things "racial" were rendered taboo, at least as applied to contemporary German society. In effect, the postwar problem of race, which had been narrowly focused on the problem of the postwar "*Mischlingskind*," was declared solved by West German officials and the media once the oldest cohort had been integrated into the workforce. Afterward, the Federal Republic embraced an antihistorical fantasy of harmonious ethnoracial homogeneity among its national citizenry.

The 1960s initiated a new era, continuing to this day, in which difference and its perceived social disruptions have been transferred to the bodies, beliefs, and cultures of Germany's immigrant populations.[76] Since then, discriminatory behavior and violence in Germany have been commonly interpreted as motivated by "xenophobia" or hatred of *foreigners*. This response is an interpretative act with significant social effects. For it casts the problem as a contemporary one born of an uncomfortable period of adjustment issuing from the end of the Cold War, the demise of socialism, the ensuing surge of immigration, and growth of Islamic radicalism. That is, it locates the *origins* of the problem as *external* to the German nation and German history, rather than treating the problem as connected to a longer, complex native history of racism and notions of race.

The refusal to speak the name of "race" has not extinguished either racialized notions of difference or expressions of racism in Germany in the six decades since 1945. What it has done, until recently, is to deprive German minorities of a critical analytical lens and language with which to effectively confront and counter everyday experiences of social exclusion—and, as important, to compare these across ethnic identification. For decades, Germans who grew up as postwar "*Mischlingskinder*" thought their problems were personal ones, due to individual inadequacies of appearance, intellect, or morality. Only as adults, and increasingly since the 1980s, have they come to recognize the problem of "race" as historical, structural, and sociological: as a persistent, powerful ideological presence that has shaped their lives in spite of who they are as individuals. Since the 1990s, invoking "race" and attending to instances of "racism" has allowed Black Germans to join with other minorities—of Turkish, African, Arabic, Asian, Latin American, and Jewish heritage—to compare shared experiences of discrimination, violence, and social marginality and to cooperate to pursue social equality and justice within Germany.[77] Acknowledging the continuing social and cultural valence of "race" in contemporary Germany need not serve to embolden racism or neofascism. Rather, it can produce—and has produced—the political and epistemological *possibilities* for exposing and eradicating ethnoracial hatred and violence through the efforts of cross-group coalitions. In this sense, reclaiming "race" as a category of analysis and action has been politically enabling, socially progressive, and historically illuminating. German minorities have begun to put this lesson to good use. It is time for historians of Germany to learn from their experiences and follow suit.

CHAPTER 2

From Victims to "Homeless Foreigners"

Jewish Survivors in Postwar Germany

Atina Grossmann

Introduction: Entangled Histories

In 1933, at the beginning of the National Socialist regime, Germany counted approximately 500,000 Jews. In 1946–47, three years after Germany had been declared *judenrein,* some quarter of a million Jews—the numbers are rough and some recent estimates top 300,000—resided in Germany, albeit on occupied and defeated territory, mostly in the American zone.[1] Only about 15,000 of them were German Jews, of whom almost half were in Berlin. Some had endured in hiding or disguised as "Aryans." Others had survived forced labor, as well as death, and concentration camps (especially elderly survivors from Theresienstadt). Most had managed a precarious above-ground existence in "privileged" mixed marriages or as *Mischlinge* (partial Jews). Still others were returned émigrés, many of them now in occupier uniform and serving as translators, interrogators, civil affairs officers, and cultural officers in all four Allied, especially the American, armed forces.

The majority, however, were Eastern European Jews, now classified by the victors as "displaced persons." As the months passed, this remnant was augmented by tens of thousands of Jewish "infiltrees" who poured into the American zone from Eastern Europe. These predominantly Polish Jews included concentration and labor camp and death march survivors, who had been freed in Germany but initially returned to their hometowns hoping, generally in vain, to find lost family members or repossess property, as well as Jews who had survived among the partisans, in hiding or passing as "Aryans." Notably, however, the largest—and the least studied—cohort of European survivors of the Final Solution comprised perhaps 200,000 Jews who had been repatriated to Poland from their difficult but life-saving refuge in the Soviet Union and then fled again, when postwar antisemitism convinced them, especially after the notorious pogrom in Kielce on 4 July 1946, that there was no future for Jews in Communist-occupied Eastern Europe.[2]

Between 1945 and 1949, and contrary to all expectation and instinct, Jewish displaced persons (DPs) in occupied Germany, centered around large refugee camps near Munich and Frankfurt and in Berlin, generated a unique transitory society. DP life was simultaneously a final efflorescence of a destroyed East European Jewish culture, a preparation for an imagined future in *Eretz Israel,* and a "waiting room" in which new lives were indeed—against all odds—begun. That this remnant of Jews gathered and constituted itself surrounded by, among, and in exchange with the Germans who had tried to exterminate them is the counterintuitive historical fact Jews, Germans, and Allied victors had to address in the immediate postwar years.

In that liminal period 1945 to 1949, before the establishment of the Federal Republic, Germans and Jews lived, as they often claimed, in different worlds on the same terrain, divided by memory, experience, and mutual antagonism. But, regulated and observed by their American occupiers, they also continually interacted, in uneasy, sometimes cordial, and mostly pragmatic, ways, in black market enterprises, and the general stuff—the nitty-gritty—of everyday life: feeding people, taking care of children and the sick, establishing local businesses and administering the camps, engaging in sports and education, and even entertainment and sexual relations. In their everyday encounters and in more public venues—demonstrations, newspapers, and political negotiations—they also contested definitions and calibrations of victimization, guilt, and responsibility, entitlement to victim status, commemoration, reparations, and a possible future for Jews in post-Nazi Germany.[3] From a ragged and exhausted group of displaced persons with very different backgrounds and wartime experiences there had emerged over several years, side by side and among a nation of defeated Germans, a new and self-conscious Jewish collectivity, which named itself the *She'erit Hapletah* (or in the Yiddish vernacular *sheyres hapleyte*), invoking biblical references to the surviving (and leftover saving) remnant that has escaped destruction and "carries the promise of a future."[4]

For the vast majority of Jewish DPs, however, that possible future meant emigration—as soon as possible but rarely before 1948—from the "blood-stained, cursed" soil of Germany. They had, in the words of one survivor interviewed in Feldafing DP camp in March 1946, "only one goal, *raus aus Europa.*"[5] Their years as displaced persons, supported by U.S. Military Government, UNRRA (United Nations Relief and Rehabilitation Administration), and international Jewish aid organizations, notably the American Joint (Jewish) Distribution Committee (JDC, Joint), had provided a frustrating—but also in many ways necessary—interregnum, a space between the trauma of war, genocide, and displacement and the burdens of starting new lives in new homelands, generally outside of Europe, in the United States, Israel, Australia, and Canada.[6] Life as Jewish DPs in the American zone of occupied Germany, whether within the protected gates of refugee camps or (for eventually up to 25 percent) outside in German villages and cities, gave the overwhelmingly young survivors time to recover physically, reestablish contact with or (more likely) mourn lost family members, establish a lively and contentious autonomous political and cultural life—conducted mostly in Yiddish—with political parties, theaters, literature, and newspapers, and in some cases learn a trade or even attend university. At the same time, the frustrations of stateless refugee existence also promoted a Zionist consciousness that served to give survivors a sense of agency and hope for the future regardless of their eventual destination. Finally—and very importantly—they began to construct a kind of human "normality" through the negotiation of encounters, both confrontational and harmonious, with defeated Germans, and the formation of new families through rapid marriage and childbirth. But this poignant and counterintuitive revival of Jewish life in the land of the murderers—albeit under the protection of reluctant but determined occupiers—was conceived from the outset as temporary, a transit station on the way to elsewhere. It was an emergency relief and rehabilitation measure that depended for its success on the firm belief that it would be short-lived.

New States and Shifting Priorities

Relations between Germans and Jews became even more complicated and confused once it became clear that some, a small minority certainly, of those survivors in transit to new lives would in fact become permanent residents of an only partially renovated post-Nazi Germany. Already by late 1947, the chaos and flux—but also the sense of openness about Germany's future—that marked the immediate postwar period was over. Political conditions and everyday life were changing for everyone: defeated Germans, American victors, and both German and DP Jewish survivors. U.S. Military Government's turn away from policies of denazification, justice, and restitution to cooperation with the former enemy in the service of intensifying Cold War conflicts and the push for German economic reconstruction and greater political autonomy became ever more pronounced. Germans were chafing for more control over their own affairs. Americans and Germans were growing ever more impatient with the dependent Jewish refugee population, especially given the social and economic pressures involved in integrating some eight million ethnic German expellees from Soviet-dominated territories.

Jewish DPs themselves were becoming more impatient and frustrated with their "waiting" life, a volatile mood that was in many ways exacerbated by the uproar over the fate of the refugee ship *Exodus* in summer 1947 and the UN vote approving partition of Palestine in November.[7] After 21 April 1947, in a signal of their weary irritation, the Military Government no longer recognized "infiltrees" as UN Displaced Persons; this meant that while the IRO (International Refugee Organization, which had taken over from UNRRA) was still in charge of maintaining the DP camps, and the borders remained essentially open, funding of refugee services devolved onto Jewish aid organizations, especially the Joint. In 1948, a DP leader took stock of the situation and sourly declared in the American-Jewish journal *Commentary* that "Jewish survivors in German DP camps are an obstacle to Cold War reconciliation with Germany . . . They are still in acute conflict with the nation which Allied occupation policy wants to make into an ally."[8] At the same time, the *Yishuv* in Palestine, struggling for statehood and foreseeing the heightening of conflict with the Arabs once the British pulled out, was increasing pressure for young and able Jews to emigrate, populate, and defend what would become a new Jewish state. And most Jewish DPs were increasingly anxious to leave a more and more assertive Germany. Nineteen forty-eight therefore would prove to be the crucial transition year, bringing the preparations for the establishment of the German Federal Republic in 1949 and the switch from Military Government to civilian "supervision" by a High Command for Germany (HICOG) led by the State Department, an easing of U.S. immigration regulations, the declaration of the state of Israel, and with the blockade and airlift, the escalation of the Cold War in the flashpoint city of Berlin.

The DP story was becoming ever more complicated. It had become clear that, despite all the reported respect for the DPs' Zionist dream and the *Yishuv*'s success in building a refuge in Palestine, the promise of the sympathetic August 1945 Harrison Report commissioned by President Truman and the subsequent recommendation of the Anglo-American Committee of Inquiry for the immediate provision of 100,000 entry permits for Palestine would not be fulfilled. Jewish DPs were trapped by the stated British refusal to consider withdrawing from Palestine unless the Jews renounced all violent resistance to their presence and by the United States' reluctance to admit them as immigrants.

The Harrison Report's warning that American treatment of Jewish survivors offered Germans an object lesson in reeducation and denazification had helped assure them a protective haven in the American zone. As U.S. priorities shifted toward reconciliation with the defeated Germans, that commitment became increasingly problematic, and the pressures for either emigration or integration of remaining DP Jews mounted. At the same time, it is important to remember that the American policy of limiting the Jewish presence in Germany and restricting—often with clear antisemitic grounding—Jewish emigration to the United States was entirely compatible with, indeed inextricably linked to, the two prime goals of Jewish survivors: supporting Jewish DP life in Germany and ultimately emigrating to a newly established state of Israel. In that sense, and in stark contrast to the situation in the British zone, American and Jewish desires, while not always reconcilable in the immediate situation, were ultimately mutually supportive.

Despite the Americans' and UNRRA/IRO's considerable efforts to organize repatriation or resettlement, this was not immediately accomplished. As Janet Flanner, the *New Yorker*'s correspondent in Europe, reported in 1948 about the mass of both Jewish and non-Jewish DPs, "after more than three years of peace, three-quarters of a million uprooted European human beings" were "still living in the American zone of Germany, all of them willing to go anywhere on earth except home." They were living side by side with the Germans "who guiltily hate them." Yet as "Genêt" (Flanner's nom de plume) pointed out, with a copious dose of romanticization, the Jewish story was distinct. Unlike non-Jewish Polish or Baltic DPs whose lands had turned Communist and who therefore now constituted themselves as necessarily uprooted "nations as exile," Jewish DPs imagined an end to exile and insisted that they did have a national home that they only needed to reach. Improbably, "Of all those now homeless in this foreign land, the Jews" were "the cheeriest," because "their faces" were "turned . . . toward Israel."[9]

The situation in the DP camps did shift drastically after the acceptance of partition in Palestine by the United Nations General Assembly in November 1947, the subsequent onset of Arab protests and riots, and the declaration of the state of Israel in May 1948. Especially young DPs were eager, or certainly faced great "moral pressure," to enlist in the fledgling defense forces of the new nation. Moreover, even the great majority of DPs who did not join the fighting force supported the struggle for the new state by contributing to a kind of national tax, publicized and collected among all DPs.[10] However, despite the collective insistence on the necessity of a Jewish state and the near universal acceptance of Zionism as the best political hope for European Jews after the Holocaust, many individual DPs, especially those with family already there, still dreamed of crossing the ocean to the United States, that other "promised land." The long-awaited June 1948 U.S. Immigration Act, however, with its 30 percent quota for agricultural workers, was much more welcoming to ethnic Germans and non-Jewish Eastern Europeans, especially from the Baltic states, than Jewish DPs, as was repeatedly noted by Jewish relief officials (and subsequent historians). Moreover, the initial provision that DPs had to have entered what was defined as American-occupied Germany, Austria, or Italy between 1 September 1939 and 22 December 1945 essentially made ineligible the great majority of Jewish DPs who had arrived in the American zone as "infiltrees" from Eastern Europe starting in 1946. The act did contain sufficient loopholes, some actually encouraged by a somewhat embarrassed President Truman, to allow entry to thousands of Jews between 1948 to 1950; the rest would arrive after the amended, more liberal DP Act of 1950. All in all, from 1945 to 1952, about 400,000 to 450,000 DPs, of whom around 72,000 to 100,000 were Jews (about 20 percent to a third of all Jewish DPs), entered the United States.[11]

In April 1948, there were perhaps 165,000 Jewish DPs left in Germany; by September their numbers had dwindled to 30,000.[12] By 1950, therefore, after the establishment of the German Federal Republic and the state of Israel as well as the shift in U.S. immigration policy, the great majority of the Jewish DPs had departed the "cursed soil" of Germany for new homelands. In 1951, when the Federal Republic of Germany formally assumed control over the DP camps from the IRO, about 12 percent of all Jews worldwide lived in Israel as compared to about 3 percent in Palestine prior to the Holocaust. In a major demographic and cultural shift, about half of all Jews resided in the United States compared to about a third before World War II. The once "flourishing" communities of Central and Eastern

Europe had been decimated, with only some concentrations left in the Soviet Union, Romania, Hungary, France, and England. Some twelve years after the Kristallnacht pogrom signaled the absolute impossibility of continuing Jewish life in Germany, and seven years after the implementation of the Final Solution designed to make Germany, and eventually Europe, *judenrein,* a quite different Germany had finally become a country with hardly any Jews.[13]

As a kind of normality was restored to a rapidly prospering West Germany, by 1950 some 30,000 Jews remained. About half of them were German Jews, often with only a marginal relationship to Judaism, and the other half, former East European DPs, the so-called hard core that was unable or unwilling to emigrate, and who stubbornly resisted either resettlement or integration. Jewish DPs who had not left with the emigration wave that followed Israeli independence or emigrated elsewhere now faced the establishment of another state, that of the Federal Republic of Germany in 1949. The Americans were relieved to hand over responsibility for the remaining DPs to the IRO and Jewish aid organizations, and then, in December 1951, officially to the West Germans. The DPs, however, regretted the loss of the Americans' reluctant, ambivalent, but ultimately benevolent authority as military occupation ended and switched to civilian "supervision."[14] Moreover, it was no secret that the vaunted currency reform that would bring good fortune to West Germans was, at least initially, bad news for the DP economy. A stabilized currency, along with the reduction of American forces from an initial high of 400,000 to about 75,000, reduced both the supply of and the need for their black market goods. As American Jewish envoy William Haber delicately put it, "The reform will, obviously, also affect the economic position of the DPs who depend upon the black market . . . With reform will come also substantially more access to imported consumer goods, so that items of barter such as foreign cigarettes will lose their value."[15] It became imperative to participate in the official West German economy in order to reap its benefits. These new possibilities in turn became an incentive for some DPs to stay.

Although some Jews stood to benefit from the developing West German welfare state and economic miracle, the birth of a stable anticommunist Germany and the essential end of an already steadily reduced denazification program dashed remaining hopes that a recognition of collective responsibility for Nazi crimes could lead to serious reparations. Reparations had become, almost immediately after the end of the war, a major issue, and not only for German Jews. Despite the many obstacles, determined surviving or returning German Jews were able to take advantage, in ways not open to DPs, of Military Government Law 59 issued by General McNarney on 10 November 1947, which assured restitution of property in the American zone to persons "who were wrongfully deprived of it between January 30, 1933 and March 8, 1945, for reasons of race, religion, nationality, ideology or political opposition to National Socialism." But Jews from Eastern Europe who had been displaced by the Nazis' war also demanded recompense. They aimed to finance rehabilitation, relief, and resettlement, as well as decrease dependence on the JDC, which had, by summer 1947, taken over the economic burden of caring for the infiltrees. All of these considerations, by both German and DP Jews, demanded a new political engagement with the still ambiguous (not occupied but "supervised") entity of the Federal Republic of Germany.[16]

Debates about a Jewish Future in Germany

In July 1949, just as the Federal Republic was being established, a remarkable conference was convened in Heidelberg by Harry Greenstein, the last Adviser on Jewish Affairs to the U.S. Military Government. Representatives of both DP and German Jews, international Jewish organizations, the "other Germany" of anti-Nazi resistance, and the American occupiers gathered to take the measure of Jewish life in the new semisovereign Germany. They argued over the future of the greatly diminished but stabilizing number of Jews, their proper relationship with Germans, and the disposition of Jewish property and claims. They debated whether there was any justification for Jews to remain in Germany, and about the nature of those justifications. Were they purely instrumental—that as long as Jews were there for whatever reason they must not be abandoned, and that Jews fleeing "from behind the iron curtain" were likely to continue to need a welcoming outpost in the West? Or were they existential and symbolic—that for all Jews to leave would be to grant Hitler a final victory? In a discussion that encompassed both the practical and the symbolic, delegates argued vigorously about the always pressing financial questions. Should the extensive cultural and monetary assets of the pre-Nazi German-Jewish community—both those already recovered and the considerable ones still to be compensated—devolve onto the tiny rump postwar *Gemeinden,* composed for the most part of people who had been only marginally Jewish? Or should they also be distributed to the much larger majority of German

Jews who had become refugees throughout the world? Greenstein tried to play the honest broker, but his very presence suggested an openness, unusual among American Jews, to the idea that there might be room for a Jewish future in Germany. "There are honest differences of opinion on the question of whether Jews should or should not remain in Germany," he noted, with some understatement. Not surprisingly, the representatives of the DP Central Committee were unalterably convinced that "there is no place for Jews in Germany," and that it would be "suicidal" to remain. Others, especially among the German Jews, believed equally strongly that "the extinction of the Jewish community in Germany would be tragic, and constitute a very dangerous precedent."[17]

By 1950, the numbers themselves told a sobering tale. With the Jewish DP population in the U.S. zone rapidly declining—in 1948 the rolls had dropped from about 165,000 to 30,000 in a matter of months—local communities (*Gemeinden* outside of DP camps) counted only 3,650 members, with an additional 3,382 in the British zone and some 7,044 in four power–controlled Berlin. In contrast to the demographic profile of the DP camps, these German-Jewish communities were elderly, with few children, and very high rates of intermarriage. At the same time it was clear that most Jews eager to go to Israel had already gone; indeed some had gone and come back. Emigration to Israel has "slowed down to a mere trickle," as disillusioned returnees and depressing letters from emigrants told of disappointment, war, and hardship in the young Jewish nation.[18]

Ironically, it was left to the American High Commissioner John Mc-Cloy, who had succeeded Military Government commander Lucius Clay when the Americans instituted civilian oversight of an independent Federal Republic, to make the most impassioned case for a Jewish future in Germany. Even if only some 30,000 remained, of the over 500,000 who had lived in Germany before 1933 and the several hundred thousand who had passed through after the war, that remnant, he insisted, had a symbolic significance. But McCloy fell back on a highly problematic argument; he asked the Jews to take on a moral obligation to the land of their murderers. The continued presence of Jews, he claimed, served as a kind of barometer of and guarantee for the moral rehabilitation of the Germans. They were a living reproach to the pervasive desire for normalization and closure of the guilt question (*Schlussstrich*), which wanted only to "forget the Auschwitzes and the Dachaus and the other concentration camps and think in terms of the new Germany we are trying to rebuild."

"To end Jewish life in Germany would be almost an acknowledgment of failure," McCloy argued. Like so many hoping for reconciliation, however, he placed the onus for taking the initiative on the victims. Resorting to his own well-meaning stereotypes, and with none too subtle reference to Jews' reputation for shady business activities, McCloy suggested that "with the tenacity, persistence, courage, and vigor of the race [sic] and with the habit of honest and fair dealing, the Jew in Germany will be restored to a position which he occupied in the past in this community and will reach even higher levels." He acknowledged, however, that "I do not know how long that will take." Presenting what would become his signature remark on the importance of the Jewish presence as a test of post-Nazi West German political maturity, McCloy stated, "What this community will be, how it forms itself, how it becomes a part and how it merges with the new Germany, will, I believe, be watched very closely and very carefully by the entire world. It will, in my judgment, be one of the real touchstones and the test of Germany's progress." Moreover, it would be the task of the Jews themselves to do the work of assimilation and integration, precisely a mission that the remaining DPs were utterly uninterested in undertaking. "The success of those that remain," the High Commissioner insisted, "will to a large extent depend upon the extent to which that community becomes less of a community in itself and merges with the general community." To his credit, McCloy fleetingly took notice of how off-base his comments must have seemed to much of his audience: "It is a little difficult for me to choose the right words to express my sympathy and my interest in the reestablishment of the Jews in Germany . . . and I realize that however sympathetic one may be, you have feelings whose depth no one can plumb."[19]

Representing a liberal antifascist "other Germany," Dr. Eugen Kogon, a non-Jewish Buchenwald survivor and editor of the journal *Frankfurter Hefte,* took a somewhat different and more credible tack to lobby for the same conclusion that Jews should not desert Germany. He expressed his deep disappointment with Germans' preoccupation with their own victimization. Not only had there been "no horrified outcry" about the atrocities they had perpetrated, but the very presence of the survivors had given rise to a new antisemitism, driven by resentment of Jews as the visible but unwanted reminders of German crimes, demanding some restitution. Yet he too still pleaded for some measure of reconciliation. His position was forcefully challenged by the energetic and controversial Philipp Auerbach, a Hamburg Jew who had survived Nazi concentration camps and had, in an unusual move, been appointed Bavarian state commissioner for racial, religious, and political persecutees in 1946. The campaign for financial reparations, Auerbach contended, was not, as so many, even ostensibly friendly, critics suggested, "an unwarranted fixation with compensation"[20] or an incitement to antisemitism. It was rather the only means left by which to force responsibility on a "German people" who had "no sense of guilt and are not held culpable by others." Where Germans saw corruption and special favor as well as confirmation of old stereotypes about money-grubbing Jews, Jews pressed the demand for minimal justice.

A broad range of opinions were represented in this open and sophisticated debate. Representatives of the scattered emigrated German Jews insisted in no uncertain terms that it would be a "travesty" (*Hohn*) if "whatever has been built up by and for 550,000 people in the course of many hundreds of years of history and designed for the needs of such a great number of people, can be claimed by 20,000 to 25,000 people," many of them with only the most tenuous relationship to the Jewish religion. There were, after all, over 200,000 surviving German Jews elsewhere in the world whose claims were being pressed by the newly established organizations, JRSO (Jewish Restitution Successor Organization, 1948) for the American zone and the Jewish Trust Corporation in the British (1949) and French (1950) zones.[21] The issues were not resolved—and they continued to be contested for many years to come—but the Heidelberg conference did establish an umbrella organization of Jewish communities in the new Germany. It quickly developed into the Central Council (*Zentralrat*) of Jews in Germany, an organization that, recognizing both the diversity of membership and the ruptures of recent history, tellingly did not refer to "German Jews" in its name.[22] A year and a half later, on Sunday 17 December 1950, the Central Committee of Liberated Jews held its last meeting in the Deutsches Museum. The Jewish DP era was officially closed, even as control of the remaining two camps passed into the hands of German authorities and more DPs were joining local German-Jewish *Gemeinden*.

By 1950, Jewish visitors were noting, with palpable regret and concern, "the almost complete normality" enjoyed by a rapidly prospering West Germany, while Jews were still displaced and austerity continued in European victor nations, notably Great Britain. Jews continued to bemoan the perceived failure of denazification, the restoration of former party members to public office, and the infuriating general absence of "public conscience." Ironically, it often seemed that those who were least "guilty," such as Kogon, were most willing to accept responsibility, while the great majority of Germans remained awash in self-pitying "moral obstinacy."

They obdurately remembered their own victimization, but, as an embit-
tered Jewish envoy reported in 1950, forgot the crimes they claimed not to
have noticed while they were happening.[23]

New Antisemitism

The putative absence of Nazis notwithstanding, Jewish officials in the Federal Republic were kept busy protesting an ever more obvious "neo" antisemitism. They had already begun to identify this tendency shortly after
the defeat of the Nazis' racial state, but once the mass of Jewish DPs had
departed, Germans were even more likely to perceive those still there not as
victims of persecution but as "asocial" and "homeless" foreigners (*heimat-
slose Ausländer*), "parasites" on West Germany's developing economy and
efforts to integrate ethnic German refugees.[24] In 1946, Jewish relief officials
suspected that traumatized DPs were inclined to "frequently see antisemitism where it may not exist."[25] After 1948, however, most were forced
to agree with the ever outspoken Auerbach when he remarked, "The antisemitism in Germany hardly needs to be exaggerated [*braucht gar nicht
überrtrieben zu werden*] because it is sufficiently present."[26]

As sympathy and memory faded (to the degree that it had ever existed), familiar stereotypes about financial and real estate speculation, endangerment of youth and women in bars owned or managed by DPs, prostitution and black market dealing, and filth and disorder became more
common and acceptable. The first year of the Federal Republic saw a wave
of cemetery desecrations. The now fully empowered German police, determined to safeguard the currency reform instituted in 1948, routinely raided
locales where Jewish black marketeers were thought to congregate. German officials, partially freed from American disciplinary control, were now
more apt simply to deny any charges of antisemitism resulting from such
actions, insisting that they were merely enforcing law and order. In a particularly blatant statement, preserved in DP files, and using vocabulary
that would have been entirely familiar to anyone who had lived through the
Third Reich, local officials in Bamberg in southern Germany, anxious to
prevent any settlement of Jewish DPs near ethnic German refugees, pre-
emptively declared in 1950, "We know that in certain circles our position
against the DPs is seen as reviving antisemitism." Absolutely not, they self-
righteously contended: "None of us are plagued by such thoughts, but the
population is justifiably defending itself against people who feel comfort-

able in dirt and vermin and therefore constitute a dangerous site of infection [*gefährlichen Ansteckungsherd*]."[27] Since it was in fact not quite proper to attack Jews as Jews, they were criticized as "foreigners" or as "certain circles," labeled as outsiders in a kind of extraterritoriality that the DPs—and indeed virtually all Jews living in Germany—would, in different and quite functional ways, also claim.[28] Indeed, there should be no doubt that the philosemitism or shamed silence that tabooized anti-Jewish acts or utterances often attributed to postwar Germany not only coexisted with but were often overwhelmed by a strong and entirely acceptable antisemitism. As Anthony D. Kauders notes in a recent study of the paradoxes of Jewish life in the Federal Republic, putative taboos on overt antisemitism notwithstanding, when it came to black market dealings and other objectionable activities by "foreigners," Germans could be quite comfortable talking about a "justified" antisemitism or distinguishing between "decent" and unacceptable [*anständige und unanständige*] Jews.[29] Even if it was clothed as resentment of, and outrage over, all manner of perceived shady dealings and social irresponsibility by especially East European Jews, and even if the explicit references to "race" had mostly (but not entirely) shifted to groups defined by skin color, especially African Americans, antisemitism was still clearly legible in a language of *Volk,* hygiene, and xenophobia that drew from both pre-Nazi and Nazi terminology and practice.[30]

DPs and Jewish organizations were, however, quick to react to such egregious incidents, as indeed were some German politicians and civic groups. At the same time, especially the JDC, which remained the major Jewish group responsible for DP welfare, fretted about how simultaneously to counter such prejudices and (with the departure of many leaders, young people, and families) the increasingly disorganized everyday reality of DP life that seemed sometimes to confirm them. In August 1949, shortly after the Heidelberg conference, Munich's liberal *Süddeutsche Zeitung* printed an article quoting approvingly McCloy's statement that "the gauge of the democratic regeneration of Germany would be the development of a new attitude on the part of the Germans toward the Jews." A week later, four letters to the editor, three of them supportive, were published, without any editorial comment. The fourth, filled with antisemitic vitriol, was signed Adolf Bleibtreu (Adolf stay faithful). With an address listed as Palestina Street, it stated, "I am employed by the *Amis* and many of them have already said that they forgive us everything except for one thing and that is that we did not gas them all, for now America is blessed with them." When the paper appeared, a crowd of DPs (several hundred or thousand, depending on the source), taking the letter as a kind of editorial opinion, decided to march on the newspaper office. Interestingly, a second spontaneous protest targeted the JDC offices. In response to these demonstrations, German police on horseback charged the crowd, which fought back with sticks and stones and set a German police bus on fire. This riotous behavior provoked the arrival of more police reinforcements, swinging their clubs and reportedly shooting into the air. JDC officials and a U.S. Army chaplain managed to calm the crowd, but order was finally restored only when American MPs—still carrying authority—ordered the Munich police officers to leave the scene.[31]

These confrontations were intensely embarrassing, of course, for the JDC, which had to invest a good deal of public relations energy in explaining incidents to their donors back in the United States while also pressuring German authorities not to overreact with more violence. The early years of the Federal Republic thus set the postwar pattern for Jewish institutions; they would spend much of their time managing a volatile constituency and on documenting and protesting antisemitic incidents, rather than on building community or religious identity.

The Hard Core

If about 30,000 Jewish DPs remained in Germany in late 1948, by 1953 perhaps half that number were registered. Of those 2,500 to 3000 had reemigrated, mostly from Israel, between 1949 and 1953.[32] This so-called hard core, which so agitated both German and Jewish authorities, stubbornly resisted either resettlement outside Germany or integration within. Some were successfully pursuing economic opportunities that had first been opened via the black or grey market; many were simply too sick or exhausted to move out of the protective DP camp confines. In June 1950, only four camps with 9,000 residents—the sick, the recalcitrant, and most uncomfortably, returnees from Israel—were still operating. Landsberg closed on 15 October 1950, Feldafing on 31 May 1951. The Bavarian state government moved to restore the Feldafing villas that had been requisitioned for the DPs to their German owners, and many of Feldafing's remaining 1,585 residents moved to Föhrenwald in Wolfratshausen near Munich, the very last haven for the hard core. These Jews, no longer DPs but rather "homeless foreigners," were now officially the responsibility of the Germans and not the international community.

Joint workers worried that they had created a population on "welfare," that did not want to leave the dubious but real comfort and safety of the camps. These survivors were unwilling and/or unable to face the economic and psychological rigors either of emigration or integration into an emerging West German society, which made no secret of its desire to rid itself of the newly imposed obligation of caring for Jewish refugees in addition to the millions of German expellees and returned prisoners of war who required assistance.[33] Those who had not left by 1949 were the ones least likely to leave, either because they couldn't or because they wouldn't. Further complicating matters, very few were willing explicitly to forswear emigration plans, creating the often cited postwar Jewish population always perched on "packed suitcases," and most comfortable in the air somewhere between New York, Tel Aviv, and Frankfurt.[34] Some claimed they still needed to make money and buy up more furniture and supplies in Germany before decamping for a harsher life in Israel; some shelved plans to emigrate at the last minute when German reparations plans that needed to be pursued on site were announced; some still hoped for a visa to the United States that had been denied them because of ill health or a criminal record. In some cases, women with babies wanted time to bring up children in familiar and easier conditions, and young people wanted to complete studies or apprenticeships. Others simply were too exhausted to contemplate another move. And, the JDC acknowledged, quite a few, especially single men, were attached to German women and the "easy" life in Germany and feared a harder life abroad.[35]

Sex and money, the two temptations of postwar German life, figured prominently in the difficult discussions about the hard core. By 1954, the JDC reported, "approximately one-third of all married women" in Föhrenwald DP camp, the last camp which held the most intractable of the DPs, were non-Jewish. This number did not even include those German women who had already converted or those living illegally in Föhrenwald as domestic workers or "camp followers." Adding to the ill will toward the returnees from Israel, these men were deemed the most likely to have taken up with German women.[36]

By the early 1950s, therefore, numerous factors coalesced to hold some Jews in Germany. The disruptions of the currency reform had eased, and the economic miracle was taking hold in West Germany. The promise of financial compensation beckoned as the German parliament, prodded by Konrad Adenauer, passed reparations (*Wiedergutmachung*) legislation in 1952, and numerous survivors, especially those who were on the verge of leaving, decided that it was more promising and practical to press their claims on site rather than from abroad. Moreover, by then, some 2,000 Jews had returned to Germany from Israel. Despite the formal prohibition on travel to Germany, Israel had no interest in preventing the departure of troublemakers and apostates who preferred life in a semisovereign West Germany, where, still subject to U.S. and JDC support and surveillance, they could rely on the reluctant but assured aid and protection of Jewish agencies and the young West German government. Of these "returnees," 690 had settled in Föhrenwald. The JDC was left to tear its hair out over how to deal with the "baffling" problem of both the DPs who refused to leave in the first place and those who, most ironically and embarrassingly, illegally slipped back in from Israel.[37]

Resentments and Reparations: The Auerbach Case and the Jewish Presence

German resentment and relief officials' frustration hardened with time. Remaining Jews, supposedly privileged by JDC "supplements," served as an unwelcome reminder of Nazi crimes and occupation authority. Germans became increasingly and unapologetically vocal about the "asocial" and criminal character of the remaining hard core. In their capacity as "Jews," survivors functioned as a kind of living memorial and reproach, to be treated with an anxious respect. But in their everyday role as foreigners and former DPs, they were viewed as unscrupulous operators and a danger to the anxiously reviving economy of postwar West Germany. Jews, for their part, sensed that defeated Germans seemed to have regained their former arrogance without losing their sense of entitlement as victims. At the same time, JDC workers, who had become more sympathetic to the Zionist aspirations of their charges, made no secret of their frustration with the endless demands and apparently undisciplined behavior of those Jewish DPs who did not act on them. They perceived those who remained as either gangsters and opportunists or demoralized victims unable or unwilling to adjust to the normal life that was now expected. Representatives of Jews living in Germany wanted more control and autonomy in their internal affairs without relinquishing the JDC's financial support. The JDC agreed that more self-sufficiency was a worthy and necessary goal, but it did not trust Jews still residing in Germany to handle their financial affairs and aid supplements properly. All of these problems were exacerbated by the disdain of most international Jewry for Jews living in Germany, on the one hand, and the resentment of Germans about the perceived material benefits and political protection that was accorded this "outsider" population, on the other hand. Ironically, this dislike was often couched in unflattering comparisons between the "good" German Jews who seemed to have mysteriously vanished and the "bad" Eastern European Jews who had taken their place.[38]

Remaining German Jews, however, also uneasily debated the feasibility of rebuilding lives and community in the place that had once been so unquestionably their homeland. For them, too, the tentative hopes and occasional euphoria of the immediate postwar period faded. As time passed, German Jews expressed more pessimism about German penitence and willingness to engage the past than they had shortly after the war ended.[39] Most German Jews understood their presence in the Federal Republic as participation in an ominously named *Liquidationsgemeinde* (a self-liquidating community) for those too old and disabled to leave. Most of their leaders, their professionals, their intellectuals, and certainly their youth had emigrated, been killed, or managed to leave a Germany in which they could never again feel at home.

Indeed, with the establishment of an independent West Germany, fellow Jews expected Jewish survivors to have left Germany, leaving those who could or would not do so feeling even more vulnerable and defensive. The World Jewish Congress expressed its view in no uncertain terms in a stark letter to all members of its executive committee, reminding Jews, "The dictate of history is not to forget." The letter added, "We neither have nor seek any power of coercion. We merely say that if Jews in small or larger groups choose to continue to live among the people who are responsible for the slaughter of six millions of our brothers, that is their affair." Unwilling to consider the possibility that "choose" might be a problematic concept in these cases, the majority of the international Jewish community, having contributed a good deal of energy and funds to the surviving remnant, now declared that they would in a sense excommunicate those who were unable or unwilling to leave the "cursed soil" of Germany. Those who stayed were unapologetically called "this vestige of the degredetion [sic] of the Jewish people" and had to pay the price: "If a Jew remains in Germany, he no longer has any portion in world Jewry."[40]

These early confrontations around antisemitism and intense debates about the future of Jews in Germany culminated in 1951 with the sensational prosecution in Munich of Bavaria's most prominent survivor, Philipp Auerbach. The brash German Jew who had become the powerful

Bavarian state commissioner for the persecuted was making common cause with the East European DPs as well as aggressively pursuing reparations and recognition for all Jews in Germany. Auerbach, dubbed the "Caesar of *Wiedergutmachung*" by the German press, was accused in a Munich court of corruption and fraud. Notorious for floating proposals, such as the grandiosely termed *Lex Auerbach,* for the payment of DM 10 to every former *KZ* inmate for each day of incarceration, his exposed and mediating position had become increasingly isolated and precarious. He was caught between the conflicting demands of German and East European Jews, and between his advocacy for Jews and his employment by the German state. He was ensnared also by his position defending the claims of the Jews living in Germany against international Jewish organizations such as the Joint and the JRSO that wanted Jews out of Germany and saw no reason why the hard core remnant of Jews in Germany should become heir to the financial and cultural legacy of a German Jewry now dispersed throughout the globe. Auerbach was convicted on lesser charges, including—ironically for a Germany always obsessed with honorifics—having illegitimately granted himself a "*Doktor*" title. In August 1952 he was sentenced to a fine and two and a half years in prison. Auerbach, who had, as numerous historians have pointed out, not always pursued his mission of political denazification and financial reparations "by the book," denounced the "terror sentence" of this new "Dreyfus case" and committed suicide.

His trial had indeed become a stage on which so many of the resentments of Germans and Jews played out. The presiding judge spoke disparagingly of Auerbach's "Aryan" wife and compared Auerbach's experiences as a concentration camp inmate with his own in Soviet captivity. The story of Philipp Auerbach's rise and fall remains one of the most dramatic and least well-researched moments in the early postwar history of Germans and Jews. Auerbach was given an impressive funeral in Munich's Jewish cemetery, and after four years of investigation, a commission of the Bavarian Parliament (*Landtag*) concluded that he should be "completely rehabilitated."[41] Returned émigré journalist Hans Habe drew the bitter conclusion that "thus an unsympathetic and controversial but innocent man became the first victim of Nazi justice seven years after our victory over Hitler's Germany."[42]

Despite the official line, and precisely because of the continuing dangers of antisemitism, the drive for reparations, and the undeniable existence of Jewish communities, the JDC did not desert the Jews who, for whatever reason, remained in this "poignant, painful, and perplexing" situation.[43] Even after Auerbach's fall, DPs continued to benefit not only from the ongoing JDC supplements but from the relatively generous if grudging welfare provisions, which were dispensed by the West German government as part of its general program for absorbing (mostly German) refugees from the East. These programs produced temptations, which only reinforced Jews' persistent and exaggerated reputation as masters of speculation and corruption. JDC records document the American Jewish organization's growing exasperation and even desperation about such incidents among the "hard core." Despite all their troubles, however, the Joint was resigned to the fact that it could not and would never renege on its commitment to its annoying brethren. Jewish officials continued to defend the (former) DPs to the federal German and Bavarian state governments, rescue from detention returnees who had entered Germany illegally from Israel (which stamped all its passports as not valid for travel to Germany), and provide welfare supplements. They continued to push emigration, while acknowledging that some Jews would remain regardless of all moral pressures or financial incentives. The DP holdouts in Germany were equally frustrated by their dependence on the Joint's grudging and, they felt, condescending, charity. But they also took full advantage of that unhappy but steadfast assistance.

An unapologetically hostile version of the events in Föhrenwald, published in a local (*Heimat*) history of the *Judenlager Föhrenwald bei Wolfratshausen* as recently as 1982 confirms historian Ron Zweig's assessment that, by the mid-1950s, the struggle over the fate of the last Jewish DP camp had led to "the worst stereotypes" being "confirmed for a large part of the German public who in any case believed that the reparations process had been an act of extortion."[44] From the perspective of local Germans, many of whom had always perceived the Jewish camps as unjustly favored centers of crime and disorder, the DPs who had dug in at Föhrenwald were now acting like "state pensioners" entitled to generous welfare, including free room and board, from both the government and the JDC. As the local historian bitingly remarked, for people who insisted that they were victims unable to work, they were surprisingly energetic in pressing their compensation claims.[45] From 1 December 1951 to 31 March 1956, the responsibility for the remaining Jewish DPs had cost the West German state almost DM 11 million, of which 4½ million went to welfare. The sum outraged Germans, while Jews pointed out that the resulting average of about DM 124 a month per person was hardly overly generous, given the recent history that had led to Jewish DPs' presence in Germany. In fact, when the last Jews left Föhrenwald on 28 February 1957, they had negotiated a settlement whereby the JDC contributed $650,000 toward emigration costs and the German government DM 3 million for resettlement—payable, however, only after the camp was truly vacated. In the end, two hundred apartments were rented in Munich (and some in Frankfurt) for those unwilling or unable to leave Germany, an arrangement that was much more economical for the German taxpayer than continued maintenance of a troubled refugee camp.[46]

In a telling example of the multiple continuities of personnel and attitude that crossed the "zero hour" divide, it was the Hamburg physician and population policy expert Hans Harmsen who quickly commissioned a study of the former Föhrenwalders. Like Fritz Burgdörfer, who had produced a 1948 memorandum on the disturbingly high birth rate of these "foreigners" in postwar Bavaria, and so many other German officials in charge of health and social welfare (and indeed restitution) in the postwar years, Harmsen had successfully—and relatively seamlessly—pursued his practical and research interests in racial and social hygiene through three German regimes. A conservative sex reformer in the Weimar Republic, he was a sterilization advocate in the Third Reich, and then became a prominent demographer and "social hygienist" in the Federal Republic and eventual cofounder of German Planned Parenthood (*Pro Familia*).[47]

Indicating how much East European Jewish DPs had transmuted from identification as victims and survivors to "homeless foreigners," the study, out of "consideration" for the subjects, did not ask questions about persecution. *KZ* experiences were only elicited if the interviewees brought them up, perhaps also a reflection of the fact that many of these DPs had spent the war in the Soviet Union, an ambiguous and convoluted fate that many evidently found even harder to talk about (and seriously listen to) than direct persecution by the Nazis.[48] Almost despite themselves and their focus on the 1950s, however, Harmsen's researchers collected testimonies about Jewish life during the war, including flight to the Soviet Union, service in the Red Army, and lengthy periods of hiding. Ironically, their interviews provide, in some ways, a more complex and differentiated picture of the Föhrenwald "hard core" than the impatient JDC reports. Many of those who remained were older and single. Most young families had left, and in some cases, families who had finally been permitted to emigrate to the United States had left behind those members too ill to travel or denied entry because of tuberculosis infection.

Following prevalent postwar "liberal" wisdom, the "social hygiene research report," published under Harmsen's aegis in 1960, urged the West German government to do precisely what the separate Jewish DP camps had tried to avoid, namely, to "disperse" the refugees to prevent any kind of "ghetto formation" in so-called foreigners' districts. The study acknowledged that this "suddenly liberated slave *Volk*" would find Germany to be a "most unsuitable" place for integration. Yet it concluded, in carefully abstract but optimistic terms, that despite their "ineradicable [*unausrottbaren*] animosity toward the former oppressor," the Föhrenwalders' "existential fear" about living among a people whose government had persecuted them had been "overcome." Dire predictions about disorderly behavior and violent confrontations had not been fulfilled. From the perspective of these German professional observers, despite continuing antisemitic incidents such as cemetery desecrations, the pragmatic coexistence and interaction that had in fact characterized Jewish/German relations during the DP era continued. "The majority lives in peace with the Germans, albeit without much further contact or friendship," they noted, adding, however, that "it remains the mission of the German neighbors to try to live in peace and with personal tolerance with these people who have, it is true [*eben*], other peculiarities than themselves." The Jews were praised, with no little surprise, for having tried to "overcome their prejudices against the Germans, and hav[ing] proven by their actions, that despite bad health and difficult conditions, they have succeeded in finding a place in the work and business world."[49] At the same time almost a third—perceived as too many by the German researchers, but actually rather on the low side from the perspective of Jews abroad—still maintained their packed suitcases stance and continued to plan for (or at least contemplate) eventual emigration.

The camps closed in the early 1950s, the last, Föhrenwald, in February 1957, just about a year after the last German prisoners of war returned from the Soviet Union and two years after the Federal Republic had attained full sovereignty. The Jewish DP era, which had been such a significant but, in most historical accounts, strangely invisible part of postwar German history, was over. But the small and fragile communities (*Gemeinden*), led by the *Zentralrat,* that took over Jewish life were substantially marked by the presence of those DPs who remained. Membership was divided between about 52 percent DP and 48 percent German Jews, although it was, as we would expect, very unevenly distributed according to place (in Berlin 71.4 percent was German; in Bavaria only 6.3 percent in 1949).[50] Jews lived in West Germany but, for the most part, still with the (by now often symbolic) packed suitcases close at hand and many familial and emotional connections around the world, and especially in Israel. The sense of transience that had facilitated everyday encounters among Jewish survivors and defeated Germans during the DP period continued to shape the lives of the minority of Jews who stayed.

The peculiar ambivalent, sometimes contradictory, orchestration of collective suspicion and individual contact, of suspicious distance and pragmatic coexistence, of participating in German life but denying any real attachment, established at a point when there were several hundred thousand Jewish survivors in Germany, continued into the early years of the Federal Republic. By 1952, about 70 percent of DPs had accepted German citizenship, albeit without any true allegiance, and a significant minority chose to remain stateless or maintain Israeli citizenship. Even those with German passports thought of themselves in many ways as dual citizens. They maintained close ties to family and friends in Israel and elsewhere, and felt only minimally committed to their German community, often speaking only a broken German (learned in concentration and labor camps and as DPs), infused with their native Yiddish. In a response that continues to challenge multicultural relations in Germany today, certainly in regard to its large Turkish minority, Germans, who tended to demand more unambiguous signs of commitment to the new state, saw—not without reason—Jews' multiple allegiances as lack of loyalty and an unwillingess to integrate. Many former DPs, for their part, approached Germans with the proverbial chip on the shoulder, quick to interpret haphazard slights—a misstep in the trolley or such—as expressions of antisemitism.[51] The pattern was not so different for most "native" German Jews and indeed set the model for the next decades of postwar relations.

Jewish life in Germany essentially fractured into two related but separate worlds. Jews inhabited a complex anxious internal society replete with sorrow and conflict. Former DPs, German Jews who had survived in Germany, or so-called rémigrés, and returnees—from both groups—from Israel clashed with each other as well as with Jewish institutions abroad that decried their very existence. Jews in West Germany, tellingly labeled, in what might be construed as an ill-conceived attempt at philosemitism, as "co-citizens" (Mitbürger), were not only alienated from the larger German society, still preoccupied with its own suffering during the war and for the most part obstinately unwilling to confront its own complicity in Nazism's crimes, but also split among themselves. German Jews, many of whom survived because of marriages to "Aryans" or because they were themselves

Mischlinge and often had only a tenuous relationship to Judaism, interacted and competed with mostly Polish East European survivors of ghettos, work and death camps, hiding and passing, or flight (and deportation)
to the Soviet Union. However, Jewish communities also made earnest efforts to care for an aging and ailing population and to build Jewish life and
Zionist identity among the small cohort of young people who had emerged
from the DP camps or been born to remaining Jews. The latter task appeared even more urgent because so many of the postwar Jewish families,
both German and East European, were in fact intermarried.[52]

At the same time, a significant portion of Jewish existence was determined by external relations and events. The leadership, in itself truncated
by the (much bemoaned) loss of an intellectual and professional elite that
had either been murdered or exiled, was preoccupied by Jews' status in regard to the politics of a young West German state seeking to establish its
international legitimacy as well as the ongoing campaigns for material
reparations. In fact, the establishment in 1950 of the *Zentralrat* was to
some extent a response to Chancellor Konrad Adenauer's frustration with
the multiple competing groups, within and outside Germany, that claimed
to represent Jewish interests and his desire (which would remain entirely
unfulfilled) for a single negotiating partner. The *Zentralrat* emerged, as Jay
Geller convincingly posits in his study of Jewish institutional life from
1945 to 1953, in part as an alternative to Adenauer's ill-fated attempt—encouraged by some of his Jewish contacts—to institute a special governmental office for Jewish Affairs within the Ministry of the Interior. Its un-
fortunate title—it was referred to as a *Referat*, evoking memories of
agencies involved with the Final Solution—did not add to its appeal
among Jewish groups already disinclined to rely on a single resource
within a German government ministry.[53] And when the Luxemburg Treaty
on German reparations to Jewish victims was finally ratified in 1952, its
provisions reflected the Federal Republic's role in international politics, including the emerging Arab-Israeli conflict and an increasingly virulent
Cold War, as well as a recognition of German responsibility. Thus, the history of these small and divided Jewish communities was not only their
own but a critical part of postwar foreign relations and international
Jewry's evolving relationship with the legacy of the Holocaust and the establishment of the state of Israel.

Some observers have spoken of a "miraculous reemergence of Jewish
life" after the Holocaust, but in fact it was neither miraculous nor incom-
prehensible.[54] Postwar Jewish life in Germany was the unexpected conse-

quence of the flight of Eastern European Jewish survivors seeking protection from postwar antisemitism into the American zone, and the precarious survival of some mostly intermarried or "partial" German Jews within the Reich. On 1 January 1959, Jewish communities in the Federal Republic counted 21,499 members; a significant number were in congregations formed by former DPs in towns where there had never been a Jewish presence before the war.[55]

The "reemergence" was numerically tiny and fraught with conflict and ambivalence; yet it became a matter of international debate and negotiation and a centerpiece of West Germany's struggle for legitimacy in the international, especially Western, community. Indeed, arguably, the fate of Jewry in postwar West Germany was of more importance to the nation's international relations than to its own domestic politics, which were much more focused on the economic miracle and the integration of millions of expellees. At the same time, and as paradoxically as everything to do with postwar Jewish life in Germany, the Jewish community was isolated, stigmatized by international Jewish groups and by the young state of Israel that refused to recognize Germany or Jews who traveled and lived there.

In Germany itself, all Jews struggled with their future, debating endlessly whether to stay or to go. DPs were more likely to insist their presence was temporary, but in reality both former DPs and "native" German Jews were conflicted about their residence in Germany. In the 1950s a relatively small if noteworthy group of 12,000 to 15,000 DPs remained in Germany, generally those with business or intimate ties, including some 1,000 who had married German women. The fragility of postwar institutional Jewish life is underscored by the importance of personal relationships and networks in shaping the delicate postwar German-Jewish relationship. In both East and West Germany, the small remnant Jewish communities relied on personal contacts to assure funding and benefits, a necessarily precarious and unstable system. For German Jews within the Federal Republic of Germany, Theodor Heuss, the ceremonial president, was the main contact and support, while the politically powerful Chancellor Adenauer operated rather on an international stage, negotiating the reparations agreements with Jewish organizations and the state of Israel. In the West, these peculiar circumstances proved remarkably enduring, but in the East they quickly fractured, with the Stalinization of the SED (Socialist Unity Party) and the escape west of many Jewish leaders—accused of "cosmopolitanism"—in 1953. This rupture in 1953 cemented the position of the Federal Republic as the postwar German state in which Jewish life could, however strangely and uneasily, continue until the fall of the Wall in 1989. By 1989 somewhere between 20 and 30 thousand Jews lived in the Federal Republic and 500 were officially registered in the German Democratic Republic.

The collapse of the Soviet bloc and the reunification of Germany in 1990 fundamentally changed the situation. Once again an unexpected influx from the East, driven by dramatic political changes, transformed the nature of Jewish life in Germany. This time it was mostly the former DPs and their offspring, now the "insiders," who had themselves come to Germany as refugees from Eastern Europe (and many of whom had spent the war in the Soviet Union), who faced a new set of "foreigners" from the East. Between 1990 and 2005, when the special regulations that had facilitated Jewish immigration were limited, some 187,000 Jews from the former Soviet Union and its successor states settled in the Federal Republic; about 105,000 have joined the official Jewish communities.[56] In yet another irony of German-Jewish history, Germany, profiting from the migration of Jews from east to west, could, at least temporarily, boast one of the fastest growing Jewish communities in the world, if not the fastest growing one. Moreover, notwithstanding the legal changes in 2005, the now unified capital of Berlin has become a magnet for many, especially young, Jews from Israel, North America, and indeed all parts of the globe. It remains to be seen whether this increased Jewish presence, both numerically and culturally, will in any lasting way conjure the "Jewish Renaissance" that many current observers greeted with anticipation, enthusiasm, and considerable skepticism. Ever more international and cosmopolitan on the one hand, and more Russian on the other hand, Jews in Germany (and the official Jewish community) face new challenges as they engage not only with the ever-present shadows of the National Socialist and wartime past but also with the transformation of Germany into a multicultural society with a growing and much larger Muslim minority. It is clear, however, that the twenty-first century has initiated a new problematic and still-evolving revival of Jewish life in a united Germany within the European community.

CHAPTER 3

Guest Worker Migration and the Unexpected Return of Race

Rita Chin

In an attempt to head off a major labor shortage precipitated by the post-war economic boom, the Federal Republic of Germany signed a worker recruitment treaty with Italy in December 1955. The agreement inaugurated an eighteen-year period of foreign labor recruitment that targeted guest workers from many southern Mediterranean countries, including Muslim Turkey. It also marked the beginning of a massive labor migration, bringing two million foreigners to West Germany by the early 1970s. This effort to obtain manpower during the *Wirtschaftswunder* produced a number of unintended consequences, most notably a radically transformed demographic, social, and cultural landscape. What began as a short-term solution to an economic crisis ultimately became the catalyst for the long-term creation of a sizeable minority community of Turks in the Federal Republic.

In many ways, the practice of importing foreign workers and the accompanying experience of demographic expansion were not new in the German context. During the Wilhelmine period, Poles from Russia and the Austro-Hungarian Empire had been recruited to work in the coal mines of the Ruhr valley and hired as seasonal workers in the eastern agricultural regions.[1] Of more immediate relevance to the period after 1955, the Nazi state—just fifteen years before—had forced tens of thousands of foreigners onto the territory of the Third Reich and exploited them as slave laborers to help fuel its war machine.[2]

Yet the Nazi legacy itself significantly altered the terms on which the postwar labor recruitment could be understood. Precisely because race had served as the primary mode of social distinction during the Nazi period, a form of categorization that determined whether a person was valued by the state or marked for destruction, one of the implicit imperatives for the reconstruction of a more fully democratic West German society was to make the question of race a nonissue. This imperative, of course, did not mean that race and racism simply disappeared from everyday interactions or even social policy in the Federal Republic. As we have already seen, policymakers had no problem absorbing the American model of a black/white binary and applying it to the offspring of African American GIs and German women; and West Germans quickly began to treat Jewish displaced persons (DPs) as "parasitic foreigners," at times drawing on language and images that the Nazis had used to brand Jews as racial Others. Guest workers did not escape this pattern. The pejorative slang word *Türkentüte,* for instance, was coined to refer to the cheap plastic bags that Turkish guest workers often used to carry groceries. At the very least, though, the horrific consequences of Nazi social policies and the regime's subsequent demise thoroughly discredited the category of "race" and made the term taboo in West German polite society and public discourse.

Despite this new reluctance to employ the word *race,* the postwar recruitment of guest workers produced a demographic landscape in which forms of essentialized thinking associated with racial ideologies became a key tool for social differentiation once again. The relationship between processes of racialization and the labor migration, however, is not as straightforward as one might expect. During the first twenty years that guest workers resided in the Federal Republic, their presence remained largely unproblematic at the level of national public debate and failed to elicit the kinds of open questioning about racial compatibility that emerged around black *Mischlingskinder* in the 1950s and 1960s.[3] Indeed, government leaders across the political spectrum, policymakers, employers in industry, and newspaper commentators actively championed the use of foreign labor as a necessary strategy to keep economic production high. There was little sense that guest workers might eventually present a social problem because everyone involved in the recruitment program assumed that labor migrants would inevitably return home.

Over the course of the 1970s, however, changes in the migrant population transformed the ways Germans thought about guest workers. By the end of the decade, the number of foreigners living in the Federal Republic surpassed four million, largely due to the influx of spouses and children. Turks, meanwhile, had outpaced other national groups and were routinely identified as the quintessential guest worker. These developments prompted political authorities to acknowledge that labor forces had become de facto immigrants, which in turn drove the establishment of new institutions, policies, and efforts at intercultural dialogue in order to facilitate integration.

At the same time, it was precisely the idea that Turks and other labor migrants now constituted a permanent presence in German society that made certain kinds of race-based thinking seem useful as a way to account for fundamental differences between peoples once again. As long as guest workers were not understood as immigrants, it was possible to suspend the whole question of difference, or more specifically, to explain it away using the language of market expediency and a rationale of mutual benefits. But it is important to be clear here: this postwar redeployment of race was not equivalent to Nazi racial practice. Recognition of de facto immigration made cultural difference an issue, and culture (rather than biology) became the primary basis for explaining fundamental incompatibilities between Turkish guest workers and Germans.

The Absence of Race?

It is one of the great ironies of postwar history that West Germany chose to embark on a massive foreign labor recruitment campaign a mere decade after the collapse of the Nazi's state-sanctioned program of racial purification. But perhaps even more incongruous is the fact that explicitly racialized ways of thinking did not become a significant rubric for public discussions of the presence of guest workers until the late 1970s, more than twenty years after federal minister of economics Ludwig Erhard signed the first labor treaty with Italy in 1955. The apparent absence of race thinking in this early period is especially remarkable when we consider that the number of foreign workers surpassed one million by 1964[4] and two million by 1970.[5] How can we explain this pattern?

An important place to begin is with the basic parameters of the labor recruitment itself. According to migration experts Stephen Castles and Mark Miller, the hallmark of guest worker programs in postwar Europe was the "legal division between the status of citizen and of foreigner."[6] West Germany's program did not even consider the possibility of recruits becoming immigrants with citizenship rights: guest workers were foreigners, while citizen status remained limited to those who could claim German ancestry.[7] This distinction, based on the principle of jus sanguinis (the right of blood) and incorporated into German law in 1913, not only determined access to work, social security, and residence, it also served as a central way to differentiate between those who belonged to the nation and those who did not. It was thus possible for foreign laborers to be physically present on West German soil and, at the same time, remain entirely separate from the social body. In this respect, the guest worker program offered a strategy for dealing with difference that did not need to draw upon an older language of race. Whereas the Nazi regime tended to rely on racial categories to distinguish between groups already within the nation, West German authorities elided this problem by marking guest workers as always outside it.[8]

Yet the category of foreigner (*Ausländer*) was not a completely neutral term in the immediate postwar period. The label surfaced in relation to Jewish Holocaust survivors who gathered in German displaced persons camps at the war's end. As we have seen, defeated Germans and occupying forces alike eventually came to understand this group not as victims of National Socialism but as intrusive foreigners claiming scarce resources.[9] Guest workers, however, initially escaped such negative associations. For one thing, they had been invited to West Germany by government and industry leaders who wanted and needed their labor power. In addition, there was no sense that these foreigners would have a permanent place on German soil. Labor migrants were imagined as a temporary phenomenon, living in the Federal Republic as transient sojourners until demand for their labor dried up. An early article in the national daily, *Frankfurter Allgemeine Zeitung,* for example, explained that "in the event of unemployment . . . , foreign workers could be sent back home again."[10]

Government authorities and business officials, moreover, presented the guest worker program in terms of a market discourse that stressed significant advantages for the nation. After the war, the Federal Republic confronted an increasingly severe labor shortage, triggered by the high casualty rate among German men during the conflict and further exacerbated by official efforts to encourage women in the wartime workforce to return to the home.[11] Labor recruitment solved this crisis by importing much-needed manpower to help rebuild the nation and fuel the *Wirtschaftswunder.* Newspaper reports and editorials from the early 1960s declared that the very health of the economy depended on a growing pool of foreign workers.[12] Meanwhile, *Der Arbeitgeber,* the newsletter of the national employers' association, summarized what industry stood to gain: "A foreigner in our employ places the best years of his labor power at our disposal. For employing firms, this results in the advantage that an older foreign worker, or one no longer fully fit and able to work, must only rarely be retained on the payroll for reasons of social policy."[13] Ordinary Germans were direct beneficiaries as well. They enjoyed better jobs, higher living standards, and an unprecedented period of economic prosperity. Above all, this market discourse relied on the presumption of limited social and cultural entanglement with guest workers, a strategy that attempted to avoid problems of race relations or racial tension altogether. The discourse, in short, operated according to a kind of cost-benefit analysis that clearly favored West Germans.

Structural conditions also helped support this conception of the guest worker program. The labor treaties initially granted employment and residence permits on a two-year basis, regularizing the principle of rotation and return to the country of origin. Early on, recruits consisted almost entirely of men between the ages of twenty and forty, but starting in the 1960s, the West German food and garment industries actively sought female guest workers, whose fine motor skills were especially prized. Whether male or female, German recruitment offices targeted laborers who were single or willing to leave their families at home. Most of these foreign workers lived in makeshift housing provided by their employers. Typically, lodgings consisted of barracks or dormitories situated near the factory site and often far removed from central neighborhoods and public transportation. Such conditions fostered a culture of isolation that seemed to corroborate the ideological fantasy: guest workers came to West Germany to contribute to its economy, but their presence was rendered largely invisible by the very social structures and institutions that supported a mass population of temporary labor.

While the language of racial differentiation remained largely absent from discussions of guest workers in the period of recruitment, then, the social and legal parameters of the program drew strict boundaries between foreign labor migrants and native Germans. In this way, assumptions about racial difference were displaced onto the figure of the guest worker. The pattern emerges especially clearly with the word *Gastarbeiter*, which became the ubiquitous term of reference for migrant laborers during the recruitment years. This euphemistic label crystallized key assumptions about the specific role that such workers would play in the Federal Republic, and functioned quite literally to define labor recruits as "guests" and "workers." It reduced their presence in West German society to economics, suggesting that their impact could be limited to the labor market; and it simultaneously insisted that their stay would be short-lived, taking for granted that most if not all foreign workers would eventually return to their home countries. In other words, the category itself presumed a racialist understanding of difference, insofar as it foregrounded the impermeable boundaries between native and foreigner, permanent and transitory. Precisely because the guest worker figure was so successful at making these distinctions appear natural and absolute (there was never any inkling that imported laborers might one day become citizens), invoking more explicit categories of race initially proved unnecessary.

Guest Workers as Immigrants

By the early 1970s, however, the advantages of the guest worker program were becoming far less clear-cut than political authorities and business leaders had originally imagined. Part of the complication arose out of a desire to extract maximum profit from the system. Once the price of importing new workers every two years exceeded the costs of keeping those who had already been trained and absorbing fluctuations in production demands, the government quietly stopped enforcing the rule of quick return—that is, it almost always granted extensions for residence and work permits, effectively allowing Turks and other labor migrants to remain in Germany indefinitely.[14]

Lengthier residences meant that more and more guest workers began to send for their families, a development that strained German social infrastructure. In 1971, a representative of the Employers' Associations (*Arbeitgeberverbände*) voiced misgivings about the new direction of migration.

> The economic dampening effect we were able to achieve until now by the employment of foreigners is turning into its opposite: the foreigners and their families now settling here have . . . heightened consumption needs. . . . To this is added the cost of public investment, far greater than when foreign workers live here housed in communal hostels. It is not merely a matter of providing suitable living quarters, as well as schoolrooms and teachers for foreign children—but also that the infrastructure of our municipalities must adjust to a larger population virtually overnight.[15]

A 1972–73 report by the Bundesanstalt für Arbeit (Federal Labor Office) outlined similar changes, highlighting in particular the dramatic rise in foreigners who were not employed at all. In 1973, there were 1.37 million non-

Germans outside the workforce, which represented a tenfold increase over a six-year period.[16] This shift gradually led many officials to conclude that the costs of the guest worker program now outweighed its benefits.[17] Later that year, the first major recession since the end of the war further substantiated this conclusion. The economic downturn resulted in massive layoffs and made the overall burden of labor migrants and their families feel even heavier.

In response, the Federal Republic issued the *Anwerbestopp* on 23 November 1973 to halt foreign labor recruitment. The decision, in a sense, aimed to make the increasingly complicated ground-level situation conform to the ideological fantasy of the guest worker program. In keeping with West Germany's market-oriented approach, the *Anwerbestopp* attempted to limit unwanted social entanglements by cutting off the supply of foreigners. But the act was also supposed to trigger the unspoken half of the recruitment compact: now that the economy no longer required supplemental manpower, it was time for foreign laborers to return home. This strategy, however, did not achieve the desired effect. The *Anwerbestopp* lowered the absolute numbers of foreigners for a couple of years, but it ultimately produced the opposite result. The new law made guest workers fear further restrictions and acted as a catalyst for a dramatic rise in family reunions.[18] By the end of the 1970s, nearly 4.5 million foreigners lived in the Federal Republic, while only 2.1 million were employed.[19] What government officials had not reckoned with was the unexpected consequences of the triumphalist market rhetoric. Even though the presence of guest workers and their families ceased to be advantageous for Germans, Germany continued to offer significant benefits for guest workers and their families.

Around this time, the labor migrant population began to change in another important way. Starting in 1971, the number of Turks in the Federal Republic surpassed all other national groups, and between 1970 and 1973, the Turkish population itself nearly doubled.[20] The trend was, in part, a result of the establishment of the European Economic Community, which granted citizens of member states reciprocal labor rights. This meant that Italians (and eventually Spaniards and Portuguese) could work in the Federal Republic without special permits, relieving the pressure to choose permanent residence because they could come and go quite easily. Turks, by contrast, were reluctant to leave, wary that they might not be able to return. The highly unstable political situation in Turkey during the late 1960s and 1970s provided additional incentive for Turks to stay in the Federal Republic and send for their families.[21] By the mid-1970s, in short, guest worker recruitment looked much more like immigration: family units displaced single laborers; so-called migrant ghettos in urban centers replaced worker barracks on the outskirts of town; and Turks (furthest from Germans in terms of religion and cultural practice) supplanted the earlier multinational guest worker community.

These structural transformations produced a gradual shift in the government's approach to the guest worker question. Initially, federal and state authorities were ill-equipped to deal with the new challenges presented by the changing migrant population. Little information existed about aspects of foreigners' lives not directly related to labor and the economy. This lack of basic knowledge led political and government agencies to solicit and fund social-scientific research on foreigners, a task that involved compiling data on the living conditions, income, savings patterns, family status and structure, education, religion, and long-term plans of recruited laborers.[22] Many of the scholars who carried out this work were sociologists influenced by systems theory. Their approach focused on the potential problems created when people from a "traditional system" such as Turkey come into contact with the Federal Republic's "modern system." Integration, these scholars argued, provided the crucial antidote for the instability created by the clash of systems.[23] The studies tended to concentrate on second-generation Turks, diagnosing the children as caught between their parents' desire to preserve cultural traditions and the influence of modern West German society.[24] Because of their liminal status, these researchers surmised, Turkish children possessed a greater propensity for social conflict, which could manifest itself in unemployment, delinquency, crime, and even violence. Schools functioned as particularly important sites of integration, since they served as the primary point of contact between Turks and German society.

By the second half of the 1970s, the need to integrate foreigners emerged as a new emphasis in policy-making, and the three leading political parties began to formulate positions on how this process might work.[25] In 1978, Chancellor Helmut Schmidt (SPD) created the Ausländerbeauftragte (Commissioner for Foreigners' Affairs), a new government position responsible for organizing and promoting national integration efforts, and appointed Heinz Kühn (SPD), the former president of North Rhine-Westphalia, to fill the post. The following year, Kühn released a memorandum that condemned foreigner policy for failing to take responsibility for the social consequences of the labor recruitment. He openly criticized the government's approach for being "obviously too much shaped by the priority

of political, labor-market points of view."[26] Kühn instead proclaimed that
"here a development has occurred that is *no longer reversible,* and the majority of those affected are no longer 'guest workers' but rather immigrants."[27] This statement marked a major watershed in the official thinking
about guest workers: the principal government spokesman on foreigner issues finally acknowledged the inadequacy of treating migrant workers
solely as a convenient labor market corrective and publicly recognized their
permanent presence in West Germany.

In many ways, though, Kühn's acknowledgment of de facto immigration only made official a set of circumstances that had been evident at the
ground level for some time. From the beginning of recruitment, charity organizations such as Catholic Caritas, Protestant Diakonisches Werk, and
the SPD's Arbeiterwohlfahrt attended to the rudimentary social needs of
guest workers, relieving federal, state, and local authorities of this obligation. The groups offered translation services, German-language classes, as
well as counseling on legal rights, apartment rental, unemployment
benefits, and job hunting. In close contact with migrants, these charities
registered the impacts of family reunions much earlier than policymakers
and consequently were the first to develop programs for the broader social
integration of spouses and children.

Nevertheless, the shift in official approach did produce important new
policy initiatives under Schmidt's socialist-liberal ruling coalition. Kühn,
for example, advocated making guest workers and their families into full
members of German society. He proposed an intensification of integrative
measures through the schools, the elimination of all segregation, the op-
tional right for foreign youth to be naturalized, and the support of foreigners' political rights through local voting.[28] In particular, Kühn stressed
the urgent need for programs at every educational level that would enable
young foreigners to overcome language difficulties, obtain the best possible
education, and give them equal opportunities for success.[29] This agenda
placed intercultural understanding at the center of the push for integration: specific recommendations included teaching German and foreign
pupils together in ethnically mixed classrooms and revising curricula to incorporate customs and traditions practiced by migrant groups.

Such initiatives, it is important to emphasize, were not merely a political effect of changes taking place at the ground level. Rather, these policies
also helped shape new modes of ideology and discourse for thinking about
the place of guest workers. Kühn's proposal for ethnically mixed class-

rooms, for instance, sought to create learning environments that would expose German students to a heterogeneous model of society, teach foreign pupils the basic values of Western democracy, and give each group the opportunity to form affective social bonds with one other. Similarly, Kühn's insistence that "teaching plans and teaching material show consideration for the multinational composition of classes" signaled a new awareness of migrant differences.[30] Along with the call for at least 5,000 more teachers trained in *Ausländerpädagogik* (foreigner pedagogy), this initiative sought to make cross-cultural sensitivity central to Germany's public education program. Integration, according to this view, would only occur through more openness and knowledge about how other cultures worked—and this process involved Germans as much as foreigners. In the course of developing new policies, then, government officials and social welfare workers began to flesh out the more specific meanings of de facto immigration. And the basic message that ran through their policy language contradicted the core assumption that had dominated public discussions on the labor migration for the previous twenty-five years: guest workers and their families were now understood as fully embedded in the day-to-day messiness of German social relations.

The Racialization of Culture

The predominance of integrationist discourse in the second half of the 1970s had two major effects on the relationship between more explicitly racialized thinking and the guest worker question. First, integration relied on the idea of cultural difference to explain the inherent difficulty of Germans and guest workers (primarily Turks) living together in the same society. As elaborated in SPD policies and programs, the implicit goal of integration was to overcome differences and facilitate peaceful, mutually enriching coexistence. Yet this preoccupation with cultural difference also served as the starting point for other, more skeptical views about the possibility of multiethnic cohabitation. Second, the Schmidt government's vigorous promotion of integration reoriented the focus of federal engagement with labor migrants from foreign relations to domestic politics, labor policy to social services. Here again, there were unexpected political consequences. Once labor migrants were perceived as a major issue on the domestic agenda, other political parties felt free to assess the effectiveness of integration. Indeed, it was only in the wake of Schmidt's integration initiatives that the presence of guest workers became a recurring flash point of ideological struggle and campaign politics at the federal level.

These two trends came together somewhat contentiously when the main opposition party, the Christian Democratic Union (CDU), began to make *Ausländerpolitik* (foreigner policy) a subject of partisan politics. In a key debate during the 4 February 1982 session of the Bundestag, Alfred Dregger, a longtime representative and the outspoken leader of the CDU/CSU caucus, accused the SPD of creating the so-called foreigner problem by failing to take decisive action against permanent residence and family reunions.[31] The CDU, in contrast, pledged to tackle the issue of migrants head-on, explicitly repudiating the right of foreigners to become German citizens. Dregger justified this position by pointing to a lack of acculturation: "As the example of Turks already shows, there are foreigners even in the second generation who have remained and want to remain foreigners in terms of mentality and language. If that is the case, naturalization is not possible."[32] For the CDU, in other words, naturalization required full "Germanization." The party additionally put forward new parameters for social integration, arguing that this task "lies squarely with the foreigners who do not want to become German, who come from other cultural circles, and who want to protect their characteristics."[33] Successful integration, the pronouncement implied, left no room for non-German "characteristics." And in stark contrast to the SPD, which defined social integration as a mutual process that would transform both Germans and foreigners, the CDU transferred the work of integration to migrants alone.

Along with these specific positions, Dregger offered a more general statement on the question of foreigners. "It is always false," he asserted, "to disregard human nature and people's ways of thinking when making political decisions. Not just Germans, but people more generally place value on preserving their national identity in principle. This permits the acceptance of only a limited number of foreigners."[34] In this view, "human nature" drove Germans to protect their collective sense of self against encroachment by other cultures. The presence of too many unassimilated migrants would make it impossible to maintain the integrity of German "national identity."

At the same time, Dregger distinguished between four categories of foreigners, suggesting that some were more compatible with Germans than others. People from the south Tyrol, Austria, and Switzerland, who were foreign citizens but spoke German, presented no integration problem.

Other Europeans shared the common Christian roots of European culture, which made integration and eventual assimilation likely. But Turks, along with people from Asian and African countries, brought such unfamiliar cultures, religions, and values that accommodation was virtually impossible.

Turks, Dregger argued, were the key group of unassimilable foreigners because of differences in culture and mentality. "The Turkish people," he asserted:

> were not shaped by Christianity, rather by Islam—another high culture, and I stress, high culture. The fact that the state founded by Ataturk in 1918 is secular and understands itself as European changes nothing, anymore than the fact that our state is also secular rather than the earlier Holy Roman Empire. Even in its more secular form, the cultural impulses of Christian and Islamic high culture have a lasting effect on our peoples. This contributes, in addition to a pronounced national pride of the Turks, to the fact that they are not assimilable. They want to remain what they are, namely Turks. And we should respect this.[35]

Despite Turkey's outward trappings of European secularism, in other words, fundamental differences between Turkish and German culture continued to exist and were simply intractable. As evidence of this, Dregger observed that largely insular Turkish "ghettos" had developed in all the major German cities. While he praised the instinct of Turks to keep to themselves and maintain their unique culture, he argued that they should do so in Turkey rather than Germany.

What Dregger offered here was a particular theory of ethnicity and culture. German culture, in this conception, was neither superior nor inferior to Turkish culture; both were simply different. Dregger did not question the legitimacy or value of multiple cultural traditions. Indeed, he celebrated the fact that significant, historically rich cultures, by definition, operated according to distinct and specific logics. Yet the very strength and persistence of Islamic culture presented a new dilemma for postwar German society. Turkish "ghettos" created pockets of an enduring minority culture within an equally strong majority culture. Dregger likened this form of mixing to the unstable combination of oil and water, in which both cultures—discrete, impenetrable, and with fundamentally incompatible interests—coexisted uneasily in isolated enclaves. Deeming such a scenario unacceptable, Dregger's solution was to relocate Turks to their natural and historical home. Ultimately, his was a theory of culture that posited an unwavering, largely immutable ethnic core or essence. Culture, in short, functioned in the same way as the older, now discredited category of race: it served to explain fundamental, incommensurable differences among peoples.

It is worth noting that similar arguments were circulating in Great Britain around this same time. As Martin Barker first demonstrated in 1981, Margaret Thatcher's rise to power (and the rebirth of conservative ideology that preceded it) was supported by what he termed "new racism," a mode of public discourse based on the assumption that immigrants threatened the British "way of life." British conservatives advocating this position emphatically eschewed any connection to racists, whom they claimed propagated hatred by insisting on the superiority of one group over another. Instead, according to Barker, Tories suggested that "human nature" impelled people "to form a bounded community, a nation, aware of its differences from other nations."[36] The instinctive desire to defend one's "way of life, traditions and customs against outsiders" arose not because immigrants were "inferior," but because they belonged to "different cultures."[37] This new theorization of race by British conservatives, like that of their German counterparts, drew considerable power from its ability both to avoid older, biologically based explanations of race and to reframe distinctions traditionally associated with race in terms of national and cultural difference.[38] In the process, a new commonsense emerged: it viewed cultural differences as fundamentally irreconcilable and thus understood immigration as antithetical to the natural desire for a homogeneous national community.[39]

In both Britain and Germany, this conservative mode of explanation was especially successful because it took seriously the fears and concerns articulated by an increasingly popular radical Right, while simultaneously providing a somewhat softer approach to the foreigner problem. Echoing right-wing critics, the CDU condemned the SPD for placing the interests of guest workers above those of Germans. Dregger even warned that if Germany became a country of immigration, it would "pave the way for a new right radicalism."[40] At the same time, he sought to distinguish the CDU position from that of extremists. In contrast to right radicals, who openly invoked Nazi-like language and insisted on "genetically transmitted" differences between groups of peoples, Dregger claimed that such distinctions resulted from strong cultural traditions.[41] On one level, this stance foregrounded a public expression of respect for others; and it used the characteristics of cultural strength and durability not so much to demonize foreigners explicitly but to construct a more reasoned argument about the impracticality of expecting migrants to assimilate. Yet Dregger's theory ultimately produced the same kinds of conclusions as the "gene"-based theories of the far Right. Whether defined in biological or cultural terms, both lines of argument presumed that migrant identities were immutable and therefore incompatible with an equally immutable German culture.

In this sense, the CDU introduced into West German public discourse a mode of racialized thinking that was at once more respectable and more insidious. Respectable because the new focus on cultural incommensurability deftly avoided any taint of association with older Nazi racial ideology, even as it espoused a similar set of assumptions about difference: the presence of a long-standing minority population on German soil threatened the basic integrity of the nation. Insidious because this framework performed a kind of sleight of hand with the category of culture, presenting cultural differences conventionally understood as the product of mutable social practices as unchanging and permanent. Yet this oblique return to racial thinking only became necessary once the federal government openly acknowledged the increasing rootedness of minority culture. As long as Turks continued to be seen as transient outsiders, the cohesiveness of German society remained intact. But once these outsiders were recognized as de facto immigrants, conservatives sought out new ideological tools for reasserting homogeneity. A racialized notion of cultural difference thus served to explain integration's inevitable failure and justify stiff opposition to immigration.

The CDU's new approach to the foreigner problem, it is important to note, coincided with significant changes in public attitudes toward guest workers. Opinion surveys from the late 1970s and early 1980s demonstrate the changing views: whereas only 39 percent of the native population had believed guest workers should return home in 1979, over 60 percent affirmed this statement in 1982; and the 42 percent of Germans who had endorsed active integration efforts in 1979 dropped to a mere 11 percent in 1982.[42] This ideological shift contributed to the larger political crisis facing the Social Democrats, which came to a head when the liberal Free Democratic Party (FDP) decided to leave the ruling coalition and partner with the Christian Democrats. Without a clear parliamentary majority for his party, Schmidt called for a vote of confidence on 1 October 1982. The subsequent SPD defeat ushered the CDU's Helmut Kohl into the chancellorship; and the general elections held the following spring produced a landslide victory for the CDU/CSU. Ultimately, this sea change underscored the extent to which SPD integrationist politics had lost its public mandate.[43]

These shifting political tides put Social Democrats on the defensive and forced the party to revise its own ideas about integration. Shortly before collapsing, the Schmidt government began to espouse a more restrictive *Ausländerpolitik,* proposing, for example, to limit the numbers of foreigners entering the country under the principle of family reunion.[44] In early 1982, the Interior Ministry declared: "There is unity [in the government] that the Federal Republic . . . is *not* a country of immigration and should not become one. The cabinet agrees that a further influx of foreigners from outside the European Community should be prevented by all possible legal means. . . . Only by a consistent and effective policy of limitation can the indispensable agreement of the German population for the integration of foreigners be secured. This is essential for the maintenance of social peace."[45]

The party as a whole strongly affirmed this position during the *Ausländerpolitik* debate in the Bundestag in February 1982. The speaker for the Social Democrats was Hans-Eberhard Urbaniak, an established Bundestag representative from Dortmund active in trade union politics. "We are for integration and consolidation," Urbaniak declared, outlining his party's new two-pronged approach to the opposition.[46] Without jettisoning integration altogether, he insisted on "consolidation"—measures to reduce the size of the foreigner population. The Federal Republic, Urbaniak claimed, had reached a threshold for absorbing foreigners, especially Turks, and allowing more to enter "would be irresponsible for both population groups in our country and would work against integration."[47] The growing conviction that integration measures were ineffective, along with a general rise in xenophobia, seems to have forced the SPD to rethink the basic conditions under which integrationist initiatives would work. Germans, this statement suggested, possessed the capacity to tolerate difference, but only when they did not feel overwhelmed by it. The SPD retreat from its earlier progressive stance on migrants thus moved socialists much closer to their conservative opponents: limiting the number of migrants was now seen as a necessary prerequisite for successful integration policy.

At the grassroots level of progressive reform, too, it is possible to detect an epistemological shift taking place in the discourse of integration, a shift that had important repercussions for the racialization of the guest worker question. During the early 1980s, this pattern can be grasped most clearly in the rising number of German-language publications on migrant women and especially the recurring trope of the imprisoned, imperiled Turkish woman. The trope itself was inextricably connected to the emergence of a new context for the debate about guest workers: what in Germany is often described as "reportage." Trope and context are not easily separated here. It was precisely the movement of guest worker representations into a domain associated with popularly accessible, journalistic treatments of contemporary social problems that fueled the new trope's force.

One of the earliest examples of reportage on migrant women was *Die verkauften Bräute: Türkische Frauen zwischen Kreuzberg und Anatolien* (Sold Brides: Turkish Women between Kreuzberg and Anatolia) published by Rowohlt Verlag.[48] The fact that a widely distributed, sales-driven press like Rowohlt began to exhibit interest in foreign (especially Turkish) women is itself instructive. For the first time, public fascination with the migrant experience began to move beyond the context of academic studies and specialty presses into the commercial mainstream. It is also instructive to consider the promotional process. While it is difficult to determine who precisely constituted the audience for this kind of reportage, Rowohlt's marketing choices for *Die verkauften Bräute* offer some useful clues. The book appeared in the "Frauen aktuell" (contemporary women) series, a list that also included works about women's self-help organizing, the role of women in mainstream political parties, and the involvement of women in political struggles such as apartheid.[49] Advertisements for the entire series ran in national feminist magazines such as *Courage*. From the vantage point of the Rowohlt marketing department, at least, the target audience for *Die verkauften Bräute* seems relatively clear. This was a book specifically addressed to German women sympathetic to leftist political causes and grassroots activism.

The book's foreword, written by the well-known and highly respected feminist Susanne von Paczensky, demonstrates a similar mode of public address. For Paczensky, the larger purpose of the project was to "make visible the difficulties and discrimination of Turkish women in the Federal Republic of Germany—with the goal of changing them. Whoever wants to help or work with them must first of all understand their situation, and that can only happen when one knows about their origin."[50] Like the Rowohlt advertisements, Paczensky's foreword hails a broad constituency of liberal-oriented teachers, social workers, counselors, and feminist sympathizers. Yet how exactly should her simultaneous invocation to ameliorate migrant "difficulties" by going to the source of their "origin" be interpreted?

To some extent, the project introduced by Paczensky operated within a broader pattern of leftist discourse. Following German academic scholarship on Turkish women, *Die verkauften Bräute* looked to Turkey, and especially to the social customs of the village, to diagnose the problems migrant women faced in Germany. Still, it is possible to detect a difference in tone and emphasis from one genre to the other. In the academic studies, the goal was to account for the impacts of the migration process on women by comparing social practices across cultures.[51] The reportage in *Die verkauften Bräute,* by contrast, presented Islam as the root cause of a fundamental crisis within Turkish gender relations. "In almost all areas of women's lives," the authors Andrea Baumgartner-Karabak and Gisela Landesberger explained,

> the influence of Islam is recognizable. Marriage and divorce are often carried out according to Islamic law. The Koran contains exact prescriptions relating to the treatment of women, against whom it discriminates strongly. Orientation to the world, moral ideas, and customary behavior are prescribed by religion, whose content is enforced by relatives and the village community. Firmly fitted within the patriarchal family, the trajectory of women's lives is completely predetermined. Decisions are first made for them by the father; after the wedding, by the husband. They have little influence on the choice of marriage partner. Their role in the household is characterized by unconditional subordination to the husband and the head of the household. Their social place within the family and in the village is defined by their sons.[52]

Islamic custom, in this view, left virtually no room for female agency. Women's lives were "predetermined"; decisions were "made for them"; their "social place" was fully defined by the men around them. The larger point of the argument, however, was not so much to critique village customs as to comment upon their transfer to West Germany via the labor migration. In the foreword, Paczensky made this clear by instructing German readers to consider the book's information about village culture in relation to the behavior of the migrant women in their midst. "Turkish women now live in our cities," she declared,

> as unassimilable, strange bodies. It is no wonder that they provoke prejudice. . . . They walk humbly two steps behind their husbands, and

even relinquish the particular domain of women—shopping for food and clothes—to their husbands or children. They contradict every imaginable image of woman: they do not do justice to the traditional role of an efficient mother, who self-confidently manages the house-hold, much less do they meet emancipated demands in their own ways of life.[53]

As the passage unfolds, it becomes clear that the problem facing migrant women is also a threat to the liberal, democratic values upheld by West German feminists. Turkish women, according to Paczensky, failed to live up to Western society's most basic standards, not even fulfilling "tradi-tional" female roles. The implication is that Islamic customs described in *Die verkauften Bräute* "contradicted"—and ultimately proved incompati-ble with—the historical emancipation of European women.

It is important to stress that Paczensky's critique was designed, first and foremost, to invite further study by liberal-minded Germans and en-courage sympathy with migrant women. Her stated purpose was to foster intercultural understanding, as opposed to overt xenophobia or stricter foreigner policies. Yet Paczensky also makes it clear that the ultimate goal of intercultural understanding was to extricate non-Western women from customs and practices deemed illiberal or even destructive. Certain types of behavior, in short, simply had to be discarded for integration into West German society to succeed. This stance was not unexpected given that most of those working with migrants at the ground level were self-identified feminists, who read the situation of Turkish women through the lens of their own struggles. The prospect of migrant women wearing headscarves, walking behind their husbands, and being cooped up in their homes seemed to undermine the basic gender equality for which West German feminists had fought so hard. What thus began as an expression of concern and a desire to study gender relations among Turks eventually became an articulation of thresholds between West and East, progressive politics and reactionary tradition, feminist practice and unreformed patriarchy.

Similar reservations arose in the day-to-day work of putting integra-tion into practice. In 1985, for example, a social-democratic Berlin city councilman publicly objected when a Turkish woman arrived at a local school for her duties as a teaching intern wearing a headscarf. Here again, intercultural understanding came into conflict with leftist principles. As the SPD councilman explained: "The headscarf is a signal and a form of discrimination . . . [that] has negative pedagogic effects on the children. For me, the claim of equality between men and women is such an important educational goal that I will not make any concessions. A teacher with a headscarf would contradict this educational mission."[54] This SPD politician drew the line at mutual understanding when the issue in question was contact between headscarved Turkish women and German children. Cultural integration, he seemed to suggest, should not come at the expense of German youth, who might absorb "discriminatory" attitudes about gender through the headscarf. Because the veiled Turkish woman served as an agent of socialization—as a professional empowered to transmit basic values to children—she became a target of particular concern.

The fact that the perceived problems of Turkish women became a major lightning rod for German feminists and leftists should come as no surprise. Migrant women have been the targets of intense interest and scrutiny in most Western European countries since the 1970s and have often served to measure an immigrant group's level of integration. But in the Federal Republic, the stakes of this concern were understood as particularly high. Historian Dagmar Herzog has argued recently that the German New Left framed its efforts to come to terms with the nation's Nazi past through a critique of postwar sexual conservatism. The push for sexual liberation, in other words, was not simply a side effect of alternative lifestyles. Rather, sexual repression offered a key explanation for why Nazism took root in Germany.[55] Precisely because the question of sexual domination was inextricably bound up with the New Left's view of fascism, Turkish gender relations posed a major concern for leftist critics.

At the same time, it was the very invocation of progressive political discourse and the language of liberal democracy that enabled a more explicit articulation of racial or ethnic difference on the Left. Turks, the argument went, threatened to reintroduce reactionary behaviors into a country that had worked tirelessly to transform itself into a modern, firmly democratic society. Such foreigners endangered the nation not so much in the older sense of anxieties about Jews as harbingers of modernity, capitalism, and liberalism.[56] Turks, rather, posed precisely the opposite problem: they potentially undermined Germany's hard-won progressivism, especially in terms of women's rights, marriage, and gender roles. It was therefore by making these kinds of progressive claims that leftists—so wary of association with tainted Nazi racial discourse—began to draw harder distinctions between Germans and Turks and require stricter standards for integration.

Even Germans on the Left, then, placed limits on how far German society should go to accommodate cultural difference. Certain core values of liberalism and Western democracy, most gradually concluded, could not be sacrificed to cultural relativism or mutual understanding. In this peculiar and unexpected way, the terms of integration set out in more progressive circles began to converge with the conservative logic of cultural incommensurability. By the mid-1980s, both ends of the political spectrum framed integration according to a strict set of parameters and defined it as a one-way process. What continued to separate these positions were the models of culture maintained by each group. Whereas most German conservatives understood migrant culture as timeless, essential, and fixed, German liberals tended to insist on the mutability of migrant culture and devoted enormous energy to the ground-level work of cultural reform.

The Paradox of Postwar Race

It is especially striking that even with the political and ideological shift toward cultural incommensurability in the early 1980s, the older language of race never explicitly surfaced in public discourse. This absence is a legacy of the Third Reich. After a twelve-year dictatorship in which racial prejudice determined state policy and suffused everyday practice, West German leaders sought to construct a stable liberal democracy in which categories based on race were irrelevant. After a regime in which racial distinctions served as justification for mass murder, the very word *race* became taboo and was largely unspeakable in a reconstructed Germany. Yet the injunction against invoking race did not prevent the fundamental components of racial formation—ideologies of essentialism and absolute difference, as well as social and economic hierarchies of differential rights—from operating in postwar German society.[57] Indeed, the taboo only prevented the process of racialization from being recognized as such. This inadvertent Nazi inheritance, in other words, produced a kind of blindness to the more subtle ways that Germans have constructed barriers to the inclusion and incorporation of guest workers and their descendants.

The larger contours of this pattern can be seen especially clearly in one final example, the Rock gegen Rechts (Rock against the Right) concert staged at roughly the same historical moment considered in this essay. On 16 June 1979, approximately 50,000 young people gathered in Frankfurt for what the *Süddeutsche Zeitung* described as a "music festival under the open sky, where individual musicians and bands played for free in order to support a political cause."[58] The cause, in this case, was to protest a major rally by the extreme right-wing National Democratic Party (NPD) taking place simultaneously in the city. German concert organizers—a coalition of leftist activists, social democrats, environmentalists, and trade union members—modeled the event on the better-known Rock against Racism movement established in Britain three years earlier. Intended as a counterdemonstration, the concert offered a more peaceful means to combat the NPD, which for five previous years had held national meetings and bloody marches in Frankfurt as part of an effort to create the "first national-democratic city in Germany." Udo Lindenberg, a musical participant in the festival, explained: "We must stop the right-wing blockheads, that's why we're here."[59]

Several aspects of the public discourse around Rock gegen Rechts immediately stand out. Most newspapers, for example, focused almost entirely on a potential clash of right- and left-wing demonstrators. The single article to appear in the respected weekly *Die Zeit,* "Fear over the State of Emergency," discussed at length preparations for a possible fight in the streets, which included "5,000 officers ready to be sent into the anticipated battle."[60] Such reports, moreover, devoted greater column space to the history of NPD provocations than to the current leftist response, reading the emergence of far right activity in terms of an older Nazi template. Commentators made much of the fact that the NPD dubbed its annual rally in Frankfurt the Deutschlandtreffen (Germany Meeting), a decision that seemed to conjure associations with the famous Nuremberg rallies of the Nazi Party and its ideal of a united Fatherland.[61]

But perhaps the most remarkable feature of the public discussion around Rock gegen Rechts was that the ostensible targets of NPD protest and violence—guest workers—did not surface at all: not in the press coverage of the far right rallies, not in the leftist response. Foreign laborers and their families, of course, provided a crucial touchstone for the NPD's political appeal and were often victims of right-wing attacks. Indeed, from the party's very inception in 1964, guest workers were identified as the primary reason for German unemployment, and the push to rid the Federal Republic of foreigners constituted a key item on the NPD agenda.[62] Yet a curious silence about these seemingly obvious connections prevailed. The cloak of neo-Nazism seemed to focus attention on the specter of Germany's troubled past, obscuring the fact that racial prejudice and violence were alive and well in the present.

The specific name for the event chosen by concert organizers illustrates how this elision operated in leftist thinking. What had been Rock against Racism in the British context became Rock gegen Rechts in the German. This change sent an important message: it was one thing to acknowledge and fight right-wing extremists, but it was quite another to suggest the reemergence of a virulent and widespread racism within the Federal Republic. Neo-Nazis, in other words, could be viewed as a fringe group, divorced from mainstream society and condemned by Germans across the political spectrum as an obvious evil. Racism, however, pointed to a broader social malady, whose existence might raise questions about whether democratization itself had worked.

These semantic shifts underscore the postwar German tendency to understand racism as something that happens in other countries such as Britain and the United States, or as a highly circumscribed problem of NPD members, *Republikaner,* and skinheads. They also demonstrate a lingering pattern of ideological evasion, which assumed that racialized thinking was antithetical to the liberal democracy the Federal Republic had become. In a sense, the legacy of the Nazi past and the postwar efforts to reenter the fraternity of Western capitalist democracies produced a paradoxical situation. The very act of speaking the word *race*—that is, allowing it into public discourse—often seemed like the first step to opening the door for ra*cism* to creep back into German society. Yet this set of assumptions also created confusion between aspiration and reality. It was easy to assume that just because Germans had eradicated the word *race* from their vocabulary, they had also purged racism from actual conditions and practices.

Ultimately, the postwar project of democratization defined the very category of race as un-German and therefore (mostly) unspeakable. Within this framework, it became possible both to idealize social and ideological distance from the Nazi past as well as to condemn overt forms of neo-Nazi violence in the present. But what this has left out are the more elusive forms of racialized thinking that have long surrounded the labor migration and ways of understanding difference in the Federal Republic.

CHAPTER 4

German Democracy and the Question of Difference, 1945–1995

Rita Chin and Heide Fehrenbach

With the collapse of the Third Reich, democratization became one of the most urgent political and ideological tasks facing West Germans. The ideal of democracy (liberty, equality, popular representation) as well as its concrete institutions (a constitution and popularly elected representative bodies) promised to protect the new state against repeating the barbarity of the Nazi dictatorship and the political tradition of German authoritarianism. By the mid-1980s, as the Federal Republic marked the fortieth anniversary of the war's end, many Germans—first and foremost, Chancellor Helmut Kohl—believed that the process of democratization was largely complete. West Germany, they argued, had proven its unwavering commitment to the values and fraternity of Western capitalist democracies.

Yet creating a stable democracy and measuring its success turned out to be more complicated than either the fathers of the Federal Republic or their heirs anticipated. In the early postwar period, the issue of democratization became linked to a robust economy and a functioning social welfare state—in no small measure because enemies of the Weimar Republic (Germany's first democratic experiment) had exploited a volatile economic situation and the state's drastically inadequate social welfare provisions to undermine the regime. After 1945, quick economic recovery was deemed essential to secure political legitimacy and social stability. The *Wirtschaftswunder*, in this respect, helped ensure that the new Bonn Republic was on the right path. But by the 1950s the postwar economic explosion required more manpower than the West German population could provide, and the government quickly turned to foreign guest workers to fill the shortage. Ultimately, the mandate to foster democracy through economic prosperity and expensive social welfare guarantees inadvertently produced an extensive labor migration that brought two million foreigners onto German soil.

By the late 1960s, democratization acquired a different set of meanings, as a younger generation of Germans, born during or immediately after the war, came of age. What had seemed to their parents like a grueling, yet courageous effort to rebuild the country and embrace Western-style democracy often appeared to a vocal minority of mostly middle-class, university-educated youth as an attempt to avoid coming to terms with the Nazi past.[1] Critics on the Left went so far as to condemn the Federal Republic's efforts to secure democracy through capitalism as a structural, political, and moral continuity from the Third Reich. It was precisely the obsession with ever-expanding economic production and the self-congratulatory attitude toward prosperity, according to 1968ers, that obscured West German society's failure to deal with its troubling historical legacy.

For guest workers, their descendants, and other out-groups, though, neither of these frameworks seemed adequate. As early as the mid-1970s, minority intellectuals began to address both the obvious and more subtle barriers to incorporation into German society. Prompted by the reunification of East and West Germany, the second-generation Turkish-German author and cultural critic Zafer Şenocak formulated a key question with major implications for assessing democratization: "Is Germany a home for Turks?" This rather innocent query suggested a radically new definition of democracy. In Şenocak's view, it was no longer enough to evaluate Germany's democratic credentials according to criteria of economic stability or even a critical attitude toward the Nazi past. Somewhat paradoxically, postwar labor recruitment had produced the demographic and cultural conditions for multiethnic democracy. Yet the ideological and political framework for democratization imagined by most Germans included little sense that guest workers might eventually become part of the nation's social and cultural fabric.

This essay explores the contested concept of democracy in the Federal Republic, a concept intimately bound up with the burden of the nation's past, the struggle over collective memory, and assumptions about ethnic belonging and national identity.[2] It deliberately focuses on public discourse in order to highlight the ways that official national memory culture has often obscured the narratives and experiences of guest workers and other minorities, both residents and citizens, in German society. The essay revisits some of the milestone moments in the Federal Republic's history and offers an extended analysis of German reunification and its aftermath. Ultimately, it aims to rethink the very meanings of postwar democratization.

Democratization, Economic Recovery, and Labor Immigration

As the U.S., British, and Soviet armies converged on Berlin in May 1945, a top priority for the Allied forces was to prevent history from repeating itself. Less than thirty years before, the victorious powers laid the blame for the First World War on Germany. The result was a punitive peace treaty that demanded stiff reparations and German acknowledgment of war guilt. Though the terms were not unreasonable for such a costly war, they did not aid postwar stability. Instead they became the rallying point for nationalist fervor, sowing the seeds of a corrosive debate among Germans about their country's shameful defeat and future course, which (with the onset of worldwide economic depression) culminated in growing popular support for the National Socialist solution. When World War II came to an end, by contrast, the Allies vowed to practice restraint in implementing the peace. Not only did the victors wish to avoid creating new German resentments, they also sought to forestall the possibility of another dictatorship that might threaten world peace for a third time.[3] For the American, British, and eventually French occupying powers, this meant helping democratic institutions take firm root and preempting political upheaval by bolstering the economy.[4]

In order to lay a firm ideological foundation for democracy, the Western Allies imposed a number of key policies, two of which are relevant here. The first, reeducation, sought to wean Germans from their undue respect for authority. The second, denazification, attempted to weed out Nazis and Nazi ideology from public life and civil service. This task included assessing individual guilt in war crimes trials such as Nuremberg.[5] During the occupation period, the Allies interned 200,000 former Nazi officials. In the first half of 1946 alone, 150,000 Germans lost their jobs in government and civil service, and 73,000 were removed from their positions in industry and commerce.[6] In practice, however, neither initiative proved as far reaching or thorough as originally envisioned. The nature of Allied occupation meant that each zone pursued these policies in different ways. The end result was an uneven and inconsistent reeducation program, prosecution of Nazi criminals, and treatment of former Nazi party members.

It is also important to acknowledge that the Allies defined these initiatives somewhat narrowly. Reeducation, for instance, targeted Germans' perceptions of authority rather than their feelings about racial difference, while denazification focused on party membership rather than social attitudes. Significantly, the Nuremberg Trials—the prime showcase for meting out justice for Nazi crimes—discussed the victims in terms of nationality and not in terms of ethnicity, race, or even religion.[7] Thus, it is not particularly surprising that just a few months into the Allied occupation, the practice of reeducation turned out to be more of a readjustment to ground-level social relations and included the persistence (if in a somewhat revised valence) of anti-Jewish, racist, and ethnocentric biases.[8] As one U.S. government official complained, "denazification, which began with a bang, has since died with a whimper . . . it opened the way toward renewed control of German public, social, economic and cultural life by forces which only partially and temporarily had been deprived of the influence they had exerted under the Nazi regime."[9] According to a 1947 survey conducted by the U.S. Office of Military Government (known as OMGUS), even though most Germans were democratically inclined, a significant minority was undemocratic and continued to hold authoritarian views. Moreover, a substantial minority of Germans, regardless of political disposition, evidenced antisemitic and racist attitudes.[10]

Despite the limitations of U.S. reeducation and denazification programs, John McCloy, head of the American administration in Germany, stated in 1949 that the behavior of Germans toward the few Jews in their midst would "be one of the real touchstones and the test of Germany's progress" in building a new state.[11] At least for some U.S. officials, then, German attitudes toward their Jewish victims served as a social barometer of democratization. But as divisions hardened between the Western Allies and the Soviet Union along Cold War lines, the United States and Britain prioritized efforts to rebuild the economy in their zones over reeducation and denazification initiatives. One consequence of this new concern was that economic recovery and entry into the Western security alliance (NATO) eclipsed justice and memory as the primary measure of West German democratization.

This shift emerged especially clearly in May 1949 when West Germany became a formal and democratic, if semisovereign, state.[12] In his inaugural address to the new Bundestag, Chancellor Konrad Adenauer expressed his concern at the lingering tendency toward antisemitism. In the face of hostile public opinion and even resistance from members of his own party, Adenauer spearheaded a compensation package for Jewish victims of the Holocaust.[13] But these acts, in a sense, completed the phase of democratization begun under American tutelage. As Diethelm Prowe has observed, "since Germans associated denazification with the occupation, they considered punishment of the guilty completed with the founding of their new democratic state."[14] The task of democratization for the young West German republic lay with building a strong and stable economy, shoring up the political democracy, and forging close economic and military relations with the Western powers.[15]

Meanwhile, the unexpectedly quick economic recovery from the war proved extremely effective. For a majority of Germans, rising prosperity went a long way toward establishing political legitimacy and quelled doubts about liberal democracy as the basic foundation for the West German state.[16] Economic success began, at least, as a kind of insurance policy against a return to barbarism or resort to Communism. Yet this path to democratization inadvertently introduced a new wrinkle into West German society. The *Wirtschaftswunder* created an urgent demand for manpower, which the native population appeared ill-equipped to provide. As a result of the high casualty rate among German men during the war and a broad consensus among political parties to encourage women in the wartime workforce to return to the home, authorities faced a massive labor shortage.[17] The Federal Republic's solution was to implement a guest worker program, signing a labor recruitment treaty with Italy on 22 December 1955 and concluding subsequent agreements with Spain, Portugal, Turkey, Greece, and Yugoslavia. With the construction of the Berlin Wall in 1961, the significant flow of East German workers dried up, and West German firms increasingly relied on non-German labor to make up the shortfall. By the autumn of 1964, the number of foreign workers in Germany surpassed one million, and five years later it topped two million.[18]

On one level, then, the large-scale importation of foreigners into the Federal Republic appeared to signal an unambiguous official retreat from state-sponsored projects of national racial purification and ethnoracial nationalism. After all, West German officials were actively pursuing a policy of foreign immigration that, in contrast to the forced labor programs of the Third Reich, was understood to be both completely voluntary and mutually beneficial. Nonetheless, despite the apparent expectations of some male immigrants, West German plans to build an ethnically diverse (if ethnically segmented) economy stopped well short of social integration.[19] The seemingly logical connection between the massive influx of foreign labor and the question of integration—including the ethnic expansion of German democracy—went largely unacknowledged.

One reason can be found in the basic structure of the labor recruitment program, from the length of employment and residence permits to the efforts to hire single men (and eventually women), from the practice of housing workers in isolated barracks to the plan to send redundant laborers back home. As a result, most West Germans took the euphemistic label *guest worker* literally; they assumed that foreigners were temporary sojourners, present in the Federal Republic only until demand for their labor dried up. As transient beings, labor recruits were not associated with such longer-term processes as social reconstruction or democratization.

There were a few exceptions to this pattern. In 1964, labor minister Theodor Blank offered a more expansive significance for guest worker recruitment, casting the program as a sign of goodwill toward the international community. This arrangement, he explained, facilitated "the merging together of Europe and the rapprochement between persons of highly diverse backgrounds and cultures in the spirit of friendship."[20] Blank further argued that the labor migration would help promote "international understanding" and "European integration."[21] But even here, in Blank's broader understanding of the guest worker program, there was a basic failure to recognize the larger implications of this policy decision: by relying on foreign laborers to fuel the economic miracle, the very process of postwar democratization now required a renewed engagement with the question of difference.

In practice, the Federal Republic adopted precisely the opposite approach. The postwar guest worker program perpetuated many of Germany's older tendencies of social exclusion.[22] Consider, for example, the legal status of those who came to the Federal Republic within the framework of labor recruitment. The original treaties and 1965 Ausländergesetz (Foreigner Regulation Law) categorized guest workers as foreigners. This distinction not only determined rights of work, social security, and residence but also precluded (until 2000) the right to become naturalized citizens. The Federal Republic continued to reserve citizenship status for those with German blood. The new state deliberately retained the legal definition of German citizenship from 1913, which was based upon the principle of jus sanguinis, favored patrilinear German descent, and relegitimated an ethnocultural vision of Germanness. In the immediate postwar years, this decision facilitated the repatriation of millions of ethnic Germans driven from the eastern reaches of the former Reich; over the course of the Cold War, it established a "fixed law of return" for any ethnic Germans entering from East Germany, Eastern Europe, or the Soviet Union. In contrast, the postwar guest worker program was based upon and perpetuated the assumption that West Germany was not a country of immigration—or, to put it more precisely, was not a country of *non-German* immigration.[23] Foreign laborers were recruited not to become permanent additions to German society but rather to provide labor for a limited period and then return to their own homes. Such migration, to quote Fatima El-Tayeb's pithy formulation, was understood as "reversible, coming with an expiration date."[24]

In this respect, the category of guest worker itself served to exclude labor migrants from the nation, making the distinction between foreigner and citizen appear natural and unassailable. For guest workers and succeeding generations of their offspring born in the Federal Republic, it was possible to be permanent residents of Germany and yet remain perpetual, even "hereditary," migrants entirely separate from the German social body and polity. Their legal status in West Germany was grounded in assumptions—neither explicitly articulated nor acknowledged—of their fundamental, unalterable difference, and civic, social, and cultural distance, from Germans.[25] In this way, distinctions based upon notions of ethnicity, race, and religion have continued to structure the legal parameters of immigration and citizenship in the Federal Republic since 1945.

In general, political and public debates about difference, and the challenges and limits of integration to West German society and democracy, only reemerged in the 1970s—a good decade and a half after the early postwar focus on the social "problem" of the so-called *Mischlingskinder* subsided.[26] Yet when such attention did resurface, it spotlighted the issue of immigration and narrowed more and more insistently on the person of the "Turk." In recent decades, "immigration" and "Turks" have become the central organizing concepts framing debates about difference and German democracy: "about what, or rather *who*, is *not* German." This focus conceives of *difference as import:* as something that crosses borders and enters from the outside, as something potentially disruptive and thoroughly external to the nation, as something alien to homegrown democracy. In doing so, it presumes a national homogeneity of the type that never existed in Germany. It excludes from national definition the social impact of historic waves of migration, mixing, and reproduction that accompanied commerce, slave trading, colonialism, war, military occupation: in short, that shaped life in the modern world. By ignoring these alternate histories, it suggests that Germany, until very recently, has been essentially Christian and, if multiethnic, then nonetheless white. [27]

The New Left, the Nazi Past, and Democratization

The initial failure to grasp the crucial place of labor recruitment in forging democracy continued through the 1960s and into the early 1970s, well after the raucous public entrée of New Left voices onto the political scene in the Federal Republic. This seems surprising in retrospect, since the 1960s marked the extended moment when the generation of war babies reached adulthood and began to level serious critiques at the democratizing process led by Adenauer.[28] Between 1963 and 1965, the Auschwitz trials in Frankfurt along with a controversial parliamentary debate over extending the statute of limitations for Nazi war crimes drew public attention once again to the presence of the National Socialist past.[29] During these same years, the far-Right National Democratic Party was founded. These events "helped remind left-wing intellectuals that the Federal Republic had not yet fully shed its anti-democratic culture" and Nazi legacy.[30] In response, 1968ers demanded a painstaking *Vergangenheitsbewältigung* (coming to terms with the past) and an end to their parents' silence concerning the Third Reich. However, they did not address the issue of the Holocaust or the implications of the Auschwitz trials. Despite its later mythology, "1968" did not represent a historical rupture, but rather a dramatic culmination of processes begun in the 1950s. Nonetheless, if the 1968ers were not the first to initiate open engagement with the Nazi past, they certainly did popularize and theorize it.[31] To members of this younger generation,

> Adenauer Germany's coming to terms with its past seemed shallow and false. Instead of really getting to the roots of . . . the origins of fascism, West Germany was busily constructing a self-serving ideology of rabid anti-communism. This credo . . . had blocked the process of democratic reform in West Germany. Just as anti-communism had replaced democracy in this "feel good" Germany, so too did general prosperity mask the immense social costs of capitalism. It was necessary, the Left argued, to confront the brutal facts of the past head on.[32]

For members of the New Left, then, the hollowness of West German democracy was bound up with the nation's unself-conscious embrace of capitalism and endless pursuit of prosperity, which served as cover for the failure to deal with its shameful Nazi past.

Pivotal to the New Left's analysis was their condemnation of West Germany's ideological alignment with the United States of America. Unlike the more moderate, "Old Left" Social Democratic Party (the SPD, which in 1966 became the governing partner in a Grand Coalition with the conservative Christian Democratic Party, or CDU/CSU), the New Left energetically rejected the image of the United States as democracy's international helpmate. Rather, New Left critics vilified American foreign and domestic policy (in Vietnam and in relation to Black Americans) as baldly participating in capitalist, imperialist, and racist exploitation at home and abroad. For the German New Left, the United States represented oppression on a global scale. In this sense, it was viewed on a historical continuum with fascism, since fascism was understood by the Left as a product of the highest stage of capitalism. Thus the epithet *fascist* was applied liberally to both the West German state (as "heir" of Nazis) and to its U.S. patron. These preoccupations shaped the analytical lens through which the New Left interpreted West German democracy and conditioned the nature of their social critique.[33]

The New Left's myopic fixation on the intersection of capitalism and fascism unwittingly led to their neglect of both systems' social and material impacts in the Federal Republic. At the most basic level, this focus "subsumed the singularity of the Nazis' systematic annihilation of the Jews under the generic term and structural concept of fascism."[34] To read history forward, German New Left intellectuals—and the more politically conservative West German historical profession—had not yet come to an understanding of the uniqueness of National Socialist crimes or the single-mindedness with which the Nazi regime pursued its Jewish victims. The historical centrality of the Jewish Holocaust for understanding National Socialism would only tentatively emerge in West Germany in the 1970s and gain momentum in the 1980s and beyond.[35]

At the same time, condemning international capitalism as a root cause of fascism did lead some New Left artists and intellectuals to extend their criticism to the Federal Republic's guest worker program. Rainer Werner Fassbinder's 1969 feature film, *Katzelmacher,* for example, depicted a vicious group of working-class friends and their dealings with an imported laborer. That same year, the social activist Günter Walraff published a book of reportage on the living conditions of guest workers, *Bilder aus Deutschland—"Gastarbeiter" oder der gewöhnliche Kapitalismus* (*Images from Germany—"Guest Workers" or Capitalism as Usual*).[36] In each case, however, self-congratulatory economic prosperity, social conformity, and ideological complacency emerged as the primary targets of critique. Foreign labor recruitment, in this view, simply represented the most extreme example of the Federal Republic's indifference to the human costs of the unbridled pursuit of capitalism. In *Katzelmacher,* for instance, the foreign laborer Jorgos functions as an abstract figure with no individual identity. He is virtually silent because of his inability to understand or speak much German, and his background remains obscure except for the fact that he has come from Greece.[37] Similarly, Walraff's book sought to challenge the idea of a surplus army of laborers, whose flexibility helped facilitate "capitalism as usual." Both guest workers and Jews remained remote as subjects, reduced (albeit in different ways) to ancillary aspects of what were perceived as the more systemic problems of capitalism and fascism.

Due to their conceptual tools and ideological commitments, this highly critical younger generation of leftist intellectuals had trouble seeing just how central the question of ethnic and racial difference had become to postwar democratization within the Federal Republic. To the extent that members of the New Left registered and responded to issues of contemporary racial oppression they treated them as a product of capitalism and imperialism. And to the degree that they adopted antiracism as a political cause, they did so by criticizing the social conditions in other countries, particularly but not exclusively in the United States. For the German New Left, the focus of antiracist and anti-imperialist struggles was directed primarily outside their country and against globalizing powers, processes, and exploitation.[38]

As early as 1966, the conservative weekly *Welt am Sonntag* recognized the paradox: "Germans who work through their past by being outraged about apartheid in South Africa or race riots in America obviously do not have anything against the apartheid of alien workers [*Fremdarbeiter*] in the Federal Republic, against their social boycott and their displacement into ghettos."[39] Consciously or not, the 1968ers, like their parents, conceived of German society as essentially homogeneous in ethnic terms. As a result, calls for democratic reform at home invoked the Nazi past and condemned selective continuities with it, while keeping virtually mum on Germany's treatment of minorities, both historically and in its multiethnic present.

Nonetheless, New Left analysis did stimulate grassroots activism. West German university students in the SDS, for example, joined with African students in their midst to protest South African apartheid and other third world injustices. Yet unlike their African counterparts, who invoked international law and human rights, these young German New Leftists ultimately mobilized representations of exotic black bodies to publicize and propagandize their politics.[40] By the turn of the 1970s, a small group of students, inspired by the putatively "authentic" revolutionary potential of American ghettoized Blacks, formed Black Panther Solidarity Committees and sought strategic alliance with disgruntled African American GIs stationed in West Germany. Although they condemned the discriminatory practices of German landlords and bar owners toward black soldiers, the students declared as their primary ambition "to expose the fascist terror of the ruling classes in the United States" and to "overthrow American centers of imperialism" and the "militarist war machine." Some young Germans permed their hair to approximate Afros and raised their white fists in Black Power salutes in an attempt to create a radical persona through the selective embodiment of hip Blackness—a racialized mimicry that awaits careful historical analysis.[41] The point here is that while interracial grassroots political activism emerged on a very small scale in the 1960s and 1970s, these alliances were conditioned by both white German ambitions of interracial solidarity *and* expressions of racial difference. After all, it was the perceived powerful revolutionary potential embodied by Blacks and Blackness that attracted the German students in the first place.

During the 1970s, grassroots organizing emerged as a new form of democratic politics in Germany. This was an important development and one that became an organizational model for the growth of community-based assistance programs for immigrants and their children in the 1970s; collective self-help groups for minorities (such as Black Germans) in the 1980s; and for intercultural, human rights, and antiracist organizations of the 1990s and beyond. These initiatives complicated the political landscape of the Federal Republic and, at certain junctures, commanded positive governmental attention to social issues or served to limit discriminatory treatment and policies toward immigrant and minority groups. Ironically, the existence of a shameful Nazi past worked to the advantage of such groups, since the West German government evidenced both a marked sensitivity to comparisons (or allegations of policy or ideological continuities) with that earlier regime and a marked determination to protect the reputation of West German democracy. Over the course of the 1970s, the growth of pluralist politics, along with official West German concerns regarding international opinion and diplomatic repercussions, encouraged the government to support programs for the integration of immigrants in German society and soften proposed policies of compulsory repatriation and family restriction for immigrants. Unlike that of the Third Reich, the power of the postwar German state was not absolute. Rather, it was mitigated by the political voice and interests of citizen groups domestically and by participation in regional alliances, such as the EU and NATO, internationally.[42]

Christian Democracy and the Normalization of German Nationalism in the 1980s

The question of democratization resurfaced as a topic of heated public debate around 1982, when Helmut Kohl and other conservatives began to declare that the Federal Republic had proven itself a mature liberal democracy. This claim heralded the completion of the nation's democratizing process and was integral to Kohl's larger push to restore German patriotism and promote a more positive sense of national identity. Along the same lines, Kohl helped establish the Deutsche Historische Museum in Berlin and the Haus der Geschichte in Bonn in order to provide Germans with historical narratives that would instill pride rather than shame or guilt. This return to nationalism also inspired revisionist histories of the Third Reich, precipitating the highly charged *Historikerstreit* (historians' debate) in 1986.[43]

The broader ideological stakes of Kohl's efforts emerge especially clearly in the 1985 Bitburg affair, when the chancellor invited U.S. president Ronald Reagan to lay a wreath at the Bitburg military cemetery to commemorate the fortieth anniversary of Germany's unconditional surrender at the end of World War II.[44] Although the request provoked an international uproar once it became known that SS soldiers had been buried there, Reagan completed the visit as planned. He justified the decision by explaining that the ceremony was intended not to reawaken bad memories but to commemorate the restoration of peace and to celebrate the stable Atlantic alliance that had been achieved in the wake of Nazism's defeat.[45] In many ways, the Bitburg ceremony was an audacious feat. As Geoff Eley has argued, Kohl orchestrated the event as "an act of symbolic resolution . . . the consummation of Germany's long-earned return to normalcy."[46] Central to this process was an interweaving of democratic self-congratulation and the production of new historical narratives. Precisely because the Federal Republic had been democratically stable for four decades, Kohl's actions suggested, it had earned the right to honor its war dead (many of whom had no specific ties to the Nazi Party) like other democratic nations. In the surrounding furor, leftist intellectuals such as Jürgen Habermas criticized what they considered a neoconservative attempt to "defuse the past."[47]

For critics on the Left, Bitburg was especially problematic because it suggested that democratization and *Vergangenheitsbewältigung* were finite processes. With that work now complete, West Germans could leave the unpleasant and shameful Nazi legacy in the past and construct a revitalized national identity for the future. Yet one striking feature of this controversy was the common belief that democratic values should be gauged in terms of German attitudes toward Nazi crimes against Jews, the nation's largest minority group prior to 1945. This shared assumption between conservatives and progressives meant that the entire debate elided the possibility of multiethnic democracy in the present. Indeed, by driving home the importance of Germany's thorny past for any attempt to resuscitate national identity, Bitburg obscured the other major aspect of such a project: namely, that the effort to reclaim a patriotic nationalism also involved defining the parameters of Germanness, a process that necessarily took place in relation to the millions of guest workers and other people of color or foreign birth now residing on West German soil.

By 1985, after all, the Federal Republic was home to the largest population of foreign residents in Western Europe. And as both Kohl and his critics knew quite well, the issue of the labor recruitment's domestic social (as opposed to economic) impact had already emerged as a topic of intense national debate. In 1979, Helmut Schmidt's socialist-liberal coalition had called for a major reformulation of the guest worker question. Leading Social Democratic officials proposed abandoning the older notion of guest workers as temporary "labor forces" in favor of open acknowledgment that nearly two million foreign workers and their families were de facto immigrants in need of social, cultural, and economic "integration." During the early 1980s, moreover, guest worker integration had become an issue of partisan politics. CDU members of the Bundestag, in particular, played a leading role in formulating a much narrower and harder notion of integration, one that imagined Turks and other foreigners as belonging to separate cultures well outside the sphere of the German nation. Whereas previous SPD integration policy had assumed that some kind of cultural adaptation or fluidity was possible, and desirable, the CDU view of culture foreclosed the potential for—and indeed the value of—reciprocal influence.[48]

The CDU's theory of self-contained national cultures helps us to see that the energetic nationalism championed by conservatives in the early 1980s was never simply an issue of moving beyond war guilt or *Wiedergut-*

machung (restitution). The renewal of national identity also required a reassertion of borders and clear definitions of cultural membership. The new push for patriotism, moreover, seems to have undergirded the zero-sum logic central to CDU foreigner policy: migrants had to choose full assimilation or return to their countries of origin. Thus, as the party sought to restore national self-esteem based on the Federal Republic's position as a now mature liberal democracy, it increasingly maintained that strong national cultures could not cross-pollinate but belonged to wholly separate natural native habitats.

Neither Kohl nor his leftist opponents, in other words, recognized (or at least were willing to admit) that the effort to resuscitate German national identity involved both rewriting the Nazi past as a twelve-year lapse redressed through democratization *and* advocating a culturally homogeneous conception of belonging. Indeed, conservatives as well as progressives seemed to assume that these interrelated tasks were entirely separate processes. For precisely this reason, leftist critics of Bitburg attacked Kohl for attempting to replace collective remembrance and atonement with unapologetic nationalism. But they, too, failed to acknowledge that the particular vision of national identity being advanced offered little room for the very guest workers whose labor did so much to secure postwar democratization.

Reverberations of Reunification

Almost a decade later, the question of national identity reemerged as a major topic of public debate, precipitated by the sudden fall of the Berlin Wall and the crumbling of the East German state. In these discussions, too, guest workers and their descendants, along with other minority groups, initially remained peripheral. The issue of national belonging first surfaced at the Monday demonstrations in Leipzig in October and November 1989. Protesters quickly moved from a universalist claim of "Wir sind DAS Volk" (We are THE people) to the more particularist declaration "Wir sind EIN Volk" (We are ONE people). Whereas the former slogan seemed directed at the German Democratic Republic's (GDR) repressive policies and called for representative democracy, the latter proclaimed a desire to reconstitute a single German people. Part of this shift had to do with a growing belief on the part of East Germans that unification offered the quickest path to a better life. Kohl's cabinet, in fact, made economic help for the East contingent upon the restoration of a national state.[49] Yet the question of what precisely the phrase "one people" signified was largely taken for granted as the push toward reunification gained momentum.

During the period from November 1989 to October 1990, public debate generally treated reunification as a foregone conclusion; most discussion focused on the practical aspects of the merger such as a single currency, the permanent resolution of Eastern borders, the privatization of GDR state property, and NATO membership. To the extent that doubts about a restored German nation emerged, they tended to come from voices abroad raising questions about the effects of this imminent change on European integration. The *New York Times,* for example, issued an editorial on the rush to German unity that highlighted the misgivings expressed by the major powers in Europe. France, according to the editorial, viewed reunification as an obstacle in its attempt to move forward with Western European economic integration, while Britain perceived this development as a potential disruption of the current balance of power.[50] One of the few Germans to voice concern was the prominent intellectual Günter Grass, who specifically linked unification with the problem of a reinvigorated nationalism. "Once again," he observed, "it looks as if a reasonable sense of nationhood is being inundated by diffuse nationalist emotion. Our neighbors watch with anxiety, even with alarm, as Germans recklessly talk themselves into the will to unity."[51] For all of these skeptics, anxiety around reunification had to do with the persistent German question: could this major power in the center of Europe sustain itself peacefully, without encroaching on its neighbors either in terms of territorial and economic expansion or nationalistic fervor?

It was not until the political process of reunification was complete that public debate explicitly turned to the question of what becoming "one people" again might mean. This conversation had two key focal points: the spate of brutal hate crimes between 1991 and 1993, and the renewed effort to deal with the burden of the German past, which crystallized in the building of a Holocaust memorial in Berlin. One clear vision of how the German people should be defined was offered by young hooligans, skinheads, and right-wing extremists who carried out a series of vicious assaults against foreigners, German minorities, and other out-groups in both eastern and western parts of the new Federal Republic, often to the chorus of "Foreigners out" and "Germany for the Germans." In September 1991, the hostility flared in the depressed eastern town of Hoyerswerda.[52] Although this was not the first violent attack in unified Germany, it was one of the largest and most protracted.[53] For nearly a week, gangs of young men, cheered on by hundreds of residents, besieged two apartment complexes that housed contract laborers from Mozambique and Vietnam who had been hired by the now defunct GDR. Armed with knives, rocks, bottles, and Molotov cocktails, the youths surrounded and blockaded the buildings. One man told newspaper reporters, "We are going to stay here until the blacks are gone."[54] Despite dozens of arrests, local police could not contain the violence and eventually used the cover of night to evacuate all 230 foreigners to safety. Significantly, this escalated aggression broke out in the weeks leading up to the first anniversary of German reunification. In the aftermath of the violence, Hoyerswerda residents appeared on national television and jubilantly proclaimed their town "foreigner-free."[55] A similar assault took place on a refugee hostel in the eastern German city of Rostock in August 1992.

Within months, ethnonational violence turned fatal in western Germany. On 23 November 1992, two skinheads set fire to the home of a Turkish family in Mölln, killing two girls, Yeliz Arslan, age ten, and Ayşe Yilmaz, age fourteen, and their grandmother, Bahide Arslan, age fifty-one. Six months later, four German youths firebombed the house of another Turkish family in Solingen, killing five women and girls.[56] These xenophobic attacks functioned as a kind of grassroots referendum on who counted as members of "ein Volk." On one level, the violence attempted to excise alien elements from the newly reconstituted nation. But there were clearly socioeconomic issues in play here, too. As numerous commentators have noted, skyrocketing unemployment plagued much of the East immediately following unification, fueling deep disappointment about the material rewards of a reunited German state. Meanwhile, resentment grew in the West as the federal government allocated large sums of money and resources to aid the new eastern states. Yet these economic factors cannot fully explain the ideological significance of the cheering onlookers in Hoyerswerda and Rostock. One source of the applause seems to have been a collective desire to remove any foreign body from the national imaginary—to create a "foreigner-free" Germany. Or perhaps the goal was more modest: to insist that the very presence of non-Germans on German soil represented an affront to the bystanders' dreams of reunification.

The views driving these antiforeigner attacks, it is important to note, represented an extreme position rejected by most Germans. After the riots in Hoyerswerda and Rostock, several thousand demonstrators from western Germany descended on both cities to condemn the brutality, provoking clashes with the police and local residents. According to a *U.S. News & World Report* journalist on the scene, even casual conversations had the potential to "erupt in rage." When Rostock resident Klaus Goetze criticized Georg Classen for coming from the West to demonstrate, for example, a furious Classen "shouted back: 'I'm here because I'm German, and it's the duty of all Germans to stand up at this moment and protest!' "[57] This sentiment was reaffirmed by tens of thousands who took to the streets all over the country to denounce the attacks in Mölln and Solingen. Between December 1992 and January 1993, nearly two million people (or one in every forty) participated in candlelight vigils, publicly repudiating the extreme Right's exclusionary vision of the nation.[58] A spokesperson for the 400,000-person-strong march in Munich pointed to the large turnout as a sign that "the majority of Germans are not secretly hostile to foreigners or sympathetic to fascism."[59] Over the next few years, grassroots efforts led to the creation of numerous German organizations devoted to the promotion of intercultural and interethnic understanding.[60] The shocking events at Mölln and Solingen served as the catalyst for a groundswell of antiracist activism around the country.

Even before most of the peace demonstrations took place, editors of the *Süddeutsche Zeitung* sought emphatically to counter any suggestion that migrants did not belong in the new Germany: "We demand protection of the constitution, police, and justice. We demand a politics which opposes extremism. . . . The integration of the foreigners residing here must no longer be the sole task of the groups we call the 'foreigner lobby.' The legal state must begin an offensive against the hatred of foreigners."[61] Taking a strong stand against the xenophobic attacks, the editorial board called on the government to formulate a proactive policy to root out "hatred" and affirm democratic protections for all residents of the Federal Republic.

In striking contrast, government leaders responded to the right-wing violence by skirting the issue of national belonging and pushing in a very different policy direction. Local officials such as the interior minister of Saxony, Rudolf Krause, explained the Hoyerswerda attacks by pointing to the abuse of Germany's asylum law.[62] His colleague, Saxon minister president Kurt Biedenkopf, in turn, demanded a drastic reduction in the number of asylum seekers sent to the new (eastern) states.[63] At the federal level, interior minister Wolfgang Schäuble repeatedly attributed the antiforeigner violence to the massive influx of refugees, adding that "large portions of the population" were alarmed at the "increase in asylum seekers."[64] He urged Kohl to take immediate steps to stem the "uncontrollable flow" of foreigners.[65] Leading policymakers, that is, emphasized a causal relationship between the nation's liberal asylum provision and xenophobic attacks, effectively avoiding the question at the heart of the violence: which social vision of Germany ought to guide the newly unified nation's future?

The political strategy of combating antiforeigner sentiment by blaming refugees dominated the country's domestic agenda for well over a year, as the Kohl administration worked to pass a more restrictive asylum law. While opponents of the effort initially balked at the prospect of amending Article 16 of the Basic Law (which provided the right of asylum for the politically persecuted) because of its historic anti-Nazi significance, the CDU managed to push through a constitutional change that went into effect in early 1993. In one sense, the widespread public hand-wringing about asylum seekers can be read as a response to the immediate problem of post-unification violence against migrants of varying types and backgrounds.

The revision of the asylum law enabled a kind of ideological quick fix. By stanching the flow of refugees, government officials positioned themselves as attentive to public discontent about foreigners and minorities more generally. Yet the decision to focus on asylum seekers ultimately meant that Germany's leaders ignored the vast majority of foreigners, most of whom were longtime residents and came to the Federal Republic through some connection to the postwar labor recruitment. Reducing the numbers of refugees, that is, said nothing about the more fundamental question of whether guest workers and their descendants *ought* to count as part of the new German nation. In this way, the debate about national belonging continued to be framed in terms that facilely excluded multiple generations of resident migrants.

Another focal point for postreunification discussions of "ein Volk" was the building of a Memorial for the Murdered Jews of Europe in the new capital city of Berlin. The project actually began in 1988 but only gained serious momentum in 1993 after political reunification was complete. Indeed, the memorial took on particular urgency in the wake of East-West consolidation because it served as a vehicle to incorporate former East Germans into the work of commemoration, a process central to the West German path to democratization. Such work seemed especially necessary in light of the GDR's key founding myth, which maintained that "East Germany was the successor state to the antifascist resistance fighters, while West Germany was the successor to the fascists and Nazis."[66] One effect of this ideology, as Jeffrey Herf has argued, was that GDR *Vergangen-*

heitsbewältigung focused on celebrating antifascist resistance and fighting the Cold War, rather than acknowledging East German implication in the Third Reich or responsibility toward Jewish victims of the Holocaust.[67] The Berlin monument thus represented the first act of commemoration on behalf of Germans as an entire people.

But the construction of the Holocaust memorial was also crucial to the production of a collective national identity. As one of the first major public undertakings of the reunified Germany, the project placed the nation's relationship to its genocidal past at the center of the process. Even the plot of land set aside for the monument underscored this vital function. Located in the heart of Berlin, the site stands adjacent to other major symbols of the united nation and its historical antecedents: the Brandenburg Gate, the Reichstag, and Hitler's bunker. After nearly two decades of wrangling—over such questions as whether Germany needed a memorial, what form it should take, and whether it should commemorate the murdered Jews of Europe or all Nazi victims—the monument was finally completed in May 2005. It was based on a design by American architect Peter Eisenman and comprised a vast field of undulating concrete slabs varying in height from three to ten feet. At the inauguration ceremony, president of the Bundestag Wolfgang Thierse emphasized the uniqueness of the event, explaining that no other country had erected a monument to "its biggest crime in history" in the middle of its capital. Here, in stone, was the conception of national identity that drove this German-German project. As Germany's "biggest crime in history," the Holocaust represented the national fate; it was what all Germans shared.

This idea, in fact, dominated discussions of national identity after reunification. In a 1993 op-ed piece for *Die Zeit,* the East Berlin theologian Richard Schröder suggested that Germans were linked by "a common responsibility": "We are responsible for our entire history with its highs and lows."[68] Five years later, in a public debate with Ignatz Bubis (head of the Central Council of Jews in Germany until his death in 1999), the novelist Martin Walser declared, "What we did in Auschwitz, we did as a nation and, by virtue of that alone, we must continue as a nation."[69] A subsequent commentary for the *Frankfurter Allgemeine Zeitung* by Klaus von Dohnanyi made the stakes of Walser's view explicit: "German identity, about which so many imprecise words have been spoken, this German identity cannot be defined today any more precisely than through our common descent from those who did it, who welcomed it or at least permitted it."[70]

By foregrounding a shared fate, these statements implicitly (although not necessarily self-consciously) advanced a highly particularist understanding of national belonging as well as a homogeneous conception of nation. Such a notion, Hanno Loewy has recently argued, "pushes off the German stage . . . all those who do not belong to the German community of fate because they can't be confronted with German 'disgrace': Jews, immigrant workers, refugees."[71] And as the first official effort to advance a collective identity for a reunited Germany, the Berlin Holocaust memorial ultimately suggested that national belonging would remain exclusive to ethnic Germans.

Endangered Democracy? The Perils of Integration

If German political leaders responded to the spate of hate crimes by shifting the debate to asylum seekers and consolidating national identity around collective Holocaust commemoration, German media and social scientists worried about what the attacks revealed about the reunified nation's democratic stability. The early 1990s unleashed a moral panic in the press, shaking confidence in the health and resiliency of the democratic system.[72] Unification brought not only the predictable economic challenges, but serious sociopolitical ones as well. Far from the easy integration of ethnic brethren that many expected, the rise in xenophobic violence threatened to undermine the respectable democratic political culture and habitus West Germans had gradually forged—and come to rely on—as their ethical polestar and public face to the world.

To some extent, this sense of crisis was stimulated and nourished by the international distress evident in American, European, and Israeli media reports on the electoral success of radical right parties and the increase in right-wing extremism, violence, and neofascist symbols in unified Germany.[73] The German press also took up the story and warned that taboos that had grown up after 1945 were for the first time being brazenly broken on a daily basis throughout the country. In November 1992, the national magazine *Der Spiegel* ran a feature story following the arson murders in Mölln, noting that the shocking incident "made clear for the first time just how far things have gone in the supposedly most free and liberal state ever to exist on German soil." That year alone, police registered more than 1,600 violent attacks, including over 500 involving arson or explosives, which left 17 dead and more than 800 injured.[74] The magazine blamed the audacious behavior of a growing "new brown milieu" and argued that right-wing violence was targeting not only foreigners, in the form of migrant laborers, asylum seekers, and refugees, but also other minority groups—such as homosexuals and the mentally and physically disabled—who had been institutionalized, sterilized, and killed for eugenic reasons during the Third Reich. As illustration, *Der Spiegel* printed an annotated photo spread of 17 murder victims under the headline "Terror 1992."[75]

Blasting the equivocation of state and federal officials as "thoroughly Weimar," and pointing to the signs of a resurgent fascism, *Spiegel* editor Rolf Lamprecht demanded action:

> Homes for asylum seekers burn, police save babies from asphyxiation, protect Vietnamese women from rape. Jewish cemeteries are desecrated, concentration camp memorials in Sachsenhausen, Ravensbrück, and Überlingen are ravaged . . . Where are the special forces, where are the units to protect personal integrity and property that were used against the terrorism of the RAF [Red Army Faction]? . . . The state powers have assembled and employed exquisite and efficient weapons to fight the terror of the streets—and now allow them to rust in the arsenal.

Public officials, he argued, must subdue violence from the radical right, just as they quelled attacks from the radical Left in the 1970s. State power must be marshaled to protect all inhabitants, not only its prominent citizens. At the same time, he suggested, the potential enemy of constitutional guarantees was not only the state, but "also us"—its citizens. Democracy, Lamprecht declared, cannot be "suicide."[76]

"Democracy as suicide" invoked a number of salient legal, political, and historic issues in the German context. These ranged from the proper use of state power and acceptable mobilization of state violence, through the desirable balance between democratic freedoms and expression on the one hand and democratic protections on the other, to the question of political bias of federal, state, and judicial officials when assessing threats to the republic. What is significant for our purposes is the sense of intense crisis and soul-searching that ethnonationalist violence and the right-radical surge provoked. The specter of 1933 and the first Republic's demise became the reigning historical analogy in the western German press, in part because of that earlier era's protection of the right-wing enemies of liberal-

ism. Democracy seemed to have reached a crossroads, and it was imperative to avoid taking a wrong turn.

In addition to condemning the increase in right radical violence, *Der
Spiegel* highlighted a significant and troubling cultural shift following
unification: namely, the overt *public* practice and tolerance of antisemitic
and racist speech that had formerly been taboo. "Germans have gotten used
to things that would have been unthinkable ten years ago. . . . Jewish jokes
and racist rhymes are again socially acceptable (*salonfähig*). Slanderous
xenophobic poems hang in police headquarters and state offices." In western German towns, it had now become "*ganz normal*" for soccer fans to yell
"Jews to Auschwitz" at referees who made unpopular calls; for taxi patrons
to refuse service from foreign drivers; for a CDU parliament representative
to urge denying asylum rights to homosexual foreigners; and for television
talk shows to repeatedly invite right-wing extremists as guests, thereby providing them free airtime and respectability.[77] "Now many are daring to say
what before they only thought," observed Ignatz Bubis, chairman of the
Central Council of Jews in Germany. Heiner Geißler, a former general secretary of the CDU, also detected a change in the political culture due to the
"de-tabooization of right-radical themes." This new license, he proposed,
was connected to recent political debates about asylum law in united Germany: "Through our arguments over foreigners," he suggested, "the soul of
our *Volk* has become twisted."[78] Like his fellow political allies and numerous social scientists, Geißler assumed that the political focus on immigration—and heated, open debates regarding its regulation and its social and
economic effects—somehow helped authorize public prejudice toward foreigners and other out-groups and encouraged the resurgence of right-wing
ideology and violence. Democratic debate over immigration policy, in short,
seemed to release suppressed emotions and biases that now shook the public sphere and postwar settlement.

The murders in Mölln also provoked a more sober stock-taking. German journalists, psychologists, sociologists, and political scientists increasingly grappled with the question of how such behavior could arise so
suddenly on the territory of the old Federal Republic: how and why violence against minorities had become prevalent even in the democratic
west.[79] When xenophobic violence initially erupted in the territories of the
former East, western German politicians and academics appeared to find
it, if not acceptable, then at least understandable. East Germans, after all,
had not benefited from the Holocaust education programs that were a

fixture in West German schools by the 1970s and 1980s. The socialist state had disavowed all connection with the fascist Nazi state and instead built its founding myths and its educational system on the argument that the GDR was heir to the resistance against National Socialism. Unlike the Federal Republic, the East German state had not assumed any moral or financial responsibility for the crimes of the Nazi regime and, into the 1980s, pursued an overtly anti-Israeli foreign policy.[80] According to western German critics, then, the two postwar Germanys developed distinctive political cultures and processes of socialization. And only one of them was based upon democratic values and practices and had made public commemoration of, and public contrition for, the Jewish Holocaust a central focus of civic education.

In 1990, West Germans expected to transfer their democratic capitalist culture eastward, to the benefit of all Germans. The Berlin Memorial for Murdered Jews represented one such initiative. In the early years following unification, however, the evolved political culture and social habitus of public life in the Federal Republic appeared unstable as regressive tendencies emerged. Media coverage suggested that the source of the instability was a kind of westward seepage of retrograde social attitudes and behaviors associated with the troubled eastern provinces. This explanation unleashed a profound, if ultimately temporary, crisis of confidence: Could the Federal Republic's democratic political maturity be illusory? Did unification "represent a reversal in the continuously progressive movement in German tolerance and democratic culture" since 1945?[81] These were the questions the (west) German media and concerned social scientists began investigating in earnest in the early 1990s.[82]

What's Going On? Antisemitism, Xenophobia, but No Racism

In an attempt to make sense of these troubling developments, western German social scientists, in scholarly publications and the press, focused on what they saw as two distinct historical and sociological phenomena: antisemitism and xenophobia.[83] Der Spiegel broke the news of one large opinion survey in January 1992, announcing in bold headlines that "One in eight Germans is an Antisemite." According to survey results, Germans preferred "Jews in Israel" to "Jews in Germany": "For most citizens of the Federal Republic, native German Jews are not compatriots, but foreigners . . . [and] foreigners are most likeable when they stay away."[84] Although the survey also polled "Jews" regarding their attitudes toward "Germans," all of those polled were Israelis. The opinions of Jewish German citizens and Jewish immigrants residing in Germany were not sought, despite the fact that non-Jewish Germans were questioned on their attitudes toward both Jews in Israel and Jews in their midst. In this period of perceived crisis, it was *national* attitudes toward significant Others that were being interrogated. And, tellingly, those national attitudes excluded minority opinion itself.

There have been studies on the persistence and virulence of antisemitism in West Germany every decade since the late 1940s. The U.S. Military Government initially explored these questions through opinion surveys. At the turn of the 1950s, West German institutes for public opinion research (Institut für Demoskopie and EMNID Institut) also undertook investigations. By the late 1950s and early 1960s, an upsurge in antisemitic incidents and the Eichmann trial in Israel drove the development of international collaborative projects and prompted the Frankfurt Institute for Social Research to take up the topic. After a brief lull in the mid- to late 1960s, sociological research on antisemitism resumed around the question of political extremism in the late 1970s and continued through the 1980s, when West Germany again experienced an increase in antisemitic activity (during the years 1982 and 1987–88).[85]

In sum, studies of antisemitism for the half century following Nazi defeat showed a very slow but steady decrease in overt antisemitic attitudes among West Germans. From a high of 40 percent in the late 1940s, the percentage of West Germans judged unambiguously antisemitic decreased to between 12 and 16 percent by 1989.[86] Some scholars of Germany interpreted this trend as a cause for celebration and a mark of normality. They argued that West Germans learned from the murderous Nazi past, benefited from denazification and reeducation, embraced democratic values, and engaged in *Vergangenheitsaufarbeitung* (confrontation with the Nazi past). This ideological work, over the long run, extinguished dangerous forms of manifest antisemitism and left a residual trace of latent antisemitism of the type acceptable in functioning democracies and comparable to that in the United States, France, and Britain. Other scholars, however, denied the efficacy of *Vergangenheitsaufarbeitung* and doubted the willingness of West Germans to engage in the process. Instead, these critics focused on the ways in which Germans have "silenced, relativized, minimized," and subjected to historical revisionism the crimes of the past to avoid acknowledging national or personal responsibility and culpability.[87] Instead of touting the gains of West German democracy, they suggested its limits and demanded a broader recognition of the historical, systemic persistence of social inequality, prejudicial practices, and ethnonational identity in the Federal Republic.

With unification, the question of an antisemitic tradition in East Germany entered the debate. Not much was known about this topic because no studies had been conducted on antisemitic attitudes among East Germans under socialism.[88] The SED assumed this phenomenon would die out along with capitalist organization and classes; over the decades the Party merely asserted it had. After 1990, however, western German social scientists were keen to conduct comparative studies of antisemitism among west and east Germans. The results came as a surprise: East Germans consistently registered much lower levels of antisemitism than their West German counterparts (4 to 16 percent respectively).[89] Suddenly, scholars began to question the impact of two decades of determined Holocaust education in West German schools, of mandatory school trips to Nazi-era concentration and death camps, of the proliferation of Holocaust commemorations, literature, and film. Given this emphasis in the Federal Republic since the late 1970s, they wondered, what did it mean that the East German population proved to be both more informed about Nazi atrocities and more tolerant in their contemporary attitudes toward Jews?[90]

Around this same time, German social scientists and the media began to highlight a phenomenon that Werner Bergmann has come to call "secondary antisemitism," namely, that

> aside from persistent traditional prejudices, the relationship between [West] Germans and Jews is influenced more and more by the way in which Germans deal with the Nazi past and the resulting responsibility toward Jews. . . . [T]he discrepancy between the desire to forget, that is, not be reminded, on the one hand, and the continuing confrontation with German crimes, on the other, *provides a new motive for prejudice,* which to some extent is expressed in the revitalization of traditional accusations made against Jews (vindictiveness, greed, striving for power).[91]

West Germans' higher levels of antisemitism, in other words, were due to a kind of "Holocaust fatigue": the sense of exasperation, frustration, anger, guilt, and most especially victimization at feeling called to task, again and again, for the crimes of their Nazi forebears. In this view, West Germans were tired of being educated; they were tired of the seemingly endless flow of commemorations and media coverage; they were tired of international accusation and condescension; they were tired of perceived Jewish hectoring. And polls seemed to confirm this interpretation: the majority of West Germans (66 percent) yearned for a "Schlußstrich"—a final end to discussions, as well as moral and financial demands, regarding the Nazi past.[92] Ultimately, the very measures employed to forge democratic stability were understood as provoking renewed antisemitism.

Xenophobia, by contrast, appeared to be an eastern malady, particularly in the trying times following unification. The onset of economic uncertainty and collapse of socialist ideals in the former East Germany led to a "return to the natural categories [*sic!*] of skin color, race, and nation," according to Wilhelm Heitmeyer, an expert on right-wing extremism at the University of Bielefeld. "For many kids [from the former GDR], the only thing that remains is the certainty of being German," he maintained. Heitmeyer's analysis was one of many that characterized xenophobic ethnonationalism as a sociological feature of the increasingly impressionable, rudderless, maladjusted eastern German youth.[93] In a 1991 study of one thousand German students, aged fourteen to nineteen, in the eastern state of Thüringen and western state of Rheinland-Pfalz, more than one in five (21 percent) of eastern German students were deemed to "hate foreigners" while only a miniscule 3 percent of their western counterparts shared that trait.[94] These distinctions were captured in more spectacular fashion the following year when a Leipzig study concluded that a whopping 54 percent of eastern German youth were xenophobic, while the corresponding nationwide percentage hovered around 28 percent—presumably due to the dilution effect of lower prevalence among western youth.[95]

On the question of xenophobia, then, western Germans initially found grounds for self-congratulation. They appeared to be more tolerant of foreigners and less prone to ethnonational outbursts, which, sociologists speculated, was due to the prevalence of social contact with migrants, minorities, and foreign visitors. East Germans, on the other hand, grew up in a "relatively monocultural society" and were unaccustomed to interacting with other peoples. Although the GDR played host to migrant laborers and students (predominantly from Vietnam, Mozambique, Cuba, and Poland), foreign nationals constituted a mere 1 percent of the population (excluding Soviet troops) and were isolated from, rather than integrated into, society at large. Like antisemitism, xenophobia and racism were taboo in the GDR, and their incidence was officially denied by the state.

Nonetheless, according to these scholars, the decline of SED credibility in the 1980s fed the formation of youth subgroups. In addition to peace, environmental, and punk groups, a small percentage of East German youth embraced neo-Nazi symbols and self-styling in protest against the socialist regime.[96] Significantly, organized right-wing political extremism remained low among eastern German youth even after unification.[97] Social scientists, by the mid-1990s, attributed xenophobic violence among these young people to a crisis of values, role models, and family relations following the demise of socialism; to inadequate policing and after-school programs in the former GDR; and to the subsequent attractions of anomic violence and youthful "Unkultur," as one critic had it. In more neutral terms, eastern teenagers tended to succumb to the lures of a youthful consumption that romanticized violent music, fashion, and behavior in order to "become someone." Absent proper socialization and guidance, these youth often turned to an ethic and commodified aesthetic of violence to cement their social identity, social circle, and social status. Xenophobia, in this analysis, was the expression of a new "youth revolt." But unlike the *Halbstarken* during the 1950s rock 'n' roll invasion, "for the first time in the history of the Federal Republic," one contemporary argued, "the revolt is coming from the right."[98]

By the second half of the 1990s, when cooler analytic heads prevailed and there was time to digest the aggregate data collected since unification, social scientists reversed themselves and declared that levels of xenophobia—like levels of antisemitism—were not markedly different between eastern and western Germans.[99] While racist attitudes had been polled by OMGUS during military occupation, and some ALLBUS and Eurobarometer surveys queried German attitudes toward guest workers and foreigners in the 1970s and 1980s, xenophobia (unlike antisemitism) had not been the subject of decades-long study in West Germany.[100] This paucity of long-range data and the perception of immigration and asylum seekers as "new" social problems meant that critical analysis of xenophobia tended to be couched in narratives of rupture and crisis, rather than in terms of broader trends and continuity across 1990. As a result, initial responses to the overt prejudice and hate crimes in the early 1990s failed to note that these were not new phenomena but an intensification of already existing patterns—at least in West Germany. In fact, the Federal Republic had experienced both an increase in racist incidents and a steady proliferation of radical right political parties during the 1980s under the watch of Kohl's CDU government. It was precisely at this moment, when public debates first emerged around asylum seekers and the newly discovered "foreigner problem," that West Germany transformed "from a receptive society into a rejectionist one."[101] Beginning in 1982, West German membership in right-wing parties rose steadily until 1986, when it dipped briefly before resuming its climb during and after 1989. Violent "antiforeigner acts" also surged in the Federal Republic in 1986 and again in 1989, before skyrocketing in 1991.[102]

While "xenophobic" attitudes and activity did increase in the eastern states after 1990, this upsurge coincided with the influx of western political organization, social ideologies, and consumerism. Yet the question of western influence was rarely explored. It is worth bearing in mind that not only established West German parties like the CDU/CSU, SPD, and FDP recruited membership in the former GDR. Right-wing extremist parties also sought to establish a base, affect electoral behavior, shape political discourse, and impose a political agenda there. How these influences interacted with political and social conceptions and behavior is still unclear. An intriguing bit of evidence from a poll on attitudes toward "foreigners" suggests that western German media and political debates may have played a role in transferring to east Germans what had, until then, been an exclusively west German preoccupation since the early 1980s. In the survey of East Germans, Turks (who at the time had no demographic presence in the former GDR) "were vicariously imported as early as 1990 onto the list of bad foreigners."[103] Moreover, although antisemitic activity by the late 1980s elicited speedy and consistent response by West German authorities, xenophobic activity did not[104]—that is, until mounting international and domestic public criticism began to erode such inaction following the Mölln massacre. It is reasonable to ask, then, whether rising xenophobic violence should be attributed primarily to ineffective policing in eastern Germany or to inattentive policing in West Germany before 1990 and, initially at least, throughout the *entire* Federal Republic afterward.[105]

The point here is not to deny the persistence of historical prejudices (against Poles and so-called Gypsies, for example, which remained high among East and West Germans) or the revaluation of racial and ethnic ideologies under socialism. Nor is it to claim that prejudicial attitudes and hate crimes were a wholesale import from West Germany. Rather, it is to suggest that unification unleashed an *interactive* process in which ethnonational identity and notions of racial and ethnic difference both achieved a heightened urgency and were transformed. By raising such questions, we do not intend to vilify Germans—West, East, or unified—as somehow more antisemitic or xenophobic than citizens of other democratic nations. In fact, comparative studies for Europe and the United States have shown that Germany falls well within the "normal" range when it comes to both.[106] Our argument here does *not* concern German peculiarities in the incidence and exercise of ethnic or racial bias and violence. Rather, it concerns German peculiarities in the *interpretation* of those common social phenomena—peculiarities of interpretation that have been relentlessly shaped by the Nazi past and retrospective engagement with it over the past six decades.

This leads us back to the specific sociological categories of analysis—namely, antisemitism and xenophobia—employed by social scientists attempting to apprehend the hate speech and grapple with the prospect of a destabilized democracy following unification. Why, for example, did scholars insist on maintaining two separate, yet ultimately indistinct, categories of analysis that, one could argue, ultimately obscured as much as they illuminated? What, in other words, are the *epistemological implications* and *social consequences* of employing separate terms for bias and violence toward minorities, migrants, and out-groups?

The logic for retaining a separate category for Jews seems obvious. It shows that Germans have internalized the lessons of the past and have acquired a laudable sensitivity to the mundane and vicious ways that Jews, as a group, have been repeatedly victimized in modern German history. Studying "antisemitism" allows one to register and gauge the waxing and waning, over time, of bias and violence toward Jews. This is surely a worthwhile endeavor. And yet, we would suggest, the wrinkle is *not* with the category "antisemitism" per se, but with what happens when one tries to understand a broader, puzzling social phenomenon like the increase in hate speech and hate crimes toward a multiplicity of groups by imposing a priori categories of analysis. Antisemitism investigates hateful attitudes and actions toward Jews. Who are the "Jews" invoked in Germans' attitudes? Are they fellow German citizens? Are they foreigners? Are they both? There is an imprecision in such polling that sometimes appears to nativize Jews, rendering them German, but at other times (as in the *Spiegel* poll that began this section) other-nationalizes or internationalizes them. One concern, then, is that such an insistently segregationist approach to examining German attitudes toward Jews does not just *register* German conceptions of difference but *reproduces* them. In addition, even in cases when Jews are non-German nationals, they are not included in studies of xenophobia. There is an inconsistency here that doesn't allow Jews to be brought into the same analytic field as other perceived Others in the study of German attitudes—even though German sociologists now recognize a correlation between the incidence of antisemitism and xenophobia in German society.[107]

On the other hand, the recent trend of studying "xenophobia" also has limitations. First and foremost, it assumes that all non-Jewish targets of hate speech and hate crimes are foreigners: that is, that they are not German citizens. This has the significant social and political effect of rendering invisible and unspeakable bias and violence against German minorities—such as Black Germans and so-called Gypsies. By employing the paradigm of immigration, the analytic category of "xenophobia" transforms German citizens into foreigners *and* refuses them the conceptual tools—such as "racism"—with which to fight this transformation.[108] It denies both their existence *as Germans* and the very possibility of imagining and accommodating "difference" *within* the nation.

The implications of this dual analysis (antisemitism/xenophobia) were evident in whose voices were heard, and whose were silenced, in German opinion polls and sociological studies of the early 1990s. "German" opinion—east and west—meant the white, non-Jewish majority, who were asked for their views of "Jews" in studies of antisemitism, and on "Turks," "Gypsies," "Blacks," "Poles," among others, in studies of xenophobia. Jews did get to participate, but only as Israelis (in the *Spiegel/Emnid* survey) or as prominent representatives (such as Ignatz Bubis) of the "Jewish community" in Germany when reaction was sought by the media to instances of antisemitism. Beyond that, the voices of real or potential victims—whether minorities, migrants, or other out-groups—were not studied; their opinions were not polled. In the end, sociological studies and opinion polls of the early 1990s structurally reproduced the very phenomenon they purported to explain.[109]

Claiming Subjectivity: Toward a Multiethnic Democracy

Although their views were not solicited by German sociologists or in German surveys of the early 1990s, minorities did weigh in.[110] Minority intellectuals, in fact, were among the first group to articulate the fundamental limits of the discourse around German democracy and national identity. For the Turkish-German Zafer Şenocak, in particular, the fall of the Berlin Wall and events in the GDR brought previously unspoken questions of national belonging into the open and seemed to offer an opportunity for radically new answers. As thousands of ethnic Germans from the East arrived in the Federal Republic, Şenocak asked whether Germany was also a "homeland for Turks," criticizing the restrictive citizens' rights available to guest workers and their descendants.[111] The genealogical definition of German citizenship, he pointed out, created a paradoxical situation. An Eastern European who could demonstrate German descent was deemed German irrespective of that person's knowledge of German language or culture, but a Turk who lived his or her entire life in Germany was still considered foreign. This moment of upheaval threw into stark relief one of the fundamental contradictions of West German democracy: namely, that its foundations had been laid with the labor of Turks and other foreign workers who continued to exist outside the legal parameters of the nation. In order to fulfill the promise of democratization, he argued, the Federal Republic needed to liberalize the definition of German citizenship.

Beyond the legal framework, Şenocak called for "a profound change of consciousness" on the part of both Germans and Turks to ensure that "native and future German citizens really live together successfully."[112] As an antidote to the tempting "phantasm of the lost homeland," he urged second-generation Turks to reject the one-sided orientation to Turkey of their parents and immerse themselves in questions of Germany's past and future. For Germans, on the other hand, "an important corrective in the process of rediscovering a new German national feeling," Şenocak reasoned, could be the "presence of a historical, cultural, and religious minority."[113] Writing just two months after the breaching of the Wall, he declared somewhat optimistically, "We have the good fortune, which unfortunately goes unrecognized, of living in a time when concepts like fatherland, home, and nation can be seen from different perspectives and when they no longer function as key words that fit only one certain lock."[114]

Yet in the face of rising xenophobic utterances and violence, and the accompanying political fixation on stanching immigration, this sense of hopefulness and possibility dissipated quickly. Two years later, in January 1992, Şenocak again wondered whether Germany could become a home for Turks. This time his answer was quite different: "We have been asking ourselves this question for a year and a half. German unification was in process and stopped past us like a train that we ourselves were sitting on. We were inside this country that we grew up in, bound to its streets, plazas, cities, and people, but we were also outside it because the symbols which were suddenly resuscitated from the dusty files of history said nothing to us."[115] Part of the problem, he suggested, was that "rapid reunification [. . .] created the illusion that current events and contemporary phenomena [could] be described with nineteenth-century language, with concepts such as *nation* and *Volk*. We have no concepts for the emotions and psychic structures to which recent historical ruptures have given rise, no concepts for the disarray of the new arrangements. The ones that are used are ripped out of context."[116] Şenocak, then, began his critique by calling for a new set of terms as well as a new way of thinking about the problem of difference in German history. But what exactly would this entail?

Part of an answer came in response to the spate of events in 1995 marking the fiftieth anniversary of the war's end. In an interview published by the Berlin daily *Der Tagesspiegel*, Şenocak drew attention to the relationship between the boundaries of national identity and the injunction to Holocaust remembrance. When asked what the commemorative events meant to him as a Turkish author in Germany, he responded, "Can immigrants participate in shaping the German future without having access to a shared history with the native population?"[117] At first glance, the inclination to involve Turks in coming to terms with German war crimes might seem counterintuitive. The millions of guest workers who came to the Federal Republic, after all, had no personal connection to or responsibility for the Third Reich. Şenocak's point, however, was that the process of Holocaust commemoration within its conventional framework inadvertently reproduced an ethnically homogeneous understanding of German identity. In the Federal Republic, he explained, "history is read as a diary of the 'community of fate,' the nation's personal experience, to which Others have no access. This conception of history as ethnic, collective memory was tied to the question of guilt after the crimes of the Nazis."[118] Only those who inherited the burden of responsibility for the Holocaust could lay claim to or share in German identity.

The very practices of *Vergangenheitsbewältigung*, Şenocak asserted further, tended to package "history, as one packs up things or buildings: in commemorative speeches, in commemorative plaques, in rituals."[119] This compartmentalized perspective was problematic because it obscured the ways the past reverberates in the present—in particular, the connections between German attitudes toward Jews and other minorities during the Wilhelmine era and Weimar Republic and German attitudes toward Turks in the postwar period. Dividing the nation's history into discrete periods and discontinuous episodes made it much harder to see that the question of difference represented an ongoing problem, one of the recurring issues for German democratization.

Şenocak's goal was not to reject Holocaust commemoration per se. Instead, he wanted to reformulate the nation's approach to its troubled history by disrupting the binary logic of categories such as self/other, inside/outside, German/Jew, and more expansively, German/foreigner. Critically analyzing German history and recognizing continuities between past and present, Şenocak insisted, required bringing immigrants (along with other German minorities, we would suggest) into the historical imaginary, into the shared burdens, responsibilities, and privileges that were an inevitable part of living in postwar German society. In short, he proposed introducing a third term into the compulsive, but stagnant, commemorations of Jewish victims by German perpetrators. In his 1998 novel *Gefährliche Verwandschaft* (*Perilous Kinship*), Şenocak fleshed out this triangular relationship. Describing "today's Germany," narrator Sascha Muteschem, son of a German-Jewish mother and Turkish father, observes:

> Jews and Germans no longer face one another alone. Instead, a situation has emerged which corresponds to my personal origin and situation. In Germany now, a trialogue is developing among Germans, Jews, and Turks, among Christians, Jews, and Moslems. The undoing of the German-Jewish dichotomy might release both parties from the burden of their traumatic experiences. But for this to succeed they would have to admit Turks into their domain. And for their part, the Turks in Germany would have to discover the Jews, not just as part of the German past in which they cannot share, but as part of the present in which they live. Without the Jews the Turks stand in a dichotomous relation to the Germans. They tread in the footprints of the Jews of the past.[120]

The literary critic Leslie Adelson has usefully cautioned against a linear interweaving of Turkish and German national memory cultures, suggesting that Şenocak "write[s] a new subject of remembrance into being" rather than presenting a transparent window into Germany's struggle with diversity on a sociological level.[121] Yet it is worth emphasizing that Şenocak's primary preoccupation was history, a topic that resonates in aesthetic as well as political registers. And it is precisely the perspective enabled by triangulation that made it possible for Şenocak to ask new kinds of questions about the relationship between history and contemporary German society. In "Thoughts on May 8, 1995," for instance, he recounted how his father listened to the war on the radio in his Turkish village. When the conflict ended, Şenocak explained, his father "experienced neither a liberation nor a collapse. He was neither victim nor perpetrator," adding, "This vantage point allows me to raise a few questions."[122] For Şenocak, this anniversary was an important occasion on which to connect past and present, especially in light of reunified Germany's newly attained sovereignty. "Germany lost World War II in 1945," he stated. "The Nazi regime was defeated. On the other hand, the subtle consequences of National Socialism continue to affect Germany even today. Does the Nazis' brutal effort to render Germany ethnically homogeneous have nothing to do with the present resistance to acknowledging, in Germany in 1995, the ethnic diversity that has arisen through migration?"[123] Here, in plain language, was the crux of the matter: fifty years of democratization and Holocaust commemoration had not brought West Germans any closer to recognizing the ongoing pattern of social exclusion bound up with public national memory discourse and accepted notions of collective identity. But a triangulated debate among Germans and their now iconic ethnic Others, Turks and Jews, Şenocak suggested, might help Germans begin to grasp ethnic diversity not simply as a temporary problem or a singular tragic episode from the past but as a central narrative of the nation's historical development. In this respect, Şenocak's larger goal was not so much to use Jews or Turks as analytic tools for unsettling the binary of German and foreigner, but rather to cultivate a *shared* sense of history and nationality, to redefine the very boundaries of national belonging and national self-understanding.

What Şenocak shows us with striking clarity is that the discussion about German democratization and national identity after 1945—both at key historical moments and in the historiography—has recapitulated older ideological patterns that presumed and projected ethnic homogeneity. Ultimately, one of Şenocak's greatest contributions (and what makes his work so crucial today) is his ability to see that diversity and difference have always been integral to the postwar project of German democracy.

Although German society has continued to become more ethnically diverse, the process of differentiating Germans from their Others has remained. Difference exists not in nature or biology, in culture or religion. Difference exists not in the person or behavior of others, but in the social and cultural *perception* of them as straying from some norm—even if that norm assumes an ideal of ethnic or cultural homogeneity that does not exist, that has never existed, in social reality. Rather than continue to fixate on minorities' and migrants' puzzling difference, we need to explore how certain groups have been excluded from German democracy by being "produced as different again and again."[124]

As Şenocak suggests, the work of democratization is ongoing. It is never finished and cannot be measured according to a fixed historical standard. Rather, it is precisely the shifting social relations—and the new kinds of epistemological vantage points—fostered by both migration and a genuine acknowledgment of the full diversity of German society that will continually revitalize German democracy and challenge its historians to reexamine and revise their narratives.

This chapter has focused on the specific historical trajectory of West German discourses of democracy stretching from Nazi defeat through unification some forty-five years later. Nonetheless, it is worth remembering that military victory in World War II was merely prelude to an extended period of postwar adjustment that accelerated demands for liberty, equality, and democratic representation among European and colonial populations. These insistent demands, along with the Cold War, challenged Western democracies as a whole to restructure social, economic, and political relations within and beyond their polities. In large measure, the postwar settlement centered on the question of how Western democracies would confront liberationist struggles at home and in their colonies abroad: whether and how they would accommodate those perceived as different in their national democratic life. More than a half century later, Germany and other European countries are still searching for an adequate answer.

CHAPTER 5

The Trouble with "Race"

Migrancy, Cultural Difference, and the Remaking of Europe

Geoff Eley

I am a refugee from South Africa, but have lived twenty-two years in Europe. My entire professional life is situated here. I am not 'the other' if you aren't it also. I haven't come in order to disappear. I am the new European. I am neither a position nor an object for ethnographic studies. I am here to alter the conception of nations and national cultures. More and more of my kind are coming. Even if Europe builds itself into a [migrant- and refugee-repelling] fortress.

—Gavin Jantjes, British artist

In what follows I want to develop some general thoughts about the acute discomforts experienced by western European politicians, social commentators, and cultural critics whenever "race" enters the agenda of political debate or erupts violently into the main territories of public life. These thoughts might be keyed to any number of major happenings of the past few years but were prompted most immediately by a continuing series of flash points occurring across Europe's sociocultural and political landscapes in the aftermath of the Iraq War. Such eruptions vary widely in form and severity. Some are prompted by security concerns associated with the so-called war on terror. Some display angry violence of a verbal or physical variety against asylum-seekers, refugees, or the economically displaced or deprived, who invariably reach Europe after traveling over vast distances. Most incidents usually involve migrant populations of a "legal" or "illegal" category, however long-term or settled these actually turn out to be. Increasingly they center around "European" differences with "Islam." But whatever the particular antagonism, "race" repeatedly figures somewhere in the discursive field, either in the primary languages and understandings of the principals, in the aggressively explicit interventions of Far Right and conservative political groupings, in the surrounding noise of popular culture, or in the deep structure of the assumptions and prejudices in play.

I began writing this essay in the wake of the astonishingly obtuse response of French politicians and commentators to the urban insurrection that swept through the Parisian *banlieues* and other French towns during October and November 2005. In the time that elapsed between the first version and the final revisions in early 2008 a steady stream of fresh occurrences, usually angry and frequently violent, kept this contemporary version of the scandal of "race" in the public eye. By stepping away from these immediate contexts, I want to explore aspects of the deeper, longer-standing, and more recalcitrant patterning of European political life. My remarks will be concerned with certain highly structured features of European political cultures since the defeat of fascism in 1945; with the persistent impediments against admitting certain manifest social relations and social practices into full and explicit public awareness; with the extremely slow and uneven replacement of one discursive formation of "race" and its recognitions with another; and with the shifting place of "race" inside western Europe's postwar political imaginaries.

In seeking to make sense of these questions, it is important to keep in mind the necessary realms of complexity that lie beyond the possible terms of my immediate discussion. Like any contemporary term of individual and collective recognition, the category of "race" has to be tracked back and forth between different contexts of political understanding. Some of these contexts will be *temporal,* involving different periods in the construction of "race" as an available category of social and political understanding. Some of them will be *comparative,* affecting the construction of "race" in different places, whether these are socially, institutionally, politically, or territorially defined. Some of them will be *epistemological,* concerning different contexts and dynamics of racialized understanding. Some of them will also concern matters of *scale,* ranging from particular localities of neighborhood, city, and region to particular national settings, and thence to the overarching frameworks of European integration, and further still to the larger transnational or globalized processes and logics operating at the level of the planet. Although in what follows I will be talking very generally, we should remember that extremely particularized histories of time, culture, and place always have to be presupposed, either as already existing funds of historiography or as future desiderata. This is not just a rhetorical nod to the immense complexity of things but a vital caveat for the various points I am trying to make.

I have two primary purposes in what follows. On the one hand, I want to trace the changing valence of "race" in European political life between the 1950s and now. On the other hand, I would like to explore certain aspects of the creation of a putatively "European" culture in the period since the 1980s. What holds these two goals together, at certain very important levels, is the centrality of "race" to Western Europe's political unconscious. In that sense my essay is as much about "Europe" and "culture" as it is about "race."

This is extraordinarily difficult territory. But the importance of examining how "race" functions in European social and political life can surely be separable from the ethical and epistemological urgencies of continuing to challenge its existence. Neither the legitimacy of racial theories nor the reification of racial differences should be entailed as a result. To argue the necessity of tackling "race" head on, by acknowledging the ways in which its presence has become only too *real,* is not to succumb to its claims. Openly confronting the terms of that presence, I want to argue, can be a step in the possibilities of superseding it. Moreover, by focusing on the persisting power of racial thought and practice I am not diminishing the countervailing efficacies of either antiracial contestations or manifold forms of actualized cultural coexistence—of that space *beyond race* altogether which Mica Nava has called "vernacular cosmopolitanism."[1] My subject is rather the difficulty that "race" describes.[2]

Is There a European Culture?

To speak sensibly of a specifically European culture we need to begin from the changing structural circumstances of European life. In that respect, even after the major ratcheting forward of European integration via the Single Europe Act and the Treaty of Maastricht in 1992–94, the most easily recognizable bases of societal commonality remain absent from "Europe" per se: language, territory, religion, history, and other recognized credentials or attributes of Europe's previously existing nation-states. In this most obvious sense, a European culture remains nascent and prefigurative, insufficiently coherent, too weak a source for the leading coordinates of collective belonging. There remain mainly a series of nationally organized cultures situated inside the European continent, which display various kinds of convergence, are subject to similar structural pressures and institutional logics of policy-making and legal regulation, and may replicate broadly commensurable processes of internal development. These days, there are certainly far stronger patterns of individual and collective experiential interaction across already-instituted national boundaries than before. There are also far denser networks of integrative relations operating institutionally and discursively across Europe as such. Yet at a level of experienced reality, in the registers of common sense and everyday life, there are probably still rather few who would deem themselves in the first instance "European," as opposed to citizens of the individual states of Europe or the products and bearers of particular national cultures.

Beneath the level of a common consciousness and its discursive architectures, on the other hand, it is impossible not to notice the progress of certain integrative logics. Major economic, social, and political transformations have been unfolding, which certainly preceded the dramatic events of 1989–91 in Eastern Europe but which became impressed on the imagination more heavily as a result. The end of the Cold War and the recoalescence of Europe's different regions into a single geopolitical entity through the Single Europe Act, Maastricht, fiscal unification, and the successive Enlargements have changed the setting in which people have to think. On the one hand, that new setting embraces the transnational rhythms of capitalist economics, the legal and institutional integration provided by supranational economic entities, and the migrancy of the expanding continental labor markets (Europe's "regime of regulation"). On the other hand, it extends to new projects of political cooperation and the circulation of associated ideas, to the relentless internationalizing of consumption and style, to the remarkably successful Europeanizing of soccer and other sports, and to the impact of new globally reaching technologies of communication (Europe's "regime of signification").[3]

If cultural change remains far more than the mere effect of such developments, they are nonetheless restructuring the environment in which cultures need to be understood. People in Europe are increasingly encouraged to see themselves—in the enactment of their identities and the self-conscious positioning of their lives—in transnational, subnational or nonnational, even postnational, as well as conventionally national, systems of meaning. To an extent, these processes are not exactly new. The commercially driven diffusion of mass-cultural forms (advertising, cinema, gramophone records, and so forth) and popular taste in food and dress, from Coca-Cola to blue jeans, normally conceived as "Americanization," was a major cultural reality of the 1950s and 1960s, and in many ways goes back to the 1920s.[4] Self-consciously international appropriations of style by particular social groups or subcultures have been much studied since the 1960s, for which the internationalist élan of the political networks of Communists, Maoists, Trotskyists, and other parts of the Left provide a particularly elaborate case. Certain categories of people have long seen themselves in an international culture of such a kind, from financiers and top managers to students and the celebrity fractions of the sporting and entertainment industries, notably in soccer, Grand Prix racing, and tennis, or rock and classical music. The transnational cultures of mass consumption have also attracted cultural critics for several decades. Yet in all of these respects, the present's special distinctiveness may be claimed. As the European Community became restructured into the European Union, the later 1980s definitely *accelerated* these processes. There was thus a much stronger *European* logic to such developments than before, as opposed to the earlier American cast of internationalization.

The meanings of "culture" itself need to be unpacked. At the level of "high" culture, the arts, and aesthetics, literally the most highly valued of cultural goods, a European culture goes back several centuries. The same is true in the more anthropological dimensions of aristocratic and bourgeois culture, most easily grasped as fashion, taste, and style—in food, dress, vacations, the social rhythms of the season, family relations, sexual mores, the international circuits of education, and the general accumulation of cultural capital. In the discourse of U.S. higher education, this is the sociocultural complex that became abstracted and hypertrophied into the reigning ideology of Western Civilization in the deeply entrenched, finely elaborated humanistic pedagogy of liberal arts education. But as we know from the various "culture wars" that have continued to unfold since the late 1980s, such conceptions entail neglects and exclusions that have not gone uncontested—powerful assumptions affecting which cultural goods are to be validated, which achievements become recognized and incorporated into tradition, and which groups acquire recognized voice. The very definition of "high" culture implies the definition of something else, the opposing of high culture to something far less valued, to culture that is "low." In the twentieth century this other understanding or location of culture has taken two principal forms. One involved the colonial representation of extra-European peoples, externalizing its distinctions within racialized frameworks of cultural difference and hierarchy. Primitivism and savagery, backwardness and lower evolutionary stages, have all figured as part of this syndrome, not always in negative ways. But a second syndrome has cohered inside western cultures themselves around the language of the "mass." Here "the popular" in popular culture came to be negatively distinguished via ideas of authenticity, whether marked by romantic notions of the rural "folk" or socialist notions of industrial community, while being reattached pejoratively to commercialized cultures of entertainment and leisure. That idea of mass culture became further linked to ideas of the city and a distinctive early-twentieth-century structure of public communication based on the cheap technologies of film, radio, gramophone, photography, television, motorization, pulp fiction, and mass advertising.

Along with the notion of the mass, as social and cultural commentators confronted the emergent social formation of the new capitalist metropolis, invariably came a discourse of corruption and moral endangerment, of "degeneration," as the polite observers of popular everydayness tended to regard it. Inside this new social imaginary, there developed a negative representational repertoire of "un-culture" and disorder, of drunkenness, gambling, undisciplined sexuality, violence, criminality, unstable patriarchy, and dissolute family life, organized around anxieties about youth in ways more or less explicitly gendered. The political valence of this thinking has always been complex. Oppositions of "high" and "low" are neither Right nor Left in themselves. Socialist and other progressive traditions have drawn just as sharp a line between, on the one hand, the ideal of an educative culture of uplift in the arts and public enlightenment and, on the other hand, an actually existing popular culture of base gratification, roughness, and disorder, which the commercialized apparatus of mass provision (or the "culture industry") was accused of being only too glad to exploit. Socialist no less than liberal cultural policies stressed the virtues of self-improvement and sobriety over the disorderly habits of much ordinary working-class existence. For socialists, places of commercial popular entertainment were a source of frivolity and backwardness in working-class culture, whether these were the music halls, circuses, fairs, and all kinds of rough sports of the later nineteenth century, or the dance halls and the movie palaces of the early twentieth century and the dance clubs, rock concerts, and commercialized television programming that followed World War II. Against that machinery of escapist dissipation they counterposed the devoutly pursued desideratum of working people organizing their own free time collectively in morally uplifting ways.

More recently, with the late-twentieth-century crisis of the inner cities, the opposition between culture that is seen to be healthy and culture that is not, in whatever the particular political or analytical and interpretive notations, became transcribed into the racially constructed image of the immigrant urban poor. That powerful ideological syndrome is itself historically reminiscent of earlier subsets of the dominant "high" versus "low" distinction, involving the xenophobic reactions against a variety of ethnically distinct refugee movements and labor migrations between the 1880s and the 1960s from the southern and eastern parts of Europe to its north and west. To that extent, socialists, liberals, and conservatives inhabited a common discursive landscape. The precise frontiers between the "high" and the "low," between the "cultured" and the "not," have been differently drawn. However, the power of the *distinctions themselves* structured the languages of national cultural identification across political divisions in ways that remained pervasive. In Antonio Gramsci's terms, they delivered some vital contours of commonsense understanding. During the course of the twentieth century they became hegemonic.[5]

A now-familiar move within cultural studies has been to refuse the very terms of this dichotomy. Cultural studies disputed the idea that cultural value can only be guaranteed by separating it from ordinary life and walling it off behind special institutions and rules of appreciation, to which special kinds of knowledge, education, and sensibility should organize the privileged access. Beyond the belief in "great" literature, "serious" music, and "fine" art (and their implied opposites of the frivolous, the vulgar, and the crude) lies the more anthropological understanding of culture as "a whole way of life," a "signifying system," or "system of meanings."[6] This may include the creative realm in the formal sense, the realm of artistic and intellectual activities, but it extends much further to encompass not only other signifying practices like journalism, fashion, advertising, and the general use of language, but also entertainment and recreation (the areas commonly disregarded as "low" culture), ordinary people's pursuit of creative arts in private and organized ways, and the general production of meaning in everyday life.[7]

Raymond Williams directly counterposed the "ordinariness" of culture, its universality, against the elitist conception, what he called "this extraordinary decision to call certain things culture and then separate them, as with a park wall, from ordinary people and ordinary work."[8] Furthermore, the contrast between "high culture" and "low culture" has often, perhaps usually, been presented as a story of decline, in which the preservation of cultural value is continuously compromised and besmirched by processes of commercialization and massification, in which standards of excellence become ever more vulnerable, threatened and diluted by opportunistic and irresponsible pandering to the dictates of popularity and fashion. This is a claim repeatedly made during expansions of democracy, whether these bring extensions of rights or improvements of living, and it was a story told once again during the 1980s and 1990s by the upholders of high-cultural tradition. But only when we deconstruct the sufficiency of the "high culture" versus "low culture" opposition can we explore the processes of change this set of anxieties reflects without the pejorative language and the antidemocratic sneer.

These observations need to be kept in mind once we turn to the contemporary problematic of "Europe" in its specifically cultural dimensions. Thus the urgent plea for a common European vision ("the consciousness of a shared political fate, and the prospect of a common future") grounded in shared cultural goods issued by Jürgen Habermas and Jacques Derrida in the spring of 2003 in response to the massed opposition against the buildup to the Iraq War not only bespeaks the codified heritage of "Western civilization"; it also needs to be filtered through assumptions about popular culture in the way indicated here.[9] Yet the available or default political context in which such an appeal to an imputed commonalty of values or cultural heritage could be issued has become profoundly different from that of an earlier time, whether we consider the most confrontational years of the Cold War in the late 1940s and 1950s, the era of decolonization, national liberation movements, and the Vietnam War, or the time of the great transnational peace movement of the early 1980s. In each case such appeals to culture could imagine the mobilized heft of social movements behind them, whether we think of the dense and elaborate associational worlds of the labor movements, the networks of progressive Christianity, or the intricate webs of affiliation later composing the new social movements. However partial and particularized these milieus and subcultures may have been in relation to the whole society, they at least composed the ground from which the cultural values of ordinary citizens could be connected to the leadership provided by parties and other forms of national coalition.

Yet in the circumstances of the early 2000s, in the new social landscapes being shaped by capitalist restructuring, with their deindustrialized ruins, class decomposition, and post-Fordist disarray, those popular cultures can no longer be treated as a source of oppositional meanings as they might once have been. The old and resilient political cultures of the Left, which between the late nineteenth century and the 1970s proved so effective in allowing society's dominant values to be contested in collective and organized ways, no longer command democratic capacities as before. The "ordinariness" of culture can no longer be imagined in the earlier registers of a socialist and class-based collectivism, which still retained extensive social purchase in the 1950s and 1960s when Raymond Williams was writing.[10] From our own vantage point, in fact, culture's "ordinariness" needs to be engaged on at least two other fronts, which had little place in the older social and political imaginaries of Europe's mobilized democracies and about which Williams also had little directly to say: that of a multicultural or multiethnic social heterogeneity certainly; but also that of an introspectively nationalist populism, which takes the presence of "foreigners" or ethnically isolable minorities as an incitement to violent boundary-drawing and cultural demarcation. In neither of *these* contexts does the imagining of a European future in the particular manner envisioned by Habermas and Derrida have much purchase.[11]

That invoking of a "common European home," as Mikhail Gorbachev once called it, usually rests upon the claim to a distinctive and coherent history. This is what in his contribution to the Habermas/Derrida initiative Adolf Muschg called "sharing a common destiny."

> What holds Europe together and what divides it are at heart the same thing: common memories and habits, acquired step by step through the process of distancing itself from fatal habits. Europe is what Europe is becoming. It is neither the Occident nor the cradle of civilization; it does not have a monopoly on science, enlightenment, and modernity. It shouldn't attempt to ground its identity in any other way than through its own experiences: any claims for exclusivity can only lead into the same delusion and pretension through which Europe of the nineteenth century believed itself to represent the rest of the world, and entitled to dominate it.[12]

But for all the new modesty and affected humility of its terms, this claim to a common culture is predicated on a silence. Europe's actually existing diversity of contemporary populations, whether considered via the bare bones demography of migrancy, ethnicity, language, and religious affiliation, or through more complex sociologies and cultural formations, uncomfortably exceeds such appeals to discretely unfolding histories held in common. In fact, far more than a mere silence is entailed here: such advocacy for the vaunted political community of "Europe" requires an active *disremembering* or *repression* of certain other histories before the hoped-for "official memory" of liberal or social democratic intellectuals like Habermas can become enabled. Instantiating this "Europe" as a widely agreed object of political aspiration, no less than earlier political and cultural constructions of the nation, *presupposes* such a work of forgetting and repression.

That emerges with unfailing clarity from Hans-Ulrich Wehler's response to the Habermas/Derrida manifesto. For Wehler, whose impeccably liberal advocacy has helped define the historical groundedness of contemporary political debates in Germany across four decades, one of the key problems left unresolved by Habermas and Derrida remains the issue of "Europe's borders." More specifically, this is a problem of Europe's opening to "the east and southeast."

> White Russia [*sic*], the [*sic*] Ukraine (which has already introduced a parliamentary and governmental resolution to join the EU by 2011), Moldova, Russia itself, and Turkey in particular *have never been part of a historic Europe.* They do not live off the legacy of Judaic, Greek, or Roman antiquity that is present in Europe to this day. They have not fought their way through the far-reaching separation of state and church, and have even returned, as they did after the Bolshevik or Kemalist intermezzo, to a symbiotic relationship between the two. They have not experienced any Reformation and, even more importantly, hardly any "Enlightenment." They have produced no European bourgeoisie, no autonomous European bourgeois cities, no European nobility, and no European peasantry. They have not participated in the greatest achievement of European political culture since the late nineteenth century: the construction of the social welfare state. Cultural divergences are deeply engraved in Europe. Orthodox Christendom still differs greatly from a Protestant and Roman Catholic Europe that also remains separated from the Islam of Turkey by an obvious cultural barrier.[13]

In its guileless iteration of the most classical of Eurocentrisms, this is a remarkable statement, which speaks as much to an exclusionary logic of cultural centeredness *inside* German society as it does to the maintenance of Europe's boundaries against a particular external state. Wehler had ignited controversy several years before with an article in *Die Zeit* arguing unambiguously against Turkey's putative accession to the European Union. In an associated interview, moreover, he insisted that "peaceful co-existence" with Germany's Turkish immigrants "really does not work": "The Federal Republic does not have a foreigner problem, it has a Turkish problem. The Muslim diaspora is essentially not capable of integration." Germany had dealt successfully with its various immigrations since the Republic's foundation, "but at some point a boundary is reached."[14] This standpoint was further embedded in an orientalist outlook of startling simplicity, questioning the Islamic world's capacity for democracy, invoking many centuries of a "clash of civilizations" between the Ottoman Empire and Christendom, and generalizing its arguments onto a European scale ("Everywhere in Europe Muslim minorities are showing themselves not assimilable, huddling defensively in their subculture").[15] Wehler painted a lurid picture of the great Anatolian unwashed, massing on the frontier in their millions, waiting only for the opening of the EU's labor market before finally flooding in. As Rita Chin remarks, "he even revived one of the Enlightenment's oldest tropes of absolute difference, comparing 65 million contemporary Turks to Ottoman hordes at the gates of Vienna."[16]

Race and the Europe Problem

What has been striking about Western European debates such as these is the degree to which the racialized terms of so many contemporary anxieties about the workability of received and emergent political arrangements, as well as the stability of their social bases, are at the same time so profoundly embedded in the discursive architecture of political debate yet still remain unspoken. Of course, in actuality "race" is speaking itself with troubling volubility, whether now or forty years ago, in a growing cacophony of conflicting and frequently violent ways. On the one hand the overt racisms of the Far Right, and on the other hand the collective actions of beleaguered minorities, have been marking out the social and cultural space of racialized political understanding for some three or four decades, varying of course from country to country and locality to locality. What remains remarkable is the performance of reluctance and disavowal through which so many European commentators still seek to avoid arriving at a language—of politics, of culture, of theory—that can openly address this phenomenon.

Thus the opening sentence of a recent collection of essays entitled *Race in France: Interdisciplinary Perspectives on the Politics of Difference* comments immediately on "the absence in France of race as a category of analysis, or likewise its rarity as a subject for serious historical and sociological examination."[17] The volume's individual contributors then explore how the doggedly entrenched French "republican tradition of color-blindness in public discourse" has decisively structured, skewed, and precluded effective policy interventions on matters of race, whether historically in the context of the earlier twentieth-century Third Republic or contemporaneously since the 1960s. As a growing body of historiography has finally begun to explore with respect to the genealogies of racialized political thought in France, the historical departure point for that republican universalism, which makes the access to Frenchness so strictly conditional on an ideal of juridical citizenship supposedly blind to any consideration of cultural difference, was provided by the French Revolution itself and the complicated ways in which its nineteenth-century legacies became disputed and reworked.[18] The classical framing for such discussions in France remains the 1804 Napoleonic Code. As one of the primary historians of immigration in France has argued:

> In the United States the immigration issue is invariably associated in theory, practice, and attitude with race and ethnicity, whereas in France the Declaration of the Rights of Man marks the triumph (or at any rate the legal triumph) of a repudiation of any form of segregation based on race, religion, or ethnic origin.[19]

No one has done more than Laurent Dubois to recuperate the complex relationship of present-day French debates over race to the deep circumstances of the Revolutionary era in that sense, charting the process by which citizenship became extended in the 1790s to the emancipated slaves of the island colonies of the Caribbean while exploring the tense renormalizing of racialized distinctions through which the colonial effect became reinstated nevertheless. As slave insurgencies precipitated an expansion of the republican ideal by their own force of action, racial equality became unexpectedly secured in St. Domingue, Martinique, and Guadeloupe between the decree of April 1792, which gave *gens de couleur* equal rights, and the ending of slavery in June 1794. Yet while this inaugurated the constitutional integration of the French Caribbean into the metropolis for the purposes of citizenship, the governing republican regimes in the three islands quickly instituted fresh forms of distinction to contain the effects. As Dubois points out, "the abstract project of eliminating distinctions depended on the assertion of difference in capacity between those who were simply 'citizens' and those who were new to political participation." The latter would still need to undergo "a moral transformation, an apprenticeship in legitimacy, before they could truly fulfill the responsibilities of citizens of the Republic."[20] In practice, accordingly, "racialized distinctions" still remained.[21]

In other words, even as the emancipated slaves of African descent became admitted into the abstracted juridical identity of citizenship and accepted as equals, they were also made subject to new forms of exclusion, whose actual basis in social relations, material practices, and situated understandings, if not always in the explicit languages of politics, was certainly to be found in *race*. If the outcome to the early debates over Caribbean citizenship during the French Revolution, which brought the enfranchising of Martinicans and Guadeloupians, had "helped to produce the erasure of race as a distinct category of difference" inside the languages of republicanism in France itself, then race as an actualized and operative set of practices defining the colonial relationship remained nonetheless as powerful and pervasive as ever.[22] This simultaneous distancing and reincorporating, erasure and reinscription, repeatedly recurred during French republican debates of the nineteenth century, becoming especially compulsive during the colonizing adventures of the new imperialism after the 1870s. Thus Third Republican policymakers "perpetuated the revolutionary tradition of avoiding formal recognition of race as a legally recognizable marker of difference, even as the country embarked on its most aggressive period of colonial expansion."[23]

But if some contributors to *Race in France* analyze the complicated ideological work needed in order to bring racialized differences under erasure, others concentrate on getting behind "the formal discursive silence about race" in order to show "race's salience as a marker of difference in practice."[24] This disjunction rested on more than mere ideological blinders, cynicism, or mechanisms of self-delusion. In fact, as a growing body of recent work attests, "racial" difference was actually a term constantly in play in the interwar years among French republican politicians and policymakers. It was deployed most far-reachingly via the systems of policing and social classification entailed by an emergent machinery of population policies, labor regulation, and social hygiene. In the practice of such policy-making, operative understandings of race were actively produced by the administrative treatment of foreigners, immigrants, and colonial subjects, subsisting in the complex interplay between republican axioms of assimilation and all the ways in which segregation was nonetheless becoming practically enacted.[25] On the one side were the liberal Republic's "rules and principles that made citizenship and a settled life a real option for immigrants," but on the other side were these new machineries of social discipline that marked out territories of discrimination and assembled "a capacity for repression."[26] This steadily emergent twentieth-century system of practice and distinction was ineluctably structured into a racialized formation, the specifically French version of the "color line."[27]

These dialectics of discursive preemption and practical or disciplinary marking, the complicated tensions between on the one hand the promises and appeals of republican universalism and on the other hand the instituted practices of racialized nonrecognition or misrecognition, have in large part continued to define the landscape of French public life around matters of "race" down to the present day, from the debates surrounding the wearing of the Muslim headscarf (*hijab*) in schools since the late 1980s to the urban explosion of violent protests in autumn 2005.[28] The key to the more contemporary discourse, obviously, is provided by the acceleration of immigration to France from the late 1950s and the growing importance during those years of people from North Africa, Spain, and Portugal rather than migrants from Italy and elsewhere inside the European Economic Community (EEC). An early sharpening of social tensions continuously agitated public awareness between the climax of the Algerian War in the early 1960s and the abrupt suspension of all further immigration by the new government of Valéry Giscard d'Estaing on 3 July 1974.[29]

How typical was this French story? At one very fundamental level it was not typical at all, one might argue, given the French Revolution's perduring consequences for the terms through which all questions of citizenship, belonging, identity, and national difference in France remained organized and understood. By the factor of the French Revolution alone, and the default reflexes of republican universalism, France has to be considered different. At the same time the complex transmission of the French Revolutionary ideals to the rest of the continent, particularly as subsequently reworked during the nineteenth century through the liberal, radical, and socialist political traditions, with varying but indelible affiliations to the spirit of 1789, gave them a vital presence elsewhere too. Not only were the French Revolution and its ethicopolitical languages of citizenship exported, in other words, but so too were the complicated silencings and suppressions that this set of universalizing ideals entailed for the various parts of the republican, socialist, and reforming Left. With varying degrees of self-consciousness, democrats in the rest of Europe easily adopted the French universalist paradigm, especially in the central and northern European regions where before 1914 the democratic Left achieved its greatest and earliest resonance. Yet they simultaneously kept a tacit silence around universalism's dark secret. Whether or not people of color were technically admitted to citizenship in its various dimensions (usually they were not), racialized distinctions invariably placed them outside the operative democratic community of the people.

What else can be said about these deeper European histories? How might we begin further unraveling the complicated backstory to our present-day crisis of racialized political anxieties? My earlier reference to the French biopolitical history of registrative policing, social discipline, and discriminatory governmentality during the earlier twentieth century provides one vital thread of racial thought. Historians now accept that versions of a eugenicist paradigm, the spreading of interest in scientific racism and biological determinism across the academic disciplines so powerfully informing the practices of social administration, were entirely continuous across European intellectual and social policy circuits of the early twentieth century. That was as true of the major capitalist countries of the developed north and west of the continent as it was of the more backward ones in the south and east, where the drive for a technocratic and modernizing project of science and social policy seemed all the more urgent and consuming, not least because of its avant-garde intimations.[30] As becomes ever more apparent from the latest historiography, the pervasiveness of scientistic modes of understanding in the domain of the social—including objective and experimental methods, the deployment of expertise, the recourse to measurement and testing, the authorizing power of statistics, the hubris of planning, the enticements of classification and universal registration, in general the appeal of the applied sciences for elaborate projects of social engineering—extended across the expanding territories of emergent twentieth-century governmentality, describing welfarism in Social Democatic Sweden no less than in Nazi Germany, enlisting the ambitions of socialists and other progressives no less than of fascists. After 1945 the overwhelming impact of the crimes of Nazism sharply severed the continuity of such thinking, as the shocking revelations of the systematic excesses of the Nazi "racial state" now profoundly compromised the future accessibility of eugenicist ideas.[31] Yet in many sectors of social administration, public health, nutrition, population planning, and the medical sciences those ideas left a very deep imprint, especially in the areas of international development and policy-making for the Third World. How exactly these legacies articulated with racialized forms of thought later in the twentieth century remains an important and underinvestigated set of problems.[32]

A second deeper context is provided by colonialism. At one level important distinctions among national cases must certainly be made. That some of Europe's sovereign states possessed colonial empires of impressive longevity dating back to the sixteenth century clearly made a difference in how racialized understandings of exotic, primitive, and savage peoples in other parts of the world contributed to shaping the national imaginary later on, whether in official, popular, or intellectual terms. Yet regardless of such deeper patterning of the relations between "Europe and its others," the genealogies of racial thinking today owe far more to the period of the so-called new imperialism during the last quarter of the nineteenth century, which took the global integration of the world economy into a period of dramatic acceleration.[33] Between the 1880s and 1914 the military, administrative, and technological superiority of the industrializing capitalist countries bore down on the defenseless and less developed parts of the globe in a restless and rapacious onslaught of exploitative, coercive, and civilizationist power. This was qualitatively different in its consequences from the much older structures of thought and relations symbolized by 1492. Thus the imposing territorial extent of the Spanish empire in the Americas was largely a thing of the past after the independence revolutions of the late eighteenth and early nineteenth centuries; the Portuguese colonial presence had become a byword for administrative and cultural decrepitude by the late nineteenth century; and after being dismantled in the wake of the Napoleonic Wars the French colonial empire only experienced a partial and faltering renewal until the general imperialist upsurge got under way in the 1880s. Rather than these instances of direct colonial rule, arguably, it was in much wider forms of commercial and missionary penetration that Europe's older relations with the rest of the world tended more substantially to consist. From *those* histories, until the late nineteenth century, only the British empire had coalesced into a significant territorial colonialism.

Thus the more pervasive cultural impact of colonialism inside the societies of the European metropole really dated from the larger-scale and more violent colonial encounters of the period since the later nineteenth century, when the intensified rivalries of the Great Powers precipitated the territorial division of the globe, whether via direct colonial annexation or the establishing of neocolonial spheres of dominance. How this expansionism exactly occurred, empire by empire, had consequences for how colonial aspirations and legacies would later be processed. But at a more fundamental level of convergence, dramatized especially in the so-called scramble for Africa, the new imperialism had cultural and ideological effects that went beyond such distinctions among national cases, seeping into the societies of the European metropole whether or not the states concerned made a grab for colonies. In those terms, it scarcely mattered whether the empire was dramatically expanding (as in the case of the British), experienced more modest increments (like the French), consolidated older trading outposts and circuits into a territorial dominion (the Dutch in Southeast Asia), took the form of a single spectacular land grab (the Belgian Congo), or persisted as the mainly moribund remnant of an older imperium (the Spanish and Portuguese).

To continue this mapping of the late-nineteenth-century European colonialisms, the German and Italian cases were distinguished both by the spectacular novelty of the two national states themselves, emerging as they did only from the unifications of the 1860s, and by the subsequent loss of their newly acquired colonies either in 1918 or 1943. The history of colonialism in Germany and Italy was necessarily imbricated with the very process of making the nation itself, whether in state-institutional terms, culturally and ideologically, or in the place imagined for the national economy in the world economy. Given the established presence of the older "world empires" and the degree to which the available territories had already been divided up, nationalist agitations for a German or Italian "place in the sun" also acquired a particular edge of frustrated aggression. Finally, the earlier loss of colonial possessions meant that Germany and Italy avoided the particular violence and divisiveness accompanying the decolonization process and its longer-lasting legacies in Britain, France, Belgium, the Netherlands, and Portugal.

Yet at the more fundamental level, *colonialism* per se, whether as the bare acquisition of colonial territories overseas or in the scale and success of the colonial empire as a system of governance, was largely irrelevant. For by the turn of the twentieth century a far more pervasive system of unequal and exploitative relations increasingly bound together the societies of the European metropole and those of the exotic and exploitable overseas, which unfolded beneath and beyond any formal structures of direct colonial rule, whether those territories might be governed formally from Europe or not. The expanding commercial penetration of extra-European markets since the boom years of 1849 through 1873, the growth of mass production and the associated machineries of advertising and packaging, the new "exhibitionary complex" of colonial museums and colonial expositions, entertainment spectacles like circuses, forms of minstrelsy, and *Völkerschauen* (ethnographic performances and exhibitions of exotic peoples), writings of travel and exploration, adventure stories and other pulp fictions, a new visual landscape of posters, postcards, advertisements, collectors' picture cards, all kinds of bric-a-brac, photographs, moving pictures, and so forth—all these produced a generic and brutally simplified field of images, ideas, and assumptions increasingly divorced from indebtedness to any particular colonial event, colonial relationship, or colonial commodity. In these terms, the Scandinavian countries, which barely participated in the colonial scrambles of the late nineteenth century, were just as susceptible to the power of colonial discourse as were Britain, Germany, and France who possessed substantial territorial empires. Whether or not ordinary Europeans had any concrete or practical connection to this reservoir of experience, they could hardly hope to set themselves outside it, whatever their social background, gender, or age. Moreover, as the enormous weight of scholarship makes ever more clear, this new machinery of representation and understanding was explicitly *racialized*. At the fin de siècle, the disorderly profusion of Europe's relations with the non-European colonial worlds was being powerfully shaped into an evidently racial matrix.

Over the longer term of the twentieth century, it is these wider cultural consequences of colonialism—of the colonial relationship in the widest sense—that become the most important from our point of view. From an accumulating wealth of powerfully argued and finely grounded empirical histories, the degree to which racialized discourses of European cultural superiority produced in the colonies migrated back into the metropolitan societies to permeate them becomes ever more apparent. From such historiography, we know far more about the complex relays back and forth between the worlds of colony and metropole than we did before. With particular intensity during the period between the 1880s and World War I, European citizens came to know themselves—their national self-identifications, their locations in society and national culture, their claims to national citizenship, their access to varieties of personhood—by means of representations of the wider-than-European overseas world as they encountered such images and ideas in the newly commodified and mass-mediated public spheres of the time. Sometimes these ideas might be explicitly promulgated by governments or disseminated by parties and pressure groups, often in highly manipulative or demagogic ways, whether in an election campaign, in the mobilization behind a particular policy or piece of legislation, or simply as generalized propaganda. But far more insidiously, they were becoming part of the general texture of the public discourse, worked into the basic architecture of public belief.

These racialized assumptions included not just formal ideas and easily legible prejudices about colonial peoples. The insidiousness resided with semiconsciously or unconsciously internalized patterns of belief, as well as with all the racialized systems of distinction, whether sophisticated or crude, that defined the British, French, Germans, Italians, and other Europeans so persistently against the patent inferiority of their colonial or neocolonial subjects. Inside metropolitan social life particular elements of political subjectivity were produced in this way out of the complicated relations that linked Europeans through webs of ideas to the overseas worlds of the colony. We might think of this "colonial effect" as the sum of the transference and translation of meanings made far away from European homelands during the course of the relentless drives of European expansionism. Such meanings were based in an entire complex of perceptions and encounters, including disorderly and heterogeneous knowledge; idioms of thought; direct and vicarious experiences; spectacular events; arresting and seductive images; compelling arguments about economics, prosperity, and global survival; a visual repertoire of fantasy and desire; manifold forms of everyday consumption; and all the relevant registers of government action. Over time, that aggregative, malleable, and extraordinarily ramified discursive presence could acquire an interpellative coherence that we have come to call, in summary form, colonialism.[34] When deployed in the domestic arenas of European politics, it has demonstrated a sustained capacity to produce active forms of political agency, with lasting presence and many particular effects.[35]

Again, once decolonization occurred during the second half of the twentieth century, with its violent and traumatizing consequences for settlers, colonial administrators, and other expatriate populations, together with all the accompanying fallout at home in the European metropole, the possession or nonpossession of a directly ruled colonial empire necessarily made for huge differences. Thus if Indian independence and Partition may have left the metropolitan stabilities of British society relatively unscathed, for example, the subsequent process of extrication from empire produced a decade of continuously reverberating contentiousness, with political disasters exploding one after another: from the Malayan counterinsurgency and Mau Mau in Kenya, through the running violence in Cyprus and the spectacular debacle of Suez, to the destructive endgame in Aden and the Unilateral Declaration of Independence in Southern Rhodesia. In parallel to that history, the French litany of crisis ran from the suppression of the Madagascar uprising, the war in Indochina, and the debacle of Dien Bien Phu to the protracted and bloody denouement of the Algerian War. Dutch withdrawal from what became Indonesia, the Belgian colonial apocalypse in the Congo, and later the Portuguese retreat from Mozambique, Guiné Bissau, and Angola all translated into severe ructions in the domestic polity in Europe.[36] Each of these immediate crises of decolonization, moreover, was succeeded by flows of postcolonial migration. Empire's legacies were varied and complex, but this was certainly most visible among them: namely, the recruitment, immigration, and long-term residence of large numbers of workers and their families from the former colonial territories—most notably from the West Indies and South Asia in Britain, from North Africa, the Caribbean, and West Africa in France. Whether via the repatriating of colonial whites to the metropole of origin or by this subsequent dynamic of immigration, Europe's colonial pasts endowed powerful consequences, visibly and materially, for the present.

Yet on the other hand, the impetus for immigration did not *require* this prior context of the directly colonial relationship. While Indonesian independence in 1949–50 necessarily engendered large-scale repatriation to the Netherlands, amounting to some 300,000 Dutch Eurasians or "Indos" by 1960, and a dribble of immigration ensued during the 1950s and 1960s from the Antilles and Surinam, for example, it was only under the differing circumstances of the 1970s that Surinamese migrancy attained mass proportions, boosting the Dutch domiciled population from some 30,000 in 1970 to around 140,000 by the end of the decade. More to the point, the Dutch state had also been recruiting labor systematically from outside the former colonial sphere altogether, signing a battery of bilateral agreements for labor importation from Italy in 1960, Spain in 1961, Portugal in 1963, Turkey in 1964, Greece in 1966, Morocco in 1969, and Yugoslavia and Tunisia in 1970. Once family members began arriving too, by far the largest ethnic groups became those from Turkey and Morocco. By the end of the 1970s, the Dutch encounter with immigration, elaborately racialized around practical, ethnographic, and cultural understandings of foreignness and difference, had lost its relationship to the colonial era as such.[37] The West German case, where there were no colonies since 1918, makes the point still more compellingly. As Rita Chin shows, by the early 1970s labor migration to West Germany had attained French and British proportions, even without the impetus of any comparable colonial past. Like the Dutch, the West German state turned to the southern European and Mediterranean periphery, concluding contracts with Italy (1955), Spain and Greece (1960), Turkey (1961), Morocco (1963), Portugal (1964), Tunisia (1965), and Yugoslavia (1968) for the putatively short-term importation of labor power. From 95,000 aliens resident in West Germany in 1956, numbers reached 1.3 million ten years later, and 2.6 million by 1973.[38]

This postwar labor migration delivers the third and most vital context of European racialization. In contrast with the overwhelmingly intra-European continental labor market of the immediate postwar years, western European labor recruitment during the 1960s reached increasingly into the non-European world. If in the earlier period the British economy continued to tap historic sources of labor supply in Ireland (957,830 Irish-born inhabitants by 1971, or 2 percent of total population), together with some new ones on the continent (for example, a peak of 103,500 Italians by 1971), by the start of the 1960s it was drawing massively on the extra-European colonial and former colonial world: namely, Guyana and the Caribbean islands; India, Pakistan, and Bangladesh; Hong Kong and the Chinese populations of Malaya and Singapore.[39] In France and Belgium the early postwar sources of immigrant labor were Italy (until the turn of the 1960s), Spain, and Portugal. Luxemburg displayed an extreme version of the same relations, making southern Europeans into some 30 percent of total population by the late 1960s.[40] Until the mid-1950s West Germany met its postwar labor needs principally from the ethnic Germans fleeing Eastern Europe and the German Democratic Republic (GDR), as did the GDR itself and Austria: by 1960 German refugees accounted for 23.8 percent of the West German population, around 20 percent of that in East Germany, and some 10 percent of that in Austria. Once this ready-made labor reserve ran out in the 1960s, the Austrian state replicated Dutch and West German examples by signing bilateral agreements to recruit foreign labor from Mediterranean countries, so that by 1973 foreign workers accounted for 8.7 percent of total employment. Italian migrants overwhelmingly predominated in Switzerland, comprising 71.5 percent of foreigners with work permits in 1961, falling to 50 percent two decades later, but otherwise the same transition recurred: German, French, and Austrian workers recruited until the 1960s, increasingly giving way to "guest workers" from the Mediterranean thereafter.[41]

Each of these contexts is important to an understanding of the place of race in the European collective memory and political unconscious: first, residual reliance on eugenicist and scientistic beliefs concerning social pathology and social problems, however disguised or recoded; second, legacies of colonialism and decolonization; third, the consequences of the postwar labor migration.[42] The case of Sweden is especially instructive here, as it falls somewhat outside these generic contexts while reemphasizing the decisiveness of a fourth factor, namely, the contemporary European preoccupation with "foreigners," increasingly voiced during the past two decades in the rhetorics of "fortress Europe."[43] From the early 1990s the increasingly visible presence in Europe of people seeking refuge or asylum from civil wars, political repression, drought and famine, and horrendous economic collapse in their countries of origin galvanized racist political mobilizations and collective violence all around the continent. The growing fixation of racialized attentions from all parts of the political spectrum on issues concerning refugees and asylum seekers was both continuous with older forms of hostility against immigrants and distinct from them.[44]

Thus in Sweden there was no history of colonial empire, although Swedish society certainly shared in the wider colonial effect described here. Likewise, if eugenicist ideas of social engineering enjoyed influence in Sweden earlier in the 1920s and 1930s, Swedes nonetheless boasted a social democratic welfare state claiming a humane and universalist vision of public goods and societal reform. Finally, Sweden lacked the major labor migrations characterizing other western European countries during the 1960s and 1970s. Indeed, Sweden's transnational labor market remained more specifically regional than these other cases, drawing workers especially from Finland, but more generally from Scandinavia under the common Nordic labor agreement of July 1954: by 1980, 42.9 percent of the foreigners in Sweden were Finns, with another 14 percent from elsewhere in Scandinavia. Some modest labor recruitment from Yugoslavia, Turkey, and Greece began during the 1960s, while non-Europeans among the annual intake of immigrants rose steadily to a sustained peak of some 40 percent in 1980. Significantly, a large part of this increase comprised refugees and asylum seekers from Yugoslavia and all parts of the Middle East, who began arriving en masse in 1989–90, peaking in the mid-1990s. By 1996, migrants and refugees together made up 18.5 percent of Sweden's overall population.[45] And here is the rub: these big facts of the arrival in Sweden of foreigners, which during the 1990s were entirely convergent with other western European experiences, resulted in the growth of racialized consciousness, an efflorescence of xenophobia and antirefugee violence, the political growth of a radical Right, and the bringing of tolerance and civility under extreme duress. In other words, even despite Sweden's lack of a colonial past, despite the acknowledged decency of its political culture, and despite its generous policies on asylum, Swedish politics demonstrated exactly the same propensities toward racialized violence and cultural racism as elsewhere. "Even in Sweden," to use the title of Alan Pred's remarkable book, the racisms disfiguring Europe's social landscape could now distressingly be seen.

In the new international conjuncture shaped in the 1990s by the juggernaut advance of neoliberal globalization, introduced in Europe first by the collapse of Communism and the ending of the Cold War, then by the ratcheting forward of integration via the Single Europe Act and the Treaty of Maastricht, the new racialized animosities have disordered Europe's social landscapes of participation, civility, and citizenship. To the Yugoslav wars of the early 1990s were soon added a further series of violent ethnic conflicts on Europe's southeastern periphery: between Serbs and Albanians, Bulgarians and Turks, Armenians and Azeris. Aside from those resulting refugee movements, displaced and impoverished peoples also began traveling from vast regions of the non-European world in Europe's direction, extruded on the one hand by the descent of African polities into a condition of ruinously persistent civil war, on the other hand by the chronic geopolitical instabilities of the entire Near Eastern and Central Asian world region. These migrations conjoined with the new forms of exploitation of labor increasingly structuring western European labor markets since the deindustrializing of the 1970s and 1980s, whose functioning presupposed precisely such an insecure and mobile reserve army of labor. As Europe's capitalism became restructured, the growing prevalence of minimum-wage, dequalified and deskilled, disorganized and deregulated, illegal and semilegal conditions of work systematically stripped workers of security and organized protections in a new system of stratified and segmented employment for which the new migrants became perfectly fitted. Thus the complicated dynamics of the restructuring of labor markets, rising unemployment, loss of security, and general social decay worked together with the visible ethnicizing of large areas of the social topography to produce repeated flash points of social and political conflict. Given the patterns of racialization discussed earlier, and their genealogies deep in Europe's nineteenth- and earlier-twentieth-century pasts, the tendency to address these tensions using the languages of "race" rapidly became endemic.

There is a further dimension to these conflicts. For some four decades now the most visible of the new migrants, country by country, have been Muslim. That was already true of the immigrant workers arriving from the late 1950s, including South Asians in Britain, North Africans in France, and Turks in West Germany, Austria, the Netherlands, and Sweden. It was still true of refugees and asylum seekers, whether East African Asians, Palestinians, and Iranians in earlier waves of the 1970s, or the former Yugoslavs, West Africans, Somalis and others from northeast Africa, and Middle Easterners of all kinds later on. The ethnic violence in Europe's southeast—in Bosnia, Albania, and Kosovo, in Bulgaria, in the Caucasus, and earlier in the Turkish occupation of Cyprus—also ranged Christians of various kinds against Muslims. By the end of the 1990s, the two narrowest of Europe's continental bridgeheads to elsewhere, from Morocco across the Straits of Gibraltar to Spain and from Albania across the Adriatic to Italy, were the scenes of particularly fevered conflict as Europe policed its southern and eastern Mediterranean frontiers.

In the aftermath of the security anxieties surrounding 9/11 the perceived threats to the integrity of this geopolitical imaginary then became still more heavily Islamized. On the cultural front, a stream of sensations, country by country, from the Salman Rushdie affair through the various controversies over the *hijab* to the Danish cartoon controversy, the killing of Theo Van Gogh, and the posturing of Ayaan Hirsi Ali helped suture these disparate yet converging phenomena into a powerful discursive equivalence. During the accompanying public debates, lent impetus by further stages in the putative enlargement and solidifying of the EU, surprisingly forthright atavisms could also be heard. First in the ill-fated drive for a European Constitution and then in the opposition against Turkish accession, the Papacy and traditionalist Christian Democrats were not the only voices to be heard invoking "Western Christendom." At the high tide of Europeanism, in other words, glued together by the so-called war on terror, there emerged an in-turned and recentered pan-European, anti-Islamic racism.

Race Recognition

A complex equivalence of what I described as the French syndrome may be found across the Channel in Britain. As in the French situation, a con-

frontational and cumulative challenge-and-response of racist and antiracist histories has been troubling public life since the mid-1960s, and if
the willingness to name racism as such has made more headway inside the
British public sphere, there are still serious inhibitions against fully acknowledging the existence of race as something *socially,* as well as ideologically, "real." This is a fundamentally important distinction. For it is not
enough to treat "race" as a form of false consciousness, as "wrong" ideas,
and as an unfounded or inappropriate language for describing phenomena
whose "objective" basis is to be found somewhere else, I would argue.
Rather than being defined just by ideational habits of thought, unexamined assumptions, bodies of prejudice, and reflexive representations existing inside people's heads, race needs also to be approached as a social formation structured around instituted practices and organized relations,
which entail both material continuities and processes of reproduction. But
in British political discourse, race tends to be addressed only unevenly and
ambivalently in that more complicated way.

British commentators remain extremely reluctant to analyze race as a
practical and material presence in social life, as opposed to seeing it as a set
of misguided, ignorant, and intolerant atttitudes and beliefs—that is, as
"prejudice" in the long-established parlance. In the postwar British case, in
common with the rest of western Europe, race initially became named in
the languages of antipathy, phobia, and rejection wielded by the largely
disreputable Far Right. By the turn of the 1960s, an awareness of shameful
practices had begun steadily intruding onto public decorum from the
trenches of social life: evidence of racial discrimination in hiring, on-the-
job practices, and all aspects of employment; racial slurs and racial tensions during everyday encounters; and especially the racialized structure of
the housing market. Escalating sociocultural anxieties around immigration, brought into the centerground of public attention between the Nottingham and Notting Hill riots of 1958 and the Smethwick election scandal of 1964, then became powerfully dramatized in Enoch Powell's
notorious "rivers of blood" speech delivered in April 1968.[46]

In the decade that followed, questions of race and immigration joined
the centerground of public political debate, making these years the crucible
for a complicated decades-long agitating of the received terms of understanding of what it might take to be accepted as British. Ironically that period might have afforded grounds for a degree of imaginable optimism: the
Labour Government's two Race Relations Acts of 1965 and 1968 addressed
the issue of racial discrimination by projecting the postwar ideals of social

citizenship in the further direction of "racial equality." As the 1970s unfolded, the patient deployment of the associated machinery of social research and public policy, animated by postwar commitments to more humane and equitable social relations, then became increasingly challenged
by the new militancies of antiracist campaigning. Yet from the very inception, this movement toward "good race relations" became practically
trumped by the insistent and often hysterical demands for greater immigration controls, which made James Callaghan's 1968 Immigration Act
only the first act in a steady sequence of legislative changes that eventually
culminated in the Conservatives' British Nationality Act of 1981. By these
means the stigmatizing of "immigrants," whose elasticity as a category became effectively extended to long-resident populations in ever more racialized ways, became the price for the 1968 Race Relations Act and its
strengthened 1976 successor.[47] During this period, a radicalized right-wing
politics began permeating the Conservative Party's rhetoric and practices
during the run-up to Margaret Thatcher's election victory of 1979.[48]

Throughout the Thatcher era, racial tensions then grew harder and
harder to ignore. These were fed by a continuous cycle of racist agitation
and endemic neighborhood-level violence on the one hand, and antiracist
countermobilizing and black identitarian coalescence on the other hand.
The major explosions of urban rioting in 1980–81 combined with the insistent accretions of restrictionist legislation and policing of immigration to
bring the issue of race directly to the political forefront, centering around
the British Nationality Act of 1981. During the later 1970s, moreover, antiracist militancy invented a synthetic Black identity for all ex-colonial
peoples of color, including Caribbean, east and west African, southern
African, Indian, Bangladeshi, and Pakistani, which during the early 1980s
found institutional recognition through local Labour Parties and Labour-
controlled city governments. If this central identity claim quickly began
fragmenting into more sectional and localized constructions of ethnicity,
articulated around differences of gender, geographies of origin, religion,
generation, class, and so forth, this transitional imagining of a unified
Black Britishness proved discursively extraordinarily fertile, opening the
initial space for multicultural advocacy in the public sphere.

In the realm of intellectual critique, a key marker was the 1978 publication of *Policing the Crisis* by Stuart Hall and a collective of authors at
the Birmingham Center for Contemporary Cultural Studies (CCCS),
which at that time was the scene of an intensive encounter between British
traditions of cultural criticism and social history and various kinds of Eu-

ropean grand theory.[49] Conceived originally as the analysis of a moral panic whipped up in November 1972 around an incident of "racial mugging" in Handsworth, a major home of black British population in Birmingham, *Policing the Crisis* showed how the issue of "law and order" was in the process of radically and pervasively recasting the agenda of British politics. A recharged conservative nationalism was recentering itself around an emergent racialized imaginary, the volume's authors suggested. In an argument about the British state and its legitimacy extending back to the eighteenth century, the book attributed to the postwar settlement forged after 1945 a rapidly diminishing capacity for securing popular consent. Amid the resulting political uncertainties, racialized anxieties were being deliberately fanned, either cynically or as part of a coherent new outlook, in order to ease the passage to a more coercive and authoritarian set of rhetorics and practices. Yet whereas racism was clearly a central term of the crisis as Hall and his coauthors were seeking to diagnose it, "race" still figured mainly as a signifier for other things. If race could be seen as the red thread of the analysis, it still remained embedded inside the broader argument about the state, about hegemony, and about class.

With the publication four years later of *The Empire Strikes Back: Race and Racism in 70s Britain,* a new CCCS collective angrily focused on this earlier effacement of race.[50] Any sensible analysis of contemporary British politics had to proceed from the pervasiveness of racial ideology, Paul Gilroy and his coauthors insisted. Not only were established notions of British identity, and of the "Englishness" at their heart, deeply structured around markers of racial difference, but those prejudices were also in process of being aggressively inflamed. Contemporary rhetorics of national identification now fed partly on nostalgias about the imperial past, partly on the postimperial pathologies resulting from Britain's decline. The overt racism of fascist campaigning organizations like the National Front and later the British National Party (BNP), together with the everyday violence practiced against Afro-Caribbean and especially South Asian communities, were only the most blatant symptoms of this racialized crisis of national identification. Far more insidiously, such racially recharged logics of patriotism were also recasting the outlook of the Thatcherized Conservative Party. In appealing to British traditions and British "heritage," Conservative languages of national assertiveness were becoming ever more pervasively centered around an unmarked and unspoken whiteness, while marginalizing or demonizing the presence of Afro-Caribbean, South Asian, and other minority populations. The silencing of the one was en-

tailed in the primacy of the other. For all its inspiring oppositional re-
sourcefulness, moreover, even the radical reworking of British traditions in
the writings of Raymond Williams, Edward Thompson, and other New
Left thinkers, whose influence on the Birmingham school was so vital, had
reinscribed the same latent ethnocentrism. By bringing those assumptions
out into the open, the authors of *The Empire Strikes Back* insisted, analysis of race could force the particular "Britishness" or "Englishness" of cultural studies into self-consciousness and voice.

   This British discussion had some obvious affinities with emerging critiques of whiteness in the United States. It also reflected the incipient
movement away from older habits of class-centered analysis toward a
recognition that consciousness, identity, and subjectivity are formed in
more complex and multiform ways. As Gilroy wrote elsewhere, this analysis "challenge[d] theories that assert the primacy of structural contradictions, economic classes, and crises in determining political consciousness
and collective action."[51] His argument drew its urgency from the new political times: if more self-conscious subcultural identities were beginning to
coalesce around British blackness during the 1970s, these were more than
matched by a mainstream Conservative drive for the recentering of national identity around an exclusivist vision of Englishness, for which race
held the key.[52] During the 1980s this continuing eruption of racialized
conflicts into public life also unnerved a widening circle of British historians and allowed earlier readings of racial attitudes to be brought slowly
into a different and increasingly prominent focus.

   Converging with this contemporary recognition of race was a new appreciation of the degree to which imperial legacies indelibly informed the
assumptions behind British national identity. The impact of such perspectives on the thinking of historians occurred only slowly and fitfully. In the
earliest stages of registering the Empire's centrality, for example, professional historians (historians by formal disciplinary affiliation, that is) remained strikingly aloof. It was no accident that much of the first impetus
came from an avowedly transdisciplinary institution like the Birmingham
CCCS, whose innovative historical work was conducted precisely beyond
the disciplinary walls of history departments and often in face of their indifference or hostility. More generally, calls for taking the consequences of
Empire seriously came from the margins even of cultural studies—for example, from the critiques of an emergent black arts movement and its interest in "diaspora aesthetics," or else from outside Britain altogether in literary studies in the United States and via the impact of Edward Said.[53] The

key benchmark volume on definitions of "Englishness" produced in this period by historians left imperialism out entirely.[54] But over the longer term, neither historiography nor wider public commentary could ignore the Empire's constitutive importance for the bases of social and cultural cohesion in metropolitan Britain, particularly in the wider domains of popular culture and the dominant sociopolitical values.[55]

Race Relations, Racism, Racialization

For a discussion of race what is most striking in the counterposing of *The Empire Strikes Back* against *Policing the Crisis* is the degree to which the earlier work both *does* and *does not* acknowledge the question. At one level race is central to its terms of discussion. Race was an essential feature of the particular events between November 1972 and March 1973 that prompted the writing of the book. In the authors' analysis, the equation of "black crime," "black urban areas," and the urban social crisis soldered together through the moral panic surrounding the mugging hysteria played a key part in ushering in the advocacy of a "law and order society." Throughout the book Hall and his coauthors wrestled to integrate their analysis of race into their analysis of class: *"class relations,"* they argued, "function as *race relations.* The two are inseparable. Race is the modality in which class is lived. It is also the medium in which class relations are experienced."[56] Yet their ulterior interest still lay in dissecting the terms of a "crisis of legitimacy" of the British state in order to expose the ways in which the bases of political order were being remade.

Thus "mugging" became not just "an example of the rising crime rate," but a metonym for this overheated and widening sense of a more generalized societal crisis: "an index of the growing tide of violence; a symbol of the breakdown of public morality; the collapse of Law and Order." Extrapolating beyond the years when *Policing the Crisis* was written and published (1974–78), we can say that its authors saw the "attempts to control and contain this crisis" as strengthening the impetus toward a markedly more austere and authoritarian climate of public policy, one that was about to culminate in the victory of the Conservative Party under Margaret Thatcher in the 1979 election. In a series of analyses begun around this same time, Hall named this new politics "authoritarian populism." Yet even though a pioneering recognition of the importance of "race," racism, and racial conflict was woven into the terms of that larger analysis, dealing with race as such still remained a second-order concern. As the blurb of *Policing the Crisis* put it: "Mugging was one theme—among many—which justified this shift by the State into a more coercive gear."[57]

This analysis was certainly extremely sophisticated. As Hall later reflected, the CCCS readings of the relationship of race to the crisis rested on a highly developed theory of ideology. They found that racism worked

> rather more like Freud's dreamwork than anything else. We found that racism expresses itself through displacement, through denial, through the capacity to say two contradictory things at the same time, the surface imagery speaking of an unspeakable content, the repressed content of a culture.[58]

In an essay written in 1978 for the Commission on Racial Equality that glossed *Policing the Crisis,* Hall put this in terms of a projection outward of severe social problems onto an external presence, where the "outward" proceeded from a psychic or cultural, as opposed to a territorial, center, and the "externality," namely, race, was a foreignness actually embedded deep in the interior of British society. Indeed, so far from being first created by the tensions consequent upon the post-1945 immigrations, "race" had been historically "constitutive" for British identity going back to the first encounters with blacks in the sixteenth and seventeenth centuries: "It is in the sugar you stir; it is in the sinews of the famous British 'sweet tooth'; it is in the tea-leaves at the bottom of the next 'British' cuppa."[59] Racism could only be made intelligible in light of these deep historical structures, Hall argued. It was "the outside history that is inside the history of the English. . . . There is no English history without that other history."[60]

But from our current vantage point the form of Hall's analysis can now be usefully historicized. His standpoint was laden with the very particular preoccupations of British Marxist debates at the turn of the 1980s. His commentaries came at the height of an antireductionist effort at the retheorizing of ideology, in the more ramified contexts of a collective generational autocritique, just before its participants fractured and dispersed into the various destinations of a post-Marxist intellectual future.[61] In other words, if Hall's writings of the late 1970s were taking immense theoretical pains in tackling the manifest actualities of race in British society and politics, whether as racism or racial identities, then they were still seeking to do so from a received ground of class analysis. While Hall insisted on the necessity of taking race seriously, he held on to the importance of class conflict as the prime mover.

Thus on the one hand race was increasingly foregrounded in Hall's thinking, particularly after the intensifying of racial tensions produced by Powell's 1968 speech. As Hall said, the political crisis was "largely thematized through race. Race is the prism through which the British people are called upon to live through, then to understand, and then to deal with the growing crisis."[62] In the same period Hall was also pioneering the analysis of racism in the media, most notably in the television program he produced in 1979, *It Ain't Half Racist Mum* (playing on the title of the popular comedy series *It Ain't Half Hot Mum* set in the British army in India during World War II).[63] Yet on the other hand, race was still being treated as the language or system of meanings needed to express something else. As Procter puts it, the gathering crisis of moral authority and social disorder after 1968 "became condensed around the *imagery* of race."[64] In effect, racism was being approached, in however sophisticated a way, as the ideological expression of a problem whose real conditions of existence would need to be sought elsewhere:

> It [the moral panic surrounding mugging] deals with those fears and anxieties, not by addressing the real problems and conditions which underlie them, but by projecting and displacing them onto the identified social group. That is to say, the moral panic crystallizes popular fear and anxieties which have a real basis and by providing them with a simple, concrete, identifiable . . . social object, seeks to resolve them.[65]

This is a very precise statement of the ideological work that Hall saw racism as being called upon to perform. But by articulating his analysis around an argument about an underlying real cause, Hall stopped short of fully recognizing the ways in which race could also itself possess such entirely "real" forms of social, cultural, and practical existence—in everyday material practices and human transactions, in formal institutions and sites of governmentality, in organized types of sociability, in actually functioning communities of common belonging, in forms of collective action, and so forth. In all of these ways, race could have consequences of its own *without* constantly having to be referred back to some prior and more fundamental origin. It is fascinating to look back on these debates of the later 1970s and early 1980s and watch someone like Hall wrestling in this way with the question of "race," simultaneously acknowledging its eruption into the public sphere, insisting on the ways in which it was now organizing primary forms of social antagonism that deserved the name of a crisis, yet still pulling back from the recognition that race could be encountered as an actually existing social formation, as something that had "real" forms of existence that were embodied and instituted rather than being displaced forms of recognition and understanding.

A further striking illustration may be found in Paul Gilroy's concluding essay in *The Empire Strikes Back.*[66] Focusing explicitly on "the cultural politics of 'black' people in this country, and the implications of their struggles for the institutions and practices of the British workers' movement," Gilroy refers his analysis to contemporary Marxist debates about socialist strategy in which Gramscians and left Eurocommunists were challenging the presumed primacy of the working class as traditionally understood.[67] Rejecting the formalistic suggestion that questions of racial justice and racial equality are primarily "political" matters to be treated separately from those relating to class, as well as the more orthodox Marxist assignment of "race consciousness" to a merely auxiliary status, he insists on the cultural specificity of the "political *forms* of struggle and organization" through which "immigrants and their children" conjoined with the wider activities of the labor movement. As well as campaigning for racial equality and stronger black representation in trade unions, accordingly, it was vital for the Left also to connect with the cultural militancy of those who "listen to reggae, build sound systems, or wear headwraps, tams and dreadlocks."[68] That would involve "giving due weight to cultural factors, understood neither as purely autonomous nor as epiphenomena of economic determinations." In this regard Gilroy took his cue directly out of *Policing the Crisis:* "The class relations which inscribe the black fractions of the working class function as race relations. The two are inseparable. Race is the modality in which class relations are experienced."[69]

It was only by analyzing "the construction, mobilization, and pertinence of different forms of racist ideology and structuration in *specific historical circumstances,*" Gilroy argued, that one might identify the particular ways in which race coalesced as a positive identity. Only by means of such careful historical deconstructions might the adoption of "race" as a category of identity become properly intelligible: "We must examine the role of these ideologies in the complex articulation of classes in a social formation, and strive to uncover the conditions of existence which permit the constitution of 'black' people in politics, ideology, and economic life."

But it was the "real" social relations that required attention, not the ideological or perceptual forms through which they were encountered and understood. Using race as a concept or category in such a way as to imply that it described something "real" was already to cede the ground or give the game away: "Thus there can be no general theory of 'race' or 'race relations situations,' only the historical resonance of racist ideologies and a specific ideological struggle by means of which real structural phenomena are misrecognized and distorted in the prisms of 'race'."[70] This commitment of Gilroy's to grounding his analysis explicitly in relation to "the class struggle" and the "class consciousness of our epoch" was a distinctive intellectual-political signature of the early 1980s, which his later writings were subsequently to shed.[71] The tension or blockage in the argument is notable. In the 1982 essay, Gilroy took great pains specifically to establish the centrality of "culture" to the grounds of black political struggle. Yet at the very end of the essay the older-established grounds of priority ("real structural phenomena" which become "misrecognized and distorted" as "race") were back.

In fact, at the turn of the 1980s Hall's was only the most sophisticated among various approaches then seeking to understand race and immigration primarily in relation to a larger set of social determinations. But if race can no longer be treated as something biologically given, but has to be seen as socially constructed, a lot then rests on how exactly one approaches the problem of ideology, for without the simultaneous rethinking of *that* problem, which preoccupied Hall just as intensely during the 1970s and 1980s, one kind of determinism (biological) would simply give way to another (social).[72] In that way, race might then be easily *reduced* to ideology, to forms of consciousness that serve to mask or conceal the real terms of social and economic existence. For Robert Miles, the leading advocate of such a materialist sociology, *racism* and not race must then become the appropriate object of analysis, because scientifically speaking *race itself* can have no demonstrable existence or validity as an object of study. The question then becomes how to locate the processes that allow "race" to become mobilized in the form of particular ideologies and their effects.

If "races" are not naturally occurring populations, the reasons and conditions for the social process whereby the discourse of 'race' is employed in an attempt to label, constitute, and exclude social collectivities should be the focus of attention rather than be assumed to be a natural and universal process.[73]

Miles accordingly proposed the concept of "racialization" for conceptualizing racism's ideological effects. He understands racialization in relation to the conflicts and disturbances associated with the regulation of migrant labor markets in an international system still mainly organized by nation-states. It results from the tensions between "on the one hand the need of the capitalist world economy for the mobility of human beings, and on the other, the drawing of territorial boundaries and the construction of citizenship as a legal category which sets boundaries for human mobility."[74] In that sense racism is seen "as integral to the development of capitalist social formations, for racisms mediate a series of contradictions that are said to arise chronically out of the commodifying logic of capitalism."

> The universalization of the commodity form creates ideologies of formal equality which are contradicted by the endemic inequalities of capitalism; racism enables a justification of inequalities by naturalizing them through conceptions of fixed attributes. Moreover, resistance to commodification and capitalist transformation allows recalcitrant populations to be racialized as primitive, thus underwriting the forcible expropriation of their labor, or even the genocide of the stigmatized populations. And the contradiction between the universalizing thrust of capitalist relations and the formation of nation-states creates populations that are constantly being collectivized through identifications that posit national and "racial" essences.[75]

One key moment in the racialization of western European politics, in this view, can be found in the large-scale labor immigrations of the 1950s and 1960s. Subsequently, in the very different conjuncture opened by the 1970s, with its drastic processes of class recomposition, the changing labor markets of a post-Fordist and deindustrializing economy, and the long-term structural crisis of the inner city, the terms of racialized political discourse became further reconfigured. By the 1990s they were increasingly being grasped through concepts of globalization.

But these sociologies of race were more than the imperfect prehistory of a subsequent cultural turn. Most important, Hall, Gilroy, and the other CCCS authors played a huge part not only in bringing problems of race centrally onto the agenda of scholarly discussion but also in precisely bridging to an analysis that was more explicitly cultural in intent. Indeed, henceforth such an analysis became increasingly hard to avoid. Likewise, in the wider context of the activities of the realigned Institute of Race Relations (IRR) under A. Sivanandan and its new mouthpiece *Race and Class,* Miles and others managed to bring racism programmatically into the centerground of social analysis. In both cases, these were gains achieved only via protracted and hard-fought intellectual confrontations with an earlier sociology of race relations, some of whose exponents really had seen race as epiphenomenal.[76] In that regard, the CCCS authors and the *Race and Class* network were each writing explicitly against predecessors whose capacity for dealing with race remained subtly blocked.[77] Here, therefore, we loop back to discussion of the French and German cases. Like French republican universalism and West German idealizing of the Enlightenment heritage of "Western" modernity, British liberalism during the 1950s and 1960s had likewise produced its own forms of resistance to the use of the category of race.

Crystallizing around the Institute of Race Relations founded in 1952 and its journal *Race* launched in 1959, the liberal race relations sociology of the immediate postwar decades arose partly in social anthropology departments and partly in the mandarin milieu of the Royal Institute of International Affairs (RIIA or Chatham House), where the IRR was housed.[78] As a field of academic knowledge, race relations was profoundly indebted to the postwar social policy consensus. While certainly inflected toward the Labour Party's social democratic vision of social integration, it also reached far into the "one nation" outlook of the post-Churchillian Conservative Party, which properly came into its own after Suez during the premiership of Harold Macmillan. The very breadth of that consensus was what made the overt racism of the successful Conservative election campaign in the West Midlands constituency of Smethwick in 1964 ("If you want a Nigger for a Neighbor, Vote Labour," in the words of the most notorious election leaflet) so shocking. The tacit observance of a code of silence in the nonnaming of the race question likewise made Enoch Powell's speech of May 1968 such a violent breach of the rules of political decorum—a "torpedo aimed at the boiler-room of consensus," as Stuart Hall puts it.[79] Thus it was both the disablement of the postwar consensus before a right-wing backlash that refused any longer to observe the embargo and the urgency of an equally radical antiracist response that opened the way for the departures outlined earlier.

The British consensus in the postwar recoding of race had two main features.[80] First, racial tensions or racial discrimination tended to be recorded as the intelligible effects of "social problems" like inadequate housing, overcrowding, educational disadvantage, high unemployment, or poverty. The key social studies, represented most classically by Sheila Patterson's *Dark Strangers* in 1963, approached their subject through that lens.[81] The great monument to this earlier body of research and empirical understanding was the enormously influential 800-page Institute of Race Relations volume edited by E. J. B. Rose in 1969 as *Colour and Citizenship: A Report on British Race Relations* (London: Oxford University Press), which was vitally keyed to the liberal "race relations" agenda of the Labour government under Roy Jenkins at the Home Office.[82] Interestingly, if "race" was treated symptomatically by the IRR and the race relations industry (as pathologies that would disappear once the relevant social problems had been sorted), then the sociologists and campaigning journalists writing about social problems per se virtually never talked about race as such except completely incidentally. Thus the hugely influential Penguin Special published in 1970 by Ken Coates and Richard Silburn, *Poverty: The Forgotten Englishmen,* was based on precisely the same slum district of St. Ann's that was the scene of the 1958 Nottingham race riot yet thought to acknowledge that racialized context nowhere in its explicit or recognizable terms of reference.[83]

Second, no less than French republican adherence to a fervently color-blind ideal of citizenship, this postwar liberal–cum–social democratic consensus placed "race" as a category completely under taboo. Here it was surely the long aftermath of the trauma of Nazism that was responsible. The shocking encounter with Nazi atrocities, genocide, and all the other consequences of the Third Reich's avowedly "racial state" fundamentally delegitimated the use of the concept. As a discursively allowable ground of reference, "race" was simply no longer available: it was scientifically meaningless and disproven; it had no basis in objective realities; and it was purely ideological. It simply should not be used.[84] Attempts were made intermittently on the part of mainly right-wing commentators of one kind or another to reopen a discussion of the relationship between "race" and "intelligence" (most notably in the writings of the prestigious psychologist Hans Eysenck), but the breadth and strength of the liberal consensus allowed them to be consistently beaten back.[85] By the 1970s, in other words, the principal academics studying race relations in British sociology, such as Michael Banton and John Rex, for the most part principled liberals or socialists ethically committed to ideals of integration, and certainly located firmly inside the postwar consensus, were dogmatically opposed to using "race" per se as a category at all. Robert Miles held to a Marxist version of that same tradition, insisting that "racism" and "racialization" do not presuppose a necessary concept of "race," let alone its real presence as social relations and social practice. Race is always about something else. That is the analytical ground that should never be given up.

The enduring power of this conviction may be glimpsed in a short opinion piece published in October 1996 in the *New Statesman* by the eminent political scientist Bernard Crick. Best known for his classic pluralist tract *In Defence of Politics* (originally published in 1962) and his official biography of George Orwell, Crick came completely out of the same postwar social democratic consensus mentioned earlier, formed both by the profound aversion against the racist ideologizing of Nazism and by the ethical aspiration for a more humane society borne by social policies of improvement.[86] Each of those commitments disallowed race as a concept. His one-page "Argument" entitled "Throw the R-Word Away: We Should Attack Racism by Ceasing to Use the Word 'Race'" insisted that race was qualitatively different from nationalism rather than merely an extreme version. It abandoned the analysis of history, sociology, and culture for the bogus belief in biology.

> For there is no such thing as race, only the destructive and false belief in the concept. It has no explanatory value whatever. Discrimination and hatred based on this false belief should be attacked, but so should the very concept. To [pursue] ideas of racial equality in the name of equality of races is to concede too much to believers in race. Councils on "race relations" should change their names. Names matter.

Further:

> So we should not attack ideas of racial superiority by asserting the equality or even the peculiarity of races. We should talk about cultures, nations, groups, not races: even when a group by being persecuted because of false racial views comes to think of itself proudly as a race. This is to be corrupted by the language of the enemy. . . . The best rebuttal is to reject the concept entirely, not its misuse or abuse.[87]

Conclusion: Race, Cultural Difference, Europe

This essay has tried to describe a vital part of the European political space. Throughout its writing, the steady drumbeat of public controversy sur-

rounding all aspects of the ethnic, religious, and cultural differences separating "Europe" from its "others" has relentlessly continued. As I composed these words, the maverick Dutch parliamentarian Geert Wilders was
in process of releasing his rabidly anti-Islamic fifteen-minute film *Fitna*. In
the absence of any sponsoring television channel, he posted Dutch and
English versions on 27 March 2008 on the internet video-sharing website
Liveleak. After being withdrawn, reposted, and withdrawn again amid a
confusing welter of legal challenges, the film seemed sure to become a veritable tinderbox of polarizing rhetorical violence.[88] A little earlier, the
Danish cartoon controversy, taking its name from the publication of a
dozen satirical depictions of the prophet Muhammad by the liberal-con-
servative daily newspaper *Jyllands-Posten* in September 2005, was once
again violently reignited. On 12 February 2008 Danish police arrested two
Tunisians and a Dane of Moroccan origins for allegedly planning the assassination of Kurt Westergaard, one of the cartoonists. In response *Jyllands-Posten* and other Danish newspapers promptly reprinted Westergaard's *Bomb in the Turban* cartoon in solidarity with the principle of free
speech, followed by other leading newspapers around the world, including
the *Observer* in Britain and the *Wall Street Journal* in the United States.
Surrounding the arrests and republication were a series of violent disturbances in Copenhagen, which developed as much from long-standing police harassment of militant squatters and the city's multiethnic alternative
scene as from the cartoon issue per se.[89] Further references such as these
can be easily multiplied: the confrontational provocations of Ayaan Hirsi
Ali; continuing headscarf debates in Turkey; Martin Amis's venting
against Islam; tensions around the shortages of mosques in Spain.[90]

A troublesome silence still marks the center of these overheated political scandals. Few seem willing to acknowledge just how powerfully ideas
about race are defining the ground from which Europeans are now able to
respond to such events. This is not an easy silence to break. As acknowledged earlier, there are good reasons to be hesitant about using a category
of race for analytical purposes. The catastrophe of Nazism disqualified
race as a concept across the academic disciplines no less than in the public
languages of politics: after 1945 it became delegitimated in Europe and effectively placed under taboo. In common with many other terms of social
understanding, it can also be argued, race functions as a category of practice rather than a category of analysis, a confusion that concepts of *racialization* and *racism* more easily avoid. Once we abandon our wariness
around the term and swallow our doubts, many continue to argue, we risk

restoring it to scientific credence and legitimacy. Yet there are strong arguments for facing race head on.[91]

First, if analysis of class formation or nation forming can be disengaged from the older structuralist or objectivist approaches, so that we emphasize both the processual constructedness and "imagined" quality of
those categories and their social realization, then there is no reason in principle why *racial formation* cannot be approached in the same way too. For
example, some years ago Rogers Brubaker and Frederick Cooper argued
that the late-twentieth-century popularity of the concept of identity was
leading precisely to the kind of reification of a category of practice mentioned earlier, and that consequently *identification* should be adopted as a
more serviceable analytical term instead.[92] Brubaker likewise advocated focusing on *nationhood* and *nationness* as a means of emphasizing the
processual quality involved in the making of a nation.[93] Yet "nation" also
signifies instituted practices, juridical definitions, regularities of government intervention at the levels of states and localities, organized activities,
machineries of socialization, an entire finely elaborated space of culture
and belief, and a great deal else besides, all of which make nations into actually existing sites of resilient solidity and stable reproduction rather than
solely something in process of becoming. Why must one perspective exclude the other? We do not need to reify the nation or assume that it pos-
sesses greater permanence and stability than it does in order to focus usefully on the structured and instituted regularities. The same goes for
"race": analyzing its regularities does not commit us to believing its reality
in some scientific or objective sense.

Second, over an extremely long period race has demonstrated extraordinary interpolative power. Ideas and assumptions about race, along
with all the associated sites and practices, circulate promiscuously through
European society. Elaborate and extensive historiographies now allow us
to periodize the terms of those histories. The postfascist conjuncture after
1945 saw a significant hiatus, for example, which then itself came to an end
by way of the new labor migrations of the late 1950s and beyond. When
such ideas circulate so profusely and acquire such powerful purchase on
social experience, I want to argue, they become *real.* A government practice, a system of policy, a set of rhetorics, a body of scientific or academic
knowledge, a religious creed, a big political idea, but also an event or chain
of events like a riot or a rash of violent incidents, a public spectacle, or a
political campaign, not to speak of deep legacies within the culture, persistent patterns of default thinking, widely diffused dogmas of commonsense

understanding, and straightforward systems of prejudice—all of these generate categories that people then have to inhabit, which interpolate them. Such interpolation is not automatic, not inevitable, not a process over which people can exercise no choice. There are competing ideas out there too. Race can also be contested. But in all sorts of ways ideas about race create places where in practice, with varying degrees of awareness, the members of a society have perforce to dwell. This describes more than just a *process* of racialization or the existence of a racist attitude or ideology somehow external or auxiliary to a materiality structured around something else. It describes a real social topography: forms of everydayness, actually existing patterns of organized community, an entire architecture of common belonging, ways of regulating public and personal space, institutional machineries, systems of governmentality. If we study only racism and racialization rather than tackling *race* head on, we miss this vital materiality. Race retains its tenacity because it inhabits an actually existing world of practices and ideas. This is the second argument for breaking the silence.

Third, if we define racism as the essentializing of "differences that might otherwise be considered ethnocultural" into characteristics that appear "innate, indelible, and unchangeable" while organizing them into systems of domination and subordination, then race becomes a source of positive identification *not only* for those in the dominant reaches of the racial hierarchy.[94] It delivers forms of political subjectivity and other ideas about the self that the racially subordinated can be capable of embracing too. The demise of scientific or biological theories of racial belonging has not prevented such racially marked populations from appropriating the category for themselves, precisely because it rested upon a recognizable material and experiential world and its histories. So negritude, black pride, and other positive ideologies of the racially subordinated suggest a further ground for taking the category of race seriously. Otherwise it becomes much harder to grasp the coherence and legitimacy of the process through which such populations have acquired a self-affirming voice. Seeing race only as a construct, socially and culturally, or arguing that it operates through fantasy and the imagination as ideology or distraction, is tacitly to place it a priori as less important than something else—than something that *does* possess "real" existence, whether as class, as the structural imperatives of capitalist labor markets, as the impact of migrancy, or as the threatened stabilities of national belonging. Unless race is allowed that kind of analytical equivalence, we will properly grasp neither the collective self-identification of racialized populations nor the material bases of their cohesion. Continuing to deconstruct the societal prevalence of "the seemingly 'natural' or 'commonsense' concept of race" will certainly retain its vital importance. But we also need to understand the materialities of race for those who become marked by it, the actualities of its presence, the experiential bases for racial identification in ordinary life.[95]

Finally, racialized understandings resonate back and forth across a number of different spheres. This interconnectedness provides race with perhaps its greatest salience of all. I began this conclusion with the spectacle of Europe's current anti-Islamic anxieties, and the febrile and hyper-security-conscious political climate of "post-9/11" has definitely endowed the perceived presence of Islam inside and outside Europe's borders with an intensely mobilized logic of racialized meaning. That logic becomes all the more apparent once we consider the other fields of divisiveness in Europe centering during the past half-century around ethnocultural, religious, and national differences. These include the consequences of the labor migrations of the period between the later 1950s and early 1970s, including the attendant growth of settled residential minority populations across Western European societies; the emergence of neofascist and other right-wing populisms around hostility to immigration during the 1970s and 1980s, common again to Western Europe as a whole; a related coalescence of identitarian politics and cultural self-assertiveness among minority populations themselves; the escalation of "antiforeigner" violence in Central and Eastern Europe accompanying the transition from Communism and the wars of Yugoslav succession during the 1990s; the new globalized migrant labor markets and the continuous traffic of illegal and semilegal itinerant workers and their dependents; the associated movements of refugees and asylum seekers, displaced partly by the same consequences of global deregulation, partly by ecological disasters, partly by politically imposed catastrophe; and last but not least, the long-running effects of decolonization and the smouldering slow burn of the legacies of colonialism. Each of these phenomena generates a particular political force field; and they all work insidiously together.

So there are many places where the materialities of race may be found. If we accept this argument—that race exists materially in social relations and practices and not just culturally as markers of difference or imaginatively as ideas in the head—then it becomes possible to build up a map of its prevalence that can accurately record all the unevenness, contingencies, and volatility while appreciating the deep embeddedness and subtle efficacies of appeal. We might begin from the parts of European society where race does patently function as a primary ordering principle, namely, within the Far Right's political imaginary of noxious immigrants and unwelcome foreigners: here at least race can be encountered as an encompassing social reality, the existential hardwiring for what seems most vital to its practitioners. We might then move out into the wider landscape of racist violence and antiforeigner enmities, where the high-impact visibility of an election campaign and the spectacle of an assassination or a cartoon scandal become sutured to the everydayness of insults and abuse on the streets. We know from the *Eurobarometer* and other survey data that since the 1980s Western European attitudes have grown consistently averse to foreigners, especially those from outside the EC/EU. By 1997 two-thirds of all Europeans surveyed *described themselves* as being in some degree racist: only in Luxemburg, Portugal, Spain, Greece, Ireland, and Sweden could more than 40 percent see themselves as free from racism, and the intervening years have removed even these few exceptions.[96] Moreover, in its noisy vociferousness the very presence of an anti-immigrant movement eventually realigns the overall climate of public policy apparently unstoppably toward its own ground. In the three decades separating the Smethwick by-election and Enoch Powell's 1968 speech from the public stigmatizing of asylum seekers in the 1990s, for example, the boundaries of acceptable discourse in British public life on questions of nationality, citizenship, and immigration lastingly shifted. Whether or not "race" supplied the polite and accredited languages of official discussion, and despite all the ways in which it continued to be forthrightly and successfully contested, racial recognitions had become textured into the discursive arena. Once again, the same story has recurred with distressing regularity around Europe more generally—"even in Sweden," as the title of Pred's book regrets.[97]

It is important to note the new "culturalist" contours of racist advocacy. In this "new racism," differences of cultural identity have notably replaced biologically founded inequalities as the main building block of racist thought. In rhetorical and pragmatic recognition of the disrepute into which racist ideas have fallen, Far Right advocacy has increasingly regrouped around the programmatic defense of the distinctiveness of national culture and its threatened integrity. In the language deployed by right-wing populists, cultural identity has become central to how the alienness of "immigrants" can be publically rationalized: such intruders are people who share neither a national heritage nor "European civilization," who do not belong, who are foreign to the way "we" live, who lack "our" cultural and moral values. This emergent ideology of race eschews the old arguments about biological inferiority in favor of a new emphasis on "rootedness" (*enracinement* in French) that "exalts the absolute, irreducible *difference* of the 'self' and the incommensurability of different cultural identities."[98] The nation's cultural identity then becomes the endangered possession, whose integrity needs to be preserved and if necessary bitterly defended. Its key referents become heritage, tradition, collective memory, geography, and an elaborate representational repertoire of differences in culture, rather than "blood" or even race per se.[99]

Country by country, this new "culturalized" racism is blurring the boundaries between previously isolable groupings of the Far Right and mainstream nationalisms that too remain strongly oriented around a collectively memorialized and ritually celebrated cultural patriotism based on national heritage. Here "Europe" signifies in complex ways. Since the shelving of "social Europe" and the more generous possibilities attibuted at the time to "1992," the EU has ceased for any forseeable future to be a feasible project of manageable sociopolitical and cultural integration, careening instead toward a narrowly understood market-defined geopolitical drive for the purposes of competitive globalization. The resulting giganticism of the EU's current process of Enlargement exacerbates the culturalizing of racism in a doubled way: it stokes the country-based anxieties already clustering around the territories of a vulnerable national identity; it simultaneously translates those resentments onto the meta-European plane of the defense of besieged civilizational values. This potent dialectic of national and European identifications—of defending the nation from within the larger battlements of a fortress Europe—brings together multiple fields of antagonism drawn with distressing predictability *against Muslims,* whether those Muslims are already inside Europe, situated around its borders, or perceived to be on their way.[100]

The Islamic provenance and affiliations of migrant minorities during the earlier period of the 1960s and 1970s lacked the same kind of salience. Then in the 1980s multiple sites of conflict coalesced willy-nilly toward a primary contradiction: everyday racism against Pakistanis and Bangladeshis in Britain; its analogs in the *banlieues* of France; discrimination against Turks in West Germany and Austria, against Moroccans and Turks in the Low Countries; campaigns against Muslims in Bulgaria, the slow descent toward violence in Bosnia and Kosovo; war between Armenians and Azeris over Nagorny-Karabagh. In the 1990s these hostilities exploded into sustained crisis, further articulated with a range of conflicts on the wider global stage. But the political logics of anti-Islamic concentration were still unevenly apparent. The main consequence of 9/11 has been exactly this: a further, disastrous radicalizing of all of the above in ways that simultaneously concentrate the representational energy *against* Islam.

In many of the most dangerously violent of the ensuing controversies—from Salman Rushdie to Geert Wilders—a disturbing elision occurs. The intricate dilemmas of how best to preserve pluralism, tolerance, and civil liberties, or of how to secure the values of individual emancipation and the freedoms of conscience and speech, become translated discursively into emblems of ethnonational identity and the broader humanistic heritage of European civilization. These are values, we hear with authoritative regularity, which "Islam" does not share. Étienne Balibar describes the slide of logic very well: from "*foreigners* to *aliens* (meaning second-class residents who are deemed to be of a different kind)"; "from *protection* to *discrimination*"; and "from *cultural difference* to *racial stigmatization.*"[101] Within the global field of post-9/11 antagonisms, many commentators have crudely aligned this elaborated system of differences with a differential capacity for democracy: "Islam and democracy are fully incompatible. They will never be compatible—not today, and not in a million years."[102] Inevitably, demagogy then fills much of the resulting political space. "We are in an undeclared war," Geert Wilders repeated after the killing of Theo van Gogh in November 2004. "These people are motivated by one thing: to kill everything we stand for." And more recently:

> Islam is something we can't afford any more in the Netherlands. I want the fascist Qur'an banned. We need to stop the Islamization of the Netherlands. That means no more mosques, no more Islamic schools, no more imams . . . Not all Muslims are terrorists, but almost all terrorists are Muslims.[103]

In Henning Mankell's novel *Kennedy's Brain,* the bereaved mother Louis Cantor quizzes her dead son Henrik's lover and friend about her origins ("How come that you are called Nazrin but don't speak Swedish with a foreign accent?"). Nazrin explains in response:

> I was born at Arlanda airport. We'd been hanging around there for two days, waiting to be allocated to some refugee camp or other. Mum gave birth to me on the floor next to passport control. It all went very quickly. I was born at the precise spot where Sweden begins.[104]

In this sense Europe has become a margin, an edge, a boundary, defined literally and metaphorically by its gates. The drama of migrancy unfolds most visibly and painfully at Europe's closest seaborne entry points: through Ceuta and the Canaries to Spain; from Libya to Lampedusa; from Albania to Apulia; from Turkey to Samos, Lesbos, Chios, and the Dodecanese.[105] Other frontiers materialize where the migrants, asylum seekers, and refugees are gathered on the inside—in a major cultural metropolis like Vienna or Amsterdam, in countless smaller sites of short and longer-term settlement, in the new semicarceral archipelago of processing and registration.[106] In the post-9/11 climate the Islamic character of so many of the marginalized minorities who live along this sharply defined European edge of differences has increasingly effaced many of the other diversities involved. But given the unfailing repetition around the map of the racialized political dynamics and deeper discursive patterning discussed here—especially given the signifying *nonwhiteness* of the people concerned—it becomes harder and harder to claim that race has not been doing its work.

Notes

INTRODUCTION

1. Jere Longman, "Surge in Racist Mood Raises Concern on Eve of World Cup," *New York Times* (4 June 2006): 1.

2. World-cup tourists were advised that certain parts of Potsdam should be considered a "no-go zone," for example.

3. For an expanded discussion, see chapter 4 in this volume. In making this point about how Germans have understood—and the media has represented—the geography of racism after unification, we are not denying the existence of racist bias, antagonism, or violence in eastern Germany. Nonetheless, it is worth pointing out that while xenophobic and antisemitic violence appears to have increased after 1990 in eastern Germany, it was in western Germany (Solingen and Mölln) that the horrific, lethal firebombings of Turkish homes occurred. (See Hermann Kurthen, Werner Bergmann, and Rainer Erb, eds., *Antisemitism and Xenophobia in Germany after Unification* [New York: Oxford University Press, 1997], 263–85, for an itemized list of right-wing extremist violence against property and people between 1989 and 1994. West German incidents dominate the list.) Bundesverfassungsschutzberichte through 2006 have documented criminal acts of extreme-right and/or xenophobic violence in both western and eastern Länder. In 2006, in fact, western states topped the list with the highest number of incidents per *Land* (146 in Nordrhein-Westfalen and 138 in Niedersachsen), although Sachsen-Anhalt (with 111 incidents) had the highest per-capita "politically motivated [right-wing] criminality" with 4.49 per 100,000 population. Reports of the geographic distribution of *Gewalttäten* (violent crimes) provide numbers only; there is no analysis of whether certain sorts of crimes are more highly represented in particular areas. This makes east-west comparisons challenging without resort to other forms of reporting. The *Verfassungsschutzberichte* are available online at http://verfassungsschutz.de/de/publikationen (last accessed 23 May 2007). For a good overview of German social scientists' assessments of the increase in xenophobia, right-wing extremism, and violence among East German youth after 1990 (and for some brief observations on the role of the media in propagating public perceptions) see Kurthen, Bergmann, and Erb, eds., *Antisemitism and Xenophobia.* For an analysis that emphasizes the role of East German male youth, see Wilfried Schubarth, "Xenophobia among East German Youth," in that volume, 143–58. Also Peter Förster et al., *Jugend Ost:*

Zwischen Hoffnung und Gewalt (Opladen, 1993); Wolfgang Melzer, *Jugend und Politik in Deutschland. Gesellschaftliche Einstellung, Zukunftsorientierungen und Rechtsextremismuspotential Jugendlicher in Ost- und Westdeutschland* (Opladen, 1992); Deutsches Jugendinstitut, *Schuler an der Schwelle zur deutschen Einheit* (Opladen, 1992); Wilfried Schubarth and Dorit Stenke, "'Ausländer-bilder bei ostdeutschen Schülerinnen und Schülern" in *Deutschland Archiv* 12 (1992): 1247–54; Gisela Trommsdorf and Hans-Joachim Kornadt, "Prosocial and Antisocial Motivation of Adolescents in East and West Germany," in *After the Wall: Family Adaptations in East and West Germany*, ed. James Youniss, 30–56. (San Francisco: Jossey-Bass, 1995); Meredith Watts, *Xenophobia in United Germany: Generations, Modernization, and Ideology* (New York: St. Martin's Press, 1997); and Richard Alba, Peter Schmidt, and Martina Wasmer, eds., *Germans or Foreigners? Attitudes Toward Ethnic Minorities in Post-Reunification Germany* (New York: Palgrave Macmillan, 2003). On East German exceptionalism in German historiography, see Paul Betts and Katherine Pence, "Introduction," in *Socialist Modern: East German Everyday Culture and Politics,* ed. Paul Betts and Katherine Pence (Ann Arbor: University of Michigan Press, 2008), 1–34.

4. Longman, "Surge in Racist Mood Raises Concern on Eve of World Cup," 1, *SportsSunday,* 6.

5. See, for example, Michael P. Nikolai, "Not Empty Words: Germany Is Welcoming the World," *Atlantic Times* 3, no. 6 (June 2006), 2.

6. David Goldberg, *Racist Culture* (Oxford: Blackwell, 1993), 91, quoted in John Solomos and Lisa Schuster, "Hate Speech, Violence, and Contemporary Racisms," in *Europe's New Racism? Causes, Manifestations, Solutions,* ed. Evans Foundation (New York: Berghahn Books, 2002), 46–47.

7. George M. Frederickson, *Racism: A Short History* (Princeton: Princeton University Press, 2002), 168, mentions the "bifurcation of studies of white supremacy and antisemitism." Though he is referring mostly to the American context, this holds for European scholarship as well, as we discuss later. On the post-1945 softening of Jewishness from race to ethnicity, see, for example, Matthew Frye Jacobsen's *Whiteness of a Different Color: European Immigrants and the Alchemy of Race* (Cambridge: Harvard University Press, 1998).

8. See Eric Weitz's useful, brief discussion of "ethnicity," "nationality," and "race" in "Racial Politics without the Concept of Race: Reevaluating Soviet Ethnic and National Purges," in *Slavic Review* 61, no. 1 (Spring 2002): 1–29; here, 6–7.

9. George M. Frederickson, *Racism: A Short History* (Princeton: Princeton University Press, 2002), quotations from 155, 151; more generally, see 140–55. Also Frederickson, *The Comparative Imagination: On the History of Racism, Nationalism, and Social Movements* (Berkeley: University of California Press, 1997), especially 77–83.

10. On the other hand, historians have explored the persistence of antisemitism after 1945. However, these investigations have been uncoupled from discussions of "race"—an analytical move that calls for some retrospective historical analysis. See chapter 4 in this volume; also Frank Stern, *The Whitewashing of the Yellow Badge: Antisemitism and Philosemitism in Postwar Germany,* trans. William Templer (New

York: Pergamon, 1992); Wolfgang Benz, ed., *Antisemitismus in Deutschland: Zur Aktualität eines Vorurteils* (Munich: Deutscher Taschenbuch Verlag, 1995); and Benz, *Jahrbuch für Antisemitismusforschung* (Munich: Deutscher Taschenbuch Verlag), the first annual issue appeared in 1992; Y. Michal Bodemann, *Jews, Germans, Memory: Reconstructions of Jewish Life in Germany* (Ann Arbor: University of Michigan Press, 1996); Jeffrey M. Peck, *Being Jewish in the New Germany* (New Brunswick: Rutgers University Press, 2006); and the various publications by sociologists Werner Bergmann and Rainer Erb, including Bergmann and Erb, eds., *Antisemitismus in der politischen Kultur nach 1945* (Opladen: Westdeutscher Verlag, 1990). In addition, some social activists and social scientists have begun to characterize violence toward ethnic minorities as "racism" in contemporary Germany. See, for example, Sanem Kleff, Edith Broszinsky-Schwabe, Marie-There Albert, Helga Marburger, and Marie-Elenora Karsten, *BRD-DDR. Alte und neue Rassismen im Zuge der deutsch-deutschen Einigung* (Berlin: Verlag für Interkulturelle Kommunikation, 1990); A. Kalpak and N. Räthzel, eds., *Die Schwierigkeit, nicht rassistisch zu sein* (Leer: Mundo Verlig, 1990); S. Jäger, *BrandSätze-Rassismus im Alltag* (Duisburg: Duisburger Institut für Sprach- und Sozialforschung, 1993); Nicola Piper, *Racism, Nationalism, and Citizenship: Ethnic Minorities in Britain and Germany* (Brookfield, VT: Ashgate, 1998), 33–43; Susan Arndt, ed., *Afrika-Bilder: Studien zu Rassismus in Deutschland* (Münster: Unrast Verlag, 2001); Jerome S. Legge, Jr., *Jews, Turks, and Other Strangers: The Roots of Prejudice in Modern Germany* (Madison: University of Wisconsin Press, 2003); and Helena Flam, ed., *Migranten in Deutschland. Statistiken-Fakten-Diskurse.* (Constance: UVK Verlagsgesellschaft, 2007). For a comparative discussion on France and Britain, see Geoff Eley's discussion in chapter 5 of this volume.

11. Robert Moeller, "Introduction: Writing the History of West Germany" in Robert Moeller, ed., *West Germany under Construction: Politics, Society, and Culture in the Adenauer Era* (Ann Arbor: University of Michigan Press, 1997), 1–30; here, 3–12.

12. Heide Fehrenbach, *Race after Hitler: Black Occupation Children in Postwar Germany and America* (Princeton: Princeton University Press, 2005); Atina Grossmann, *Jews, Germans, and Allies: Close Encounters in Occupied Germany* (Princeton: Princeton University Press, 2007); Rita Chin, *The Guest Worker Question in Postwar Germany* (Cambridge: Cambridge University Press, 2007).

13. Aras Ören, *Was will Niyazi in der Naunynstraße* (Berlin: Rotbuch Verlag, 1973). For an analysis of Ören's works, see Chin, *The Guest Worker Question,* especially chapter 1; and Leslie A. Adelson, *The Turkish Turn in Contemporary German Literature: Toward a New Critical Grammar of Migration* (New York: Palgrave Macmillan, 2005), chapter 3. The same year a book chronicling the experience of Blacks in West Germany appeared, Karen Thimm and DuRell Echols, *Schwarze in Deutschland* (Munich: Protokolle, 1973).

14. Katharina Oguntoye, May Opitz (later Ayim), and Dagmar Schultz, *Farbe bekennen: afro-deutsche Frauen auf den Spuren ihrer Geschichte* (Berlin: Orlanda Verlag, 1986), trans. by Anne V. Adams as *Showing Our Colors: Afro-German Women Speak Out* (Amherst: University of Massachusetts Press, 1992), xxi–xxii.

15. Zafer Şenocak, *Atlas des tropischen Deutschlands* (Berlin: Babel, 1992), trans. by Leslie A. Adelson as *Atlas of a Tropical Germany: Essays on Politics and Culture, 1990–1998* (Lincoln: University of Nebraska Press, 2000), 1–2.

16. For example, Peter Weingart, Jürgen Kroll, and Kurt Bayertz, *Rasse, Blut und Gene. Geschichte der Eugenik und Rassenhygiene in Deutschland* (Frankfurt am Main: Suhrkamp, 1988), Paul Weindling, *Health, Race, and National Politics between National Unification and Nazism, 1870–1945* (New York: Cambridge University Press, 1989), as well as the recent work of Fatima El-Tayeb, Lora Wildenthal, Tina Campt, Pascal Grosse, and Isabel Hull, among others. On the question of colonialist continuities, see Birthe Kundrus, "Kontinuitäten, Parallelen, Rezeptionen. Überlegungen zur 'Kolonisierung' des Nationalsozialismus," *Werkstatt-Geschichte* 43 (2006): 45–62.

17. Claudia Koonz, *The Nazi Conscience* (Cambridge: Harvard Belknap Press, 2003); Stern, *Whitewashing.* Hanna Schissler, "Introduction," in *The Miracle Years,* ed. H. Schissler (Princeton: Princeton University Press, 2000).

18. Uta G. Poiger, *Jazz, Rock, and Rebels: Cold War Politics and American Culture in Divided Germany* (Berkeley: University of California Press, 2000); also Poiger, "Imperialism and Empire in Twentieth-Century Germany," *History and Memory* (2006); Maria Höhn, *GIs and Fräuleins: German-American Encounter in 1950s West Germany* (Chapel Hill: University of North Carolina Press, 2002); Fehrenbach, *Race after Hitler;* Grossmann, *Jews, German, Allies.* Other recent publications (not all by historians) that devote some attention to the issue of difference in post-1945 Germany are Rogers Brubaker, *Citizenship and Nationhood in France and Germany* (Cambridge: Harvard University Press, 1992); Tina Campt, Pascal Grosse, and Yara-Colette Lemke-Muniz de Faria, "Blacks, Germans, and the Politics of the Imperial Imagination, 1920–1960," *The Imperialist Imagination: German Colonialism and Its Legacy,* ed. Sara Friedrichsmeyer, Sara Lennox, and Susanne Zantop (Ann Arbor: University of Michigan Press, 1998), 205–29; Patricia Mazón and Reinhild Steingröver, eds., *Not So Plain as Black and White: Afro-German History and Culture from 1890–2000* (Rochester: University of Rochester Press, 2005); Katrin Sieg, *Ethnic Drag: Performing Race, Nation, Sexuality in Postwar Germany* (Ann Arbor: University of Michigan Press, 2002); Neil Gregor, Nils Roemer, and Mark Roseman, *German History from the Margins* (Bloomington: University of Indiana Press, 2006).

19. Y. Michel Bodemann and Gökce Yurdakul, eds., *Migration, Citizenship, Ethos* (New York: Palgrave Macmillan, 2006); Chin, *The Guest Worker Question in Postwar Germany.*

20. In this connection, it is notable that historians of Germany have not yet produced a synthetic interpretation of the role of difference in the development of the German nation comparable to Jacobsen's *Whiteness of a Different Color,* which spans from the inception of the American Republic through the late twentieth century. This is certainly not due to the paucity of migration to Germany or to that modern nation's need to integrate minority populations.

21. German Historical Institute Database, *German History in Documents and Images.* "Report of the District Government of the Prussian District of Koblenz on the Jewish Population," 1820. From Vormärz to Prussian Dominance (1815–

1866): Documents—Government and Administration: Emancipation of the Jews. http://germanhistorydocs.ghi-dc.org/sub_document.cfm?document_id=434 (accessed 16 May 2007).

22. Recently, historians of Germany have begun to reexamine the role of religion, and their assumptions regarding secularization, in the constitution of German modernity and the nation. See, for example, Rudy Koshar, "The History of Christianity Beyond the Residual" H-Net Book Review of Sheridan Gilley and Brian Stanley, eds., *World Christianities, c. 1815–c.1914.* Vol. 8. Cambridge History of Christianity (Cambridge: Cambridge University Press, 2006) and Hugh McLeod, ed., *World Christianities, c. 1914–c. 2000,* vol. 9. Cambridge History of Christianity. (Cambridge: Cambridge University Press, 2006), dated July 2007.

23. For an early example of this thesis, see Fritz Stern, *The Politics of Cultural Despair: A Study in the Rise of Germanic Ideology* (Berkeley: University of California Press, 1974). More recent examples include Philippe Burrin, *Nazi Anti-Semitism: From Prejudice to the Holocaust* (New York: New Press, 2005), and Shulamit Volkov, *Germans, Jews, and Antisemites: Trials in Emancipation* (New York: Cambridge University Press, 2006).

24. See Art. 3 of the West German Basic Law (*Grundgesetz*) and Arts. 6 and 11 of the East German constitution (*Verfassung*).

25. For an expanded discussion, see Chin, *The Guest Worker Question,* especially chaps. 3–4.

26. Martin Barker, *The New Racism* (London: Junction Books, 1980); Paul Gilroy, *There Ain't No Black in the Union Jack;* and Etienne Balibar, "Is There a Neo-Racism," in Etienne Balibar and Immanuel Wallerstein, *Race, Nation, Class: Ambiguous Identities* (London: Verso, 1991), 21–23.

27. For an interesting discussion of historical and cultural understandings informing Nazi policies in sorting Germans from Czechs, in effect deciding who of the latter were "Aryanizable," see Tara Zahra, "Your Child Belongs to the Nation: Nationalization, Germanization, and Democracy in the Bohemian Lands, 1900–1945" (doctoral diss., University of Michigan, 2005), 503ff.

28. Here we agree with Rogers Brubaker who has argued, "Ethnicity, race, and nation should be conceptualized not as substances or things or entities or organisms or collective individuals—as the imagery of discrete, concrete, tangible, bounded and enduring 'groups' encourages us to do—but rather in relational, processual, dynamic, eventful, and disaggregated terms. This means thinking of ethnicity, race, and nation not in terms of substantial groups or entities but in terms of practical categories, situated actions, cultural idioms, cognitive schemas, discursive frames, organizational routes, institutional forms, political projects, and contingent events. *It means thinking of ethnicization, racialization, and nationalization as political, social, cultural, and psychological processes. And it means taking as a basic analytical category not the 'group' as an entity but groupness as a contextually fluctuating conceptual variable*" (emphasis added). Rogers Brubaker, *Ethnicity without Groups* (Cambridge: Harvard University Press, 2004), 11.

29. Brubaker helpfully argues that "by treating ethnicity as a way of understanding, interpreting, and framing experience, [cognitive] perspectives provide an alternative to substantialist or groupist ontologies. They afford strong reasons for

treating ethnicity, race, and nationalism as one domain rather than several."
Brubaker, *Ethnicity without Groups*, 86.

30. Maxim Silverman, *Deconstructing the Nation: Immigration, Racism, and Citizenship in Modern France* (London: Routledge, 1992), 1290.

31. As Brubaker puts it, racial and ethnic "common sense"—"the tendency to partition the social world into putatively deeply constituted, quasi-natural intrinsic kinds . . .—is a key part of what we want to explain, not what we want to explain things with; it belongs to our empirical data, not our analytical toolkit." Brubaker, *Ethnicity without Groups*, 9. Brubaker notes that "'Groupness' is a variable, not a constant" (4).

32. Brubaker, *Citizenship and Nationhood;* Balibar and Wallerstein, *Race, Nation, Class;* A. Rattsani and S. Westwood, eds., *Racism, Modernity, and Identity* (Cambridge: Polity Press, 1994); Piper, *Racism, Nationalism, and Citizenship;* I. Pinn and M. Nebelung, *Vom "klassichen" zum aktuellen Rassismus in Deutschland. Das Menschenbild der Bevölkerungstheorie und Bevölkerungpolitik* (Duisburg: Duisburger Institut für Sprach- und Sozialforschung, 1992). H. Glenn Penny and Matti Bunzl, eds., *Worldly Provincialism: German Anthropology in the Age of Empire* (Ann Arbor: University of Michigan Press, 2003); Fatima El-Tayeb, *Schwarze Deutsche. Der Diskurs um Rasse und nationale Identität* (Frankfurt am Main Campus, 2001); Andrew Zimmerman, *Anthropology and Antihumanism in Imperial Germany* (Chicago: University of Chicago Press, 2001); Isabell Hull, *Absolute Destruction: Military Culture and the Practices of War in Imperial Germany* (Ithaca: Cornell University Press, 2004); Reiner Pommerin, *Sterilisierung der Rheinlandbastarde. Das Schicksal einer farbigen deutschen Minderheit 1918–1937* (Düsseldorf: Droste, 1979); Tina Campt, *Other Germans: Black Germans and the Politics of Race, Gender, and Memory in the Third Reich* (Ann Arbor: University of Michigan Press, 2003); Mazón and Steingröver, eds., *Not So Plain as Black and White;* Atina Grossmann, *Reforming Sex: The German Movement for Birth Control and Abortion Reform, 1920–1950* (New York: Oxford University Press, 1995); Michelle Mouton, *From Nurturing the Nation to Purifying the Volk: Weimar and Nazi Family Policy, 1918–1945* (New York: Cambridge University Press, 2007); Uwe Mai, *"Rasse und Raum": Agrarpolitik, Sozial- und Raumplanung im NS-Staat* (Munich: Schöningh, 2002); Bayertz, *Rasse, Blut und Gene;* Roger Bartlett and Karen Schönwalder, eds., *The German Lands and Eastern Europe* (New York: St. Martin's Press, 1999); Eduard Mühle, ed., *Germany and the European East in the Twentieth Century* (New York: Berg, 2003); and Krista O'Donnell, Renate Bridenthal, and Nancy Reagin, eds., *The Heimat Abroad: The Boundaries of Germanness* (Ann Arbor: University of Michigan Press, 2005).

33. George Fredrickson has noted that racism "is always nationally specific. It invariably becomes enmeshed with searches for national identity and cohesion that vary with the historical experience of the country." *Racism*, 75.

34. George M. Fredrickson has similarly observed that it "is high time that historians devoted the same effort to understanding 'race' as a transnational social and historical phenomenon that they have sometimes applied to class, gender, and nationalism." *The Comparative Imagination: On the History of Racism, Nationalism, and Social Movements* (Berkeley: University of California Press, 1997), 77.

35. Robert Bernasconi, "After the Invention of Race: Racial Discourse in Germany from Kant to National Socialism," talk presented at "Remapping Black Germany" conference, University of Massachusetts, Amherst, 22 April 2006.

36. For the German context, see the work of Michael Kater, *Different Drummers: Jazz in the Culture of Nazi Germany* (New York: Oxford University Press, 1992); Uta Poiger, *Jazz, Rock, and Rebels;* Katrin Sieg, *Ethnic Drag;* and David Ciarlo, "Consuming Race, Envisioning Empire: Colonialism and German Mass Culture, 1887–1914" (doctoral diss., University of Wisconsin, Madison, 2003), among others.

37. See, for example, Uta G. Poiger, "Beauty, Business, and German International Relations," in *WerkstattGeschichte* 45 (2007): 53–71; Alys Weinbaum, Lynn M. Thomas, Priti Ramamurthy, Uta G. Poiger, Madeleine Yue Dong, and Tani Barlow, *The Modern Girl Around the World* (Durham: Duke University Press, 2008); and Heide Fehrenbach and Uta G. Poiger, *Transactions, Transgressions, Transformations: American Culture in Western Europe and Japan* (New York: Berghahn Books, 2000).

38. Jan Gross, *Fear: Antisemitism in Poland after Auschwitz* (New York: Random House, 2007).

39. Poiger, *Jazz, Rock, and Rebels;* Maria Höhn, *GIs and Fräuleins;* Heide Fehrenbach, *Race after Hitler.*

40. See, for example, Young-Sun Hong, " 'The Benefits of Health Must Spread among All': International Solidarity, Health, and Race in the East German Encounter with the Third World," in Katherine Pence and Paul Betts, eds., *Socialist Modern: East German Everyday Culture and Politics* (Ann Arbor: University of Michigan Press, 2008), 183–210.

41. See chapter 4 in this volume. Also Martin Klimke, "The 'Other' Alliance: Global Protest and Student Unrest in West Germany and the U.S., 1962–1972" (doctoral diss., Universität Heidelberg, 2005), and Victor Grossmann, "The GDR Newspaper *Junge Welt* and Solidarity with African-Americans (especially in the Angela Davis case)," paper presented at the 2006 German Studies Association Meeting, Pittsburgh, October 2006.

42. Höhn, *GIs and Fräuleins;* Fehrenbach, *Race after Hitler,* esp. chapter 1.

43. Frank Stern, *Whitewashing;* Grossmann, *Jews, Germans, and Allies.* For a discussion of how the Nuremberg Trials organized knowledge about Nazi crimes and victims, see Donald Bloxham, *Genocide on Trial: War Crimes Trials and the Formation of Holocast History and Memory* (New York: Oxford University Press, 2003).

44. Diethelm Prowe, "The 'Miracle' of the Political-Culture Shift: Democratization between Americanization and Conservative Reintegration," in Schissler, ed., *The Miracle Years,* 451–58; here, 456. Also Stern, *Whitewashing.*

45. For an expanded discussion, see chapter 4 in this volume.

46. Daniel Goldhagen has been a prominent, if controversial, proponent of this view. For more nuanced versions that discuss problems of immigration and "foreignness," although not questions of race after 1945, see Konrad H. Jarausch and Michael Geyer, *Shattered Past: Reconstructing German Histories* (Princeton: Princeton University Press, 2003), especially the chapter on "redefining national

identities," 221–44, esp. 235–41; also Konrad H. Jarausch, *After Hitler: Recivilizing Germans, 1945–1995,* trans. Brandon Hunziker (New York: Oxford University Press, 2006).

47. A notable exception is Flam, ed., *Migranten in Deutschland.*

48. Robert G. Moeller, "Remembering the War in a Nation of Victims: West German Pasts in the 1950s," in Schissler, ed., *The Miracle Years,* 83–109; here, 86–87; for a more comprehensive discussion see R. G. Moeller, *War Stories: The Search for a Useable Past in the Federal Republic of Germany* (Berkeley: University of California Press, 1999). Also Stern, *Whitewashing.*

49. See Geoff Eley's discussion in chapter 5.

50. For a brief, related discussion of whether the post-1945 radical right should be characterized as "fascist,"see Diethelm Prowe, "The Fascist Phantom and Anti-Immigrant Violence: The Power of (False) Equation," in Angelica Fenner and Eric D. Weitz, *Fascism and Neofascism: Critical Writings on the Radical Right in Europe* (New York: Palgrave Macmillan, 2004), especially 132–34.

51. See, for example, Peter Bethge, "Welchen Stand haben ausländische Arbeiter bei uns?" *Junge Welt* (28 September 1972) in Deniz Göktürk, David Gramling, and Anton Kaes, eds., *Germany in Transit: Nation and Migration, 1955–2005* (Berkeley: University of California Press, 2007).

52. Atina Grossmann, "A Question of Silence," in Robert G. Moeller, *West Germany under Construction* (Ann Arbor: University of Michigan Press, 1997); Norman Naimark, *Russians in Germany: A History of the Soviet Zone of Occupation, 1945–1949* (Cambridge: Harvard Belknap Press, 1995), chap. 2; W. Karin Hall, "Humanity or Hegemony: Orphans, Abandoned Children, and the Sovietization of the Youth Welfare System in Mecklenberg, Germany, 1945–1952" (doctoral diss., Stanford University, 1998); Jeffrey Herf, *Divided Memory: The Nazi Past in the Two Germanies* (Cambridge, 1996).

53. Hermann W. Schönmeier, ed., *Prüfung der Möglichkeiten eines Fachkräfteprogramms Mosambik* (Saarbrucken: Verlag Breitenbach, 1991); Eva-Maria Elsner and Lothar Elsner, *Ausländer und Ausländerpolitik in der DDR* (Berlin: Gesellschaftswissenschaftliches Forum, 1992); Eva-Maria Elsner and Lothar Elsner, *Zwischen Nationalismus und Internationalismus: Über Ausländer und Ausländerpolitik in der DDR 1949–1990* (Rostock: Norddeutscher Hochschulschriften Verlag, 1994); Jan C. Behrends, Thomas Lindenberger, and Patrice G. Poutrus, eds., *Fremde und Fremd-Sein in der DDR: zu historischen Ursachen der Fremdenfeindlichkeit in Ostdeutschland* (Berlin: Metropol, 2003); Eva Kolinsky, "Meanings of Migration in East Germany and the West German Model," in Mike Dennis and Eva Kolinsky, eds., *United and Divided: Germany since 1990* (New York: Berghahn Books, 2004), 145–75; Christian Müller and Patrice G. Poutrus, eds., *Ankunft, Alltag, Ausreise: Migration und interkulturelle Begegnung in der DDR-Gesellschaft* (Cologne: Böhlau, 2005); Göktürk, Gramling, and Kaes, eds., *Germany in Transit,* especially chapter 2; and Hong, "'The Benefits of Health.'"

54. Jonathan Zatlin is a recent exception; see his "Scarcity and Resentment: Economic Sources of Xenophobia in the GDR, 1971–1989," in *Central European History* 40, no. 4 (December 2007): 683–720, which appeared after this introduction

was authored. Victoria de Grazia's magisterial *Irresistible Empire: America's Advance through Twentieth Century Europe* (Cambridge: Harvard University Press, 2005) does not consider the role of foreign labor.

55. A notable recent exception is Rita Chin, *The Guest Worker Question.*

56. See Gross, *Fear;* Joshua D. Zimmerman, ed., *Contested Memories: Poles and Jews during the Holocaust and Its Aftermath* (New Brunswick: Rutgers University Press, 2003); Peggy Piesche, et al., *Mythen, Maske, und Subjekte: Kritische Weißseinsforschung in Deutschland* (Münster: Unrast, 2006). Since 2005, the Black European Studies Initiative (BEST) has begun to hold a series of international conferences.

57. Brubaker, *Ethnicity Without Groups,* 11.

58. Five million Slavs were forcibly transferred to the German Reich as slave labor by the German military; thousands of ethnic Germans settled in western Poland and other Eastern European territories; Jews were transported by the millions to ghettos and concentration and death camps, leading to six million deaths. In addition, beginning in 1939, with the division of Poland between Nazi Germany and the USSR, Soviet troops deported 1.5 million people from Poland, including 600,000 Poles, as slave labor to Siberia, Soviet Central Asia, and the Soveit Arctic, a tenth of whom died. A further 30,000 Poles were shot in Poland. See Mark Kramer, "Introduction," *Redrawing Nations: Ethnic Cleansing in East-Central Europe, 1944–1948,* ed. Philipp Ther and Ana Siljak (Lanham, MD: Rowman and Littlefield, 2001), 3, 5. Also Ulrich Herbert, *Hitler's Foreign Workers: Enforced Foreign Labor in Germany under the Third Reich,* trans. William Templer (Cambridge: Cambridge University Press, 1997); Mark Spoerer, *Zwangsarbeit unter dem Hakenkreuz. Ausländische Zivilarbeiter, Kriegsgefangene und Häftlinge im Deutschen Reich und im besetzten Europa 1939–1945* (Stuttgart: Deutsche Verlags-Anhalt, 2001); Elizabeth Harvey, *Women and the Nazi East: Agents and Witnesses of Germanization* (New Haven: Yale University Press, 2003); Wolfgang Jacobmeyer, *Vom Zwangsarbeiter zum Heimatlosen Ausländer: die Displaced Persons in Westdeutschland* (Göttingen: Vandenhoeck und Ruprecht, 1985); Eugen Lemberg and Friedrich Edding, *Die Vertriebenen in Westdeutschland. Ihre Eingliederung und ihr Einfluss auf Gesellschaft, Wirtschaft, Politik und Geistesleben* (Kiel: Hirt, 1959).

59. The groups affected were Chechens, Ingush, Kalmyks, Meskhetian Turks, Karachais, Bashkirs, Balkars, Volga Germans, and Crimean Tatars. For an overview of ethnic cleansing in Eastern Europe, see Kramer, "Introduction," 4–21; here, 4, 15.

60. Those affected were Greeks, Bulgars, Kurds, Khemshils, Kabardines, Poles, Finns, Moldavians, Armenians, Lithuanians, Latvians, and Estonians. Kramer, "Introduction," 4.

61. Speech on Poland, 15 December 1944. Quoted in Kramer, "Introduction," 6–7.

62. See Kramer, "Introduction," 17.

63. See the excellent essays in Ther and Siljak, eds., *Redrawing Nations.* For the expulsion of Germans from Czechoslovakia, see Eagle Glassheim, "National Mythologies and Ethnic Cleansing: The Expulsion of Czechoslovak Germans after 1945," *Central European History* 33, no. 4 (2000): 463–86.

64. It might be useful to ask if the postwar politics of ethnic cleansing in Europe fits the description of "differentialist racism," which Etienne Balibar defines as one "whose dominant theme is not biological heredity but the insurmountability of cultural differences, a racism which, at first sight, does not postulate the superiority of certain groups or peoples in relation to others but 'only' the harmfulness of abolishing frontiers, the incompatibility of life-styles and traditions." Etienne Balibar and Immanuel Wallerstein, *Race, Nation, Class,* 21.

65. For the beginnings of a historiography on this question for Poland and eastern Europe, see Gross, *Fear;* Robert Blobaum, ed., *Antisemitism and Its Opponents in Modern Poland* (Ithaca: Cornell University Press, 2005); Timothy Snyder, *The Reconstruction of Nations: Poland, Ukraine, Lithuania, Belarus, 1569–1999* (New Haven: Yale University Press, 2003); and Omer Bartov, *Erased: Vanishing Traces of Jewish Galicia in Present-Day Ukraine* (Princeton: Princeton University Press, 2007). Padraic Kenney discusses the first two of these books in an illuminating overview of recent historiography on modern Poland, "After the Blank Spots are Filled: Recent Perspectives on Modern Poland" in *Journal of Modern History* 79 (March 2007): 134–61. In his essay Kenney observes how the writing of Polish history remains grounded in unexamined ethnic identification. While historiography on Poland is increasingly concerned with issues of difference and nation over the longue durée—see, for example, the recent book by Joanna Beata Michlic, *Poland's Threatening Other: The Image of the Jew from 1880 to the Present* (Lincoln: University of Nebraska Press, 2006)—it still lacks a systematic focus on ethnicization/racialization as a broader social and cultural process after 1945. On the expulsion of ethnic Germans from central and eastern Europe and the Yugoslav wars, see Norman Naimark, *Fires of Hatred: Ethnic Cleansing in Twentieth-Century Europe* (Cambridge: Harvard University Press, 2001). Also Peter Gatrell, "Introduction: World Wars and Population Displacement in Europe in the Twentieth Century," and Gatrell, "Displacing and Re-Placing Population in the Two World Wars: Armenia and Poland Compared," in *Contemporary European History* 16, no. 4 (2007): 415–26, 511–27.

66. Heide Fehrenbach, "War Orphans and Postfascist Families: Kinship and Belonging after 1945," in Frank Biess and Robert Moeller, eds., *Histories of the Aftermath: The Legacies of World War II in Comparative European Perspective* (New York: Berghahn Books, forthcoming 2009). Also Kjersti Ericsson and Eva Simonsen, eds., *Children of World War II: The Hidden Enemy Legacy* (New York: Berg, 2005); Diane L. Wolf, *Beyond Anne Frank: Hidden Children and Postwar Families in Holland* (Berkeley: University of California Press, 2007); and Tara Zahra, "Lost Children: Displaced Families and the Rehabilitation of Postwar Europe," in *Journal of Modern History* 81, no. 1 (March 2009).

67. Examples of recent scholarship are Kathleen Paul, *Whitewashing Britain: Race and Citizenship in the Postwar Era* (Ithaca: Cornell University Press, 1997); Alec G. Hargreaves and Mark McKinney, eds., *Post-Colonial Cultures in France* (New York: Routledge, 1997); Maud S. Mandel, *In the Aftermath of Genocide: Armenians and Jews in Twentieth Century France* (Durham: Duke University Press, 2003); Paul A. Silverstein, *Algeria in France: Transpolitics, Race, and Nation* (Bloomington: Indiana University Press, 2004); Herman Lebovics, *Bringing the*

Empire Back Home: France in the Global Age (Durham: Duke University Press, 2004); David Beriss, *Black Skins, French Voices: Caribbean Ethnicity and Activism in Urban France* (Boulder: Westview Press, 2004); Todd Shepard, *The Invention of Decolonization: The Algerian War and the Remaking of France* (Ithaca: Cornell University Press, 2006); Andrea L. Smith, *Colonial Memory and Postcolonial Europe: Maltese Settlers in Algeria and France* (Bloomington: Indiana University Press, 2006).

68. For a useful discussion of the ideological and conceptual problems informing the binary of civic and ethnic nationalism, see Brubaker, *Ethnicity without Groups,* 135ff.; for a discussion that favors a focus on "liberal stateness" to avoid the ethnic/civic dichotomy, see Christian Joppke, *Selecting by Origin: Ethnic Migration in the Liberal State* (Cambridge: Harvard University Press, 2005). For an attempt to retheorize the relationship between East and West Europe, see Attila Melegh, *On the East-West Slope: Globalization, Nationalism, Racism, and Discourses on Central and Eastern Europe* (New York: Central European University Press, 2006).

69. This would encompass, for example, state belonging and citizenship, processes of social and economic integration or segregation, employment and labor practices, immigration and emigration, school, social welfare, family and reproduction policies, and processes of individual and group self-definition.

70. Recent scholarly publications include Steven Vertovec and Ceri Peach, eds., *Islam in Europe: The Politics of Religion and Community,* Migration, Minorities, and Citizenship Series (New York: St. Martin's Press, 1997); Joel S. Fetzer and J. Christopher Soper, eds., *Muslims and the State in Britain, France, and Germany* (New York: Cambridge University Press, 2005); Jonathan Laurence and Justin Vaisse, *Integrating Islam: Political and Religious Challenges in Contemporary France* (Washington, DC: Brookings Institution, 2006).

CHAPTER 1

1. The literature on this subject is vast, though children are rarely its exclusive focus. For these examples, see Michael Burleigh and Wolfgang Wippermann, *The Racial State: Germany, 1933–1945* (New York: Cambridge University Press, 1993); Marion Kaplan, *Beyond Dignity and Despair* (New York: Oxford University Press, 1998); Atina Grossmann, *Reforming Sex: The German Movement for Birth Control and Abortion Reform, 1920–1950* (New York: Oxford University Press, 1995), esp. 136–65. Nazi amendments to adoption law included "Gesetz über Vermittlung der Annahme an Kindesstat vom 19.4.1939," the text of which appeared in *Reichsgesetzblatt I,* 795; commentary on the law can be found in *Deutsche Justiz* (1939): 701. Also "The Law to Change and Supplement the Regulations on Family Relations and to Regulate the Legal Status of Stateless Persons" of 14 April 1938 (*Reichsgesetzblatt* I, 380); and "The Marriage Law of 6 July 1938" (*Reichsgesetzblatt* I, 807). These laws were preceded in the fall of 1935 by the "Law for the Protection of German Blood" that prohibited sexual relations or marriage between "Aryan" Germans and "Jews, Negroes, or Gypsies [Sinti and Roma] or their bastards." See also Michelle Mouton, "Rescuing Children and Policing Families: Adoption Policy in

Weimar and Nazi Germany," *Central European History* 38, no. 4 (December 2005): 545–71.

2. For example, the work of Atina Grossmann, Elizabeth Heinemann, Dagmar Herzog, and Anette Timm. On children as victims, see Debórah Dwork, *Children with a Star: Jewish Youth in Nazi Europe* (New Haven: Yale University Press, 1991); Jane Marks, *The Hidden Children: The Secret Survivors of the Holocaust* (New York: Ballantine Books, 1993); Richard C. Lukas, *Did the Children Cry? Hitler's War against Jewish and Polish Children, 1939–1945* (New York: Hippocrene, 1994); Center for Advanced Holocaust Studies, *Children and the Holocaust: Symposium Presentations* (Washington, DC, 2004); Lynn Nichols, *Cruel World: The Children of Europe in the Nazi Web* (New York: Knopf, 2005); Nicholas Stargardt, *Witnesses of War: Children's Lives Under the Nazis* (New York: Knopf, 2006); as well as memoirs or autobiographies, such as those by Anne Frank and Ruth Kluger.

3. This essay summarizes some of the arguments made in my recent book. For a more expansive analysis of this process, and a detailed discussion of evidence, see Heide Fehrenbach, *Race after Hitler: Black Occupation Children in Postwar Germany and America* (Princeton: Princeton University Press, 2005).

4. Fatima El Tayeb, *Schwarze Deutsche. Der Diskurs um 'Rasse' und nationale Identität* (Frankfurt am Main: Campus, 2001); Lora Wildenthal, "Race, Gender, and Citizenship in the German Colonial Empire," in *Tensions of Empire*, ed. F. Cooper and A. Stoler (Berkeley: University of California Press, 1997). On this shift, Fehrenbach, *Race after Hitler*, chapter 3.

5. Frank Stern, *The Whitewashing of the Yellow Badge: Antisemitism and Philosemitism in Postwar Germany* (New York: Pergamon, 1992).

6. Alexander Perry Biddiscombe, "Dangerous Liaisons: The Anti-fraternization Movement in the U.S. Occupation Zones of Germany and Austria, 1945–1948," in *Journal of Social History* 34, no. 3 (2001): 611–47.

7. The transcript of interviews can be found in the U.S. National Archives, College Park (NACP), RG 107, Civ. Aide to Sec'y. of War, Entry 189, Box 265, Technical Intelligence Reports. See also Walter White, *A Rising Wind* (Garden City, NY: Doubleday, 1945), for descriptions of white violence toward black GIs in wartime Europe and the U.K; and E. T. Hall, Jr., "Race Prejudice and Negro-White Relations in the Army," *American Journal of Sociology* 52, no. 5 (March 1947): 401–9. For a discussion of interracial tensions between U.S. servicemen in 1950s West Germany, see Maria Höhn, *GIs and Fräuleins: The German-American Encounter in 1950s West Germany* (Chapel Hill: University of North Carolina Press, 2002), 95–108; Johannes Kleinschmidt, "Besatzer und Deutsche. Schwarze GIs nach 1945," *Amerika Studien* 40, no. 4 (1995): 646–65; Biddiscombe, "Dangerous Liaisons"; Timothy L. Schroer, *Recasting Race after World War II: Germans and African Americans in American-Occupied Germany* (Boulder: University of Colorado Press, 2007).

8. See Fehrenbach, *Race after Hitler*, chapter 1.

9. Anette F. Timm, "Sex with a Purpose," *Journal of the History of Sexuality* 11, no. 1–2 (2002): 223–55.

10. The girl's youth worker from the prewar period reportedly intervened to pre-

vent the girl from being shipped to the eastern front and prostituted against her will. See Archiv des Diakonischen Werkes der Evangelische Kirche Deutschlands [ADW], HGSt 1161, letter of Frl. Bäcker to Schwester Elisabeth Müller, 19 July 1952.

11. This phrase is borrowed from Dagmar Herzog, "Hubris and Hyprocrisy, Incitement and Disavowal: Sexuality and German Fascism," *Journal of the History of Sexuality* 11, no. 1–2 (2002): 9; Regina Mühlhäuser, "Between Extermination and Germanization: Children of German Men in the 'Occupied Eastern Territories,' 1942–1945," in Kjersti Ericsson and Eva Simonsen, eds., *Children of World War II: The Hidden Enemy Legacy* (New York: Berg, 2005), 167–89.

12. Timm, "Sex with a Purpose," 246; special double issue, "Sexuality and German Fascism," ed. Dagmar Herzog, *Journal of the History of Sexuality* 11, no. 1–2 (January–April 2002), particularly the essays by Herzog, Timm, Szobar, and Kundrus. Also Gabriele Czarnowski, "Hereditary and Racial Welfare (*Erb- und Rassenpflege*): The Politics of Sexuality and Reproduction in Nazi Germany," *Social Politics* (Spring 1997): 114–35.

13. Not all sexual contact between the "liberators and liberated" was elective. For a discussion of the social experience and national mythology of rape in and after 1945, see Atina Grossmann, "A Question of Silence: The Rape of German Women by Occupation Soldiers," in *October* 72 (1995): 43–63; Norman Naimark, *The Russians in Germany* (Cambridge, MA: Harvard University Press, 1995); Atina Grossmann, "Victims, Villains, and Survivors," *Journal of the History of Sexuality* 11, no. 1–2 (2002): 306–7; Marlene Epp, "The Memory of Violence," *Journal of Women's History* 9, no. 1 (1997): 58–87; Robert G. Moeller, *War Stories: The Search for a Usable Past in the Federal Republic of Germany* (Berkeley: University of California Press, 2000), 51–87; Ingrid Schmidt-Harzbach, "Eine Woche im April: Berlin 1945—Vergewaltigung als Massenschicksal," *Feministische Studien* 2 (1984): 51–65; Annemarie Tröger, "Between Rape and Prostitution," in *Women in Culture and Politics*, ed. J. Friedlander et al., 97–117 (Bloomington: Indiana University Press, 1986); Special issue of *October* 72 (Spring 1995), "Berlin 1945: War and Rape. Liberators Take Liberties," especially the essays by Helke Sander, Gertrud Koch, and Atina Grossmann; Elizabeth Heinemann, "The 'Hour of the Woman'" in *American Historical Review* 101 (1996). On rape by black soldiers, see Fehrenbach, *Race after Hitler*, chap. 2, and the somewhat problematic study by J. Robert Lilly, *Taken By Force: Rape and American GIs in Europe during World War II* (New York: Palgrave Macmillan, 2007).

14. Grossmann, *Reforming Sex*, 150–52, and in general chapter 6. Also Gisela Bock, "Antinatalism, Maternity, and Paternity" in David Crew, ed., *Nazism and German Society* (New York: Routledge, 1993); Gabriele Czarnowski, "Frauen als Mütter der Rasse'. Abtreibungsverfolgung und Zwangssterilisation im Nationalsozialismus," in Gisela Staupe and Lisa Vieth, eds., *Unter anderen Umständen. Zur Geschichte der Abtreibung* (Dresden, 1993).

15. Grossmann, *Reforming Sex*, 193, also 153. Kirsten Poutrus, "Von den Massenvergewaltigungen zum Mutterschutzgesetz. Abtreibungspolitik und Abtreibungspraxis in Ostdeutschland, 1945–1950," *Die Grenzen der Diktatur. Staat und Gesellschaft in der DDR*, ed. Richard Bessel and Ralph Jessen (Göttingen: Vandenhoeck und Ruprecht, 1996), 170–98; and Grossmann, "A Question of Silence," 56.

16. Staatsarchiv Augsburg, Nr. 30: Gesundheitsamt Sonthofen, Memo from the Bürgermeister des Marktes Sonthofen, regarding "Schwangerschaftsunterbrechung," 7 June 1945. Also Staatsarchiv Augsburg, Nr. 30: Gesundheitsamt Sonthofen, Memo of Reichsministerium des Innern, "Unterbrechung von Schwangerschaften," 14 March 1945.

17. Estimates range from 350,000 to one million in a German population of 64.5 million. Poutrus, "Von den Massenvergewaltigungen zum Mutterschutzgesetz," 193, 178–80.

18. On antinatalism in the Third Reich, see Gisela Bock and Charles Johnson, ed., *Rassenpolitik und Geschlechterpolitik in Nationalsozialismus* (Göttingen: Vandenhoeck und Ruprecht, 1993); Grossmann, *Reforming Sex,* 194–95; Timm, "The Legacy of *Bevölkerungspolitik*"; and Fehrenbach, *Race after Hitler,* chapter 2.

19. Grossmann, *Reforming Sex,* chapter 8; Poutrus, "Von den Massenvergewaltigungen."

20. Staatsarchiv Augsburg, Nr. 30, Gesundheitsamt Sonthofen; Nr. 19, Gesundheitsamt Neuburg; and VA Lindau 1946: Einzelfälle.

21. Ibid.

22. For an expanded discussion, see Fehrenbach, *Race after Hitler,* chapter 2. Staatsarchiv Augsburg, Nr. 30: Gesundheitsamt Sonthofen, applications for abortions, 1945–46; and Gesundheitsamt (GA), Nr. 19: Neuburg. Also NACP, OMGUS, Executive Office, Office of the Adjutant General, General Correspondence, Box 43, File: Incidents-American. On *"Amiliebchen"* and *"Negerliebchen,"* see Heinemann, "The Hour of the Woman," and Höhn, *GIs and Fräuleins.* On the issue of rape, see Naimark, *Russians in Germany;* Atina Grossmann, "A Question of Silence"; and Lilly, *Taken By Force.*

23. Staatsarchiv Augsburg, VA Lindau, 1946, Einzelfälle. Also Luise Frankenstein, *Soldatenkinder. Die uneheliche Kinder ausländischer Soldaten mit besonderer Berücksichtigung der Mischlinge* (Munich: W. Steinebach, 1954), 29.

24. Frankenstein, *Soldatenkinder,* 16–19, 23–24; Höhn, *GIs and Fräuleins.* Fehrenbach, *Race after Hitler,* chaps. 1–2.

25. NACP, RG 306, USIA, Research Reports on German Public Opinion, Box 9, Report C-1 "Assessment of Troop-Community Relations," 30–32; Vernon W. Stone, "German Baby Crop Left by Negro GIs," *Survey* 85 (November 1949): 579–83; Frankenstein, *Soldatenkinder,* 23. Also Hermann Ebeling, "Zum Problem der deutschen Mischlingskinder," *Bild und Erziehung* 7, no. 10 (1954): 612–30; Rudolf Sieg, "Mischlingskinder in Westdeutschland," *Beiträge zur Anthropologie* 4 (1955): 9–79; Gustav von Mann, "Zum Problem der farbigen Mischlingskinder in Deutschland," *Jugendwohl* 36, no. 1 (January 1955): 50–53; Hans Pfaffenberger, "Zur Situation der Mischlingskinder," *Unsere Jugend* 8, no. 2 (1956): 64–71; Herbert Hurka, "Die Mischlingskinder in Deutschland," *Jugendwohl* 6 (1956): 257–75.

26. Stadtarchiv Nürnberg, C88/I Pflegeamt/Allgemeine Akten 1908–1993, Nr. 5, 7, 13. Also Schroer, *Recasting Race.*

27. After 1949, with the founding of the West German state, German officials unsuccessfully pursued child support by American soldiers for out-of-wedlock "occupation children." American authorities refused to permit U.S. soldiers to appear before German courts. When German women attempted to press paternity suits,

soldiers were suddenly shipped back to the United States. Although cast as economic grievances, official German pursuit of child support by American soldiers also represented an attempt to rein in the underregulated social and sexual behavior of foreign troops on German soil, subject them to German law and custom, and reestablish the prerogatives of native German men in domestic public and private life.

28. NARA-CP, OMGUS, Circular 181. For small sample numbers of marriage applications by African American GIs and German women, see Vernon W. Stone, "German Baby Crop Left by Negro GIs," in *Survey* (November 1949): 579–83, and Luise Frankenstein, *Soldatenkinder.*

29. For a full discussion of these issues, see Fehrenbach, *Race after Hitler,* chapter 3.

30. Rogers Brubaker, *Citizenship and Nationhood in France and Germany* (Cambridge: Harvard University Press, 1992). For discussion of pre-1933 racial science and notions of race, see P. Weingart, J. Kroll, and K. Bayertz, *Rasse, Blut und Gene. Geschichte der Eugenik und Rassenhygiene in Deutschland* (Frankfurt am Main: Suhrkamp, 1992), and El-Tayeb, *Schwarze Deutsche.* For an instructive discussion of racial studies during World War I, see Andrew D. Evans, "Anthropology at War: Race Studies of POWs during World War I," in H. Glenn Penny and Matti Bunzl, eds., *Worldly Provincialism: German Anthropology in the Age of Empire* (Ann Arbor: University of Michigan Press, 2003), 198–229. Also Gerhard Hirschfeld, "Nazi Germany and Eastern Europe," and Michael Müller, "Poland and Germany from the Interwar Period through to the Time of *Détente,*" in Eduard Mühle, ed., *Germany and the European East in the Twentieth Century* (New York: Berg, 2003), 67–90, 91–106, respectively; also Elizabeth Harvey, *Women in the Nazi East: Agents and Witnesses of Germanization* (New Haven: Yale University Press, 2003).

31. Statistisches Bundesamt/Wiesbaden, "Statistische Berichte: Die unehelichen Kinder von Besatzungsangehörigen im Bundesgebiet und Berlin (West)" Arb.-Nr. VI/29/6, 10 October 1956.

32. Walter Kirchner, "Eine anthropologische Studie an Mulattenkinder in Berlin unter Berücksichtigung der soziale Verhältnisse (doctoral diss., Free University Berlin, 1952), 10, 49; Rudolf Sieg, "Mischlingskinder in Westdeutschland. Eine Anthropologische Studie an farbigen Kinder," *Beitrage zur Anthropologie* 4 (1955), 10–11. Sieg received permission from the Central-Ausschuss für die Innere Mission and from the Caritas Verband to conduct his examination of *Mischlingskinder* in their orphanages (Kinderheime) located in the regions of Bremen/Bremerhaven, Heidelberg/Mannheim, Kaiserlautern, Mainz/Wiesbaden, Nuremberg, and Stuttgart (16). For a compatible analysis, see Tina Campt and Pascal Grosse, "'Mischlingskinder' in Nachkriegdeutschland: Zum Verhältnis von Psychologie, Anthropologie und Gesellschaftpolitik nach 1945," *Psychologie und Geschichte* 6, no. 1–2 (1994): 48–78.

33. Carola Sachse and Benoit Massin, *Biowissenschaftliche Forschung an Kaiser-Wilhelm-Instituten und die Verbrechen des NS-Regimes. Informationen über den Gegenwärtigen Wissenstand* (Berlin, 2000); Fatima El-Tayeb, *Schwarze Deutsche;* Reiner Pommerin, *"Sterilisierung der Rheinlandbastarde." Das Schicksal einer farbigen deutschen Minderheit 1918–1937* (Düsseldorf: Droste, 1979).

34. In total, 4,776 "children of colored paternity" were recorded in the 1955 census. Of these, the most resided in Bavaria (1,681), Baden-Württemberg (1,346), Hesse (881), and Rheinland-Pfalz (488). The balance were scattered among Nordrhein-Westfalen (151), Bremen (95), [West] Berlin (72), Lower Saxony (51), Hamburg (10), and Schleswig-Holstein (1). Statistisches Bundesamt, "Statistische Berichte: Die uneheliche Kinder von Besatzungsangehörigen im Bundesgebiet und Berlin (West)," 10 October 1956, 9. These numbers do not include children who had already been adopted abroad by the mid-1950s.

35. Atina Grossmann, "Trauma, Memory, and Motherhood: Germans and Jewish Displaced Persons in Post-Nazi Germany, 1945–1949," *Archiv für Sozialgeschichte* 38 (1998): 215–39; Grossmann, "Victims, Villains, and Survivors"; Yehuda Bauer, *Out of the Ashes* (New York, 1989). On *"Russenkinder"* see W. Karin Hall, "Humanity or Hegemony: Orphans, Abandoned Children, and the Sovietization of the Youth Welfare System in Mecklenburg, Germany, 1945–1952" (doctoral diss., Stanford University, 1998), 146–61.

36. As Atina Grossmann notes, however, demographer and population policy expert Hans Harmsen (whose career spanned the Weimar, Nazi, and postwar years) commissioned a "social hygiene research report" on the so-called hard core of Jews still resident in the Föhrenwald DP camp in 1957, several years after the administration of the DP camps had passed into official West German hands. It is worth noting, however, that the study targeted adults and was based on a total of 100 questionnaires, interviews, and home visits; unlike Black German children, the subjects voluntarily participated in the study and were not subjected to physical-anthropological or psychological testing. See chapter 2 in this volume.

37. Walter Kirchner, "Eine anthropologische Studie an Mulattenkindern in Berlin under Berücksichtigung der sozialen Verhältnisse" (phil. diss., Freie Universität, 1952), 12, 35; also Rudolf Sieg, *Mischlingskinder in Westdeutschland. Festschrift für Frederic Falkenburger* (Baden-Baden, 1955), 27.

38. Kirchner, "Eine anthropologische Studie," 40–49; Sieg, *Mischlingskinder,* 25–62. It bears noting that these same attributes were mentioned in 1954–55 school reports on the children that were ordered by the federal Ministry of the Interior.

39. Kirchner, "Eine anthropologische Studie," 61, 35; Sieg, *Mischlingskinder,* 65, emphasis added.

40. Arguing that the "psychical" legacy of racial inheritance need not be an insurmountable burden, Kirchner concluded by urging that "everything possible be done" to improve the living conditions of the children. Kirchner, "Eine anthropologische Studie," 62.

41. I am not addressing popular attitudes in this argument. For a discussion of these issues at the grassroots level see, for example, Werner Bergmann and Rainer Erb, *Anti-Semitism in Germany: The Post-Nazi Epoch since 1945,* trans. Belinda Cooper and Allison Brown (New Brunswick, NJ: Transaction, 1997); Stern, *Whitewashing of the Yellow Badge;* Julius H. Schoeps, ed., *Leben im Land der Täter: Juden im Nachkriegsdeutschland* (Berlin: Jüdische Verlagsanstalt, 2001); Wolfgang Benz, *Feindbild und Vorurteil* (Munich, 1996); Höhn, *GIs and Fräuleins.*

42. On shifts in U.S. understandings of race, see Matthew Frye Jacobsen, *Whiteness of a Different Color: European Immigrants and the Alchemy of Race*

(Cambridge, MA: Harvard University Press, 1999); Matthew Pratt Guterl, *The Color of Race in America, 1900–1940* (Cambridge, MA: Harvard University Press, 2001); and Eric Goldstein, *The Price of Whiteness: Jews, Race, and American Identity* (Princeton: Princeton University Press, 2006).

43. Frank Stern, "Deutsch-Jüdisches Neubeginnen nach 1945? Ein Rückblick auf die Gründung der Gesellschaften für Christlich-Jüdisches Zusammenarbeit," in *Journal Geschichte* 6 (1989); Josef Foschepoth, *Im Schatten der Vergangenheit. Die Anfänge der Gesellschaft für Christlich-Jüdische Zusammenarbeit* (Göttingen, 1993), 155–203.

44. The boy's name has been changed to protect his identity. Stadtarchiv Nürnberg, C25/I, F Reg: Gesamtbestand Sozialamt, Nr. 489. Memo from Frau Dr. Struve to the Landesfürsorgeverband Mittelfranken, 23 March 1955. Also Stadtarchiv Nürnberg, C33/V: Adoptionsakten.

45. Percentages on Bavarian schoolchildren come from Stadtarchiv Nürnberg, C24 Amt für Volksschulung und Schulverwaltungsamt 1821–1986, Nr. 723, 724. Ulrich Herbert, *A History of Foreign Labor in Germany, 1880–1980,* trans. W. Templer (Ann Arbor, 1990), 195.

46. Staatsarchiv Freiburg, F110/1, Nr. 176: Oberschulamt Freiburg; Bayrisches Hauptstaatsarchiv [HStA], MK 62245, Memo from Ständige Konferenz der Kultusminister, Bonn, 27 February 1956, summarizing report results from the Länder.

47. Coverage in the *Chicago Defender* and Baltimore *Afro-American* began in 1947; by 1948 the *Pittsburgh Courier* also ran stories on so-called brown babies in Germany, as did *Ebony* by the turn of the 1950s.

48. In part the origin of this social imaginary was the popular West German film *Toxi* (a top-ten box office hit in 1952) that scripted the general fate of black occupation children as abandoned, unwanted, and institutionalized. See Fehrenbach, *Race after Hitler,* chap. 4, for a discussion of this movie and its broader impact.

49. Edmund C. Jann, "The Law of Adoption in Germany," Typescript, Library of Congress, Law Library, Foreign Law Section (Washington, DC, 1955). Nazi amendments included "Gesetz über Vermittlung der Annahme an Kindesstat vom 19.4.1939," the text of which appeared in *Reichsgesetzblatt I,* 795; commentary on the law can be found in *Deutsche Justiz* (1939): 701. Also "The Law to Change and Supplement the Regulations on Family Relations and to Regulate the Legal Status of Stateless Persons" of 14 April 1938 (*Reichsgesetzblatt* I, 380); and "The Marriage Law of 6 July 1938" (*Reichsgesetzblatt* I, 807). These laws were preceded in the fall of 1935 by the "Law for the Protection of German Blood" that prohibited sexual relations or marriage between "Aryan" Germans and "Jews, Negroes, or Gypsies [Sinti and Roma] or their bastards." For an English overview of German legislation on adoption through the early postwar period, see Jann, "Law."

50. The Americans did allow adoptive parents or children to petition for the reinstatement of adoptions that were terminated against their will by German authorities between 1933 and 1945. Jann, "Law," 4; Helmut Glässing, *Voraussetzungen der Adoption* (Frankfurt am Main: Alfred Metzner Verlag, 1957). On the U.S. response, ADW, CAW 843. On American adoption practices, see E. Wayne Carp, ed., *Adoption in America: Historical Perspectives* (Ann Arbor: University of Michigan

Press, 2004), and Barbara Melosh, *Strangers and Kin: The American Way of Adoption* (Cambridge, MA: Harvard University Press, 2002).

51. In 1948 Bavaria, for example, the justification for the amendment of the state adoption law invoked the "great losses of many families due to the war and the availability of a huge number of orphans," arguing: "It is also especially important to think such cases in which people, married with children, desire to adopt children of relatives, friends, or neighbors, above all from the eastern regions [of the former German empire (Ostgebieten)] whose parents were killed in the war or its aftermath. Often it is the illegitimate child of a fallen son one wants to adopt." Bayerisches Hauptstaatsarchiv (BHStA), Staatskanzlei (StK) 130324. "Rechtsausschuss, Antrag aus der Ausschusssitzung vom 5. November 1948." In August 1950, a temporary modification of the adoption law was passed by the Bundestag ("Gesetz zur Erleichterung der Annahme an Kindes Statt") to allow German families with children to adopt. This law was renewed in 1952 to extend to 1955. ADW, CAW 843, Deutscher Bundestag, 1. Wahlperiode 1949, Drucksache Nr. 3931.

52. Bundesarchiv Koblenz [BAK], B153/342, "Vermerk" to Dr. Rothe, 25 May 1951.

53. Yara-Colette Lemke Muniz de Faria mentions these initiatives in *Zwischen Fürsorge und Ausgrenzung* (Berlin: Metropol, 2002), 102–3.

54. Meeting of the Committee to consider . . . the Immigration of . . . German orphans of Negro Blood, 29 Jan 1951. NAACP papers, Reel 8: Group II, Box G11, "Brown Babies, 1950–58."

55. Walter White press release, 18 September 1952. NAACP, Reel 8: Group II, Box G11 "Brown Babies 1950–58."

56. For a detailed discussion of Mabel Grammer's activities, the response of the International Social Service, and the shifting policy of West Germans, see Fehrenbach, *Race after Hitler,* chapter 5, and Lemke Muniz de Faria, *Zwischen Fürsorge und Ausgrenzung.*

57. Heinrich Webler, "Adoptions-Markt" in *Zentralblatt für Jugendrecht und Jugendwohl* 42, no. 5 (May 1955): 123–24. Also BAK, B153: Bundesministerium für Familien- und Jugendfragen, File 1335, I–II: "Material über Probleme des Internationalen Adoptionsrechts"; Hauptstaatsarchiv Stuttgart, Akten des Innenministeriums, EA2/007: Vermittlung der Annahme an Kindesstatt, Band II, 1955–66; and Franz Klein, "Kinderhandel als strafbare Handlung," in *Jugendwohl,* Heft 3 (1956): 95. ADW, HGST 1161, "Kurzbericht über die Sitzung . . . dem 12. Juli 1955 im Bundesministerium des Innern; Bayerisches Hauptstaatsarchiv, MInn 81906.

58. ADW, HGSt 3949, Auszug aus dem Bericht über die Tätigkeit der Adoptionszentrale für den Verwendungsnachweise, Zuschuss 1961 and 1963.

59. BAK, B153: Bundesministerium für Familien- und Jugendfragen, File 1335, I–II: "Material über Probleme des Internationalen Adoptionsrechts." HStAStg, Akten des Innenministeriums, EA2/007: Vermittlung der Annahme an Kindesstatt, Band II, 1955–66; Heinrich Webler, "Adoptions-Markt," in *Zentralblatt für Jugendrecht und Jugendwohl* 42, no. 5 (May 1955): 123–24; Franz Klein, "Zur gegenwärtige Situation der Auslandsadoption," *Unsere Jugend* 9 (1955): 401–8; Franz Klein, "Kinderhandel als strafbare Handlung," 95.

60. ADW, HGst 3949. Also BAK, B189/6858: File: Besatzungs- und Mischlingskinder—Allgemein.

61. Klaus Eyferth, "Das Problem der deutschen Mischlingskind"; and Klaus Eyferth, Ursula Brandt, and Wolfgang Hawel, *Farbige Kinder in Deutschland* (Munich, 1960).

62. Eyferth remained the exception to this trend. BAK, B149: Bundesministerium für Arbeit und Sozialordnung, no. 8679; BayHStA, MInn 81126, press clippings on "Mischlingskinder," 1960–61; BayHStA, MK62245, "Volksschulwesen Negerkinder"; Hessisches Hauptstaatsarchiv, Abt. 940/77; Elly Waltz, "Mischlinge werden jetzt Lehrlinge," *Münchner Merkur* 164 (9–10 July 1960); "Farbige Lehrlinge—wieder sehr gefragt," in *Münchner Merkur* 63 (15 March 1961); and Klaus Eyferth, "Gedanken über die zukünftige Berufseingliederung der Mischlingskinder in Westdeutschland," in *Neues Beginnen* 5 (May 1959), 65–68.

63. "Wiedersehen macht Freude," *Quick* (28 April 1963): 38; "Toxi: Alle Menschen sind nett zu mir," c. 1964, no periodical title given, photo essay filed in Stiftung Deutsche Kinemathek, Berlin, Nachlass R. A. Stemmle; "Die 'Toxis' since erwachsen—und haben Heiratssorgen," *Welt am Sonntag* (26 March 1967), 6; Ruth Bahn-Flessburg, "Sie haben die gleichen Chancen wie die Weissen: Auf der Suche nach den farbigen Besatzungskindern," *Unsere Jugend* 20 (1968): 295–303; and Ruth Bahn-Flessburg, "Die Hautfarbe ist kein Problem: Farbige 'Besatzungskinder'—Vierzehn Lebensläufe," *Frankfurter Allgemeine Zeitung* (1968, filed in ADW, HGSt 3949 295–303); "Adam und Eva: Ein Mädchen wie Toxi fand sein Glück an der Elbe," *Neue illustrierte Revue* 7 (10 February 1975), 47–50; "Die Deutschen mit der dunkler Haut," *Quick* 46 (3–9 November 1977): 82–89. A couple of serialized novels featuring black German teenaged girls were also published in West German magazines in the early 1960s. See Ursula Schaake, *"Meine schwarze Schwester,"* *Revue* no. 42 (Weihnachten 1960) through no. 15 (9 April 1961); Stefan Doerner, *"Mach mich weiss, Mutti!"* *Quick* 16, no. 17 (28 April 1963) through no. 27 (7 July 1963). For an early study of representations of Blacks in the West German press, see Rosemarie K. Lester, *Trivialneger. Das Bild des Schwarzen im westdeutschen Illustriertenroman* (Stuttgart: Akademischer Verlag H.-D Heinz, 1982).

64. "Lehrlinge mit dunkler Haut," *Frankfurter Allgemeine Zeitung* (12 August 1961), clipping in ADW, HGSt 3949.

65. For example, "Adam und Eva: Ein Mädchen wie Toxi fand sein Glück an der Elbe," *Neue illustrierte Revue* 7 (10 February 1975), 47–50; see also my analysis in Fehrenbach, *Race after Hitler*, 176–79.

66. Rainer Werner Fassbinder's film *Ali: Fear Eats the Soul,* released in 1974, was a provocative exception and certainly not widely seen in Germany at the time.

67. In a somewhat surprising omission, Dagmar Herzog does not discuss interracial sex and its social, political, or symbolic significance in post-1945 Germany in her recent book, *Sex after Fascism: Memory and Morality in Twentieth-Century Germany* (Princeton: Princeton University Press, 2005). On the New Left's use of exoticized black bodies in political representation, see Quinn Slobodian, "Radical Empathy: Third World Politics in 1960s West Germany" (Ph.D. diss., New York University, 2008).

68. "Adam und Eva," 47–48; also Bahn-Flessburg, "Die Hautfarbe."

69. This last example is from a personal acquaintance. See also Karen Thimm and DuRell Echols, *Schwarze in Deutschland* (Munich: Protokolle, 1973); Gisela Fremgen, . . . *und wenn du dazu noch Schwarz bist. Berichte schwarzer Frauen in der Bundesrepublik* (Bremen: Edition CON, 1984); May Opitz (Ayim), Katharina Oguntoye, and Dagmar Schultz, eds., *Showing Our Colors: Afro-German Women Speak Out,* trans. Anne V. Adams (Amherst, MA: University of Massachusetts Press, 1992); and Ika Hügel-Marshall, *Daheim unterwegs. Ein deutsches Leben* (Berlin, 1998), and English translation, Ika Hügel-Marshall, *Invisible Woman: Growing Up Black in Germany,* trans. Elizabeth Gaffney (New York: Continuum, 2001).

70. Audre Lorde, "Foreword to the English Language Edition," Opitz (Ayim), Oguntoye, and Schultz, eds., *Showing Our Colors,* vii–viii. Originally published in German as *Farbe bekennen. Afro-deutsche Frauen auf den Spuren ihrer Geschichte* (Berlin: Orlanda, 1986).

71. *Farbe Bekennen*'s 1986 publication in the Federal Republic postdated two other volumes that have not been given as much critical attention. These are Thimm and Echols, *Schwarze in Deutschland,* and Fremgen, . . . *und wenn du dazu noch Schwarz bist.*

72. The publication of *Farbe Bekennen* has been recognized as a milestone since it helped stimulate the creation of a national movement committed to the empowerment and political solidarity of Black Germans. This has been accomplished, with some degree of success, through the creation of organizations such as *Initiative Schwarze Deutsche* (ISD) in 1985 and *Afro-deutsche Frauen* (ADeFra) in 1986; by founding black German publications (such as *afro-look, Afrakete,* and *Afro-Courier*); and by sponsoring a German Black History month (after the American model) and annual Bundestreffen, or nationwide conferences of Black Germans.

Farbe Bekennen appeared in English translation as *Showing Our Colors: Afro-German Women Speak Out.* The following discussion is based upon *Showing Our Colors;* Tina Campt, "Afro-German Cultural Identity and the Politics of Positionality: Contests and Contexts in the Formation of a German Ethnic Identity," *New German Critique* 58 (Winter 1993): 109–26; "Special Issue on the Black German Experience," *Callaloo* 26, no. 2 (2003); Erin Crawley, "Rethinking Germanness: Two Afro-German Women Journey Home" in K. Jankowsky and C. Love, eds., *Other Germanies* (Albany, 1997), 75–95; Leroy Hopkins, Jr., ed., *Who Is German? Historical and Modern Perspectives on Africans in Germany,* Harry and Helen Gray Humanities Program Series, vol. 5 (Washington, DC, 1999). See also Patricia Mazón and Reinhild Steingröver, *Not So Plain as Black and White: Afro-German History and Culture from 1890–2000* (Rochester: University of Rochester Press, 2005).

73. For example, Karen Thimm and DuRell Echols, *Schwarze in Deutschland* (Munich, 1973); Katharina Oguntoya, "Die Schwarze deutsche Bewegung und die Frauenbewegung in Deutschland," *Afrekete: Zeitung von afro-deutschen und Schwarzen Frauen* 4 (1989): 3–5, 33–37; Opitz et al., *Showing Our Colors;* Campt, "Afro-German Cultural Identity"; and May Ayim, "Die afro-deutsche Minderheit," *Ethnische Minderheiten in der Bundesrepublik Deutschland,* ed. Cornelia Schmalz-Jacobsen and Georg Hansen (Munich: Beck, 1995).

74. Paul Gilroy and Stuart Hall have been influential voices on Blacks and Blackness in a European context; see Geoff Eley's essay in this volume. For a biographical portrait of one Black German woman who decides to see her extended family, see the 1995 ZDF production *Ich wollte immer blond sein auf der Haut.*

75. BayHStA, MInn 81094, "Mischlingskinder," 1960–61.

76. See Chapters 3 and 4.

77. Campt, "Afro-German Cultural Identity"; Special Issue on the Black German Experience, *Callaloo* 26, no. 2 (2003); Francine Jobatey, *"Afro-Look:* Die Geschichte einer Zeitschrift von Schwarzen Deutschen" (doctoral diss., University of Massachusetts, 2000).

CHAPTER 2

1. Statistical data is inexact and bewildering, largely because of changes over time, inconsistencies in categorizations among those collecting data, and the difficulties of counting a highly mobile and sometimes illegal population. Most sources now agree that by spring 1947, the Jewish DP population in Germany was approximately 200,000, but that "some 300,000 Jewish DPs and refugees are believed to have passed through Austria and/or Germany for longer or shorter periods of time." The higher figures for 1946 and 1947 include the influx into the American zone of mostly Polish Jews who had been repatriated from the Soviet Union, and a later wave in 1947 from Czechoslovakia, Hungary, and Romania. For discussion of the confusing statistics, see Atina Grossmann, *Jews, Germans, and Allies: Close Encounters in Occupied Germany* (Princeton: Princeton University Press, 2007), especially 131–32. Much of this article draws directly on my discussion in the concluding chapter 6 of *Jews, Germans, and Allies.*

2. See, for example, Jan T. Gross, *Fear: Anti-Semitism in Poland after Auschwitz, An Essay in Historical Interpretation* (New York: Random House, 2006).

3. On these interactions, see Grossmann, *Jews, Germans, and Allies,* especially chapters 4 and 5.

4. On the biblical references from Genesis, First Chronicles, and Jeremiah driving the use of the term *She'erit Hapletah* (or its spoken Yiddish variant *sheyres hapleyte*) see among many other discussions Zeev W. Mankowitz, *Life between Memory and Hope: The Survivors of the Holocaust in Occupied Germany* (Cambridge: Cambridge University Press, 2002), 2.

5. Taped interview by David P. Boder with Helen Tichauer, Feldafing, Germany, 23 September 1946, USHMMA RG-50.472.

6. Displaced persons (DPs) were defined as all those who had been expelled, deported, or fled as a result of German wartime policies; ethnic Germans who fled or were expelled from the Soviet occupied East were not included. Initially, Jews constituted a small percentage of all DPs, but as repatriations proceeded, they became an increasingly large and visible part of the DP population.

7. On the complexities of the Exodus Affair, in which mostly young Zionist DPs battled British troops in the port of Haifa before being forced to return to

Germany—a Pyrrhic victory for the British who clearly lost the propaganda battle to the Zionists, see Hagit Lavsky, *New Beginnings: Holocaust Survivors in Bergen-Belsen and the British Zone in Germany* (Detroit: Wayne State University Press, 2002), and Arieh J. Kochavi, *Post-Holocaust Politics: Britain, the United States, and Jewish Refugees, 1945–1948* (Chapel Hill: University of North Carolina Press, 2001).

8. Samuel Gringauz, "Our New German Policy and the DPs: Why Immediate Resettlement Is Imperative," *Commentary* 5 (1948): 508, 509; "golden age" comment on 509.

9. Genêt, "Letter from Aschaffenburg, October 20," *New Yorker* (30 October 1948): 98–101. On non-Jewish DPs, see Laura Hilton, "Prisoners of Peace: Rebuilding Community, Identity and Nationality in Displaced Persons Camps in Germany, 1945–52" (Ph.D. diss., Ohio State University, 2001).

10. Hanna Yablonka, *Survivors of the Holocaust: Israel after the War* (London: Macmillan Press, 1999), 142. For an excellent judicious untangling of the many issues involved, including the motivation and agency of the young DPs, see Avinoam Patt "Finding Home and Homeland: Jewish Youth Groups in the Aftermath of the Holocaust" (Ph.D. diss., New York University, 2005, forthcoming Wayne State University Press), especially chapter 5, "Between Hope and Disappointment: Jewish DP Youth and *Aliyah*."

11. Lower numbers from Michael Brenner, entry on DPs, *Encyclopedia of the Holocaust*, 154; higher numbers from Mark Wyman, *DPs: Europe's Displaced Persons, 1945–1951* (Ithaca: Cornell University Press, 1989), 155, 178–204.

12. Brenner, *Encyclopedia of the Holocaust*, 154.

13. U. O. Schmelz, "The Demographic Impact of the Holocaust," in *Terms of Survival: The Jewish World since 1945* (New York: Routledge, 1995), ed. Robert Wistrich, 45. David Weinberg (paper, USHMM DP workshop, July 2005) counters assertions of a "void" in postwar Jewish life by pointing to significant reconstruction and renewal efforts, especially in France and Britain. In 1948 there were about 625,000 Jews left in Eastern Europe outside of the Soviet Union. See Ron Zweig, *German Reparations and the Jewish World: A History of the Claims Conference* (Boulder: Westview Press, 1987), 44.

14. Rebecca Boehling, *A Question of Priorities: Democratic Reform and Economic Recovery in Postwar Germany* (Providence: Berghahn Books, 1996), 7. The State Department, which had been so chary of giving visas to desperate German Jews in the 1930s and had vigorously resisted Morgenthau's plans to fully deindustrialize a defeated Germany, was viewed as being more hostile to Jews than the Military Government had been.

15. Report from William Haber, Adviser on Jewish Affairs in American zone of Germany to Meir Grossman, American Jewish Conference, New York, 10 June 1948, in Abraham J. Peck, ed. *Archives of the Holocaust*, vol. 9 (New York: Garland, 1990), 312, see 319–21.

16. In general see Zweig, *German Reparations*. On the end of denazification, see especially John H. Herz, "The Fiasco of Denazification," *Political Science Quarterly* 62, no. 4 (1948); also Boehling, *A Question of Priorities*. Already in 1948, émigré political scientist John Herz had concluded, "Nothing could be more revealing than the strange modification of meaning that the term 'de-

nazification' itself has undergone. While at first signifying the elimination of Nazis from public life, it has now in German everyday language come to mean the removal of the Nazi stigma from the individual concerned; that is, the procedure by which he gets rid of certain inhibitions or restrictions." Herz, "Fiasco," 590, also cited in Boehling, 239.

17. All quotes from conference entitled "The Future of the Jews in Germany," Heidelberg, 31 July 1949. Minutes edited by Harry Greenstein, Adviser on Jewish Affairs, United States Military Government in Germany dated 1 September 1949. See especially 5–6, 10–14, 19–22, 24, 29, 41, 45–46, 52. A preliminary meeting had taken place in March. See also Jay Geller, *Jews in Post-Holocaust Germany, 1945–1953* (New York: Cambridge University Press, 2005), 72–77, and Michael Brenner, *After the Holocaust: Rebuilding Jewish Lives in Postwar Germany* (Princeton: Princeton University Press, 1997), 74–77.

18. In Berlin with 80 percent of the community German-Jewish, 34 percent were over 55 and only 11 percent under 17; in Frankfurt where only 45 percent were German, 16 percent were 55 and over, 14 percent under 17. See also Eva Kolinsky, *After the Holocaust: Jewish Survivors in Germany after 1945* (London: Pimlico, 2004), 213–15, who claims, 215, that intermarriage rates in cities were up to 75 percent, with only 2 of 10 non-Jewish partners converting.

19. In contrast to McCloy's remarks about the status of Jews as a test of West German "progress," Heide Fehrenbach, *Race after Hitler: Black Occupation Children in Postwar Germany and America* (Princeton: Princeton University Press, 2005), 94, points out that many "liberal" Germans preferred to point to their treatment of "colored" *Mischlinge,* generally the offspring of German women and African American soldiers, as the test of their "social maturity." Her book in general opens up many possible questions about comparisons between postwar West German reactions to Jews and the new racial others, especially African Americans. Geller, *Jews in Post-Holocaust Germany* (which I read after I had completed my own research) also notes McCloy's placing "onus" on Jews. It is worth noting as well that at the same time McCloy was under enormous pressure from German church and political officials to release incarcerated Nazi war criminals. In March 1950 he set up an "Advisory Board on Clemency for War Criminals" which led by 1951 to many releases and reduced punishments. See, for example, Norbert Frei, *Adenauer's Germany and the Nazi Past: The Politics of Amnesty and Integration,* trans. Joel Gold (New York: Columbia University Press, 2002).

20. Ronald Webster, "American Relief and Jews in Germany, 1945–1960," *Leo Baeck Institute Yearbook,* 38, 1993, 293–321, 304, referring to the Joint.

21. On this conflict, see Zweig, *German Reparations,* 57ff.

22. On the history of the Zentralrat, see Harry Maor, "Über den Wiederaufbau der jüdischen Gemeinden in Deutschland Seit 1945" (diss., Mainz, 1961); Geller, *Jews in Post-Holocaust Germany;* and Udi Chadasch, "Der Zentralrat der Juden in Deutschland von seiner Entstehung Bis zum Ende der Adenauer-Ära," master's thesis, Cologne, 1992.

23. Report by Dr. B. Sagalowitz, April 1950, Report on trip to Germany (translated from German original), *Archives of the Holocaust,* vol. 9, 361–62, 368, 377–78. Hannah Arendt made the same observation in 1950, "Germans who confess their

own guilt are in many cases altogether innocent in the ordinary, down-to-earth sense, whereas those who are guilty of something real have the calmest consciences in the world," in "The Aftermath of Nazi Rule: Report from Germany," *Commentary* 10 (October 1950), 348. For a later reflection by someone who had been deeply involved in both DP and restitution matters, see Kurt R. Grossmann, "The Problem of Forgetting: Thoughts on the Nazi War Crimes Trials," *Patterns of Prejudice,* Institute of Jewish Affairs, vol. 2, no. 6 (November–December 1968): 10–16. There is by now a vast literature on this "problem of forgetting"; see especially Robert G. Moeller, *War Stories: The Search for a Usable Past in the Federal Republic of Germany* (Berkeley: University of California Press, 2001), and Frei, *Adenauer's Germany and the Nazi Past.*

24. Despite resentments and tensions, the much more numerous expellees were integrated into the German national community, in ways that Jewish DPs would and could never be. See for example, Perrti Ahonen, *After the Expulsion: West Germany and Eastern Europe, 1945–60* (Oxford: Oxford University Press, 2003).

25. Report of Oscar A. Mintzer, "The Legal Situation of Jewish DPs in the American Zone," Germany. September 23, 1946. AJDC Archives/ 390.

26. Werner Bergmann, "'Der Antisemitismus in Deutschland braucht gar nicht übertrieben zu werden . . . 'Die Jahre 1945–1953," in Julius H. Schoeps, ed. *Leben im Land der Täter: Juden im Nachkriegsdeutschland, 1945–1952* (Berlin: Judische Verlagsanstalt, 2001), 205.

27. Quoted from *Neues Volksblatt,* 13 July 1950. Also from *Fränkischer Tag,* 8 July 1950. The local refugee office (*Flüchtlingsausschuss*) protested housing "foreigners" together with expellees (*Heimatvertriebenen*) "because they are heavily involved in the black market and constitute a moral danger to the [German] refugee youth." See YIVO DPG 294.2/49 MK483/R5. Numerous such press accounts were collected and retyped by the DP organizations, to be used as evidence with both the West German and the American authorities. See Maria Höhn, *GIs and Fräuleins: The German-American Encounter in 1950s West Germany* (Chapel Hill: University of North Carolina Press), for later period.

28. For further discussion of this self-imposed outsider status, see, for example, Y. Michal Bodemann, "Mentalitäten des Verweilens. Der Neubeginn judischen Lebens in Deutschland," in Schoeps, *Leben im Land der Täter,* 15–29.

29. Anthony D. Kauders, *Unmögliche Heimat: Eine deutsch-jüdische Geschichte der Bundesrepublik* (Munich: Deutsche-Verlags-Anstalt, 2007), 28, 33. On philosemitism, see Frank Stern, *The Whitewashing of the Yellow Badge: Antisemitism and Philosemitism in Postwar Germany,* trans. William Templar (Oxford: Pergamon Press, 1992).

30. On shifting the language of "race" from Jews to groups defined by skin color, especially African Americans, see Fehrenbach, *Race after Hitler.* At some points, however, as Kauders has pointed out, the language of "race" was specifically employed as a kind of cover for the direct mention of antisemitism, for example, in general calls for tolerance that preached the rejection of *Rassenhass* (racial hatred) precisely in order to avoid explicit reference to the antisemitism that was in fact at issue. See Kauders, *Unmögliche Heimat,* 29. As the articles in this volume suggest, the complicated intersections and overlappings of discourses around race/racism, antisemitism, and xenophobia in post-Nazi Germany are by no means clear.

31. 31 August 1949, Report from Mr. Harry Greenstein, Adviser on Jewish Af-

fairs to US Commander in Germany on riot of 10 August 1949. AJDC file 499. Here too there are myriad somewhat different versions of the events. See, for example, Norbert Mühlen, *The Return of Germany: A Tale of Two Countries* (Chicago: Henry Regnery, 1953), 163–65; Anthony Kauders, *Democratization and the Jews: Munich, 1945–1965* (Lincoln: University of Nebraska Press, 2004), 139. The *Süddeutsche Zeitung* had a year earlier on 17 April 1948 published an article in its "Debate" section entitled "Antisemitismus-1948" that blamed the "asocial behavior" of the DPs for antisemitism and favorably contrasted the "unobtrusive" profile of remaining German Jews. See also Bergmann, "Der Antisemitismus," 195, and Juliane Wetzel, "Trauma und Tabu, Jüdisches Leben in Deutschland nach dem Holocaust," in Hans-Erich Volkmann, ed., *Ende des Dritten Reiches-Ende des Zweiten Weltkriegs* (Munich: Piper, 1995), 433–44, 454 n. 30.

32. The statistics are inconsistent and confusing. Webster, "American Relief and Jews in Germany," says that in 1953, there were still 30,000 former DPs and their families in the Federal Republic, 309. Brenner in *Encyclopedia of the Holocaust* lists 30,000 in late 1948 and only 12,000 in 1952, 159.

33. See, for example, JDC reports, note 35.

34. Y. Michal Bodemann in *A Jewish Family in Germany Today: An Intimate Portrait* (Durham, NC: Duke University Press, 2005) uses the sociological term *Verweiler*, borrowed from Simmel to categorize this long-term commitment to transience; see Introduction, 1–35, also in Julius Schoeps, ed., *Leben im Land der Täter*, 15–29. Zweig, *Reparations* refers to "sojourners," 58, and "itinerants," 56; Jeffrey Peck and John Borneman titled their book about Jews in postwar Germany *Sojourners: The Return of German Jews and the Question of Identity* (Lincoln, NE: University of Nebraska Press, 1995).

35. JDC Report, 26 January 1949. AJDC file 392. YIVO DPG 294.2/65/MK 483/R6, also 163–66. Also see YIVO 294.2/ 580 and AJDC File 398 on Föhrenwald "hard core."

36. Anthony Kauders, *Democratization and the Jews*, 61–62 n. 28, quoting JDC reports from 1954, 1952, and 1951. By 1950, there are also many reports, similar in language and intent to those dealing with the absent American GI fathers of illegitimate German children, about local welfare agencies' search for Jewish DP fathers and efforts to claim child support. As was the case with the Americans, the DPs had invariably decamped (or were said to have) for Israel or elsewhere, leaving responsibility (*Vormundschaft*) for German women's babies—who, if illegitimate, were automatically German citizens—with the West German state. See examples in YIVO DPG/294.2/559/MK483/R42. On the situation of American "occupation children," see Fehrenbach, *Race after Hitler*, 74ff.

37. Minutes of Administration Committee of Joint Distribution Committee, 3 November 1953. Marked "highly confidential." See also Zweig, *German Reparations*, 124.

38. See among many sources Brenner, *After the Holocaust;* Schoeps, *Leben im Land der Täter;* Kauders, *Democratization and the Jews*.

39. See for example, articles in *Der Weg* (journal of the Berlin Gemeinde) no. 1 (3 January 1947).

40. Memorandum from Oscar Karlbach to Robert S. Marcus, 16 June 1950, in *Archives of the Holocaust* 9, 398–99.

41. Elke Fröhlich, "Philipp Auerbach (1906–1952), 'Generalanwalt für Wiedergutmachung,'" in Manfred Treml and Wolf Weigand, eds., *Geschichte und Kultur der Juden in Bayern: Lebensläufe," Veröffentlichung zur Bayerischen Geschochte und Kultur* 18/88: 315–20; here, 320. This complicated story has not yet been fully told or unraveled. For a judicious analysis, see Constantin Goschler, "The Attitude towards Jews in Bavaria after the Second World War," *Leo Baeck Institute Yearbook* 36 (1991): 443–58; reprint in Robert G. Moeller, ed., *West Germany under Construction: Politics, Society, and Culture in the Adenauer Era* (Ann Arbor: University of Michigan Press, 1997), 231–50; Moeller, "Der Fall Philipp Auerbach, Wiedergutmachung in Bayern," in Ludolf Herbst and Constantin Goschler, eds., *Wiedergutmchung in der Bundesrepublik Deutschland* (Munich, 1989), 77–98. See also among other sources, Wolfgang Kraushaar, "Die Auerbach-Affäre," in Julius H. Schoeps, ed., *Leben im Land der Täter,* 209–18. The tensions around restitution and conflicts with Auerbach were exacerbated by the Nazi past of his German counterpart, Theodor Oberländer, the Bavarian State Secretary for Refugee Affairs. See Zweig, *German Reparations,* 124. Auerbach's papers are now open for researchers in the Bavarian State Archives. The Munich *Landessrabbiner* Aron Ohrenstein, who had been charged along with Auerbach, had made himself particularly unpopular with Jewish organizations not only because he was perceived as corrupt but because he was known for "his willingness to convert Christian women." See Kauders, *Democratization and the Jews,* 141–42, 61–62 n. 28. The accusation of a new Dreyfus case in the Bavarian courts was not new; it had been used in the Weimar Republic; see Douglas Morris, *Justice Imperiled: The Anti-Nazi Lawyer Max Hirschberg in the Weimar Republic* (Ann Arbor: University of Michigan Press, 2005).

42. Haus Habe, *Our Love Affair with Germany* (New York: G. P. Putnam's Sons, 1953), 128. According to Leo W. Schwarz, *The Redeemers: A Saga on the Years 1945–1952* with an introduction by General Lucius D. Clay (New York: Farrar, Strauss, and Young, 1953), 208–11, citing a *New York Times* report of 17 August 1952, John J. McCloy rejected appeals by Auerbach and his friends to move the case from a German to an Allied court.

43. "Our Unfinished Job in Germany," 13 October 1953. A Report by David Rosenstein. JDC File 398.

44. Zweig, *German Reparations,* 124.

45. Eugen Steppan, *Waldram: "Anspruch auf Vergangenheit und Zukunft" Die Geschichte des Wolfratshauser Ortsteiles Waldram,* 1982, 67–68; in Zentral Archiv der deutschen Juden, Heidelberg, file 033.5 (433.6).

46. In 1956, 633 people remained in Föhrenwald; 12 turned the key in February 1957, Webster, "American Relief and Jews in Germany," 292. According to Zweig, most of those who emigrated went to Australia, *German Reparations,* 125. It should be noted that the sensational descriptions from both Germans and Jews of Föhrenwald as a center of crime and asocial behavior contrast to the much more rosy memories of the young Jewish children who grew up and went to school there in the early 1950s. See, for example, contributions by Rahel Salamander and Sam Norich at 1995 DP conference in Munich, a combined scholarly and camp reunion occasion. On Föhrenwald, see especially Angelika Königseder and Juliane Wetzel,

Waiting for Hope: Jewish Displaced Persons in Post–World War II Germany (Evanston: Northwestern University Press, 2001), 148–66 on costs, especially 163–64.

47. For a discussion of Harmsen's long career, see Atina Grossmann, *Reforming Sex: The German Movement for Birth Control and Abortion Reform, 1920–1950* (New York: Oxford University Press, 1995), esp. 204–11.

48. For example, the Historical Commissions set up by survivors in Poland and the DP camps apparently did not collect testimonies about experiences in the Soviet Union. See Laura Jockusch, "Jüdische Geschichtsforschung im Lande Amaleks. Jüdische historische Kommissionen in Deutschland 1945–1949," in Suzanne Schönborn, ed. *Zwischen Erinnerung und Neubeginn: Zur deutsch-jüdischen Geschichte nach 1945* (Munich: Martin Meidenbauer, 2006), 20–41.

49. Johannes Menke, "Die soziale Integration jüdischer Flüchtlinge des ehemaligen Regierungslagers 'Föhrenwald' in den drei Westdeutschen Grossstädten Düsseldorf, Frankfurt und München, Nach im Sommer 1959 (vom 6.8.–25.9) durchgeführten sozialhygienischen Feldstudien über die ehemaligen Lagerinsassen," vol. 2, *Sozialhygienische Forschungen* 2 (Hamburg 1960), ed. Hans Harmsen, esp. 3, 6, 27–29, 59–68. The study was based on 100 completed questionnaires as well as interviews and home visits. It is worth comparing the language and tone of this report to similar ones prepared on the integration of ethnic German refugees from the East and also on the "mixed breed" children of German women and African American GIs. On the latter, especially the "liberal" postwar discourse on race, see Fehrenbach, *Race after Hitler*, 74–106.

50. Harry Maor, "Über den Wiederaufbau der jüdischen Gemeinden," 19. Maor's unfortunately still unpublished thesis remains the best and most comprehensive study of Jewish *Gemeinden* in early postwar Germany. According to his early statistics, in March 1949, Jewish communities in Germany, including the Soviet zone, had 21,645 members; 50.7 percent were German, 49.3 percent DP; without the East, which had admitted no DPs, the balance was 52 percent DP and 48 percent German Jewish. See also Geller, *Jews in Post-Holocaust Germany.*

51. Maor, *Wiederaufbau*, 25ff.

52. Anthony Kauders, *Unmögliche Heimat,* argues strenuously that the strong attachment to Israel, including significant financial support, was driven by a powerful sense of guilt (*Schuld*) among Jews who remained in Germany. See Maor, *Wiederaufbau,* for discussion of the high rate of intermarriage among both East European and German Jews in Germany after the war.

53. See Geller, *Jews in Post-Holocaust Germany,* 78–89.

54. Geller, *Jews in Post-Holocaust Germany,* 2.

55. Maor, *Wiederaufbau,* 32.

56. See Kauders, *Unmögliche Heimat,* 201. On the latest wave of Jewish immigration, see also, among many sources, Jeffrey M. Peck, *Being Jewish in the New Germany* (New Brunswick, NJ, 2006), 40–41. Determining the actual number of Jews living in Germany today is virtually impossible. Official community statistics clearly underestimate the actual population because of numerous factors including its transience and mobility, the reluctance to join "official" congregations that are mostly (but no longer only) orthodox, and most important, the fact that many of

the new arrivals from the former Soviet Union are not considered Jewish in a religious (*Halachic*) sense (generally because their mothers are not recognized as Jewish).

CHAPTER 3

1. For more on Polish workers in Germany during the late nineteenth and early twentieth centuries, see Christoph Kleßmann, *Polnische Bergarbeiter im Ruhrgebiet, 1870–1945* (Göttingen: Vandenhoeck und Ruprecht, 1978); Richard C. Murphy, *Gastarbeiter im Deutschen Reich. Polen in Bottrop, 1891–1933* (Wuppertal: Peter Hammer Verlag, 1982); Ulrich Herbert, *Geschichte der Ausländerbeschäftigung in Deutschland 1880 bis 1980* (Bonn: Verlag J. H. W. Dietz, 1986), trans. by William Templer as *A History of Foreign Labor in Germany, 1880–1980: Seasonal Workers/Forced Laborers/Guest Workers* (Ann Arbor: University of Michigan Press, 1990), especially chapter 1; John J. Kulczycki, *The Foreign Worker and the German Labor Movement: Xenophobia and Solidarity in the Coal Fields of the Ruhr, 1871–1914* (Oxford and Providence: Berg, 1994); Kulczycki, *The Polish Coal Miners' Union and the German Labor Movement in the Ruhr, 1902–1934: National and Social Solidarity* (Oxford and New York: Berg, 1997).

2. Herbert, especially chapters 2 and 4. See also Ulrich Herbert, *Fremdarbeiter: Politik und Praxis des "Ausländer-Einsatzes" in der Kriegswirtschaft des Dritten Reiches* (Berlin: J. H. W. Dietz, 1999).

3. For an important discussion of Afro-German children and the Federal Republic's social policy toward this population, see Heide Fehrenbach, *Race after Hitler* (Princeton: Princeton University Press, 2005). For more on African American GIs and German women, see Maria Höhn, *GIs and Fräuleins: The German-American Encounter in 1950s West Germany* (Chapel Hill: University of North Carolina Press, 2002).

4. On 10 September 1964, the Federal Republic welcomed the one-millionth guest worker—Armando Rodrigues of Portugal—at the Cologne-Dietz train station. There was some question about whether Rodrigues was actually number 1,000,000, but he was officially celebrated as such, and the event made news throughout West Germany. See, for example, Wolfgang Kuballa, "Großer Bahnhof für Armando Sá Rodrigues: Der millionste Gastarbeiter in der Bundesrepublik mit einer Feier in Köln begrüßt," *Süddeutsche Zeitung,* 11 September 1964; n.a., "'Großer Bahnhof' für den millionsten Gastarbeiter," *Der Tagesspiegel,* 11 September 1964, 5; n.a., "Gastarbeiter Nr. 1000000," *Bild-Zeitung,* 11 September 1964, 1; n.a., "'Großer Bahnhof' erschreckte den Zimmermann aus Portugal," *Westdeutsche Allgemeine Zeitung,* 11 September 1964, 3.

5. By 30 September 1970, there were 2,976,500 foreigners in the Federal Republic. See Statistisches Bundesamt, *Statistisches Jahrbuch für die Bundesrepublik Deutschland* (Stuttgart: Kohlhammer, 1971), 42.

6. Stephen Castles and Mark J. Miller, *The Age of Migration: International Population Movements in the Modern World,* 3rd ed. (New York: Guilford Press, 2003), 72.

7. This definition of German citizenship was not revised until the year 2000, forty-five years after the Federal Republic initiated foreign labor recruitment. The new law augmented the 1913 definition of German nationality, which had determined belonging on the basis of ethnic descent or blood (the principle of jus sanguinis). The revision now also granted citizenship according to place of birth (the principle of jus soli) and, for the first time, automatically bestowed this status on children born in the Federal Republic to non-German parents. In terms of process, the right to automatic citizenship only accrued to children with at least one parent who had resided in the Federal Republic for eight or more years and held either an *unbefristete Aufenthaltserlaubnis* (unrestricted residence permit) for a minimum of three years or an *Aufenthaltsberechtigung* (residence entitlement). The new law also required any child receiving German citizenship on the basis of jus soli formally to choose German citizenship upon reaching the age of majority or lose German nationality by the age of twenty-three.

8. It is worth noting that Slavs, a category of people that was crucial in the Nazi racial imagination, existed primarily outside the nation.

9. See Grossmann, "Defeated Germans and Surviving Jews," 5–6.

10. During the recruitment program's first few years, the mobility of foreign workers was perceived as yet another advantage of this already advantageous solution to the labor shortage. See "Italiener in der deutschen Industrie-Ergebnis eines Experiments," *Frankfurter Allgemeine Zeitung,* 21 October 1959. Quoted in Ulrich Herbert, *A History of Foreign Labor in Germany, 1880–1980* (Ann Arbor: University of Michigan Press, 1990), 211.

11. For more on the push to redomesticate women after 1945, see Robert Moeller, *Protecting Motherhood: Women and the Family in the Politics of Postwar West Germany* (Berkeley: University of California Press, 1993).

12. See, for example, "Die Beschäftigung erreicht einen neuer Höchststand," *Frankfurter Allgemeine Zeitung,* 15 July 1963; Ernst Günter Vetter, "Das Übel der Überbeschäftigung," *Frankfurter Allgemeine Zeitung,* 23 August 1963.

13. H. Stirn, ed., *Ausländische Arbeiter im Betrieb: Ergebnisse der Betriebserfahrung* (Frechen/Cologne: Bartmann-Verlag, 1964), 47.

14. There is some debate about *when* the West German government actually stopped enforcing the rotation policy. Marilyn Hoskins and Roy Fitzgerald maintain that rotation was not enforced from the very beginning, or at least once recruitment began in earnest; whereas Ertekin Özcan claims that the government maintained it until the recession of 1966–67. See Marilyn Hoskins and Roy C. Fitzgerald, "German Immigration Policy and Politics," in Michael C. LeMay, ed., *The Gatekeepers: Comparative Immigration Policy* (New York: Praeger, 1989), 97–98; Ertekin Özcan, *Türkische Immigrantenorganizationen in der Bundesrepublik Deutschland* (Berlin: Hitit Verlag, 1989), 44–45.

15. Rolf Weber, "Die BRD ist kein Einwanderungsland," *Handelsblatt,* 12 November 1971. Quoted in Herbert, 232.

16. Bundesanstalt für Arbeit, ed., *Ausländische Arbeitnehmer 1972–1973. Erfahrungsbericht* (Nuremberg: Bundesanstalt für Arbeit, 1974).

17. See also Herbert, 231; Karen Schönwälder, "Migration, Refugees, and Ethnic Plurality as Issues of Public and Political Debates in (West) Germany," in David

212 Notes to Pages 86–90

Cesarani and Mary Fulbrook, eds., *Citizenship, Nationality, and Migration in Europe* (London: Routledge, 1996), 164–66.

18. Hoskins and Fitzgerald, 98.

19. Rainer Münz and Ralf Ulrich, "Changing Patterns of Immigration to Germany," in Klaus J. Bade and Myron Weiner, eds., *Migration Past, Migration Future: Germany and the United States* (Providence: Berghahn Press, 1997), 83.

20. Turks numbered 469,200 in 1970; 652,800 in 1971; and 893,600 in 1973. See Statistisches Bundesamt, 1971, 42; Statistisches Bundesamt, 1973, 52; Statistisches Bundesamt, 1974, 51.

21. Heinz Kühn, "*Stand und Weiterentwicklung der Integration der ausländischen Arbeitnehmer und ihrer Familien in der Bundesrepublik Deutschland. Memorandum des Beauftragten der Bundesregierung*" (Bonn, 1979), 8.

22. The most active agencies in this regard were the Labor Ministry, the SPD's Friedrich-Ebert-Stiftung, and the CDU's Konrad-Adenauer-Stiftung. Peter O'Brien's dissertation offers an informative examination of social scientific research on foreigners commissioned by West German governmental agencies from the mid-1970s to the mid-1980s. See Peter O'Brien, "The Paradoxical Paradigm: Turkish Migrants and German Policies" (Ph.D. diss., University of Wisconsin, Madison, 1988), especially 100–220.

23. The most important systems-theory-oriented studies of integration are Hans-Joachim Hoffmann-Nowotny, *Soziologie des Fremdarbeiterproblems* (Stuttgart: Enke, 1973); Hartmut Esser, Eduard Gaugler, and Karl Heinz Neumann, eds., *Arbeitsmigration und Integration. Sozialwissenschaftliche Grundlagen* (Konigstein: Hanstein, 1979); Hartmut Esser, *Aspekte der Wanderungssoziologie. Assimilation und Integration von Wandern, ethnischen Gruppen und Minderheiten* (Darmstadt: Luchterhand, 1980).

24. Some of the earliest and most significant empirical studies of guest workers and their families include: Bundesanstalt für Arbeit, ed., *Repräsentativuntersuchung 1972 über die Beschäftigung ausländischer Arbeitnehmer im Bundesgebiet und ihre Familien- und Wohnverhältnisse* (Nuremberg: Bundesanstalt für Arbeit, 1973); Ursula Mehrländer, *Soziale Aspekte der Ausländerbeschäftigung* (Bonn: Verlag Neue Gesellschaft, 1974); Ursula Boos-Nünning, Manfred Hohmann, and R. Reich, eds., *Schulbildung ausländischer Kinder* (Bonn: Eichholz Verlag, 1976).

25. For a fuller discussion of the major political positions on integration, see Rita Chin, *The Guest Worker Question in Postwar Germany* (New York and Cambridge: Cambridge University Press, 2007), Chapter 2.

26. Kühn, 2, 11. From 1966 to 1978, Kühn was minister president of North Rhine-Westphalia, the state with by far the largest numbers of foreigners. In 1979, it had a total of 1,277,000 foreign residents. See Statistisches Bundesamt, 1980, 66.

27. Kühn, 15. Emphasis added.

28. Kühn, 3–4.

29. More than half of the section outlining Kühn's policy recommendations was devoted to educational issues. Kühn, 18–36.

30. Kühn, 29.

31. Alfred Dregger served as mayor of Fulda from 1956 to 1970. In 1972 he be-

came a member of the Bundestag and served as leader of the CDU/CSU caucus in the German parliament from 1982 to 1991.

32. Bundestag, *Verhandlungen des Deutschen Bundestages: Stenographische Berichte*, 9. Wahlperiod, vol. 120 (Bonn: Deutscher Bundestag und Bundesrat, 1982), 4895.

33. Bundestag, 4895.

34. Bundestag, 4892.

35. Bundestag, 4893.

36. Martin Barker, *The New Racism: Conservatives and the Ideology of the Tribe* (London: Junction Books, 1980), 21.

37. Barker, 23–24.

38. As we emphasize in the Introduction, arguments based on biology and culture have been routinely interwoven in making claims of absolute or essential differences between groups of people.

39. Barker, 1–53. Paul Gilroy has discussed Barker's work recently within the larger context of a "crisis of raciology." See Paul Gilroy, *Against Race: Imagining Political Culture Beyond the Color Line* (Cambridge: Harvard University Press, 2000), 32–39.

40. Bundestag, 4894.

41. In November 1981, the right-wing newspaper *Deutsche Wochenzeitung* published a version of the so-called Heidelberg Manifesto, a document that raised a cry of alarm at the "infiltration of the German *Volk* by the immigration of millions of foreigners." The manifesto was written by Helmut Schröcke, a physicist and mineralogist at the University of Munich also known for his extreme right-wing views. Fourteen other professors signed the statement, including humanists, historians, theologians, and scientists with appointments at Frankfurt, Mainz, Bochum, and Munich. For more on this document, see Hanno Kühnert, "Rassistische Klänge," *Die Zeit*, 5 February 1982, 61.

42. See Schönwälder, 166.

43. The CDU/CSU won in the spring of 1983 with 48.8 percent of the vote. Only the 1957 election gave the CDU/CSU a higher margin of victory, with 50.2 percent of the vote. See Dennis L. Bark and David R. Gress, *A History of West Germany*, vol. 2 (Oxford: Basil Blackwell, 1989), 387.

44. Barbara Marshall, *The New Germany and Migration in Europe* (Manchester and New York: Manchester University Press, 2000), 13.

45. Bundesministerium des Inneren, *Aufzeichnungen zur Ausländerpolitik und zum Ausländerrecht der Bundesrepublik Deutschland* (Bonn: Bundesministerium des Inneren), 3. Quoted in Marshall, 13. Emphasis added.

46. Bundestag, 4888.

47. Bundestag, 4890.

48. The book's authors, Andrea Baumgartner-Karabak and Gisela Landesberger, described the experience of Turkish women on the basis of a visit to rural Anatolia, personalizing their discussion with journal entries and pictures from the trip.

49. The series advertisement appeared in *Courage*, November 1979, 46. The full list of advertised books includes Cheryl Benard and Edit Schlaffer, *Die ganz*

gewöhnliche Gewalt in der Ehe; Herta Däubler-Gmelin, *Frauenarbeitslosigkeit oder Reserve zurück an den Herd!;* Cornelia Edding, *Jede kann helfen;* Carmen Thomas, ed., *Die Hausfrauengruppe oder Wie elf Frauen sich selbst helfen;* Marielouise Jannssen-Jurreit, ed., *Gegen Diskriminierung;* Luc Jochimsen, *Sozialismus als Männersache oder Kennen Sie "Bebels Frau"?;* Susanne von Paczensky, ed., *Frauen und Terror;* Pro Familie Bremen, ed., *Wir wollen nicht mehr nach Holland fahren;* Carola Stern, ed., *Was haben die Parteien für die Frauen getan?;* and Ruth Weiss, ed., *Frauen gegen Apartheid.*

50. Susanne von Paczensky, "Frauen aus Anatolien: Vorwärt" in Baumgartner-Karabak and Landesberger, 8.

51. The most important studies within this genre include Franz Brandt, *Situationsanalyse nichterwerbstätiger Ehefrauen ausländischer Arbeitnehmer in der Bundesrepublik Deutschland* (Bonn: Bundesminister für Jugend, Familie und Gesundheit, 1977); Ute Welzel, ed., *Situation der Ausländerinnen: Fachtagung am 19.–21. September in Berlin* (Berlin: Institut für Zukunftsforschung, 1981); *Informationsdienst Bildungsarbeit mit ausländischer Arbeitern, Sonderheft/Frauen* (Bonn: Deutscher Volkshochschul-Verband e.V., 1981); Peter Schmuck, *Der Islam und seine Bedeutung für türkische Familien in der Bundesrepublik Deutschland* (Munich: DJI Verlag, 1982); Christine Huth and Jürgen Micksch, eds., *Ausländische Frauen: Interviews, Analysen und Anregungen für die Praxis* (Frankfurt: Verlag Otto Lembeck, 1982); Horst Westmüller, *Kultur und Emanzipation: Ausländische und deutsche Frauen in Projekten der Sozialarbeit und Sozialforschung* (Rehburg-Loccum: Evangelische Akademie Loccum, 1985). For an extensive list of the work on foreign women, see Alice Münscher, *Ausländische Frauen: Anotierte Bibliographie* (Munich: DJI Verlag, 1980). For an in-depth discussion of German academic scholarship on Turkish women in this period, see Rita Chin, *The Guest Worker Question in Postwar Germany,* chapter 3.

52. Baumgartner-Karabak and Landesberger, 67–68.

53. Paczensky, 7. Susanne von Paczensky, it is worth noting, is considered a major activist of the post-1945 period. As a young woman, she was one of the few Germans allowed to observe the Nuremberg trials. A journalist, author, and sociologist, Paczensky became very politically active and participated in the women's, peace, and environmental movements. I include this quote precisely to demonstrate that German discomfort with the possibility of reciprocal change in the process of integration has not been restricted to those on the Right.

54. Quoted in Vera Gaserow, "Die vielen Seiten eines Kopftuchs," *Die Tageszeitung,* 11 November 1985.

55. Dagmar Herzog, *Sex after Fascism: Memory and Morality in Twentieth Century Germany* (Princeton: Princeton University Press, 2005), 2.

56. The classic analysis of this mode of thinking about Jews in Imperial Germany is Fritz Stern, *The Politics of Cultural Despair* (Berkeley: University of California Press, 1961).

57. Étienne Balibar has also argued that an emphasis on absolute cultural differences over biological heredity constitutes a kind of "racism without races." See Étienne Balibar, "Is There a Neo-Racism?" in Étienne Balibar and Immanuel

Wallerstein, *Race, Nation, Class: Ambiguous Identities* (London: Verso, 1991), 21–23.

58. N.a., "Rock-Musik gegen 'rechts'," *Süddeutsche Zeitung,* 18 June 1979, 9.
59. N.a., "Ochsenköppe stoppen," http://www.wdr.de/themen/Kultur/Stich tag/2004/06/16.jhtml
60. Claudia Dillermann, "Angst vor dem Notstand," *Die Zeit,* 15 June 1979, 15.
61. Dillermann, 15; see also, n.a., "Massenkrawalle in Frankfurt vermieden," *Süddeutsche Zeitung,* 18 June 1979, 6.
62. *Der Spiegel* 15 (1966): 42. Studies of the National Democratic Party proliferated in the years immediately following its founding in 1964. These include Reinhardt Kühnl, *Die NPD: Struktur, Programm und Ideologie einer neofaschistischen Partei* (Frankfurt am Main: Suhrkamp, 1969); Lutz Niethammer, *Angepasster Faschismus: politische Praxis der NPD* (Frankfurt am Main: Fischer Verlag, 1969); Erwin K. Scheuch, Hans D. Klingemann, and Thomas A. Herz, eds., *Die NPD in den Landtagswahlen 1966–1968* (Cologne: Institut für vergleichende Sozialforschung, 1969); and John David Nagle, *The National Democratic Party: Right Radicalism in the Federal Republic of Germany* (Berkeley: University of California Press, 1970). Since then, however, scholarship has focused on other organs of the far Right, especially the *Republikaner.* For more on this phenomenon, see Gabriele Nandlinger, "Chronik der Gewalt" in Klaus Henning Rosen, ed., *Die zweite Vertreibung: Fremde in Deutschland* (Bonn: J. H. W. Dietz, 1992), 119–58; Armin Pfahl-Traughber, *Rechsextremismus: Eine kritische Bestandaufnahme nach der Wiedervereinigung* (Bonn: Bouvier, 1993); and Claus Leggewie, *Druck von rechts: Wohin treibt die Bundesrepublik?* (Munich: C. H. Beck, 1993).

CHAPTER 4

1. Youthful political and cultural criticism regarding continuities from the Nazi period emerged already in the 1950s. See, for example, Heide Fehrenbach, "From Feckless Masses to Engaged Critics" and "Local Challenges to Dominant Culture," in Fehrenbach, *Cinema in Democratizing Germany* (Chapel Hill: University of North Carolina Press, 1995), 169–233. For more recent analysis of the role of youthful consumption in democratization and its relation to politicization and political activity (whether the more general trend toward liberalization or the emergence of the New Left), see Uta G. Poiger, *Jazz, Rock, and Rebels: Cold War Politics and American Culture in a Divided Germany* (Berkeley: University of California Press, 2000) and Detlef Siegfried, *Time Is on My Side: Konsum und Politik in der westdeutschen Jugendkultur der 60er Jahre* (Göttingen: Wallstein, 2006).
2. In this respect, this essay is situated within historiographical debates about collective memory. This field has been explored in detail by Alon Confino, "Collective Memory and Cultural History: Problems of Method," *American Historical Review* 102, no. 5 (1997): 1386–1403; Susan A. Crane, "Writing the Individual Back into Collective Memory," *American Historical Review* 102, no. 5 (1997): 1372–85; and more recently, Peter Fritzsche, "The Case of Modern Memory," *Journal of*

Modern History 73 (2001): 87–117. Studies specifically on national memory in Germany include Saul Friedländer, *Memory, History, and the Extermination of the Jews of Europe* (Bloomington: Indiana University Press, 1993); Andreas Huyssen, *Twilight Memories: Marking Time in a Culture of Amnesia* (New York and London: Routledge, 1995); Wolfgang Wipperman, *Umstrittene Vergangenheit: Fakten und Kontroversen zum Nationalsozialismus* (Berlin: Espresso Verlag, 1998); and Wulf Kansteiner, *In Pursuit of German Memory: History, Television, and Politics after Auschwitz* (Athens, OH: Ohio University Press, 2006).

3. Josef Foschepoth, "German Reaction to Defeat and Occupation," in Robert G. Moeller, ed., *West Germany under Construction: Politics, Society, and Culture in the Adenauer Era* (Ann Arbor: University of Michigan Press, 1997), 73–89; here, 76, 87.

4. The Soviets were less sanguine about democracy for recent Nazi supporters. See Jeffrey Herf, *Divided Memory: The Nazi Past in the Two Germanys* (Cambridge, MA: Harvard University Press, 1997), 33–37.

5. The Soviets also advocated denazification but generally implemented it on the basis of class lines. See Herf, 74. The Soviet approach also maintained that the rise of fascism in Germany resulted from structural causes and the elimination of fascism required structural changes. See Foschepoth, 75–79.

6. Herf, 204; also Cornelia Rauh-Kühne, "Die Entnazifizierung und die deutsche Gesellschaft," in *Archiv für Sozialgeschichte* 35 (1995): 35–70.

7. See, for example, Michael R. Marrus, *The Nuremberg War Crimes Trial, 1945–1946: A Documentary History* (New York: Bedford Books, 1997), and Donald Bloxham, *Genocide on Trial: War Crimes Trials and the Formation of Holocaust History and Memory* (New York: Oxford University Press, 2001).

8. Frank Stern, "The Historic Triangle: Occupiers, Germans, and Jews in Postwar Germany," in Robert G. Moeller, ed., *West Germany under Construction,* 199–229; here, 202, and more generally Stern, *The Whitewashing of the Yellow Badge.* See also Grossmann, *Jews, Germans, and Allies;* Gilad Margalit, *Germany and Its Gypsies: A Post-Auschwitz Ordeal* (Madison: University of Wisconsin Press, 2002); Höhn, *GIs and Fräuleins,* and Fehrenbach, *Race after Hitler.*

9. Quoted in Stern, "Historic Triangle," 223.

10. Anna J. Merritt and Richard L. Merritt, *Public Opinion in Occupied Germany: The OMGUS Surveys, 1945–1949* (Urbana: University of Illinois Press, 1970), cited in Herf, 205. For a brief discussion of antisemitism as registered in postwar surveys, public opinion, and political culture in the Federal Republic, see Werner Bergmann and Rainer Erb, *Anti-Semitism in Germany: The Post-Nazi Epoch since 1945,* trans. Belinda Cooper and Allison Brown (New Brunswick: Transaction, 1997), esp. 1–17.

11. John McCloy, Remarks at the Heidelberg Conference, 1949, Truman Library, Papers of H. N. Rosenfield, Box 16. Quoted in Stern, 225. Also Atina Grossmann, *Jews, Germans, and Allies,* and Jay Geller, *Jews in Post-Holocaust Germany, 1945–1953* (New York: Cambridge University Press, 2005). Within a decade, liberal Germans were suggesting that West Germany's treatment of black occupation children—the so-called *Mischlingskinder*—would be a touchstone for German democracy. See chapter 1 in this volume.

12. The West German Federal Republic achieved full sovereignty in May 1955.

13. Robert G. Moeller, "Remembering the War in a Nation of Victims: West German Pasts in the 1950s" in Hanna Schissler, *The Miracle Years* (Princeton: Princeton University Press, 2001), 83–109; here, 86. For an expanded discussion, see Stern, *Whitewashing.* On West German approaches to the state of Israel, see the recent book by Hannfried von Hindenburg, *Demonstrating Reconciliation: State and Society in West German Foreign Policy toward Israel, 1952–1965* (New York: Berghahn Books, 2007).

14. Diethelm Prowe, "The 'Miracle of the Political-Culture Shift': Democratization between Americanization and Conservative Reintegration," in Hanna Schissler, *The Miracle Years,* 451–58; here, 456.

15. For a useful discussion of the efforts to deal with the Nazi past during the early Federal Republic, see Norbert Frei, *Adenauer's Germany and the Nazi Past* (New York: Columbia University Press, 2002).

16. For a discussion about the role of consumption and heightened access to consumer goods in this process, see Michael Wildt, *Am Beginn der Konsumgesellschaft* (Hamburg: Ergebnisse Verlag, 1994).

17. On the gendered character of early postwar Germany, see Robert Moeller, *Protecting Motherhood: Women and the Family in the Politics of Postwar Germany* (Berkeley: University of California Press, 1993) and Elizabeth Heineman, *What Difference Does a Husband Make? Women and Marital Status in Nazi and Postwar Germany* (Berkeley: University of California Press, 1999).

18. Wolfgang Seifert, "Social and Economic Integration of Foreigners in Germany," in *Paths to Inclusion: The Integration of Migrants in the United States and Germany,* ed. Peter H. Schuch and Rainer Münz (New York: Berghahn Books, 1998), 83–113, and Klaus Bade, "Paradoxen Bundesrepublik: Einwanderungssituation ohne Einwanderungsland," in *Deutsch im Ausland, Fremde in Deutschland. Migration in Geschichte und Gegenwart,* ed. Klaus Bade (Munich: Beck, 1992), 391–410.

19. For an expanded discussion of this process, see Rita Chin, *The Guest Worker Question in Postwar Germany.* Jennifer Miller (Rutgers University) is working on an interesting dissertation that explores the recruitment process of the first generation of "guest workers" in Turkey, along with their understandings and expectations prior to emigrating and the disappointments and discrimination they faced upon arrival in the Federal Republic. Early on, before the family reunion policy was put into effect, numerous Turkish men anticipated an active social life among Germans.

20. Quoted in Ulrich Herbert, *A History of Foreign Labor in Germany, 1880–1980: Seasonal Workers/Forced Laborers/Guest Workers,* trans. William Templer (Ann Arbor: University of Michigan Press, 1990), 213.

21. Theodor Blank, "Ein Schritt zur Völkerverständigung," *Der Arbeitgeber,* 17. Jg., 1965, 280.

22. For a discussion of Germany's longer history of labor immigration, see Herbert, *History of Foreign Labor.* For a discussion of historical conceptions and legal definitions of German citizenship, see Rogers Brubaker, *Citizenship and Nationhood in France and Germany* (Cambridge, MA: Harvard University Press, 1992).

23. Brubaker, *Citizenship and Nationhood,* 168–78. Also Seifert, "Social and Economic Integration of Foreigners in Germany."

24. Fatima El-Tayeb, "'The Birth of a European Public.' Race, Migration, and Identity in 'Postnational' Europe," 2, paper presented at the symposium "Histories of the Aftermath: The European 'Postwar' in Comparative Perspective," University of California, San Diego, 16–17 February 2007.

25. The term *hereditary migrant* is taken from El-Tayeb, "The Birth of a European Public," 2.

26. Public, scientific, and official discussions of "difference" and integration first emerged after 1945 in relation to the so-called mixed-race children (*Mischlingskinder*) or black occupation children (*farbige Besatzungskinder*) fathered by Allied occupation soldiers of color. See chapter 1.

27. The quote is adapted from El-Tayeb, "The Birth of a European Public," 2, and in general 1–6. Also Fehrenbach, *Race after Hitler,* 184–86.

28. For a more detailed discussion of this mounting generational critique, see Harold Marcuse, "Revival of Holocaust Awareness in West Germany, Israel, and the United States," in Carole Fink, Philipp Gassert, and Detlef Junker, eds., *1968: The World Transformed* (Cambridge: Cambridge University Press, 1998), 421–38.

29. Adalbert Rückerl, *The Investigation of Nazi Crimes, 1945–1978: A Documentation* (Heidelberg, 1979); Andrei S. Markovits and Philip S. Gorski, *The German Left: Red, Green, and Beyond* (Oxford, 1993), 51–53; and Herf, 340–44.

30. Markovits and Gorski, 52.

31. For a collection of essays that critically examines the mythologies of 1968, see Phillip Gassert and Alan E. Steinweis, eds., *Coping with the Nazi Past: West German Debates on Nazism and Generational Conflict, 1955–1975* (New York: Berghahn Books, 2006), and Kristina Meyer's useful online review of it in H-Soz-u-Kult (H-Net Reviews) dated 7 September 2007.

32. Markovits and Gorski, 52.

33. In fact, some New Left activists also condemned Israeli foreign policy as imperialistic and fascistic vis-à-vis the Palestinians, particularly following the Six Days War. In protest, a handful of West German "urban guerrillas" planted a bomb, which did not detonate, in a Jewish synagogue in Berlin on the anniversary of Kristalnacht, 9 November 1969. In his recent book, Wolfgang Kraushaar argues that manifest antisemitism was not limited to the radical right but informed the actions of the radical left as well. Wolfgang Kraushaar, *Die Bombe im Jüdischen Gemeindehaus* (Hamburg: Hamburger Edition, 2005). See also the useful September 2007 book review by Karrin M. Hanshew for H-Net Book Review Project, in which she notes, "Members of both the liberal and radical Left seconded . . . the belief that 'there are no left-wing antisemites!' and remained stubbornly deaf to traditional anti-Jewish sentiments resurfacing in anti-imperialist critiques of Israel and calls for Palestinian liberation." Also Matthias Brosch, Michael Elm, Norman Geißler, Brigitta Elise Simbürger, and Oliver von Wrochem, eds., *Exklusive Solidarität. Linker Antisemitismus in Deutschland. Vom Idealismus zur Antiglobalisierungsbewegung* (Berlin: Metropol Verlag, 2007). For a different analysis of the New Left's relationship with the Nazi past, see Dagmar Herzog, *Sex after Fascism* (Princeton: Princeton University Press, 2005).

34. Markovits and Gorski, 52.

35. On this point, see Nicolas Berg, *Der Holocaust und die westdeutschen Historiker. Erforschung und Erinnerung* (Göttingen: Wallstein, 2004). Also critical and supportive commentary on Berg's book in *Historisches Forum*, Band 2 (2004), http://edoc.hu-berlin.de/e_histfor/2/PHP/Beitraege_2-2004.php#419 (accessed 18 March 2008).

36. It is worth noting that recent scholarship has claimed that Walraff was a paid informant for the Stasi, the East German secret police. According to Hubertus Knabe, for example, Walraff received information for his books from the Stasi. See Knabe, *Die unterwanderte Republik: Stasi im Westen* (Berlin: Propyläen, 1999).

37. See Linda Alcoff, "The Problem of Speaking for Others," *Cultural Critique* 20 (1991–92): 5–32.

38. In her discussion of West German feminism's blindness to the question of race, Sara Lennox briefly notes that members of the student movement and New Left supported anti-imperialist and antiracist struggles outside of the Federal Republic during the 1960s and 1970s; however, it was not until the 1980s that West German feminists began to consider racism within the ranks of German feminism itself. See "Divided Feminism: Women, Racism, and German National Identity" in Susan Castillo, ed., *Engendering Identities* (Porto: Universidade Fernando Pessoa, 1996), 30.

39. H. von Studnitz, "Sind wir unfair zu den Gastarbeitern?" *Welt am Sonntag,* 20 March 1966. Quoted in Julia Woesthoff, "Ambiguities of Antiracism: Representations of Foreign Laborers and the West German Media, 1955–1990" (Ph.D. diss., Michigan State University, 2004), 61.

40. Quinn Slobodian discusses this in his dissertation "Radical Empathy: Third World Politics in 1960s West Germany" (Ph.D. diss., New York University, 2008).

41. See Martin Klimke, "The 'Other' Alliance: Global Protest and Student Unrest in West Germany and the United States, 1962–1972" (doctoral diss., Universität Heidelberg, 2005); Maria Höhn, "The Black Panther Solidarity Committees and the *Voice of the Lumpen*" in *German Studies Review* 31, no. 1 (2008): 133–54, quotation from 137. For an analysis of black self-fashioning in the Japanese context, see Ian Condry, "The Social Production of Difference: Imitation and Authenticity in Japanese Rap Music," in Heide Fehrenbach and Uta G. Poiger, eds., *Transactions, Transgressions, Transformations: American Culture in Western Europe and Japan* (New York: Berghahn Books, 2000), 166–84.

42. See Peter O'Brien, "Continuity and Change in Germany's Treatment of Non-Germans" in *International Migration Review* 22, no. 3 (Autumn 1988): 109–34, esp. 119–26. Maria Höhn shows that West German government officials were compelled to intervene against patterns of discrimination against African American troops in the FRG because of American concerns that Black Panther Solidarity protests in 1970s might become a "coordinated movement," draw support from "the communist East," and create instability in that sensitive Cold War region. A leading West German newspaper also suggested that some 30,000 communist "guest workers" in Germany might also join in. "The Black Panther Solidarity Committees," 142.

43. Discussions of the *Historikerstreit* and the relationship between the Nazi

past and German national identity include Richard J. Evans, "The New National-ism and the Old History: Perspectives on the West German Historikerstreit," *Journal of Modern History* 59 (1987): 761–97; Hans-Ulrich Wehler, *Entsorgung der deutschen Vergangenheit? Ein polemischer Essay zum "Historikerstreit"* (Munich: C. H. Beck, 1988); Charles Maier, *The Unmasterable Past: History, Holocaust, and German National Identity* (Cambridge, MA: Harvard University Press, 1988); Geoff Eley, "Nazism, Politics, and the Image of the Past: Thoughts on the West German Historikerstreit, 1986–1987," *Past and Present* 121(1988): 171–208.

44. For more on the Bitburg affair, see Geoffrey Hartman, ed., *Bitburg in Moral and Political Perspective* (Bloomington: Indiana University Press, 1986).

45. Evans, 789.

46. Eley, 176.

47. Jürgen Habermas, "Defusing the Past: A Politico-Cultural Tract" in Hart-mann, ed., *Bitburg in Moral and Political Perspective,* 43–44.

48. This pattern of cultural racism links the German debates to similar ideo-logical and political struggles taking place in Britain during the same time period. See, for example, Martin Barker, *The New Racism: Conservatives and the Ideology of the Tribe* (London, 1980), 1–53; Paul Gilroy, *Against Race: Imagining Political Culture beyond the Color Line* (Cambridge, MA: Harvard University Press, 2000), 32–39.

49. Konrad Jarausch and Volker Gransow, "The New Germany: Myths and Realities," in Jarausch and Gransow, eds., *Uniting Germany: Documents and De-bates, 1944–1993* (Providence: Berghahn Books, 1994), xxvi.

50. *New York Times* editorial, 19 November 1989, cited in Jarausch and Gransow, 83–84.

51. Günter Grass, n.t., *New York Times,* 7 January 1990.

52. Already during 1991, there had been sporadic attacks against foreigners, in-cluding an incident in Dresden, where a Mozambican contract laborer hired by the GDR was pushed to his death from a moving streetcar.

53. For a chronology of hate crimes in western and eastern Germany between 1989 and 1994, see Hermann Kurthen, Werner Bergmann, and Rainer Erb, eds., *An-tisemitism and Xenophobia in Germany after Unification* (New York: Oxford Uni-versity Press, 1997), 263–85. For a statistical chart entitled "Right-Wing Extrem-ism, Immigration, and Violence against Foreigners and Jews in Germany, 1980–1994" see ibid., 8.

54. Leon Mangasarian, "Police Evacuate Mozambicans after Racist Attacks in Eastern Germany," United Press International, 21 September 1991.

55. Stephen Kinzer, "A Wave of Attacks on Foreigners Stirs Shock in Ger-many," *New York Times,* 1 October 1991, A1.

56. For analysis of the violence against foreigners in the Federal Republic dur-ing the early 1990s, see Gabriele Nandlinger, "Chronik der Gewalt," in Klaus Hen-ning Rosen, ed., *Die zweite Vertreibung: Fremde in Deutschland* (Bonn: Dietz, 1992), 119–58; Armin Pfahl-Traughber, *Rechtsextremismus: Eine kritische Bestandauf-nahme nach der Wiedervereinigung* (Bonn: Bouvier, 1993); and Claus Leggewie, *Druck von rechts: Wohin treibt die Bundesrepublik?* (Munich: C. H. Beck, 1993).

57. John Marks, "The Fight for a New Germany's Soul," *U.S. News and World*

Report, vol. 113, no. 10 (14 September 1992): 22. This American news source provides a perspective on the riots quite unlike any of those captured in the German media.

58. Stephen Kinzer, "Germany Ablaze: It's Candlelight, Not Firebombs," *New York Times* (13 January 1993), A4, cited in Jarausch and Gransow, 268.

59. Kinzer, "Germany Ablaze," 268.

60. For a partial list, see the German organizations affiliated with the European Network Against Racism (founded 1997); many were founded during the mid- to late 1990s, http://www.enar-eu.org. See also the antiracist newspaper ZAG, founded in Berlin in 1991 and its links to like-minded German organizations. http://www .zag-berlin.de/antirassismus/links/links.html. (Both websites last accessed 19 March 2008).

61. Heribert Prantl, "Eine deutsche Pubertät," *Süddeutsche Zeitung,* 10 October 1991.

62. Knut Pries, "Die Krawalle in Hoyerswerda," *Süddeutsche Zeitung,* 24 September 1991, 3.

63. Giovanni di Lorenzo, "Der Mob siegt in Hoyerswerda," *Süddeutsche Zeitung,* 25 September 1991.

64. David Gow, "Bonn Condemns Neo-Nazi Clashes," *Guardian,* 24 September 1991.

65. Kinzer, A1.

66. Herf, 177.

67. For a useful analysis of how this political discourse developed, see Herf, 13–200.

68. Richard Schröder, *Die Zeit,* 29 January 1993, cited in Jarausch and Gransow, 273–74.

69. Martin Walser, "Erfahrungen beim Verfassen einer Sonntagsrede," *Frankfurter Rundschau* (12 October 1998): 10, cited in Hanno Loewy, "A History of Ambivalence: Post-Reunification German Identity and the Holocaust," *Patterns of Prejudice* 36, no. 2 (2002): 3–13; here, 10. The Walser-Bubis debate was sparked by remarks—most famously that Auschwitz should not be a "moral cudgel"—which Walser made during his acceptance speech for the Peace Prize of the German Book Trade in October 1998.

70. Klaus von Dohnanyi, "Eine Friedensrede. Martin Walsers notwendige Klage," *Frankfurter Allgemeine Zeitung,* 14 November 1998, cited in Loewy, 11.

71. Loewy, 11.

72. American political scientist Meredith Watts used the term *moral panic* to describe alarmist media coverage of the social problems accompanying unification and increased immigration after 1990. Meredith W. Watts, *Xenophobia in United Germany: Generations, Modernization, and Ideology* (New York: St. Martin's Press, 1997), 4.

73. Already in early 1989—before the fall of the Berlin Wall—the right-wing Republikaner Party drew 7.5 percent of the votes in the West Berlin city council election, the right-wing National Democratic Party won representation in Frankfurt am Main (March 1989), and by June, the Republikaner won 7.1 percent in all of West Germany in a European election (in Bavaria, the Republikaner received

14.6 percent in the same election). In state elections in the former East Germany in October 1990, in contrast, the Republikaner vote ranged from a mere 0.6 to 1.9 percent of the vote. In Berlin elections in May 1992, the Republikaner Party drew 8.3 percent of the vote (9.9 percent from Western Berlin; 5.4 percent from eastern Berlin). See Kurthen, Bergmann, and Erb, eds., *Antisemitism and Xenophobia,* 263–73. On international media reaction, see, for example, "Die Seele des Volkes verbogen," *Der Spiegel* 49 (30 November 1992): 18–19; also Herman Kurthen, Werner Bergmann, and Rainer Erb, "Introduction: Postunification Challenges to German Democracy," and Holli A. Semetko and Wolfgang G. Gibowski, "The Image of Germany in the News and U.S. Public Opinion after Unification," in Kurthen, Bergmann, and Erb, eds., *Antisemitism and Xenophobia,* 3–17, 242–56.

74. "Die Seele des Volkes verbogen," *Der Spiegel* 49 (30 November 1992): 14, 17.

75. With the exception of the Mölln murders, the victims were male. They were identified as a Romanian, a "Gypsy," a Vietnamese, an Albanian, a Pole, and nine Germans, four of whom were homeless and at least two of whom were critics of Nazism and neo-Nazism. *Der Spiegel* 49 (1992): 15.

76. Rolf Lamprecht, "Die wehrhafte Demokratie," *Der Spiegel* 45 (2 November 1992): 24–55; here, 25.

77. Ibid.; Watts, 20.

78. Lamprecht, "Die wehrhafte Demokratie," 17, 20. Geißler, it should be noted, represented a rather idiosyncratic voice within the CDU in that he was more open to debates regarding how best to facilitate integration. His early support of a multicultural German society led to his ouster as general secretary in 1989. See Chin, chapter 4.

79. The perception of right-wing or racist violence as "suddenly" appearing with unification ignores the recurrent cycles of antisemitic, xenophobic, and racist violence against people and property in the Federal Republic since the 1950s as well as the appearance of right-wing action in the German Democratic Republic since the 1980s. See Bergmann and Erb, *Antisemitism in Germany;* Watts, *Xenophobia in United Germany,* chap. 1, esp. 21–43; Eva Kolinsky, "Meanings of Migration in East Germany and the West German Model," in Mike Dennis and Eva Kolinsky, *United and Divided: Germany since 1900* (New York: Berghahn Books, 2004), 145–75.

80. The Socialist Unity Party (SED, ruling party of the GDR) did condemn the crimes of the Nazi Regime (although they interpreted the Nazi Regime as the perverse culmination of late capitalism), and East German schoolchildren did take trips to death and concentration camps as part of their antifascist education and socialization. Nonetheless, since the GDR officially refused to interpret itself as a successor state to the Nazi Regime, it refused responsibility (moral or financial) for its crimes, and instead took credit for helping to defeat it. On the SED's policy toward Jews in the early GDR, see Mario Kessler, "Anti-Semitism in East Germany, 1952–1953: Denial to the End," in Leslie Morris and Jack Zipes, eds., *Unlikely History: The Changing German-Jewish Symbiosis, 1945–2000* (New York: Palgrave, 2002), 141–54. Also Kurthen, Bergmann, and Erb, "Introduction: Postunification Challenges to German Democracy," 12–13, and Hermann Kurthen, "Antisemitism and Xenophobia in United Germany: How the Burden of the Past Affects the Present," in Kurthen, Bergmann, and Erb, *Antisemitism and Xenophobia,* 39–41.

81. Watts, 214.

82. This is not to suggest that unified Germany actually witnessed the return of "fossil fascism," as National Socialism and its direct political heirs have been dubbed. Indeed, since the 1990s, academics have spilled much ink suggesting that the changed historical context, socioeconomic and political systems, popular attitudes, and global order make such comparisons facile and fundamentally unsound. Nonetheless, what is significant is that they *were* made. And they were made in the early 1990s precisely because observers—in Germany and abroad—detected an abrupt, perceptible change in the political culture of the Federal Republic. The term *fossil fascism* is taken from Meredith Watts, *Xenophobia in United Germany*, who has shown that while the early 1990s saw an increase in the "number and membership of neo-Nazi groups, . . . they remained on the fringe . . . and the actual extent of their influence is open to debate" even as ethnocentric violence toward outgroups rose, 250, see also chap. 2. Diethelm Prowe has argued for distinctions between fascism, neofascism or "mimetic" or "nostalgic" fascism of the "lunatic fringe," and the right radicalism of the 1990s in his essay "The Fascist Phantom and Anti-Immigrant Violence: The Power of (False) Equation," in Angelica Fenner and Eric D. Weitz, eds., *Fascism and Neofascism: Critical Writings on the Radical Right in Europe* (New York: Palgrave Macmillan, 2004), 125–40; here, 132. On developments in Germany and Europe as a whole since the 1980s and 1990s, see Peter H. Merkl and Leonard Weinberg, eds., *Right-Wing Extremism in the Twenty-First Century* (London: Frank Cass, 2003).

83. The German terms used for xenophobia are *Fremdenfeindlichkeit, Ausländerfeindlichkeit,* or *Ausländerhaß*.

84. "Jeder achte Deutsche ein Antisemit. Spiegel-Umfrage über die Einstellung der Bundesbürger und der Juden zueinander," *Der Spiegel* 4 (20 January 1992): 41. The survey was commissioned by *Spiegel* and conducted by the Bielefeld Emnid-Institut and the Tel Aviv Gallup Institute. It surveyed the opinions of 2,000 "West Germans," 1,000 "East Germans," and 1,000 "Jews," all of whom were Israelis.

85. For a discussion of research and surveys on antisemitism in West Germany, see Bergmann, *Antisemitism in Germany,* 1–24; on the increase of antisemitic violence in the 1980s, see table 1.1, "Right-Wing Extremism, Immigration, and Violence against Foreigners and Jews in Germany, 1980–94," in Kurthen, Bergmann, and Erb, "Introduction: Postunification Challenges to German Democracy," in Kurthen, Bergmann, and Erb, eds., *Antisemitism and Xenophobia,* 8.

86. This did not include respondents judged "mildly antisemitic." The survey questions and design rationales differed over the decades, therefore exact comparisons are not possible across categories. For more information, see Bergmann, *Anti-Semitism in Germany,* 1–8.

87. For a more detailed discussion of "optimists" and "pessimists," and a list of representative authors and works for each camp, see Kurthen, "Antisemitism and Xenophobia in United Germany," 40–45.

88. Kurthen, Bergmann, and Erb, "Introduction: Postunification Challenges to German Democracy," 12.

89. This held true for attitude surveys from 1991 through 1994. "Jeder achte Deutsche ein Antisemit. Spiegel-Umfrage über die Einstellung der Bundesbürger

und der Juden zueinander," *Der Spiegel* 4 (20 January 1992); also Bergmann, "Antisemitism and Xenophobia in Germany since Unification," 23–27.

90. Bergmann, "Antisemitism and Xenophobia in Germany since Unification," 23–27.

91. Emphasis added. Bergmann, *Anti-Semitism in Germany,* 226–27.

92. The corresponding number for east Germans was 46 percent. In a survey taken in 1994, east Germans remained 20 points behind west Germans on the issue (36 to 56 percent). See "Mehr verdrängt als bewältigt?" 65; also the comparative discussion of western and eastern Germans' perception of Jews (polled in 1990 and again in 1994) in Werner Bergmann, "Antisemitism and Xenophobia in Germany since Unification," in Kurthen, Bergmann, and Erb, eds., *Antisemitism and Xenophobia,* 22–28.

93. Heitmeyer quotation is from "Die Seele des Volkes verbogen" in *Der Spiegel* 49 (30 November 1992): 24. For an overview of opinion polls and research on the issue of xenophobia among eastern and western Germans, see Kurthen, Bergmann, and Erb, *Antisemitism and Xenophobia.* For a discussion of the generational dimension of German xenophobia, see Watts, *Xenophobia.*

94. "Schüler: Schließt die Wessis ein," *Der Spiegel* 48 (23 November 1992): 52.

95. Reported in "Bestie aus deutschem Blut," *Der Spiegel* 50 (7 December 1992): 25.

96. Bergmann cites a number of 10 to 15 percent, drawn from a 1988 study by the Central Institute for Research on Youth in Leipzig. Kurthen, Bergmann, and Erb, *Antisemitism and Xenophobia,* 7, 23.

97. Bergmann, "Antisemitism and Xenophobia in Germany since Unification," in Kurthen, Bergmann, and Erb, eds., *Antisemitism and Xenophobia,* 26. It is worth noting, though, that xenophobic attitudes increased during the first half of the 1990s.

98. "Bestie aus deutschem Blut," *Der Spiegel* 50 (7 December 1992): 22–33; here, 23, 25. For a more comprehensive assessment that is critical of the analysis I am summarizing here, see Watts, *Xenophobia,* esp. 250–54. As contemporaries and later studies showed, most xenophobic violence was perpetrated by youth between the ages of fourteen and twenty-two in both eastern and western Germany; a higher percentage of hate crimes perpetrated in western Germany was tied to right-wing extremist political organization. See Watts, *Xenophobia;* also Beate Vossen, "Police Initiatives against Racism and Xenophobic Violence in North Rhine-Westphalia," and Karl-Heinz Schamberger, "Role of the Federal Criminal Police in Germany," in Robin Oakley, ed., *Tackling Racist and Xenophobic Violence in Europe: Case Studies* (Strasbourg: Council of Europe, 1997), 81–92, 93–104; and Wilfried Schubart, "Xenophobia among East German Youth," in Kurthen, Bergmann, and Erb, eds., *Antisemitism and Xenophobia,* 143–58. On the 1950s and the *Halbstarken,* see Uta G. Poiger, *Jazz, Rock, and Rebels: Cold War Politics and American Culture in Divided Germany* (Berkeley: University of California Press, 2000).

99. Aside from political geography, there were differences in generation, class, educational levels, and urban or rural residence. For a summary, see Bergmann, "Antisemitism and Xenophobia in Germany since Unification," esp. 28–35, and Watts, *Xenophobia,* 232–37. In addition, some of the highest levels of xenophobic

activity had been registered in the west in the early 1990s. See, for example, Beate Vossen, "Police Initiatives against Racism and Xenophobic Violence in North Rhine-Westphalia."

100. For a brief discussion, see Watts, *Xenophobia,* 46–48.

101. Klaus J. Bade, *Ausländer, Aussiedler, Asyl in der Bundesrepublic Deutschland* (Bonn: 1992), quoted in Bergmann, "Antisemitism and Xenophobia in Germany since Unification," 28.

102. Kurthen, Bergmann, and Erb, "Introduction" (table 1.1), 8.

103. Watts, *Xenophobia,* 257, and in general chapter 5.

104. Kurthen, Bergmann, and Erb, *Antisemitism and Xenophobia,* 9.

105. Effective action and coordination among police only began to increase in 1992. Even after the Mölln and Solingen murders, for example, the Berlin police bureaucratically referred a fearful Turkish couple, who reported an arson incident in their apartment building (someone set a baby stroller on fire) and were seeking protection, to the fire department, which promptly declined action because the fire was extinguished and there was "no immediate danger." By mid-decade, however, the Berlin police were beginning to borrow strategies from their colleagues in the multiethnic United States. See Barbara John, "Local Government Initiatives in Berlin," in Oakley, *Tackling Racist and Xenophobic Violence in Europe,* 105–8.

106. See discussion in Watts, *Xenophobia,* 58–61, and Hermann Kurthen, "Antisemitism and Xenophobia in United Germany," in Kurthen, Bergmann, and Erb, eds., *Antisemitism and Xenophobia,* esp. 45–48.

107. Kurthen, Bergmann, and Erb, eds., *Antisemitism and Xenophobia,* and Watts, *Xenophobia.*

108. Oddly, the broad category of racism (and racist violence) figures legally as a subcategory of "xenophobic offenses." These are defined as "acts committed, due to intolerance, against individuals for their actual or potential [*sic!*] nationality or ethnicity; race or skin colour; religion or ideology; origin; appearance." Karl-Heinz Schamberger (Federal Criminal Police Agency), "Role of the Federal Criminal Police in Germany," in Oakley, "Tackling Racist and Xenophobic Violence in Europe," 93–104; here, 96.

109. One exception we have come across actually manages to prove the rule. In a study of schoolchildren, Richard D. Alba, Johann Handl, and Walter Müller studied the "ethnic characteristics" of Turkish, Yugoslav, Italian, and Greek children in Germany. The children were polled for the food eaten and language spoken at home, number of good "German" friends they had, and the like, and were ultimately rated for their ethnic "distinctiveness"—how ethnically different they were from normative German children! Tellingly, Jewish German children were *not* included in the study, presumably because it would be deemed insensitive or worse to rate their ethnic quotient. It seems worth noting that the researchers appear to have had a "liberal" goal: to understand the "roots of ethnic educational disadvantage" and facilitate integration into German schools. Richard D. Alba, Johann Handl, and Walter Müller, "Ethnic Inequalities in the German School System," in Schuck and Münz, eds., *Paths to Inclusion,* 116–54, and especially 133–47. See Flam for a more critical assessment of ethnic inequality in German schools. Over the course of the 1990s, sociological surveys have begun to integrate "foreigner" opinion; see

Steffen Kühnel and Jürgen Leibold, "The Others and We: Relationships between Germans and Non-Germans from the Point of View of Foreigners Living in Germany," and Ferdinand Böltken, "Social Distance and Physical Proximity: Day-to-Day Attitudes and Experiences of Foreigners and Germans Living in the Same Residential Areas," in Richard Alba, Peter Schmidt, and Martina Wasmer, eds., *Germans for Foreigners? Attitudes toward Ethnic Minorities in Post-Reunification Germany* (New York: Palgrave Macmillan, 2003), 143–62, 233–54.

110. For example, May Ayim, "Das Jahr 1990: Heimat und Einheit aus afrodeutscher Perspektive," which appears in English translation as "The Year 1990: Homeland and Unity from an Afro-German Perspective," in Göktürk, Gramling, and Kaes, *Germany in Transit,* 126–29.

111. Zafer Şenocak and Bülent Tulay, "Germany—Home for Turks? A Plea for Overcoming the Crisis between Orient and Occident," in Şenocak, *Atlas of a Tropical Germany: Essays on Politics and Culture, 1990–1998,* trans. Leslie Adelson (Lincoln: University of Nebraska Press, 2000).

112. Şenocak and Tulay, 2.

113. Şenocak and Tulay, 7.

114. Şenocak and Tulay, 3.

115. Zafer Şenocak, "Ein Türke geht nicht in die Oper," *Die Tageszeitung* 21 (January 1992): 11.

116. Zafer Şenocak, "What Does the Forest Dying Have to Do with Multiculturalism?" in Şenocak, 26.

117. Zafer Şenocak, "May One Compare Turks and Jews, Mr. Şenocak?" in Şenocak, 53.

118. Şenocak, 53.

119. Şenocak, 53.

120. Zafer Şenocak, *Gefährliche Verwandschaft* (Munich: Babel, 1998), 40. Literary scholar Andreas Huyssen has argued that the perilous kinships confronted by the novel's protagonist emerge in the shrouded family history of his Turkish grandfather, a history that Germany and Turkey share around "genocides that have left a burden of guilt to successive generations." But the real stakes of this legacy, according to Huyssen, involve the question of "how such histories are remembered and how they can be imagined and written at a time when the changing memory culture of Germany poses new problems of memory for the Turkish immigrants and their descendants." See Andreas Huyssen, "Diaspora and Nation: Migration into Other Pasts," *New German Critique* 88 (Winter 2003): 147–64; here, 160.

121. Leslie A. Adelson, "The Turkish Turn in Contemporary German Literature and Memory Work," *Germanic Review* 77, no. 4 (2002): 333.

122. Zafer Şenocak, "Thoughts on May 8, 1995" in Şenocak, 58–59.

123. Şenocak, 59–60.

124. El-Tayeb, "The Birth of a European Public," 21. This focus is similar to R. Miles's notion of racialization, which emphasizes difference making as a "representational process." R. Miles, *Racism* (London: Routledge, 1989), 74, quoted in Nicola Piper, *Racism, Nationalism, and Citizenship: Ethnic Minorities in Britain and Germany* (Brookfield, VT: Ashgate, 1998), 39. For a more recent discussion, see Rogers Brubaker, *Ethnicity without Groups.*

CHAPTER 5

The ideas in this chapter focus on some broader European contexts for considering the themes of "race" and politics, building partly on an earlier essay: "Culture, Britain, and Europe," *Journal of British Studies* 31 (1992), 390–414; and some arguments in *A Crooked Line: From Cultural History to the History of Society* (Ann Arbor: University of Michigan Press, 2005), 133–48.

The opening epigraph is from Ingela Lind, "Den nye europén kommer från Afrika," *Daagens Nyheter*, 26 June 1994, cited by Allan Pred, *Even in Sweden: Racisms, Racialized Spaces, and the Popular Geographical Imagination* (Berkeley: University of California Press, 2000), 56.

1. See Mica Nava, *Visceral Cosmopolitanism: Gender, Culture, and the Normalisation of Difference* (Oxford: Berg, 2007).

2. See here Paul Gilroy, "Race Ends Here," and Sophie Body-Gendrot, "'Now You See, Now You Don't': Comments on Paul Gilroy's Article," *Ethnic and Racial Studies* 21 (1998), 838–47, and 848–58. See also Gilroy's two books: *Against Race: Imagining Political Culture beyond Color Line* (Cambridge: Harvard University Press, 2001); and *Postcolonial Melancholia* (New York: Columbia University Press, 2004).

3. Still exemplary in this regard: William Wallace, *The Transformation of Western Europe* (London: Pinter and Royal Institute of International Affairs, 1990), and "Introduction: The Dynamics of European Integration," in Wallace, ed., *The Dynamics of European Integration* (London: Pinter and Royal Institute of International Affairs, 1990), 1–24. See also Mikael af Malmborg and Bo Strath, eds., *The Meaning of Europe* (Oxford: Berg, 2002); Chris Shore, ed., *The Building of Europe: The Cultural Politics of European Integration* (London: Routledge, 2000). The distinction between "regime of regulation" and "regime of signification" was originally suggested to me by Michael Geyer in a paper called "After the Revolution of 1989" presented to a symposium "Neither East Nor West? Undergraduate European Studies and the Transformation of Europe," at Kalamazoo College on 4–5 May 1990. See also his essay "Historical Fictions of Autonomy and the Europeanization of National History," *Central European History* 22 (1989): 316–42, which provides a benchmark for the vastly proliferating preoccupation with "Europeanization" among historians in Germany during the 1990s and since.

4. See now especially Victoria de Grazia, *Irresistible Empire: America's Advance through Twentieth-Century Europe* (Cambridge: Harvard University Press, 2005).

5. For succinct introductions to how I am using these terms (*common sense, hegemony*), see Raymond Williams, *Marxism and Literature* (Oxford: Oxford University Press, 1977), 108–14; Stuart Hall, Bob Lumley, and Gregor McLennon, "Politics and Ideology: Gramsci," in *Working Papers on Cultural Studies, 10: On Ideology* (Birmingham: Center for Contemporary Cultural Studies, 1977), 45–76; Anna Marie Smith, *Laclau and Mouffe: The Radical Democratic Imaginary* (London: Routledge, 1998), 151–76; Geoff Eley, "Reading Gramsci in English: Observations on the Reception of Antonio Gramsci in the English-Speaking World, 1957–1982," *European History Quarterly* 14 (1984): 456–64.

6. This understanding of culture is usually traced back to Raymond Williams, especially *Culture and Society, 1780–1950* (London: Hogarth Press, 1958), 16, 120–36; see also John Higgins, *Raymond Williams: Literature, Marxism, and Cultural Materialism* (London: Routledge, 1999), 37–42; Lesley Johnson, *The Cultural Critics: From Matthew Arnold to Raymond Williams* (London: Routledge and Kegan Paul, 1979), 2–4, 27–34. For later developments, see the following essays of Stuart Hall: "Cultural Studies: Two Paradigms," in Nicholas B. Dirks, Geoff Eley, and Sherry B. Ortner, eds., *Culture/Power/History: A Reader in Contemporary Social Theory* (Princeton: Princeton University Press, 1994), 520–38; "Cultural Studies and the Centre: Some Problematics and Problems," in Stuart Hall, Dorothy Hobson, Andrew Lowe, and Paul Willis, eds., *Culture, Media, Language: Working Papers in Cultural Studies* (London: Hutchinson, 1980), 15–47; "Notes on Deconstructing 'the Popular'," in Raphael Samuel, ed., *People's History and Socialist Theory* (London: Routledge, 1981), 227–40; "Cultural Studies and Its Theoretical Legacies," in Lawrence Grossberg, Cary Nelson, and Paula Treichler, eds., *Cultural Studies* (New York: Routledge, 1992), 277–94; "Introduction: Who Needs Identity?", in Stuart Hall and Paul du Gay, eds., *Questions of Cultural Identity* (London: Sage, 1996), 1–17.

7. See Raymond Williams, "Culture Is Ordinary," in his *Resources of Hope: Culture, Democracy, Socialism* (London: Verso, 1989), 4: "Culture is ordinary: this is the first fact. Every human society has its own shape, its own purpose, its own meanings. Every human society expresses these, in institutions, in arts and learning. The making of a society is the finding of common meanings and directions, and its growth is an active debate and amendment under the pressures of experience, contact, and discovery . . . The growing society is there, yet it is also made and remade in every individual mind. The making of a mind is, first, the slow learning of shapes, purposes, and meanings, so that work, observation, and communication are possible. Then, second, but equal in importance, is the testing of these in experience, the making of new observations, comparisons, and meanings. A culture has two aspects: the known meanings and directives, which its members are trained to; the new observations and meanings, which are offered and tested. These are the ordinary processes of human societies and human minds, and we see through them the nature of a culture: that it is always both traditional and creative; that it is both the most ordinary common meanings and the finest individual meanings. We use the word culture in these two senses: to mean a whole way of life—the common meanings; to mean the arts and learning—the special processes of discovery and creative effort. Some writers reserve the word for one or other of these senses; I insist on both, and on the significance of their conjunction."

8. Ibid., 5.

9. See Jürgen Habermas and Jacques Derrida, "February 15, Or, What Binds Europeans Together. Plea for a Common Foreign Policy, Beginning in a Core Europe," in Daniel Levy, Max Pensky, and John Torpey, eds., *Old Europe, New Europe, Core Europe: Transatlantic Relations after the Iraq War* (London: Verso, 2005), 7. In Umberto Eco's contribution to the initiative proposed by Habermas and Derrida, "An Uncertain Europe between Rebirth and Decline," he itemized Western Civilization's characteristics as follows: "the fundamental principles of the

so-called Western world, the Greek and Judeo-Christian heritage, the ideas of freedom and equality born out of the French Revolution, the heritage of modern science that started with Copernicus, Galileo, Kepler, Descartes, and Francis Bacon, the capitalistic form of production, the secularization of the State, Roman or Common Law, the very idea of justice achieved through class struggle (all typical products of the European Western world, and we could cite many more) are nowadays are no longer the exclusive domain of Europe. On the contrary, they have spread and become popular in America, Australia, and—although not everywhere—in many parts of Asia and Africa." Ibid., 15.

10. For an elaboration and detailed grounding of this argument, see Geoff Eley, *Forging Democracy: The History of the Left in Europe, 1850–2000* (New York: Oxford University Press, 2002), especially 384–428, 457–69.

11. See Mabel Berezin and Martin Schain, eds., *Europe Without Borders: Remapping Territory, Citizenship, and Identity in a Transnational Age* (Baltimore: Johns Hopkins University Press, 2003).

12. Adolf Muschg, "'Core Europe': Thoughts about the European Identity," ibid., 26.

13. Hans-Ulrich Wehler, "Let the United States Be Strong! Europe Remains a Mid-Size Power: A Response to Jürgen Habermas," ibid., 121. The emphasis inside the quotation is mine. For a stunningly straightforward iteration of the same standpoint: Heinrich August Winkler, "The West: Still a Community of Values?," *Internationale Politik* 8 (Summer 2007), accessed at http://en.internationalepolitik.de/archiv/2007/summer 2007/.

14. Hans-Ulrich Wehler, interviewed by Ralph Bollmann, *TAZ*, 6849 (10 September 2002), 6.

15. Hans-Ulrich Wehler, "Das Türkenproblem," *Die Zeit* 38 (12 September 2002), "http://zeus.zeit.de/text/archiv/2002/38/200238_tuerkei.contra.xml"http://zeus.zeit.de/text/archiv /2002/38/200238_tuerkei.contra.xml, 3. See also the readers' letters in response, "Diskussion: Wie ein Schlag ins Gesicht. Lesedebatte zu Hans-Ulrich Wehler: "Der Türkenproblem," *Die Zeit*, 40 (27 September 2002), http://zeus.zeit.de/text/archiv/2002/40/200240_1-tuerken.xml. Also Hans-Ulrich Wehler, "Verblendetes Harakiri. Der Türkei-Beitritt zestrört die EU," *Aus Politik und Zeitgeschichte*, B 33-34/2004, 6–8, reprinted in a longer version in Helmut König and Manfred Sicking, eds., *Gehört die Türkei zur Europa? Wegweisungen fur ein Europa am Scheideweg* (Bielefeld: Transcript, 2005), 47–61. My reference to Samuel P. Huntington, *The Clash of Civilizations and the Remaking of World Order* (New York: Simon and Schuster, 1996), is deliberate, as Wehler invokes this book at the outset of his interview with Ralph Bollmann. See note 14, this chapter.

16. Rita Chin, *The Guest Worker Question in Postwar Germany* (Cambridge: Cambridge University Press, 2007), 273. One of the best critiques of the sources of such orientalism remains Bryan S. Turner's doubled commentary in *Marx and the End of Orientalism* (London: Allen and Unwin, 1979), and *Weber and Islam: A Critical Study* (London: Routledge and Kegan Paul, 1978). See also Edward Said, *Orientalism* (New York: Pantheon, 1978).

17. Herrick Chapman and Laura L. Frader, "Introduction: Race in France," in

Chapman and Frader, eds., *Race in France: Interdisciplinary Perspectives on the Politics of Difference* (New York: Berghahn Books, 2004), 1.

18. See especially the discussion in Laurent Dubois, "An Enslaved Enlightenment: Rethinking the Intellectual History of the French Atlantic," *Social History* 31 (2006): 1–14, which builds on the following works: Michèle Duchet, *Anthropologie et histoire au siècle des lumières: Buffon, Voltaire, Rousseau, Helvétius, Diderot* (Paris: Maspero, 1974); Louis Sala-Molins, *Dark Side of the Light: Slavery and the French Enlightenment* (Minneapolis: University of Minnesota Press, 2006); Sankar Muthu, *Enlightenment Against Empire* (Princeton: Princeton University Press, 2003). For a cognate argument, see also Jennifer Ngaire Heuer, *The Family and the Nation: Gender and Citizenship in Revolutionary France, 1789–1830* (Ithaca: Cornell University Press, 2005).

19. Gérard Noiriel, "French and Foreigners," in Pierre Nora, ed., *Realms of Memory: The Construction of the French Past,* vol. 1: *Conflicts and Divisions* (New York: Columbia University Press, 1996), 148.

20. Laurent Dubois, "Republican Anti-Racism and Racism: A Caribbean Genealogy," in Chapman and Frader, eds., *Race in France,* 32. Racial distinctions may have been excised from official language, Dubois continues, but "officials once again highlighted the difference of those who had just become citizens, not so much through racial language as through claims about their historically rooted moral capacity to be full citizens." Ibid., 33.

21. Of course, slavery was also restored by Napoleon in 1802. For full-length studies, see Laurent Dubois, *A Colony of Citizens: Revolution and Slave Emancipation in the French Caribbean, 1787–1804* (Chapel Hill: University of North Carolina Press, 2004), and *Avengers of the New World: The Story of the Haitian Revolution* (Cambridge: Harvard University Press, 2004).

22. Chapman and Frader, "Introduction," 8.

23. Ibid.

24. Ibid., 10; David Beriss, "Culture-as-Race or Culture-as-Culture: Caribbean Ethnicity and the Ambiguity of Cultural Identity in French Society," ibid., 111–40.

25. Clifford Rosenberg, "Albert Sarraut and Republican Racial Thought," ibid., 36–53. See also Clifford Rosenberg, *Policing Paris: The Origins of Modern Immigration Control Between the Wars* (Ithaca: Cornell University Press, 2006); Pierre-André Taguieff, "Face à l'immigration: Mixophobie, xénophobie ou sélection. Un débat français dans l'entre-deux-guerres," *Vingtième siècle* 47 (1995): 103–31, and "Théorie des races et biopolitique sélectionniste en France," *Sexe et Race* 3 (1990): 12–60; 4 (1990), 3–33; William H. Schneider, *Quality and Quantity: The Quest for Biological Regeneration in Twentieth-Century France* (Cambridge: Cambridge University Press, 1990).

26. Chapman and Frader, "Introduction," 10; Mary Dewhurst Lewis, *The Boundaries of the Republic: Migrant Rights and the Limits of Universalism in France, 1918–1940* (Stanford: Stanford University Press, 2007), and "The Strangeness of Foreigners: Policing Migration and Nation in Interwar Marseilles," in Chapman and Frader, eds., *Race in France,* 77–107. See also the following collections: Sue Peabody and Tyler Stovall, eds., *The Color of Liberty: Histories of Race in France* (Durham: Duke University Press, 2003); Tyler Stovall and Georges van

den Abeele, eds., *French Civilization and Its Discontents: Nationalism, Colonialism, Race* (Lanham: Lexington Books, 2003).

27. "The problem of the twentieth century is the problem of the color line, the question as to how far differences of race . . . are going to be made, hereafter, the basis of denying to over half the world the right of sharing to their utmost ability the opportunities and privileges of modern civilization." W. E. B. DuBois made this famous statement originally at the Pan-African conference in Westminster Town Hall, London, in July 1900. See "To the Nations of the World," in David Levering Lewis, ed., *W. E. B. Dubois: A Reader* (New York: Henry Holt, 1995), 639. He repeated it in "The Forethought" to *The Souls of Black Folk* (1903), in W. E. B. DuBois, *Writings* (New York: Library of America, 1986), 359. See also Brent Hayes Edwards, *The Practice of Diaspora: Literature, Translation, and the Rise of Black Internationalism* (Cambridge: Harvard University Press, 2003), especially 1–15.

28. See now especially Joan W. Scott, *The Politics of the Veil* (Princeton: Princeton University Press, 2007); also Scott's earlier *Parité: Sexual Equality and the Crisis of French Universalism* (Chicago: University of Chicago Press, 2005); and John R. Bowen, *Why the French Don't Like Headscarves: Islam, the State, and Public Space* (Princeton: Princeton University Press, 2007).

29. Giscard had just won a narrow victory in the presidential election over François Mitterand, the candidate of the Union of the Left. Despite a series of severe scandals during the early 1970s over the treatment of immigrants and a worsening of the public climate on the issue, immigration played virtually no part in the election itself, where the two principal camps maintained a studied silence. Announced somewhat out of the blue, the temporary stay on immigration (with the exception of migration internal to the European Economic Community) was meant to provide a breathing space for social policy innovation. For the trajectory of French immigration policy after 1945, see Gary P. Freeman, *Immigrant Labor and Racial Conflict in Industrial Societies: The French and British Experience, 1945–1975* (Princeton: Princeton University Press, 1979), 68–98, 22–25.

30. See, for instance, Maria Bucur, *Eugenics and Modernization in Interwar Romania* (Pittsburgh: University of Pittsburgh Press, 2001); Saul Dubow, *Scientific Racism in Modern South Africa* (Cambridge: Cambridge University Press, 1995).

31. See Michael Burleigh and Wolfgang Wippermann, *The Racial State: Germany, 1933–1945* (Cambridge: Cambridge University Press, 1991).

32. The legacies of the Nazi era in this respect, academic discipline by academic discipline, policy domain by policy domain, have been intensively explored during the past decade and a half, although mainly by investigating the Third Reich for the genealogies of postwar fields of knowledge and policy. The literature has become voluminous, but see Götz Aly and Susanne Heim, *Architects of Annihilation: Auschwitz and the Logic of Destruction* (Princeton: Princeton University Press, 2002); Götz Aly and Karl Heinz Roth, *The Nazi Census: Identification and Control in the Third Reich* (Philadelphia: Temple University Press, 2004); Susanne Heim, *Kalorien, Kautschuk, Karrieren: Pflanzenzüchtung und landwirtschaftliche Forschung in Kaiser-Wilhelm-Instituten 1933–1945* (Göttingen: Wallstein, 2003); Ingo Haar and Michael Fahlbusch, eds., *German Scholars and Ethnic Cleansing, 1919–1945* (New York: Berghahn Books, 2005); Michael Burleigh, *Germany Turns*

Eastwards: A Study of Ostforschung in the Third Reich (Cambridge: Cambridge University Press, 1988); Gretchen E. Schafft, *From Racism to Genocide: Anthropology in the Third Reich* (Urbana: University of Illinois Press, 2004), esp. 157–256; Atina Grossmann, *Reforming Sex: The German Movement for Birth Control and Abortion Reform, 1920–1950* (New York: Oxford University Press, 1995), 189–216; Michael Thad Allen, "Modernity, the Holocaust, and Machines without History," in Michael Thad Allen and Gabrielle Hecht, eds., *Technologies of Power: Essays in Honor of Thomas Parkes Hughes and Agatha Chipley Hughes* (Cambridge: MIT Press, 2001), 175–214. For the field of international population politics in this regard, see the pathbreaking work of Matthew Connelly, "To Inherit the Earth. Imagining World Population, from the Yellow Peril to the Population Bomb," *Journal of Global History* 1 (2006): 299–319; "Seeing beyond the State: The Population Control Movement and the Problem of Sovereignty," *Past and Present* 193 (November 2006): 197–203; *Unnatural Selection: The Population Control Movement and Its Struggle to Remake Humanity* (Cambridge: Harvard University Press, 2008). For the relationship between empire, colonial famine, nutritional science, and Britain's "social problem," see James Vernon, *Hunger: A Modern History* (Cambridge: Harvard University Press, 2007).

33. See Francis Barker, Peter Hulme, Margaret Iversen, and Diana Loxley, eds., *Europe and Its Others: Proceedings of the Essex Conference on the Sociology of Literature, July 1984* (Colchester: University of Essex, 1985), including Edward Said, "Orientalism Reconsidered," 14–27.

34. This is where the hugely ramified influence of Edward Said's *Orientalism* (New York: Pantheon, 1978) might also be set. See especially his subsequent *Culture and Imperialism* (New York: Knopf, 1993), and Michael Sprinker, ed., *Edward Said: A Critical Reader* (Oxford: Blackwell, 1992).

35. A brilliant investigation of these deep-lying legacies of empire descending from the late nineteenth and early twentieth centuries and subsequently redeployed as a result of the decolonization process will be Bill Schwarz's forthcoming several-volume study *Memories of Empire*, which paradigmatically historicizes the dynamics of racialization of British politics in the period since the 1960s defined by Enoch Powell's notorious "rivers of blood" speech in April 1968. Schwarz splendidly delivers on the promise of the new historiography of empire by compellingly demonstrating the pervasiveness of its presence in the cultural and political life of the home society, both in popular cultural terms and in the shaping of the social, cultural, and political imaginaries of the political class (Oxford: Oxford University Press).

36. See Caroline Elkins and Susan Pedersen, eds., *Settler Colonialism in the Twentieth Century: Projects, Practices, and Legacies* (New York: Routledge, 2005); David Anderson, *Histories of the Hanged: The Dirty War in Kenya and the End of Empire* (New York: Norton, 2005); Caroline Elkins, *Imperial Reckoning: The Untold Story of Britain's Gulag in Kenya* (New York: Henry Holt, 2005).

37. For a useful summary, see Panikos Panayi, *Outsiders: A History of European Minorities* (London: Hambledon Press, 1999), 140–41. For further insight, see Ian Buruma, *Murder in Amsterdam: The Death of Theo Van Gogh and the Limits of Tolerance* (New York: Penguin Press, 2006), and Dubravka Ugresic, *The Ministry of Pain* (New York: Ecco, 2006).

38. See Chin, *Guest Worker Question,* 7–13, 24–29, 33–52; Panayi, *Outsiders,* 139–40.

39. Panayi, *Outsiders,* 136–38. This new migrant flow included people from one British colony inside Europe but on the extreme Mediterranean periphery, namely Cyprus: numbers of resident Cypriots increased from 10,343 to 72,665 during 1951 through 1971.

40. W. R. Böhning, *The Migration of Workers in the United Kingdom and the European Community* (Oxford: Oxford University Press, 1972), 41–42.

41. Panayi, *Outsiders,* 124–25, 141–42, 135. For an excellent general overview, see Klaus J. Bade, *Legal and Illegal Immigration into Europe: Experiences and Challenges* (Wassenaar: Netherlands Institute for Advanced Study, 2003), and *Migration in European History* (Oxford: Blackwell, 2003). Also: Thomas Faist, "Migration in Contemporary Europe: European Integration, Economic Liberalization, and Protection," in Jytte Klausen and Louise A. Tilly, eds., *European Integration in Social and Historical Perspective* (Lanham: Rowman and Littlefield, 1997), 223–48; James F. Hollifield, "France: Republicanism and the Limits of Immigration Control" (Commentary by Charles P. Gomes), and Philip Muus, "The Netherlands: A Pragmatic Approach to Economic Needs and Humanitarian Considerations" (Commentary by Hans Entzinger and Arend Lijphart), in Wayne A. Cornelius, Takeyuki Tsuda, Philip L. Martin, and James F. Hollifield, eds., *Controlling Immigration: A Global Perspective,* 2nd ed. (Stanford: Stanford University Press, 2004), 183–218, 263–95; Gallya Lahav, *Immigration and Politics in the New Europe: Reinventing Borders* (Cambridge: Cambridge University Press, 2004). For two classics of early reportage: John Berger and Jean Mohr, *A Seventh Man: A Book of Images and Words about the Experience of Migrant Workers in Europe* (Harmondsworth: Penguin, 1975); Jane Kramer, *Unsettling Europe* (New York: Penguin, 1980).

42. A further reservoir of commonsense assumptions about national differences in "racial" terms remained relatively disengaged from colonialism and scientism, while being cued instead to other bases of "foreignness." Examples would be the Poles and other Slav ethnicities for Germany, or the Irish for England. For a fascinating study to this effect, see Tony Kushner, *We Europeans? Mass Observation, "Race," and British Identity in the Twentieth Century* (Aldershot: Ashgate, 2004). See also Mary J. Hickman, "Reconstructing Deconstructing 'Race': British Political Discourses about the Irish in Britain," *Ethnic and Racial Studies* 21 (1998): 288–307.

43. See especially here Jennifer Hyndman and Alison Mountz, "Refuge or Refusal: The Geography of Refusal," in Derek Gregory and Allan Pred, eds., *Violent Geographies: Fear, Terror, and Political Violence* (New York: Routledge, 2007), 77–92.

44. The single most brilliant treatment of the entire field of social, cultural, and political histories surrounding the European antiforeigner racisms of the 1990s and early 2000s is Pred, *Even in Sweden.* See also Alice Bloch and Carl Levy, eds., *Refugees, Citizenship, and Social Policy in Europe* (New York: St. Martin's, 1999).

45. Panayi, *Outsiders,* 136, 143, 151; Pred, *Even in Sweden,* 33–40. See also Jens Rydgren, *From Tax Populism to Ethnic Nationalism: Radical Right-Wing Populism in Sweden* (Oxford: Berghahn Books, 2006).

46. See Stuart Hall, "A Torpedo Aimed at the Boiler-Room of Consensus," which also reproduces the text of Enoch Powell's speech, *New Statesman,* 17 April 1998, 14–19. In many ways the best introductions to this founding period are still the various volumes of investigative analytical reportage produced at the time. E.g., Paul Foot, *Immigration and Race in British Politics* (Harmondsworth: Penguin, 1965), and *The Rise of Enoch Powell* (Harmondsworth: Penguin, 1969); Derek Humphrey, *Police Power and Black People* (London: Panther, 1972); Derek Humphrey and Michael Ward, *Passports and Politics* (Harmondsworth: Penguin, 1974).

47. See Bob Alexander Hepple, "Have Twenty-five Years of the Race Relations Acts in Britain Been a Failure?" in Hepple and Erika M. Szyszczak, eds., *Discrimination: The Limits of the Law* (London: Mansell, 1992), 28: "[The] price for the Race Relations Act 1968 was the Commonwealth Immigration Acts 1962 and 1968 and the price for the Race Relations Act 1976 was the Immigration Act of 1971 and the British Nationality Act 1981."

48. A judicious summary of this period between the advent of Powellism and the early Thatcher years can be found in Peter Clarke, *Hope and Glory: Britain, 1900–2000,* 2nd ed. (London: Penguin, 2004), 319–29. However, Clarke also backdates the more difficult politics of Muslim assimilation developing in the 1990s somewhat anachronistically into the earlier time.

49. Stuart Hall, Chas Critcher, Tony Jefferson, John Clarke, and Brian Roberts, *Policing the Crisis: Mugging, the State, and Law and Order* (London: Macmillan, 1978).

50. Center for Contemporary Cultural Studies, ed., *The Empire Strikes Back: Race and Racism in 70s Britain* (London: Hutchinson, 1982). The book's opening sentence read: "The central theme of this book is that the construction of an authoritarian state in Britain is fundamentally intertwined with the elaboration of popular racism in the 1970s." See John Solomos, Bob Findlay, Simon Jones, and Paul Gilroy, "The Organic Crisis of British Capitalism and Race: The Experience of the Seventies," ibid., 9.

51. Paul Gilroy, "One Nation under a Groove: The Cultural Politics of 'Race' and Racism in Britain," in Geoff Eley and Ronald Grigor Suny, eds., *Becoming National: A Reader* (New York: Oxford University Press, 1996), 367.

52. In a sustained series of writings beginning in the late 1970s, Stuart Hall worked this argument into a theory of "Thatcherism." By this he meant a new form of "authoritarian populism" built on the ruins of the postwar social democratic consensus, which established itself during the 1980s and then as a result of three successive election victories. A virulent discourse of the nation, sharpened via the Falklands/Malvinas War in 1982, and then turned against the striking coalminers during 1984–85 as the "enemy within," was vital to the cementing of that achievement. Constant evocations of Englishness, drawing on older imperial memories as well as the racist antagonisms of the postimperial present, were crucial. See esp. Stuart Hall, *The Hard Road to Renewal: Thatcherism and the Crisis of the Left* (London: Verso, 1988).

53. E.g., Paul Gilroy, "Nothing But Sweat inside My Hand: Diaspora Aesthetics and Black Arts in Britain," in Institute for Contemporary Arts, ed., *Black Film,*

British Cinema (London: ICA Document 7, 1988), 44–46, and "It Ain't Where You're From, It's Where You're At," *Third Text*, 13 (Winter 1990–91), 3–16; Kobena Mercer, "Diasporic Culture and the Dialogic Imagination: The Aesthetics of Black Independent Film in Britain," in Mbye Cham and Claire Andrade-Watkins, eds., *Black Frames: Critical Perspectives on Black Independent Film* (Boston: MIT Press, 1988), 50–61. See also Benita Parry, "Overlapping Territories and Intertwined Histories: Edward Said's Postcolonial Cosmopolitanism," in Sprinker, ed., *Edward Said*, 23.

54. See the preface to Robert Colls and Philip Dodd, eds., *Englishness: Politics and Culture, 1880–1920* (London: Croom Helm, 1986): "Because we could not find a suitable or willing contributor, there is no account of what 'the Empire,' or a part of it, thought of the English." See also Bill Schwarz, "Englishness and the Paradox of Modernity," *New Formations*, 1 (Spring 1987): 147–53. There were some exceptions to historians' neglect. John MacKenzie began a long series of studies of the popular culture of imperialism, which approached "Englishness . . . as a complex of historical, moral, and heroic values which justified the possession of an empire." Quoted by Parry, "Overlapping Territories," 42 n. 7. As Parry argues, the study of "ephemeral writing such as popular fiction, text-books for use in non-elite schools, advertizing, as well as official works on colonial policy . . . would enable one to construct a language of ascendancy in self-definitions of Englishness, valorizing masculinity, encouraging notions of 'supermen,' inflecting patriotism with racism, and underwriting both exercise of and deferral to authority." First published in 1972, Parry's own *Delusions and Discoveries: India in the British Imagination, 1880–1930* (London: Verso, 1998), was an early pioneering study from a literary standpoint. See her new preface, 1–28. See John M. MacKenzie, *Propaganda and Empire: The Manipulation of British Public Opinion, 1880–1960* (Manchester: Manchester University Press, 1984), and MacKenzie, ed., *Imperialism and Popular Culture* (Manchester: Manchester University Press, 1984).

55. See especially Antoinette Burton, ed., *After the Imperial Turn: Thinking with and through the Nation* (Durham: Duke University Press, 2003).

56. Hall et al., *Policing the Crisis*, 394.

57. This and the earlier phrases are taken from the back cover of *Policing the Crisis*. For Stuart Hall's analysis of Thatcherism as a new and highly distinctive form of right-wing politics, see the following: "The Great Moving Right Show," *Marxism Today*, January 1979, 14–20; "Popular-Democratic *vs.* Authoritarian Populism: Two Ways of 'Taking Democracy,'" in Alan Hunt, ed., *Marxism and Democracy* (London: Lawrence and Wishart, 1980), 157–85; "Notes on Deconstructing 'the Popular,'" in Raphael Samuel, ed., *People's History and Socialist Theory* (London: Routledge and Kegan Paul, 1981), 227–40. The latter two of these essays were delivered as papers to conferences in December 1978 and November 1979 respectively. Versions of all three were later reprinted in Hall, *Hard Road to Renewal*.

58. Stuart Hall, "Race, Culture, and Communications: Looking Backward and Forward at Cultural Studies," *Rethinking Marxism* 5 (1992), 15. Here I am following the discussion in James Procter, *Stuart Hall* (London: Routledge, 2004), 80–86. Procter uses the example of the notoriously racist British stand-up comedian Bernard Manning, who refuted charges of racism by pointing to his love of Indian

food, commenting that "there is nothing (more) contradictory about his claims: racism works unconsciously through both desire and loathing." Ibid., 81.

59. Stuart Hall, "Racism and Reaction," in *Five Views of Multi-Cultural Britain* (London: Commission on Racial Equality, 1978), 25.

60. Stuart Hall, "Old and New Identities, Old and New Ethnicities," in Anthony D. King, ed., *Culture, Globalization, and the World System* (London: Macmillan, 1991), 49.

61. The best entry into this intellectual history is through Hall, "Cultural Studies and the Center: Some Problematics and Problems," and "Cultural Studies and Its Theoretical Legacies." For the detailed process of working the problems through, see the following essays by Hall: "Culture, Media, and the 'Ideological Effect,'" in James Curran, Michael Gurevich, and Janet Woollacott, eds., *Mass Communication and Society* (London: Edward Arnold, 1977), 315–48; "Rethinking the 'Base and Superstructure' Metaphor," in Jon Bloomfield et al., eds., *Class, Hegemony, and Party* (London: Lawrence and Wishart, 1977), 43–72; "The 'Political' and the 'Economic' in Marxist Theory of Classes," in Alan Hunt, ed., *Class and Class Structure* (London: Lawrence and Wishart, 1978), 15–60; "The Rediscovery of 'Ideology': Return of the Repressed in Media Studies," in Michael Gurevich, Tony Bennett, James Curran, and Janet Woollacott, eds., *Culture, Society, and the Media* (London: Methuen, 1982), 56–90; "Signification, Representation, Ideology: Althusser and the Post-Structuralist Debates," *Critical Theories of Mass Communication* 2 (1985): 91–114. The last of these essays marks Hall's emergence onto a post-Marxist or "non-materialist" ground of theory. For a considered reflection from the "other side" of that trajectory, see Hall, "Introduction: Who Needs 'Identity'?"

62. Hall, "Racism and Reaction," 30.

63. See Stuart Hall, "The Whites of Their Eyes: Racist Ideologies and the Media," in George Bridges and Rosalind Brunt, eds., *Silver Linings: Some Strategies for the Eighties* (London: Lawrence and Wishart, 1981), 28–52; and "The Racist Within," *Listener*, 20 July 1978 (transcript of a BBC Radio talk).

64. Procter, *Stuart Hall*, 84.

65. Hall, "Racism and Reaction," 33.

66. Paul Gilroy, "Steppin' Out of Babylon—Race, Class, and Autonomy," CCCS, ed., *Empire Strikes Back*, 276–314.

67. Ibid., 276.

68. Ibid., 280.

69. Ibid., 276.

70. Ibid., 281.

71. Ibid., 306–7. See Gilroy's later extraordinarily influential works: *The Black Atlantic: Modernity and Double Consciousness* (Cambridge: Harvard University Press, 1993); *Against Race;* and *Postcolonial Melancholia;* also *Small Acts: Thoughts on the Politics of Black Cultures* (London: Serpents Tail, 1993).

72. See Hall's essays cited in note 61.

73. Robert Miles, *Racism* (London: Routledge, 1989), 73.

74. Robert Miles, "Racism, Marxism, and British Politics," *Economy and Society* 17 (1988): 438.

75. Ali Rattansi and Sallie Westwood, "Modern Racisms, Racialized Identities," in Rattansi and Westwood, eds., *Racism, Modernity, and Identity: On the Western Front* (Cambridge: Polity Press, 1994), 9. See also Robert Miles, "Explaining Racism in Contemporary Europe," ibid., 189–221.

76. The greatly valued librarian at the IRR, A. Sivanandan led a radical revolt in the Institute resulting in its capture and the withdrawal of the patrician civil service contingent (represented by Philip Mason, the director from 1952 to 1970), who had previously established its activities; Sivanandan then became director and founding editor of the journal *Race and Class*. See his account in *Race and Resistance: The IRR Story* (London: Institute of Race Relations, 1974), and his two volumes, *A Different Hunger* (London: Pluto Press, 1982), and *Communities of Resistance* (London: Verso, 1990). See also Kwesi Owusu, "The Struggle for a Radical Black Political Culture: An Interview with A. Sivanandan," in Owusu, ed., *Black British Culture and Society: A Text Reader* (London: Routledge, 2000), 416–24. For Philip Mason's works, see *Race Relations* (London: Oxford University Press, 1970) and *Patterns of Dominance* (London: Oxford University Press, 1970).

77. For a fine synthetic work that seeks to build on both the CCCS and the *Race and Class* strands of thinking, see Floya Anthias and Nira Yuval-Davis (in association with Harriet Cain), *Racialized Boundaries: Race, Nation, Gender, Colour, and Class in the Anti-Racist Struggle* (London: Routledge, 1992).

78. A succinct introduction to the IRR and its contexts can be found in Paul B. Rich, *Race and Empire in British Politics* (Cambridge: Cambridge University Press, 1986).

79. "I had recently moved to Birmingham and will never forget the impact of the 'Rivers of Blood' speech. I remember the sudden, shared feeling of fear, the sense of hostility, the huddling together against the impending violence, the unspoken aggression in the streets as little groups of black men and women came together to discuss how to respond to the violence it seemed calculated to unleash. There were already reserves of resentment in places like Birmingham, Coventry, and the Black Country against the postwar tide of immigrants looking for jobs. Now the dyke had burst, the taboos were broken; and we felt suddenly adrift and unprotected in alien country." Hall, "Torpedo," 16.

80. For a general overview, see John Solomos, *Race and Racism in Britain,* 3rd ed. (Houndmills: Palgrave Macmillan, 2003). While providing a valuable culturalist critique of the "race relations" tradition, Chris Waters, " 'Dark Strangers' in our Midst: Discourses of Race and Nation in Britain, 1947–1963," *Journal of British Studies* 36 (1997): 207–38, unfortunately effaces the sociopolitical context emphasized here. For an important dissentient view emphasizing the countervailing cultures of antiracism and social inclusivity, see Nava, *Visceral Cosmopolitanism*, especially 10–12, 97–120.

81. See Sheila Patterson, *Dark Strangers* (Harmondsworth: Penguin, 1963) and *Immigration and Race Relations in Britain, 1960–1967* (London: Oxford University Press, 1969). See also Nicholas Deakin, *Colour, Citizenship, and British Society* (London: Panther, 1970).

82. For an emblematic collection that already gestures toward the "harder" materialism emerging during the 1970s around Marxists like Sivanandan and Miles,

see Sami Zubaida, ed., *Race and Racialism* (London: Tavistock, 1970). John Rex was an important transitional figure. See his *Race Relations in Sociological Theory* (London: Routledge and Kegan Paul, 1970); *Race, Colonialism, and the City* (London: Routledge and Kegan Paul, 1973); and *Race and Ethnicity* (Milton Keynes: Open University Press, 1986).

83. Ken Coates and Richard Silburn, *Poverty: The Forgotten Englishmen* (Harmondsworth: Penguin, 1970). Neither race as such nor the ethnic composition of the St. Ann's resident population receive more than the occasional incidental mention (e.g., 96, 98, 122). Socialists of an old school, the authors clearly saw race as secondary to the underlying circumstances of social inequality and social deprivation. Ken Coates was a former coalminer teaching in the Adult Education Department of Nottingham University. In 1968 he founded the Institute of Workers Control. He also Chaired the Bertrand Russell Peace Foundation as well as editing its journal *The Spokesman*. During 1989–99 he was a Labour Party member of the European Parliament (MEP), serving for five years as president of its Human Rights Subcommittee. Coates and Silburn's book was analogous in purposes to Michael Harrington's *The Other America: Poverty in the United States* (New York: Macmillan, 1962).

84. There are various intellectual histories of the process by which race became disallowed as an available category. These are usually keyed to the various *Statements on Race and Race Prejudice* coordinated and issued by UNESCO in 1950, 1951, 1964, and 1967, which were collectively produced in the course of international conferences of academics and policymakers. For an emblematic text of the late 1960s and early 1970s in this area, see Paul Baxter and Basil Sansom, eds., *Race and Social Difference: Selected Readings* (Harmondsworth: Penguin, 1972), which basically sets out to document the invalidity of the category. The characteristic scholarly representative of this standpoint in British race relations has been Michael Banton. See his *Race Relations* (London: Tavistock, 1967); *Promoting Racial Harmony* (Cambridge: Cambridge University Press, 1985); and *Racial Theories* (Cambridge: Cambridge University Press, 1987). See also Elazar Barkan, *The Retreat of Scientific Racism: Changing Concepts of Race in Britain and the United States between the Wars* (Cambridge: Cambridge University Press, 1993).

85. Another key element in the postwar consensus which had become ever stronger by the 1960s, namely, the commitment to educational reform and comprehensive schooling, was predicated on a fundamental progressivist critique of the use of intelligence testing as a basis for secondary school selection. For Eysenck and his contexts: Hans J. Eysenck, *The IQ Argument: Race, Intelligence, and Education* (New York: Library Press, 1971), *The Inequality of Man* (London: Fontana/Collins, 1973), and *Rebel with a Cause: The Autobiography of H. J. Eysenck* (London: W. H. Allen, 1990); Alexander Alland, *Race in Mind: Race, IQ, and Other Racisms* (London: Palgrave Macmillan, 2004), 159–78.

86. See Bernard R. Crick, *In Defence of Politics*, 4th ed. (Chicago: University of Chicago Press, 1993), and *George Orwell: A Life* (Boston: Little, Brown, 1980).

87. Bernard R. Crick, "Throw the R-Word Away: We Should Attack Racism by Ceasing to Use the Word 'Race,'" *New Statesman*, 18 October 1996, 49. See also Steven Rose and Hilary Rose, "Why We Should Give Up On Race: As Geneticists and Biologists Know, the Term No Longer Has Meaning," *Guardian*, 9 April 2005.

For a useful discussion of the Crick article, see Harry Goulbourne, *Race Relations in Britain since 1945* (London: Macmillan, 1998), viii–ix, 146–54.

88. The character and status of this scabrously inflammatory visual squib may be tracked by carefully following the wealth of links assembled under the *Wikipedia* article, *"Fitna* (Film)," at http://.en.wikipedia.org.wiki/ Fitna_%28film %29 (accessed 3 April 2008). The film purports to explore Qur'anic authority for the pursuit of Islamic universalism by terrorist means, characterizing Islam as antithetical to European values, essentially antidemocratic, and equivalent to Nazism. Wilders heads the forthrightly right-wing Party for Freedom (PVV), which won nine seats in the Dutch national elections of November 2006. In an interview with *Der Spiegel* he called for a strengthening of European *Leitkultur* ("core culture") capable of withstanding the "creeping tyranny of Islamization," a culture to be founded on "Christian, Jewish, humanistic traditions." See Gerald Traufetter, "Interview with Dutch Populist Geert Wilders: Moderate Islam Is a Contradiction," *Der Spiegel,* 31 March 2008. More generally, see Toby Sterling, "Dutch Await Reaction after MP Releases Film on Qur'an," *Guardian,* 28 March 2008; Gregory Crouch, "A Dutch Antagonist of Islam Waits for His Premiere," *New York Times,* 22 March 2008. The film's title comes from the Arabic *fitna* meaning "disagreement and division among people" or a "test of faith in times of trial." For the German debate about the need for a *Leitkultur,* see Hartwig Pautz, "The Politics of Identity in Germany: The *Leitkultur* Debate," *Race and Class* 46 (April–June 2005): 39–52.

89. Again, the details of these events may be reconstructed by following the multitude of links and references in the article on *"Jyllands-Posten* Muhammad Cartoons Controversy," at http://en.wikipedia.org.wiki/ Danish_cartoon_contro versy (accessed 3 April 2008). If the issue of the cartoons was willingly appropriated by Wilders, the various elements in the political violence surrounding the cartoon issue in Denmark need to be carefully unscrambled. For the original controversy, see Art Spiegelman, "Drawing Blood: Outrageous Cartoons and the Art of Outrage," *Harper's Magazine,* June 2006, 43–52; Heiko Henkel, "'The Journalists of *Jyllands-Posten* are a Bunch of Reactionary Provocateurs': The Danish Cartoon Controversy and the Self-Image of Europe," *Radical Philosophy* 137 (May–June 2006).

90. See Ayaan Hirsi Ali, *The Caged Virgin* (New York: Free Press, 2006), and *Infidel* (New York: Free Press, 2007); Sabrina Tavernise, "In Turkey, A Step to Allow Headscarves," *New York Times,* 29 January 2008; Martin Amis, *The Second Plane: September 11, Terror, and Boredom* (New York: Knopf, 2008); Ciar Byrne, "Eagleton Stirs Up the Campus with Attack on 'Racist' Amis and Son," *Independent,* 4 October 2007; Ronan Bennett, "Shame On Us," *Guardian,* 19 November 2007; Jonathan Brown, "Amis Launches Scathing Response to Accusations of Islamophobia," *Independent,* 12 October 2007; Victoria Burnett, "Spain's Many Muslims Face Dearth of Mosques," *New York Times,* 16 March 2008; Elaine Scholing, "Socialists Re-Elected in Spain, After a Bitter Campaign," *New York Times,* 10 March 2008. Ian Buruma, *Murder in Amsterdam: The Death of Theo Van Gogh and the Limits of Tolerance* (New York: Penguin, 2006), offers a careful guide to many of these issues while studiously avoiding the issue of "race."

91. See the essays by Gilroy and Body-Gendrot cited in note 2, this chapter.

92. See Frederick Cooper and Rogers Brubaker, "Beyond Identity," *Theory and Society* 29 (2000): 1–47, reprinted in Frederick Cooper, *Colonialism in Question: Theory, Knowledge, History* (Berkeley: University of California Press, 2005), 59–90.

93. Rogers Brubaker, "Rethinking Nationhood: Nation as Institutionalized Form, Practical Category, Contingent Event," in *Nationalism Reframed: Nationhood and the National Question in the New Europe* (Cambridge: Cambridge University Press, 1996), 13–22; also Loïc Wacquant, "For an Analytic of Racial Domination," *Political Power and Social Theory* 11 (1997): 222–23.

94. This is George Fredrickson's definition of racism. He continues: "My theory or concept of racism . . . has two components: *difference* and *power*. It originates from a mind set that regards 'them' and 'us' in ways that are permanent and unbridgeable . . . In all manifestations of racism . . . what is being denied is the possibility that the racializers and the racialized can coexist in the same society, except perhaps on the basis of domination and subordination." See George M. Fredrickson, *Racism: A Short History* (Princeton: Princeton University Press, 2002), 5. See also Joan W. Scott, *The Politics of the Veil* (Princeton: Princeton University Press, 2007), 42–45.

95. Howard Winant, "The Theoretical Status of the Concept of Race," in Les Back and John Solomos, eds., *Theories of Race and Racism: A Reader* (London: Routledge, 2000), 181–82; also Brian Nero, *Race* (Houndmills, Basingstoke: Palgrave Macmillan, 2003), 8–9.

96. See the table in Lahav, *Immigration and Politics in the New Europe,* 170. Lahav's book provides a meticulous and exhaustive comparative account of the relevant country by country evidence. See also Herbert Kitschelt, *The Radical Right in Western Europe: A Comparative Analysis* (Ann Arbor: University of Michigan Press, 1995). A 2005 survey by the French National Human Rights Commission found that 55 percent of French people thought there were too many foreigners in the country. One in three described themselves as straightforwardly racist, an increase of 8 percent from the previous year. In another survey by *Le Figaro* in 2006, 51 percent felt foreigners who did not love France should get out. This was an old Le Pen slogan, which Nicolas Sarkozy paraphrased in his 2007 presidential campaign. See Angelique Crisafis, "The Crackdown," *Guardian,* 3 October 2007.

97. See Pred, *Even in Sweden;* also Allan Pred, *The Past Is Not Dead: Facts, Fictions, and Enduring Racial Stereotypes* (Minneapolis: University of Minnesota Press, 2004); Rydgren, *From Tax Populism to Ethnic Nationalism;* Dennis Sven Nordin, *A Swedish Dilemma: A Liberal European Nation's Struggle with Racism and Xenophobia, 1990–2000* (Lanham: University Press of America, 2005). More generally: Annvi Gardberg, *Against the Stranger, the Gangster, and the Establishment: A Comparative Study of the Ideologies of the Swedish Ny demokrati, the German Republikaner, the French Front National, and the Belgian Vlaams Blok* (Helsinki: Swedish School of Social Science, University of Helsinki, 1993); Hans-Georg Betz and Stefan Immerfall, eds., *The New Politics of the Right: Neo-Populist Parties and Movements in Established Democracies* (New York: St. Martin's, 1998); Martin Schain, Aristide Zolberg, and Patrick Hossay, eds., *Shadows Over Europe: The Development and Impact of the Extreme Right in Western Europe* (London: Palgrave Macmillan, 2002).

98. Verena Stolcke, "Talking Culture: New Boundaries, New Rhetorics of Ex-

clusion in Europe," *Current Anthropology* 36 (1995): 4.

99. The initial coinage of the "new racism" in these terms is usually attributed to Martin Barker in *The New Racism* (London: Junction Books, 1981); also "Racism: The New Inheritors," *Radical Philosophy* 21 (1984): 2–17. For convergent French analysis: Pierre-André Taguieff, *The Force of Prejudice: On Racism and Its Doubles* (Minneapolis: University of Minnesota Press, 2001). Of course, this cultural racism can also be turned against perceived interlopers, outsiders, and migrants from inside Europe itself or even within a particular nation; witness the rise of the Italian *Lega Nord* (Northern League) founded under Umberto Bossi in 1991, whose popular vote in national elections ranged from a peak of 10.1 percent in 1996 to 4.1 percent ten years later. Likewise in Italy, the supposed relationship between Romanian immigrants and violent criminality became the bone of bitter contention between the far Right of the two countries. In November 2007 Alessandra Mussolini, MEP and leader of the Neo-Fascist *Azione Sociale* (Social Action), declared all Romanians to be criminals, thereby triggering the departure of five MEPs of the Greater Romania Party from the European Parliament's transnational far Right grouping, Identity, Tradition, and Sovereignty (ITS). Formed in January 2007 from parties in Italy, France, Austria, Bulgaria, Romania, and Britain, ITS was the first neo-fascist transnational caucus to cross the twenty-MEP threshold qualifying such groupings for official funding inside the European Parliament. See Ian Traynor, "Xenophobia Destroys EU's Ultra-Rightwing MEP Group," *Guardian,* 15 November 2007; Ian Fisher, "Romanian Premier Tries to Calm Italy After a Killing," *New York Times,* 8 November 2007.

100. See Étienne Balibar, "Is There Such a Thing as European Racism?" in *Politics and the Other Scene* (London: Verso, 2002), 40–55. For the dynamics of contemporary "Islamization," see Oussama Cherribi, "The Growing Islamization of Europe," and Jocelyne Cesari, "Muslim Minorities in Europe: The Silent Revolution," in John L. Esposito and François Burgat, eds., *Modernizing Islam: Religion in the Public Sphere in Europe and the Middle East* (New Brunswick: Rutgers University Press, 2003), 193–213, 251–69; Yvonne Yazbek-Haddad, ed., *Muslims in the West: From Sojourners to Citizens* (Oxford: Oxford University Press, 2002), Part I: "Carving Up Muslim Space in Western Europe," 19–167.

101. Étienne Balibar, *We, The People of Europe? Reflections on Transnational Citizenship* (Princeton: Princeton University Press, 2004), 122. For the watershed moment in the elision from cultural difference to political values, see Talal Asad, "Multiculturalism and British Identity in the Wake of the Rushdie Affair," *Politics and Society* 18 (1990): 455–80; Malise Ruthven, *A Satanic Affair: Salman Rushdie and the Rage of Islam* (London: Chatto and Windus, 1990).

102. Geert Wilders, quoted in Keith B. Richburg, "In Netherlands, Anti-Islamic Polemic Comes with a Price," *Washington Post,* 1 February 2005, also for the following quotation.

103. Ian Traynor, "'I Don't Hate Muslims. I Hate Islam,' Says Holland's Rising Political Star," *Observer,* 17 February 2008.

104. Henning Mankell, *Kennedy's Brain* (New York: New Press, 2007), 47–48.

105. See Jason DeParle, "In a World on the Move, a Tiny Island Strains to Cope," *New York Times,* 24 June 2007; Ian Fischer, "For African Migrants, Europe

Becomes Further Away," *New York Times,* 26 August 2007; Caroline Brothers, "Unwilling New Frontier for Migrants: Three Greek Isles," *New York Times,* 3 January 2008 (on Samos, Lesbos, and Chios); Anthee Carassava, "Greek Islands, Overwhelmed by Refugees, Seek Help," *New York Times,* 7 May 2008 (on the Dodecanese).

106. See, for instance, Ivar Erkman, "Far From War, a Town with a Well-Used Welcome Mat," *New York Times,* 13 June 2007, on the Swedish community of Sodertalje eighteen miles southwest of Stockholm, where the 60,000 inhabitants received 1,000 mainly Christian Iraqi refugees during 2006 and almost double that number in 2007. In 2006 Sweden received 9,000 of the 22,000 Iraqis seeking asylum in industrialized countries; in 2007 the anticipated numbers were 20,000, as against only 7,000 accepted in the United States. For another of Europe's new margins, see Eamon Quin, "Ireland Learns to Adapt to a Population Growth Spurt," *New York Times,* 19 August 2007: the Irish population of 4.2 million contained a remarkable growth of 322,645 during the previous five years, roughly half of whom were immigrants.

Select Bibliography

GERMANY AFTER 1945

Alba, Richard, Peter Schmidt, and Martina Wasmer, eds. *Germans or Foreigners? Attitudes toward Ethnic Minorities in Post-Reunification Germany.* New York: Palgrave Macmillan, 2003.

Ahonen, Pertti. *After the Expulsion: West Germany and Eastern Europe, 1945–1990.* Oxford: Oxford University Press, 2003.

Arndt, Susan, ed. *AfrikaBilder. Studien zu Rassismus in Deutschland.* Münster: Unrast, 2001.

Bade, Klaus, ed. *Neue Heimat im Westen: Vertriebene, Flüchtlinge, Aussiedler.* Münster: Westfälischer Heimatbund, 1990.

Behrends, Jan C., Thomas Lindenberger, and Patrice G. Poutrus, eds. *Fremde und Fremd-Sein in der DDR: zu historischen Ursachen der Fremdenfeindlichkeit in Ostdeutschland.* Berlin: Metropol, 2003.

Benz, Wolfgang, ed. *Antisemitismus in Deutschland. Zur Aktualität eines Vorteils.* Munich: Deutscher Taschenbuch Verlag, 1995.

Benz, Wolfgang, ed. *Jahrbuch für Antisemitismusforschung.* Munich: Deutscher Taschenbuch Verlag, 1995–.

Berg, Nicolas. *Der Holocaust und die westdeutschen Historiker.* Göttingen: Wallstein, 2004.

Bergmann, Werner, and Rainer Erb. *Antisemitism in Germany: The Post-Nazi Epoch since 1945.* New Brunswick: Transaction, 1997.

Beyer, Heidemarie. "Entwicklung des Ausländerrechts in der DDR." *Zwischen Nationalstaat und multikultureller Gesellschaft. Einwanderung und Fremdenfeindlichkeit in der Bundesrepublik Deutschland,* ed. Manfred Heßler, 211–27. Berlin: Hitit Verlag, 1993.

Biess, Frank. *Homecomings: Returning POWs and the Legacies of Defeat in Postwar Germany.* Princeton: Princeton University Press, 2006.

Bloxham, Donald. *Genocide on Trial: War Crimes Trials and the Formation of Holocaust History and Memory.* New York: Oxford University Press, 2003.

Bodemann, Y. Michel. *Jews, Germans, Memory: Reconstructions of Jewish Life in Germany.* Ann Arbor: University of Michigan Press, 1996.

Bodemann, Y. Michel, and Gökç Yurdakul, eds. *Migration, Citizenship, Ethos.* New York: Palgrave Macmillan, 2006.

Brenner, Michael. *After the Holocaust: Rebuilding Jewish Lives in Postwar Germany.* Princeton: Princeton University Press, 1997.

Brubaker, Rogers. *Citizenship and Nationhood in France and Germany.* Cambridge: Harvard University Press, 1992.

Campt, Tina, Pascal Grosse, and Yara-Colette Lemke Muniz de Faria. "Blacks, Germans, and the Politic of the Imperial Imagination, 1920–1960." In Sara Friedrichsmeyer, Sara Lennox, and Susanne Zantop, eds., *The Imperialist Imagination: German Colonialism and Its Legacy.* Ann Arbor: University of Michigan Press, 1998.

Chin, Rita. *The Guest Worker Question in Postwar Germany.* New York: Cambridge University Press, 2007.

Connelly, John. "Catholic Racism and Its Opponents." *Journal of Modern History* 79 (December 2007): 813–47.

El-Tayeb, Fatima. "'Blood Is a Very Special Juice': Racialized Bodies and Citizenship in Twentieth-Century Germany." In "Complicating Categories: Gender, Class, Race, and Ethnicity," ed. Eileen Boris and Angélique Janssens, *International Review of Social History,* 149–69, Supplement 7. Cambridge: Cambridge University Press, 1999.

Elsner, Eva-Maria, and Lothar Elsner. *Ausländer und Ausländerpolitik in der DDR.* Berlin: Gesellschaftswissenschaftliches Forum, 1992.

Elsner, Eva-Maria, and Lothar Elsner. *Zwischen Nationalismus und Internationalismus. Über Ausländer und Ausländerpolitik in der DDR 1949–1990.* Rostock: Norddeutscher Hochschulschriften Verlag, 1994.

Evens Foundation, ed. *Europe's New Racism? Causes, Manifestations, and Solutions.* New York: Berghahn Books, 2002.

Fehrenbach, Heide. *Race after Hitler: Black Occupation Children in Postwar Germany and America.* Princeton: Princeton University Press, 2005.

Fehrenbach, Heide. "War Orphans and the Postfascist Family: Kinship and Belonging after 1945." In Frank Biess and Robert Moeller, eds., *Histories of the Aftermath: The Legacies of World War II in Comparative European Perspective.* New York: Berghahn Books, forthcoming 2009.

Flam, Helena, ed. *Migranten in Deutschland. Statistiken-Fakten-Diskurse.* Constance: UVK Verlagsgesellschaft, 2007.

Geller, Jay Howard. *Jews in Post-Holocaust Germany, 1945–1953.* New York: Cambridge University Press, 2005.

Göktürk, Deniz, David Gramling, and Anton Kaes, eds. *Germany in Transit: Nation and Migration, 1955–2005.* Berkeley: University of California Press, 2007.

Gregor, Neil, Nils Roemer, and Mark Roseman, eds. *German History from the Margins.* Bloomington: Indiana University Press, 2006.

Grossmann, Atina. "A Question of Silence: The Rape of German Women by Occupation Soldiers." *October* 72 (1995): 43–63.

Grossmann, Atina. *Jews, Germans, and Allies: Close Encounters in Occupied Germany.* Princeton: Princeton University Press, 2007.

Heineman, Elizabeth D. *What Difference Does a Husband Make? Women and Marital Status in Nazi and Postwar Germany.* Berkeley: University of California Press, 1999.

Herzog, Dagmar. *Sex after Fascism: Memory and Morality in Twentieth-Century Germany.* Princeton: Princeton University Press, 2005.

Höhn, Maria. *GIs and Fräuleins: The German-American Encounter in 1950s West Germany.* Chapel Hill: University of North Carolina Press, 2002.

Höhn, Maria. "The Black Panther Solidarity Committees and the *Voice of the Lumpen.*" *German Studies Review* 31, no. 1 (2008): 133–54.

Hong, Young-Sun. "'The Benefits of Health Must Spread among All': International Solidarity, Health, and Race in the East German Encounter with the Third World." In Katherine Pence and Paul Betts, eds., *Socialist Modern: East German Everyday Culture and Politics.* Ann Arbor: University of Michigan Press, 2008.

Hügel-Marshall, Ika. *Invisible Woman: Growing Up Black in Germany.* Trans. Elizabeth Gaffney. New York: Continuum, 2001.

Institut für Internationale Politik und Wirtschaft der DDR. *Gegen Rassismus, Apartheid, und Kolonialismus.* Berlin (East): Staatsverlag der Deutschen Demokratischen Republik, 1978.

Kauders, Anthony D. *Unmögliche Heimat. Eine deutsch-jüdische Geschichte der Bundesrepublik.* Munich: Deutsche Verlags-Anstalt, 2007.

Kleff, Sanem, Edith Broszinsky-Schwabe, Marie-There Albert, Helga Marburger, and Marie-Eleonora Karsten. *BRD—DDR. Alte und neue Rassismen im Zuge der deutsch-deutschen Einigung.* Werkstatt-Berichte Nr. 1. Berlin: Verlag für Interkulturelle Kommunikation, 1990.

Kochavi, Arieh J. *Post-Holocaust Politics: Britain, the United States, and Jewish Refugees, 1945–1948.* Chapel Hill: University of North Carolina Press, 2001.

Kolinsky, Eva. *After the Holocaust: Jewish Survivors in Germany after 1945.* London: Pimlico, 2004.

Kolinsky, Eva. "Meanings of Migration in East Germany and the West German Model." In *United and Divided: Germany since 1900,* ed. Mike Dennis and Eva Kolinsky, 145–75. New York: Berghan Books, 2004.

Krüger-Potratz, Marianne. *Anderssein gab es nicht. Ausländer und Minderheiten in der DDR.* Münster: Waxmann Verlag, 1991.

Kurthen, Hermann, Werner Bergmann, and Rainer Erb, eds. *Antisemitism and Xenophobia in Germany after Unification.* New York: Oxford University Press, 1997.

Laurence, Jonathan. "(Re)Constructing Community in Berlin: Turks, Jews, and German Responsibility." In Ruth A. Starkman, *Transformations of the New Germany.* New York: Palgrave Macmillan, 2006.

Legge, Jerome S., Jr. *Jews, Turks, and Other Strangers: The Roots of Prejudice in Modern Germany.* Madison: University of Wisconsin Press, 2003.

Lehmann, Albrecht. *Im Fremden ungewollt zuhaus: Flüchtlinge und Vertriebene in Westdeutschland, 1945–1990.* Munich: Beck, 1991.

Lemke Muniz de Faria, Yara-Colette. *Zwischen Fürsorge und Ausgrenzung. Afrodeutsche "Besatungskinder" im Nachkriegsdeutschland.* Berlin: Metropole, 2002.

Mankowitz, Zeev W. *Life between Memory and Hope: The Survivors of the Holocaust in Occupied Germany.* Cambridge: Cambridge University Press, 2002.

Margalit, Gilad. *Germany and Its Gypsies: A Post-Auschwitz Ordeal.* Madison: University of Wisconsin Press, 2002.

Marshall, Barbara. *The New Germany and Migration in Europe.* New York: Manchester University Press, 2000.

Mazón, Patricia, and Reinhild Steingröver. *Not So Plain as Black and White: Afro-German Culture and History, 1890–2000.* Rochester: University of Rochester Press, 2005.

Merkl, Peter H., and Leonard Weinberg, eds. *Right-Wing Extremism in the Twenty-First Century.* Portland, OR: Frank Cass, 2003.

Moeller, Robert G. *War Stories: The Search for a Usable Past in the Federal Republic of Germany.* Berkeley: University of California Press, 2001.

Morris, Leslie, and Jack Zipes, eds. *Unlikely History: The Changing German-Jewish Symbiosis, 1945–2000.* New York: Palgrave, 2002.

Müggenburg, Andreas. *Die ausländischen Vertragsarbeiter in der ehemaligen DDR. Darstellung und Dokumentation.* Bonn: Mitteilungen der Beauftragten der Bundesregierung für Belange der Ausländer, 1996.

Müller, Christian, and Patrice G. Poutrus, eds. *Ankunft, Alltag, Ausreise. Migration und interkulturelle Begegnung in der DDR-Gesellschaft.* Cologne: Böhlau, 2005.

O'Brien, Peter. "Continuity and Change in Germany's Treatment of Non-Germans." In *International Migration Review* 22, no. 3 (Autumn 1988): 109–34.

Opitz, May, Katharine Oguntoye, and Dagmar Schultz, eds. *Showing Our Colors: Afro-German Women Speak Out.* Trans. Anne V. Adams. Amherst: University of Massachusetts Press, 1986.

Peck, Jeffrey M. *Being Jewish in the New Germany.* New Brunswick: Rutgers University Press, 2006.

Piesche, Peggy, Maureen Maisha Eggers, Grada Kilomba, and Susan Arndt, eds. *Mythen, Maske, und Subjekte: Kritische Weißseinsforschung in Deutschland.* Münster: Unrast, 2006.

Piper, Nicola. *Racism, Nationalism, and Citizenship: Ethnic Minorities in Britain and Germany.* Brookfield, VT: Ashgate, 1998.

Poiger, Uta G. "Beauty, Business, and International Relations." In *WerkstattGeschichte* 45 (2007): 53–71.

Poiger, Uta G. *Jazz, Rock, and Rebels: Cold War Politics and American Culture in a Divided Germany.* Berkeley: University of California Press, 2000.

Poiger, Uta G. "Imperialism and Empire in Twentieth-Century Germany." *History and Memory,* 17, no. 1/2 (2005): 87–116.

Poutrus, Patrice G. "An den Grenzen des proletarischen Internationalismus. Algerische Flüchtlinge in der DDR." *Zeitschrift für Geschichtswissenschaft* 55, no. 2 (February 2007): 162–78.

Räthzel, Nora. "Aussiedler and Ausländer: Transforming German National Identity." In *Transformations of the New Germany,* ed. Ruth Starkman, 157–80. New York: Palgrave Macmillan, 2006.

Riedel, Almut. *"hatten ooch Chancen, ehrlich." Erfahrungen algerischer Arbeitsmigranten in der DDR.* Opladen: Leske und Budrich, 1994.

Rosen, Klaus Henning, ed. *Die zweite Vertreibung: Fremde in Deutschland.* Bonn: J. H. W. Dietz, 1992.

Schönborn, Susanne, ed. *Zwischen Erinnerung und Neubeginn: Zur deutsch-jüdischen Geschichte nach 1945.* Munich: Martin Meidenbauer, 2006.

Schoeps, Julius H., ed. *Leben im Land der Täter: Juden im Nachkriegsdeutschland 1945–1952.* Berlin: Jüdische Verlagsanstalt, 2001.

Schuck, Peter, and Rainer Münz, eds. *Paths to Inclusion: The Integration of Migrants in the United States and Germany.* Migration and Refugees Series, vol. 5. New York: Berghahn Books, 1998.

Sieg, Katrin. *Ethnic Drag: Performing Race, Nation, Sexuality in West Germany.* Ann Arbor: University of Michigan Press, 2002.

Stern, Frank. *The Whitewashing of the Yellow Badge: Antisemitism and Philosemitism in Postwar Germany.* Trans. William Templer. New York: Pergamon, 1992.

Thimm, Karen, and DuRell Echols. *Schwarze in Deutschland.* Munich: Protokolle, 1973.

Volkov, Shulamit. *Germans, Jews, and Antisemites: Trials in Emancipation.* New York: Cambridge University Press, 2006.

Watts, Meredith W. *Xenophobia in United Germany: Generations, Modernization, and Ideology.* New York: St. Martin's Press, 1997.

Zatlin, Jonathan. "Scarcity and Resentment: Economic Sources of Xenophobia in the GDR, 1971–1989." *Central European History* 40, no. 4 (December 2007): 683–720.

EUROPE AFTER 1945—GENERAL, COMPARATIVE

Barker, Francis, Peter Hulme, Margaret Iversen, and Diana Loxley, eds. *Europe and its Others: Proceedings of the Essex Conference on the Sociology of Literature, July 1984.* Colchester: University of Essex, 1985.

Baumann, Gerd. *The Multicultural Riddle: Rethinking National, Ethnic, and Religious Identities.* New York: Routledge, 1999.

Bessel, Richard, and Dirk Schumann, eds. *Life after Death: Approaches to a Cultural and Social History of Europe during the 1940s and 1950s.* Cambridge: Cambridge University Press, 2003.

Brubaker, Rogers. *Ethnicity without Groups.* Cambridge: Harvard University Press, 2004.

Buruma, Ian. *Murder in Amsterdam: The Death of Theo Van Gogh and the Limits of Tolerance.* New York: Penguin, 2006.

Connelly, Matthew. *Unnatural Selection: The Population Control Movement and Its Struggle to Remake Humanity.* Cambridge: Belknap/Harvard University Press, 2008.

Council of Europe, Directorate of Social and Economic Affairs. *Tackling Racism and Xenophobia: Practical Action at the Local Level.* Strasbourg: Council of Europe Press, 1995.

Council of Europe, Directorate of Social and Economic Affairs. *Tackling Racist and Xenophobic Violence in Europe: Case Studies.* Strasbourg: Council of Europe Press, 1997.

Deák, István, Jan T. Gross, and Tony Judt. *The Politics of Retribution in Europe: World War II and Its Aftermath.* Princeton: Princeton University Press, 2000.

Dean, Martin, Constantin Goschler, and Philipp Ther, eds. *Robbery and Restitution: The Conflict over Jewish Property in Europe.* Studies on War and Genocide. New York: Berghahn Books, 2007.

Elkins, Caroline, and Susan Pedersen, eds. *Settler Colonialism in the Twentieth Century: Projects, Practices, and Legacies.* New York: Routledge, 2005.

Esposito, John L., and François Burgat, eds. *Modernizing Islam: Religion in the Public Sphere in Europe and the Middle East.* New Brunswick: Rutgers University Press, 2003.

Evans Foundation, ed. *Europe's New Racism? Causes, Manifestations, and Solutions.* New York: Berghahn Books, 2002.

Fetzer, Joel S., and J. Christopher Soper. *Muslims and the State in Britain, France, and Germany.* New York: Cambridge University Press, 2005.

Freeman, Gary P. *Immigrant Labor and Racial Conflict in Industrial Societies: The French and British Experience, 1945–1975.* Princeton: Princeton University Press, 1979.

Gregory, Derek, and Allan Pred, eds. *Violent Geographies: Fear, Terror, and Political Violence.* New York: Routledge, 2007.

Hazekamp, Jan Laurens, and Keith Popple, eds. *Racism in Europe: A Challenge for Youth Policy and Youth Work.* London: University College London Press, 1997.

Jonker, Gerdien, and Valérie Amiraux, eds. *Politics of Visibility: Young Muslims in European Public Spaces.* Bielefeld: Transcript Verlag, 2006.

König, Helmut, and Manfred Sicking, eds. *Gehört die Türkei zur Europa? Wegweisungen fur ein Europa am Scheideweg.* Bielefeld: Transcript, 2005.

Lahav, Gallya. *Immigration and Politics in the New Europe.* New York: Cambridge University Press, 2004.

Melegh, Attila. *On the East-West Slope: Globalization, Nationalism, Racism, and Discourses on Central and Eastern Europe.* New York: Central European University Press, 2006.

Naimark, Norman M. *Fires of Hatred: Ethnic Cleansing in Twentieth-Century Europe.* Cambridge: Harvard University Press, 2001.

Panayi, Panikos. *Outsiders: A History of European Minorities.* London: Hambledon Press, 1999.

Ramet, Sabrina P. *Whose Democracy? Nationalism, Religion, and the Doctrine of Collective Rights in Post-1989 Eastern Europe.* Lanham, MD: Rowman and Littlefield, 1997.

Roemer, John E., Woojin Lee, and Karine Van der Straeten. *Racism, Xenophobia, and Distribution: Multi-Issue Politics in Advanced Democracies.* Cambridge: Harvard University Press, 2007.

Ther, Philipp, and Ana Siljak, eds. *Redrawing Nations: Ethnic Cleansing in East-Central Europe, 1944–1948.* Lanham, MD: Rowman and Littlefield, 2001.

Vertovec, Steven, and Ceri Peach, eds. *Islam in Europe: The Politics of Religion and Community.* New York: St. Martin's Press, 1997.

Weitz, Eric D. *A Century of Genocide: Utopias of Race and Nation.* Princeton: Princeton University Press, 2003.

Yazbek-Haddad, Yvonne, ed. *Muslims in the West: From Sojourners to Citizens.* Oxford: Oxford University Press, 2002.

BRITAIN AFTER 1945

Balibar, Etienne, and Immanuel Wallerstein. *Race, Nation, Class: Ambiguous Identities.* London: Verso, 1991.
Barker, Martin. *The New Racism.* London: Junction Books, 1980.
Center for Contemporary Cultural Studies, ed. *The Empire Strikes Back: Race and Racism in 70s Britain.* London: Hutchinson, 1982.
Deakin, Nicholas. *Colour, Citizenship, and British Society.* London: Panther, 1970.
Foot, Paul. *Immigration and Race in British Politics.* Harmondsworth: Penguin, 1965.
Gilroy, Paul. *The Black Atlantic: Modernity and Double Consciousness.* Cambridge: Harvard University Press, 1993.
Gilroy, Paul. "One Nation under a Groove: The Cultural Politics of 'Race' and Racism in Britain." In Geoff Eley and Ronald Grigor Suny, eds., *Becoming National: A Reader.* New York: Oxford University Press, 1996.
Gilroy, Paul. *"There Ain't No Black in the Union Jack": The Cultural Politics of Race and Nation.* London: Hutchinson, 1987.
Owusu, Kwesi, ed. *Black British Culture and Society: A Text Reader.* London: Routledge, 2000.
Patterson, Sheila. *Dark Strangers.* Harmondsworth: Penguin, 1963.
Patterson, Sheila. *Immigration and Race Relations in Britain, 1960–1967.* London: Oxford University Press, 1969.
Paul, Kathleen. *Whitewashing Britain: Race and Citizenship in the Postwar Era.* Ithaca: Cornell University Press, 1997.
Sivanandan, A. *Race and Resistance: The IRR Story.* London: Institute of Race Relations, 1974.

FRANCE AFTER 1945

Beriss, David. *Black Skins, French Voices: Caribbean Ethnicity and Activism in Urban France.* Boulder, CO: Westview Press, 2004.
Bowen, John R. *Why the French Don't Like Headscarves: Islam, the State, and Public Space.* Princeton: Princeton University Press, 2007.
Chapman, Herrick, and Laura L. Frader, eds. *Race in France: Interdisciplinary Perspectives on the Politics of Difference.* New York: Berghahn Books, 2004.
Feldblum, Miriam. *Reconstructing Citizenship: The Politics of Nationality Reform and Immigration in Contemporary France.* Albany: State University of New York Press, 1999.
Hargreaves, Alec G., and Mark McKinney, ed. *Post-Colonial Cultures in France.* New York: Routledge, 1997.
Laurence, Jonathan, and Justin Vaisse. *Integrating Islam: Political and Religious*

Challenges in Contemporary France. Washington, DC: Brookings Institution Press, 2006.

Lebovics, Herman. *Bringing the Empire Back Home: France in the Global Age.* Durham: Duke University Press, 2004.

MacMaster, Neil. *Colonial Migrants and Racism: Algerians in France, 1900–62.* New York: St. Martin's Press, 1997.

Mandel, Maud S. *In the Aftermath of Genocide: Armenians and Jews in Twentieth-Century France.* Durham: Duke University Press, 2003.

Moyn, Samuel. *A Holocaust Controversy: The Treblinka Affair in Postwar France.* Hanover, NH: University Press of New England, 2005.

Peabody, Sue, and Tyler Stovall, eds. *The Color of Liberty: Histories of Race in France.* Durham: Duke University Press, 2003.

Sayad, Abdelmalek. *The Suffering of the Immigrant.* Trans. David Macey. Malden, MA: Polity Press, 2004.

Scott, Joan W. *The Politics of the Veil.* Princeton: Princeton University Press, 2007.

Shepard, Todd. *The Invention of Decolonization: The Algerian War and the Remaking of France.* Ithaca: Cornell University Press, 2006.

Silverstein, Paul A. *Algeria in France: Transpolitics, Race, and Nation.* Bloomington: Indiana University Press, 2004.

Smith, Andrea L. *Colonial Memory and Postcolonial Europe: Maltese Settlers in Algeria and France.* Bloomington: Indiana University Press, 2006.

Stovall, Tyler, and Georges van den Abeele, eds. *French Civilization and Its Discontents: Nationalism, Colonialism, Race.* Lanham: Lexington Books, 2003.

SWEDEN, POLAND, UKRAINE, ROMANIA, THE SOVIET UNION/RUSSIA AFTER 1945

Bartov, Omer. *Erased: Vanishing Traces of Jewish Galicia in Present-Day Ukraine.* Princeton: Princeton University Press, 2007.

Berdahl, Daphne, Matti Bunzl, and Martha Lampland, eds. *Altering States: Ethnographies of Transition in Eastern Europe and the Former Soviet Union.* Ann Arbor: University of Michigan Press, 2000.

Blobaum, Robert, ed. *Antisemitism and Its Opponents in Modern Poland.* Ithaca: Cornell University Press, 2005.

Brubaker, Rogers, Margit Feischmidt, Jon Fox, and Liana Grancea. *Nationalist Politics and Everyday Ethnicity in a Transylvanian Town.* Princeton: Princeton University Press, 2006.

Gross, Jan. *Fear: Anti-Semitism in Poland after Auschwitz; An Essay in Historical Interpretation.* New York: Random House, 2006.

Hirsch, Francine. "Race without the Practice of Racial Politics." *Slavic Review* 61, no. 1 (Spring 2002): 30–43.

Kenney, Padraic. "After the Blank Spots Are Filled: Recent Perspectives on Modern Poland." *Journal of Modern History* 79 (March 2007): 134–61.

Lemon, Alaina. "Without a 'Concept'? Race as Discursive Practice." *Slavic Review* 61, no. 1 (Spring 2002): 54–61.

Michlic, Joanna Beata. *Poland's Threatening Other: The Image of the Jew from 1880 to the Present.* Lincoln: University of Nebraska Press, 2006.

Pred, Allan. *Even in Sweden: Racisms, Racialized Spaces, and the Popular Geographical Imagination.* Berkeley: University of California Press, 2000.

Slezkine, Yuri. *The Jewish Century.* Princeton: Princeton University Press, 2004.

Snyder, Timothy. *The Reconstruction of Nations: Poland, Ukraine, Lithuania, Belarus, 1569–1999.* New Haven: Yale University Press, 2003.

Weiner, Amir. "Nothing But Certainty." *Slavic Review* 61, no. 1 (Spring 2002): 44–53.

Weitz, Eric D. "Racial Politics with the Concept of Race: Reevaluating Soviet Ethnic and National Purges." *Slavic Review* 61, no. 1 (Spring 2002): 1–29.

Weitz, Eric D. "On Certainties and Ambivalencies: Reply to My Critics." *Slavic Review* 61, no. 1 (Spring 2002): 62–65.

Zimmerman, Joshua D., ed. *Contested Memories: Poles and Jews during the Holocaust and Its Aftermath.* New Brunswick, NJ: Rutgers University Press, 2003.

Index